D1289140

The Cinema of
Wim Wenders

DATE DUE

OCT 21 1997			
JAN 16 REC'D			
APR 25 1998			
APR 21 REC'D			
JUL 02 1998			
OCT 30 1999			
NOV 12 1999			
MAR 04 2000			
FEB 22 2000			
FEB 06 2002			
FEB 25 2002			
FEB 25 2002			
DEC 18 2004			
APR 13 2005			

GAYLORD | | PRINTED IN U.S.A

CONTEMPORARY FILM AND TELEVISION SERIES

A complete listing of the books in this series can be found at the back of this volume.

General Editor
Patricia B. Erens
Rosary College

Advisory Editors
Lucy Fischer
University of Pittsburgh

Miriam White
Northwestern University

Peter Lehman
University of Arizona

Caren J. Deming
University of Arizona

Robert J. Burgoyne
Wayne State University

The Cinema of Wim Wenders

Image,

Narrative,

and the

Postmodern

Condition

Edited by Roger F. Cook and Gerd Gemünden

Wayne State University Press

Library of Congress Cataloging-in-Publication Data
The cinema of Wim Wenders : image, narrative, and the postmodern condition / edited by Roger
    F. Cook and Gerd Gemünden.
        p. cm. — (Contemporary film and television series)
    Includes bibliographical references and index.
    ISBN 0-8143-2578-5 (pbk. : alk. paper)
    1. Wenders, Wim—Criticism and interpretation. 2. Wenders, Wim— Interviews. I. Cook,
Roger F., date. II. Gemünden, Gerd, date. III. Series.
    PN1998.3.W46C56   1997   96-25409
    791.43'0233'092—dc20

Designer: Mary Krzewinski

All photographs reprinted with the kind permission of Stiftung Deutsche Kinemathek Berlin.

    Acknowledgments: The co-editors of this volume are grateful to the Dartmouth College Development Fund and the Research Council at the University of Missouri-Columbia, whose generous financial support helped make this volume a reality. We owe a special thanks to Michael Töteberg at Verlag der Autoren (Frankfurt), who helped secure copyrights for the translations, gave us access to his own research files, and put us in touch with Wim Wenders. Similarly, we are indebted to Jolanda Darbyshire at Wim Wenders Produktion for providing us with video tapes of Wenders's films, in some cases prior to their commercial release or in original, full-length versions that were not released.
    Finally, we would like to thank Wim Wenders for taking time to address our questions openly and with interest.

CONTENTS

▌Contents

CONTRIBUTORS

NORA M. ALTER is Assistant Professor of German and Film and Media Studies at the University of Florida. Publications include *Vietnam Protest Theatre: The Television War on Stage* (Indiana UP, 1996), and articles on various aspects of European and North American film, theatre, literary, and cultural studies, including essays on Erich Fried, Harun Farocki, and Thich Nhat Hanh. She is currently completing a manuscript on the international essay film.

ROGER F. COOK is Associate Professor of German at the University of Missouri in Columbia. He is the author of *The Demise of the Author: Autonomy and the German Writer, 1770–1848* (1993) and various articles on German literature. He has published essays in the area of German cinema on Wenders, Helma Sanders-Brahms, and Alexander Kluge, and is currently completing the book *By the Rivers of Babylon: Heinrich Heine's Late Songs and Reflections.*

TIMOTHY J. CORRIGAN is Professor of English and Film Studies at Temple University. His books include *New German Film: The Displaced Image* (1983; rev. 1995), *The Films of Werner Herzog* (1986), *A Cinema Without Walls: Movies and Culture after Vietnam* (1991), and *Writing about Film* (2nd ed. 1994). His most recent work includes an anthology on film and literature and an essay on "immediate history."

THOMAS ELSAESSER is Professor at the University of Amsterdam, and Chair of the Department of Film and TV Studies. His essays on film theory and film history are in over sixty collections and anthologies. Books as author and editor include *New German Cinema: A History* (1989), *Early Cinema: Space, Frame, Narrative* (1990), *Writing for the Medium: Television in Transition* (1994), *Double Trouble* (1994), *Hoogste Tijd voor en speelfilm* (1995), *A Second Life: German Cinema's First Two Decades* (1996), and *Fassbinder's Germany: Identity, History, Subject* (1996).

GERD GEMÜNDEN teaches German and comparative literature at Dartmouth College. Publications include *Die hermeneutische Wende* (1990), *Wim Wenders: Einstellungen* (with Michael Töteberg, 1993), and essays on Wenders, R. W. Fassbinder, Werner Herzog, Monika Treut, and Herbert Achternbusch. He is presently completing a study of the reception of American popular culture in postwar Germany.

NORBERT GROB lives in Berlin. His publications include *Wenders* (1984; rev. 1992), *Ray* (with Manuela Reichart, 1989), and *Die Macht der Filmkritik* (with Karl Prümm, 1990). He is co-editor of Edition Filme and frequently writes for *Die Zeit*. His most recent work focuses on Erich von Strohheim and William Wyler.

ALICE KUZNIAR, Associate Professor of German and Comparative Literature at the University of North Carolina, Chapel Hill, is author of *Delayed Endings: Nonclosure in Novalis and Hölderlin* (U of Georgia P, 1987). In addition to numerous articles on German Romanticism, she has edited *Outing Goethe and His Age* (Stanford UP, 1996). In the area of cinema, she has published on David Lynch, Wim Wenders, and Monika Treut and is currently working on a book on queer German cinema.

RICHARD W. MCCORMICK teaches German film and literature at the University of Minnesota, where he is an Associate Professor. He has written *Politics of the Self: Feminism and the Postmodern in West German Literature and Film* (1991) and co-edited the two-volume anthology *Gender and German Cinema: Feminist Interventions* (1993). He has published articles on New German Cinema, German feminist cinema, and Weimar cinema; he is currently finishing a book on gender and modernity in Weimar film and literature.

Introduction:
Wim Wenders's Cinema of
Displacement

"What's wrong with a cowboy in Hamburg?" asks Tom Ripley, the title character of Wim Wenders's *The American Friend*, when questioned about his cowboy hat. Ripley's defensive tone of voice indicates that he sees nothing wrong with his Stetson-wearing, T-Bird-driving urban cowboy existence in a North German metropolis where he resides in a mansion that resembles the White House and overlooks the Hamburg harbor. Occurring early in the film and followed by the title, Ripley's line attests to a sense of dislocation central not only to *The American Friend* but to all of Wenders's films, a powerful aesthetics of displacement that informs them on the level of theme, style, and genre.

To be sure, Wenders's narratives feature a continuing cast of displaced characters, travelers, transients, exiles: the uprooted Hans, who upon his release from prison finds himself pursued by former gang members (*Summer in the City*); the retired goalkeeper and random murderer Bloch, fleeing to a remote Austrian village (*The Goalie's Anxiety at the Penalty Kick*); the English settlers imposing Puritan morals in a savage and foreign land—a film actually shot in Spain and with Catholic actors (*The Scarlet Letter*); the drifting journalist Philip Winter inflicted in America with writer's block and an incessant need to fix reality by taking Polaroids (*Alice in the Cities*); the inner emigrant Wilhelm Meister, who experiences the impossibility of travel as *Bildung* (*Wrong Move*); the solitary and taciturn Bruno and Robert, a movie repairman and a psycholinguist traveling through the wasteland of the German-German border (*Kings of the Road*); Wenders's American friends and Hollywood mavericks Nicholas Ray and Sam Fuller (*Lightning over Water, The State of Things*); the Japanese direc-

tor Ozu, Wenders's role model for a positive colonization by American cinema (*Tokyo-Ga*); the exiled director Friedrich Munro, who, like F. W. Murnau, feels "at home nowhere, in no house, in no country" and who also meets with an early death in California (*The State of Things*); the return and disappearance of the male wanderer (*Paris, Texas*); the reversed angels descending from heaven for an improbable love affair (*Wings of Desire*) or a comic crime pursuit (*Faraway, So Close!*); and Claire and Sam's futuristic chase around the world in an "ultimate road movie" leading into outer space (*Until the End of the World*). From Paris, France (where Wenders was initiated into cinephilia at the Cinémathèque), via Paris, Texas, to Paris/Tokyo (the location for his philosophical reflections on the auteurism of fashion and film in *Notebooks on Cities and Clothes*), Wenders's films could be analyzed exhaustively by their references to borders (geographic and psychological) and by the various attempts to traverse an inner and outer world by car, train, plane, ship, cinema, photography, television, and video. They comprise a cinematic universe peopled with protagonists who, like Ripley, seem to know less and less who they are or who anybody else is. Whether it is Ripley's Stetson, a symbol for the American cowboy—or more precisely, its celluloid myth propagated by Hollywood—or Jonathan Zimmermann's *Mütze*, a more practical and less conspicuous woolen cap and a prop of the German *Heimatfilm* or *Bergfilm* tradition, the question of which hat to wear is a difficult one for Wenders's protagonists, just as his films defy attempts to situate them within either one of the film traditions these two hats represent.

An Auteur Directed by Hollywood

Born Ernst Wilhelm Wenders on August 14, 1945, just a few months after the German army had surrendered to the Allied forces, Wenders, like many directors of the New German Cinema, spent his childhood under American occupation, a time he remembers for its supplies of chocolate, chewing gum, and an Indian headdress worn during carnival. If we are to believe Wenders's own sparse statements about his adolescence, all that mattered to him during those formative years were pinball machines, pool tables, Polaroids and, of course, the English and American pop music broadcast on American Forces Network radio, selected on the local jukebox, or secretly bought and played on a friend's record player. Wenders has explained how rock music offered him an alternative to all the *Kultur* forced on him in his youth. Because of the stigma of fascism associated with traditional German culture (in an often-cited reference he mentions Beethoven as an example),[1] he trusted rock and roll as a cultural form for expressing intuitively his generation's opposition. Not only for Wenders, but also for many others of his generation, it corresponded to their psychic needs within a climate of cultural pessimism and historical skepticism. His films, however, render the presence of American culture a much more complex and problematic phenomenon. Although in an often-quoted remark he once called rock music a lifesaver, he also warned, in an equally famous line of one of his characters, that it colonizes the subconscious. This paradox is typical for the double bind of the colonized, who has to articulate the critique of colonialism in the language of the colonizer, often resulting in a critical assessment of one's own upbringing and childhood memories, or even of one's very self.

In the context of a patriarchal lineage of film directors—in particular, Wenders's relation to American directors—this double bind manifests itself in oedipal terms. Nicholas Ray, Sam Fuller, and John Ford provided him with father figures, and their films served both as catalysts and as antagonists for his own development as a filmmaker. That is, they were role models for him to study and follow, but ultimately to abandon or supersede, as the transformations of style, genre, and theme from *The Goalie's Anxiety at the Penalty Kick* to *Wings of Desire* and beyond demonstrate. Even though for Wenders, as for other self-proclaimed "fatherless" filmmakers of the immediate postwar generation, the search for new beginnings took on the rhetoric of "starting out of a vacuum" and of a self-fashioned autodidacticism, he felt a close tie to the filmic vision of the 1940s and 1950s Hollywood cinema that in his youth had instilled in him a positive image of America. Thus even when he begins to question the colonizing force of American cinema (or actually of the American media industry as a whole), he does not see his own colonization as filmmaker into an American film language as problematic. While preparing to film *The American Friend* in 1976, he reaffirmed the lasting value of American cinema for his work: "Our admiration for American cinema is still right, I think. Because the way of telling a story, the language of the American cinema is still valuable . . . I mean, for me, there is no other language, no other film language . . . I'm not even sure you can call it an American one, but it was made in America at least."[2] And while some German directors cite writers, composers, painters, or philosophers as models, Wenders emphatically strove to situate himself as heir to a *film* tradition, even though it was a foreign one.

The filmmakers of Wenders's generation whose film roots were in American cinema faced certain ambiguities in their attempt to establish a national film culture. These directors had to find a way to make, produce, and distribute films that would reach an audience who, like themselves, had been reared on the American films that had flooded West Germany since the 1950s, but which would also offer this audience something the American films could not. The irony of the situation was that the American system was both the model for high proficiency to be emulated and at the same time the competition to be outdone at the box office: a big brother loved for a cinema that taught these young directors new ways of seeing, yet hated for its ideology (especially in the wake of the Vietnam War) and for its stranglehold over the German market. Genres like the thriller, the detective story, the melodrama, or, in Wenders's case, the road movie, which had been developed to perfection by the Hollywood studios, became a preferred medium for German filmmakers because they could rely on established genre conventions and calculate audience expectations. The question therefore became how to transform these genres creatively in order to make them fit the mold of a unique German context. As Wenders noted about adapting Patricia Highsmith's novel *Ripley's Game* for the screen, "Writing the script now for *Ripley's Game* [later released as *The American Friend*], I realize that this kind of story always tends to be done the way Hitchcock did it. It's very hard to be inventive, because this kind of story has been so well worked over by Hitchcock. . . . Of course, I'm trying to avoid creating the same emotions in the audience, but it's the techniques that are intruding. Hitchcock's techniques. A lot of his inventions go hand in hand with things in the Highsmith story: as if there was no other way of doing it."[3] Timothy Corrigan has argued that *The American Friend* "create[s] a Hollywood brilliance that cites and strangely moves beyond the images common to Hitchcock, Fuller, and Ford . . . at once a deconstruction of the old idiom and an approximation of its fluency."[4] While this may explain the success of Wenders's films at home, the reasons for his immense popularity abroad, particularly among American audiences, are quite different. Unlike the majority of contemporary Hollywood films, most of Wenders's films are completely free of aggression, move at a leisurely pace, and are poor on plot and suspense and rich on atmosphere and incidents. Viewer identification is less a consequence of psychological motivation than of sharing the (predominantly male) protagonists' ways of seeing—an aesthetics that, in a roundabout fashion, has been subsumed under the label "European art film."

While Wenders admired Hollywood for its proficiency and its film grammar, he resented the capitalist dimensions of its industry (it is no accident that two of his favorite American directors, Ray and Fuller, survived on the fringes of the studio system). He realized early in his career the need to control production and distribution and to liberate himself from the encroaching economic colonization of German film by the American industry. His steadfastness in working toward this independence stemmed in part from a three-month stint in 1966 at the administrative office of the Düsseldorf branch of United Artists. He reflected on his firsthand experience with the distribution system in a 1969 article with the telling title "Despising What You Sell." In it he summarizes those aspects of the media industry that left him no alternative but to carve out his own path as an independent filmmaker: "From production to distribution, the same violence was at work: the same lack of love in dealing with images, sound and language; the stupidity of German dubbing; the vulgarity of the block and blind booking system; the lack of variety in advertising; the lack of conscience involved in exploiting the cinema-owners; the idiocy involved in cutting films down, etc."[5] This first experience with the industry taught him that the final film product was inextricably coupled with the production and distribution systems. He received free tickets as a part of his job and viewed many of the films he had helped to distribute, concluding that the films he watched "were almost always a continuation of what I had experienced during the day in the distribution office."[6]

Wenders's initial desire to establish independent means of production and distribution was shared by all the directors of New German Cinema, who had to struggle to secure financing for any serious or innovative filmmaking, even after the initial successes of the years 1965–69. In 1971 Wenders founded, together with thirteen other Munich filmmakers, the Filmverlag der Autoren. When it fell into financial difficulties in 1974, he founded his own production company to make *Wrong Move* and *Kings of the Road* while remaining a shareholder in the Filmverlag, which Rudolf Augstein, the owner of *Der Spiegel*, had purchased and restructured. Then in 1975 in Berlin he formed Road Movies (with Peter Handke as partner), which has served as the primary production company for his subsequent feature films. Even after he had established himself as a leading international director, he had to struggle to maintain control of the production and distribution of his films. When *Paris, Texas* won the Golden Palm at Cannes in 1984 and seemed destined to be his first major moneymaker in both Europe and the United States, a dispute broke out over the distribution rights in Germany. Dissatisfied with the number of copies provided by the Filmverlag for German distribution, he became entangled in a nasty legal battle that delayed the release of the film for eight months and had some impatient film fans chartering buses to see it in Switzerland. As a result, Wenders and two of the other three remaining filmmakers still represented in the Filmverlag sold off their shares. This conflict was only one indication of the changes in the relationship between cinema and money he found upon returning to Germany in 1984 after seven years in the United States. He quickly discovered that the sense of adventure and willingness to experiment that had fueled the rise of New German Cinema during the late 1960s and 1970s was absent in the German film scene of the mid-1980s. Still, because he has produced all of his films himself, with the exception of *Hammett*, Wenders can be said to enjoy artistic freedom and financial independence to a degree that other filmmakers seldom approximate.

The Visual Ethics of New German Cinema

Unlike Italian neorealism or the French nouvelle vague, New German Cinema was not a new style of cinema. What unites filmmakers with diverse political and aesthetic agendas—filmmakers such as Alexander Kluge, Hans Jürgen Syberberg, Volker Schlöndorff, Margarethe von Trotta, Helma Sanders-Brahms, Rainer Werner Fassbinder, and Wim Wenders—is their effort to reach an audience that feels uncomfortable with or even suspicious of German films. Hence the admiration of many directors for Hollywood proficiency outweighed their skepticism about the colonizing and imperialist aspects of its industry. As Fassbinder put it, "American cinema is the only one I can take seriously, because it's the only one that has really reached an audience."[7] However, one must be careful to distinguish the impact American cinema has made on individual directors of New German Cinema. The ten- to fifteen-year difference in age between Alexander Kluge, Hans-Jürgen Syberberg, or Edgar Reitz and Rainer Werner Fassbinder, Werner Herzog, or Wenders created much more than a generation gap. The younger filmmakers, who had not experienced the Third Reich, seemed uninterested in salvaging and reworking the remnants of a past German culture.[8] Herzog, Fassbinder, and Wenders were drawn to the sense of freedom and opportunity promised by 1950s and (pre-Vietnam) 1960s "America," and nothing could be more alien to them than the fierce anti-Americanism of Reitz's *Heimat* or Syberberg's *Our Hitler*. Timothy Corrigan's analysis of Werner Herzog's effort to situate himself within a film tradition—in Herzog's case, that of Weimar Cinema—through his use of expressionist tropes and film models also fits the bill of Fassbinder and Wenders: "His own national heritage . . . appears as if filtered through a past that begins in 1945 and becomes displaced through Hollywood culture: . . . the terms of this new beginning are fundamentally more commercially, theatrically, and imagistically determined than any notion of a true historical beginning."[9]

This younger group of directors, among whom Wenders was a leading figure, is distinguishable from those who signed the Oberhausen Manifesto—a movement often referred to as Young German Film because of its attacks of "Opas Kino" ("grandpa's cinema")—not only by its breach with Germany's past but also by a turn away from some of the modernist tendencies of its immediate predecessors. In contrast to New German Cinema, Young German Film was pursuing a "new realism" that meant to educate the spectator and to demonstrate the viability of a certain thesis, with the films often being little more than a selection of incidents and events in the life of a character. Spectators were asked to approve or disapprove of the reality represented on the screen—film was understood as a mirror that reflects reality rather than as a window that opens up onto new worlds. In

contrast to this notion of film as a transparent medium in the service of social critique, for the filmmakers that debuted in the late 1960s and early
1970s the medium itself became the center of their aesthetic strategies.
Wenders, Fassbinder, and Herzog, but also von Trotta, Herbert Achternbusch, and Werner Schroeter, drew attention to the morality of the mis-en-
scène itself. Wenders's films in particular did not so much strive to convince as they invited viewers to participate in the mundane activities of
their protagonists, turning the cinema into a place to indulge the audience's
"hunger for experience."[10]

Thus in terms of aesthetic strategy, Wenders's filmmaking differs
radically from the often more directly ideological agenda of New German
filmmakers such as Kluge and Syberberg. In the case of Wenders and
Kluge, even where they seem to be in agreement one finds radically different approaches. In his writings on cinema Kluge has repeatedly emphasized
that "the film on the screen sets in motion a film in the head of the spectator."[11] Wenders too has maintained that the "film" should actually take
shape in the mind of the viewer.[12] However, his efforts to liberate the vision of the spectator stand in almost direct opposition to Kluge's filmmaking. The latter subjects the images, characters, and narrative of his films to
an authorial enunciation based on ideological critique. Such an agenda in
filmmaking contrasts with Wenders's (as well as Herzog's) commitment to
visual freedom and his (their) belief that cinema is, as Thomas Elsaesser
writes, "a refuge from self-consciousness and self-awareness, the search for
a kind of post-ideological space, attracting spectators to an experience of
'pure being as pure seeing.'"[13] Wenders's agenda is less that of a critical
modernist, either in Kluge's manner of ideological critique or in the mode
of aesthetic rebellion typical of Fassbinder or Syberberg.[14] The act of "pure
seeing" fostered in his films contrasts strongly with an ideologically critical
cinema of the type espoused by Kluge, which aims for "a film in the head
of the spectator"—that is, for a *particular* film. Unlike Kluge's various aesthetic strategies intended to distance the spectator—often by modifying the-
atrical devices first espoused in Brecht's theory of epic theater—Wenders's
more postmodern understanding of critique is set firmly *within* the film,
drawing viewers into the spectacle in order to lead them to an understanding of the origin of images. He employs this strategy with remarkable consistency—from the 1968 short *Alabama: 2000 Light Years* as allegory of
the death of the camera to the recent grand-scale science-fiction road movie
Until the End of the World, which centers around the ethics of making the
invisible visible.

Fostered by generous subsidy laws and promoted by the Ministries of
Culture of the individual German States, by the mid-1970s New German
Cinema had turned into an art house commodity whose recognition at home
depended largely on its international success—or more specifically, on its

success in the United States.[15] As it established itself in this fashion, the Oberhausen definition of *Autorenfilm* underwent serious modifications, ultimately leading filmmakers to criticize the subsidy system the manifesto had helped to create. Corrigan maintains that directors such as Wenders, Herzog, and Fassbinder, who no longer fulfilled the concept of the author as a solely responsible and accountable creator of art, "seem to have adapted the *auteur* tag as a convenient label and effective marketing strategy."[16] Different modes of production, distribution, and rapport with the audience distinguish the diverse styles of New German Cinema from what has traditionally been termed auteur film, since the term was first applied to the directors of the French nouvelle vague.

This break with the aesthetics of European auteurism, within a national cinema that had lost the connection to its roots, positioned the New German directors in a cinematic no-man's-land. The films of these New German filmmakers often reflect their infatuation with American culture as a cinephilic flood of allusions to genres, styles, and even particular "phrasings" from classical American cinema. This raises the question, however, of how their tendency to quote their cinematic big brother, sometimes ironically or even playfully, relates to the postmodern practice of pastiche, with its eclectic inclusion of both popular and classical culture. Elsaesser has argued that Wenders's cinephilia (which he takes as representative of a large part of New German Cinema) is not so much a matter of the filmmaker reveling in cinematic history but rather is mediated by "its extra-cinematic historical roots in a particular postwar German childhood and adolescence."[17] Moreover, because these historical roots go back to the cultural and political paralysis of the Adenauer era, one finds a loss of faith in the European modernist culture that could have offered an alternative to the influx of American cinema. Wenders strives ardently to ground the experiential dimension of his films in something more collective and more open than either the privileged authorial position of the auteur (as in the high modernist cinema of Bergman or Fellini) or in a self-reflexive film language engrossed in its own aesthetic statement.

The Death of a Mythical Landscape

Wenders's beginnings at the Munich Academy of Film and Television present more an oppositional relation to American cinema than the ambiguous infatuation that characterizes some of his later work. His early shorts feature pinball machines, jukeboxes, and pool tables, but aesthetically they have little in common with what is generally considered the forte of Hollywood cinema of the 1940s and 1950s, namely, fast-paced stories full of suspense and excitement, narrative closure, rounded characters played by glamorous stars, and witty dialogue—in short, high entertainment that holds the audience under its sway. Wenders's avant-garde beginnings, in contrast, dispense with all of the above and let rock music speak out as nonverbal protest against Hollywood aesthetics. *3 American LP's*, for instance, Wenders's first collaboration with Peter Handke, is a thirteen-minute short that consists of ten shots, most of them out of a moving car, and includes a dialogue between Wenders and Handke about the emotional and visual responses evoked by American music. The music, as Handke comments, can not only be heard but also seen, touting America as the place of liberated vision. Music in this film is clearly more than a metaphor for an alternative way of life (which it was for most members of the Woodstock generation); for Wenders and Handke it provides a different form of perception: "Music from America is more and more replacing the sensuality that the films have lost."[18] *Summer in the City*, which takes its title from a song by the Lovin' Spoonful and is dedicated to the Kinks, one of Wenders's favorite rock bands at the time, appears to move closer to American genre films because it cites elements from the gangster movie. Yet Wenders later stated that the music constitutes the only emotional contact in the otherwise (e)motionless and powerless life of the central figure. The film lacks psychological motivation; we witness the endless passage of *temps mort*, intended to draw spectator involvement away from the characters and whatever minimal story line remains and directing it toward the composition of the film.

The overriding attention to sense experiences in Wenders's early films and those by other Munich filmmakers has led critics to speak of a Sensibilist tendency. As Eric Rentschler writes, "The *Sensibilisten* eschewed logical systems and political categories, insisting on the integrity of the subjective experience in all its immediacy and directness. One relied on the momentary uniqueness of lived encounters. There existed an unspoken taboo against intellectualizing what one perceived; direct experience of the word was enough in and of itself. . . . The works had a contemplative tenor and little if any story line; they consisted of series of images meant to capture the ineffable feel of things."[19] Not unlike New Subjectivity, a contemporary literary movement that included Handke as one of its leading figures, these films feature less a naive withdrawal into inwardness than a faith in cinema's (and literature's) potential to break down cultural social forces that shackle (visual) perception. In what might seem a contradictory comparison, the subjective impulses of Sensibilist film correspond more to Kracauer's notion of "cinematic" art than to dependence on free artistic creations of the filmmaker. Thus on one level, even in these early films the underlying principle in Wenders's filmmaking steers away from aesthetic self-reflexivity and toward "'cinematic' films—films, that is, which incorporate aspects of physical reality with a view to making us experience them."[20]

A "still life" framed by a window in the short *Silver City* (1968).

While the infusion of American culture in Wenders's early films underwent complex mediations and negations, it manifested itself more readily in the film reviews he wrote during the same period. In the introduction to *Emotion Pictures*, the 1986 collection of essays and reviews (most from the years 1968–71, when he was still a student and writing for the Munich magazine *Filmkritik*), he comments that he "feels more familiar with these reviews, rereading them now, than with [his] first films from about the same period."[21] He goes on to explain that the reviews convey better the sense of vision he was trying to achieve, while the early film images now seem strange and puzzling. Some of the reviews he chose to publish describe the film vision of American cinema, primarily that of the American Western, which had reached him as a youth and helped guide his own career as a filmmaker. In a 1969 review of a retrospective of American Westerns in Munich, he summed up his own ideas on film images in the words of Anthony Mann: "You could say that the best example of a good film would be one that you would understand completely if you left off the soundtrack and only watched the image. That's what directing films is about."[22] In that same review he refers to a number of isolated images from those films that typified for him the defining language of American cinema: "Robert Mitchum carries her [Marilyn Monroe in *The River of No Return*] out of the saloon, leaving her red shoe lying in the street"; or, "Paul New-

19

man [in *The Left-Handed Gun*] shoots the sheriff, who is knocked around so violently by the bullet that he loses a boot, which stays standing upright beside the corpse! A child comes along and starts laughing heartily at the empty boot."[23] Perhaps the best description of the act of "pure seeing" he associated with American cinema in those early years is his review of Rudolf Thome's 1969 film *Rote Sonne: "Rote Sonne,"* Wenders writes, "is one of those very rare European films that don't simply try to imitate American cinema . . . but have rather taken their *stance* from American films: one of quietly and unobtrusively spreading out the surface of their world for ninety minutes and nothing else."[24]

Although in these reviews he was able to isolate and characterize this style of unobtrusive cinematic presentation, he felt that he had floundered in his attempts to achieve this "attitude" in his own films during the same period. He often refers to *The Goalie's Anxiety at the Penalty Kick* as his first feature film, preferring to bury and forget his feature-length diploma film *Summer in the City*.[25] *The Goalie* first clarified for him the need to find his own "grammar," because the "American cinema's way of showing things"[26] kept intruding unconsciously on his attempts to find his own style. With hindsight Wenders now points to a particular scene, a long sequence showing the protagonist, Bloch, in a bus headed to the Austrian-Hungarian border, as "a professional turning point" in the development of his own cinematic grammar. Dependent to some extent on unplanned occurrences during the shooting, this scene was for Wenders a foretaste of the open style that would characterize his filmmaking in general, and the road movies in particular.

Early on in his career, Wenders realized that the cinematic tradition of "pure seeing" he wanted to re-create was a thing of the past; if he was to transcend an unproductive state of nostalgia, he could not simply imitate this style but would have to transform it to fit his own aesthetic purposes. Wenders made clear the dangers of exploiting a genre like the Western in his review of Sergio Leone's *Once upon a Time in the West*, suggesting an intricate connection between an aesthetic (over)determination of film images and the widening control of the film industry. The review begins, "I don't want to see another Western. This one is the limit. This one is a killer."[27] Quoting Siegfried Kracauer's description of film as the "redemption of physical reality," Wenders bemoans the end of those Westerns that "spread out a surface that was nothing else but what you could see."[28] He sees in Leone's film an abusive preempting of the genre, where not only an intertextuality of arbitrary images but also an indifferent foregrounding of its own artistic repertoire efface the Western itself: "The film by Leone is completely indifferent to itself. It only shows the unconcerned viewer the luxury that led to its creation: the most complicated camera movements, the most refined crane-tracking shots and pans, fantastic sets, incredibly good actors, a huge railway construction site built just for show so that a coach could drive through it once. Yes, and Monument Valley, . . . I became very sad when I saw the film for a second time: I felt like a tourist, a 'Western tourist.'" Anticipating some of the theoretical notions that would later define "postmodern film," he sensed that this cynical attitude heralded the death of not only a genre, but of a whole mythology: "Their death [Woody Strode and Jack Elam, who only make a cameo appearance in the opening scene] is the death of a genre and a dream, both of them American."[29]

Wenders perceived this development and accepted it, with sadness but without resigning to the alleged death of all myth. In fact, at the end of his review in 1969 he already anticipates one aspect of his own aesthetic strategies that would counter the seemingly arbitrary exhibition of mixed codings (pastiche) with alternative, mythologically charged images: "I'm pleased that I saw Monument Valley again in another film, that I had a chance to *see* it again: in *Easy Rider*, with Peter Fonda, with an Exxon filling-station." At this point one still discerns Wenders's faith in American cinema, a faith that will erode slowly over the next decade and finally come to an abrupt end when he goes to Hollywood to make *Hammett* (1978–82). It was only then that he realized that not only was the Western dead, but the classical age of cinema itself had run its course. American cinema's ability to sustain a unified vision and narrative form, and with it a collective American myth, had succumbed to the Hollywood production/distribution system. The danger existed that the language of American cinema would now serve to make only two kinds of films: rehashed stories or imitations of the great films of the 1940s, and films made explicitly to fit consumption needs that the industry itself had for the most part created.

In this situation Wenders concluded that he would have to take a different approach in his films. Following his usual method of tackling aesthetic questions through filmmaking, he worked through to a conclusion in *The State of Things*. He came to the realization that his personal films, his stance between Hollywood and European auteur film, would be compromised by a media industry that was co-opting the images and the film language of American cinema for its commercial interests. The stance of those classical films, "one of quietly and unobtrusively spreading out the surface of their world for ninety minutes and nothing else," had fallen prey to this co-optation. The image could no longer appear on the screen in and for itself, and thus the cinema of "pure seeing" had also become its victim. In response to the cynical form of film he had first experienced in Leone's postclassical Western, Wenders envisioned another form of mixing elements from classical cinema with the visual experiences of the present. Fragments that represent the grand myth of "America"—shots of places and landscapes, grand dimensions of space and depth, classical elements of technique and style, diverse genres, and different historical periods—would all appear in the same film. But as in *Easy Rider*, they would come together in an alternative form of narrative that would overcome cynical resignation. Thus *Paris, Texas*, his first attempt to put his intentions into practice, opens with a long shot of Devil's Graveyard in Big Bend National Park (reminiscent of John Ford's Westerns) before moving gradually into the suburban environment of Burbank, California. Its protagonist, Travis, the updated self-sufficient loner of the Western, rides into town (contemporary America) to take on those corrupt forces that subvert the pursuit of the American Dream. No longer, however, are they embodied in the greedy banker or ruthless large ranch owner. In *Paris, Texas* the anachronistic outsider falls prey to a myriad of cultural and social forces to which he responds with cynical disinterest; nothing but the empty remnant shell of that once vibrant dream of America remains.

Despite this pessimistic portrayal of contemporary America, Wenders envisioned a new narrative cinema that would activate the residual forces that these images carry with them (from past films) and put them to use in the revitalization of cinema's capacity to create myths in earnest. He succeeds in this more affirmative form of alternative film only when he returns to Germany after making *Paris, Texas*. On the one hand appalled by the inroads the American media industry had made into European culture, and on the other hand heartened by the alternative national vision he discovered in the "free" city of Berlin, Wenders turned his attention to myths of German identity and national history. As the final words of *Wings of Desire* proclaim, he saw the film as a new beginning in the creation of a critical, yet affirmative film art that acknowledges the need for the restoration of German national identity, despite its problematic past. Through this unlikely fusion of the critical *Filmautor* with the affirmative national filmmaker, Wenders situates himself anew between classical Hollywood and traditional European film art. With the inclusion of diverse and fragmentary elements on the one hand, and the shift toward a more impersonal, collective form of narrative on the other, he takes significant steps away from both poles.

Postmodernism—An Opposition from Within

The ambivalent stance toward both classical high art and popular (American) culture makes Wenders's work an obvious subject in the contemporary debate about modernism and postmodernism, a debate in which Wenders's films have been cited by critics of various denominations. While terminological inconsistencies and different historical, political, and aesthetic preconceptions about what exactly defines the postmodern make it difficult to apply a definitive "modern" or "postmodern" label to Wenders's cinema, the questions that this stimulating debate has raised are quite relevant for his work. It is not difficult to see why questions about authorship, about the relation of high art and popular culture, about the appropriation of style and genre in the form of parody or pastiche, or about representation and simulation—all of which lie at the heart of the debate about postmodernism—can be discussed through Wenders's films.

It is, however, also not surprising that those critics who cite Wenders's films as an example of postmodernist cinema often register as well their affinity to the aesthetic tenets of modernism. His films generally feature a solitary male protagonist who resembles the alienated outsider typical of modernist texts. However, in all such cases the (journeying) male protagonist is neither a figure whose alienation constitutes a rejection of the social order as a whole nor the individualistic hero of American cinema who puts things back in order, at least within the fictional confines of the film narrative. On the contrary, Wenders's films call into question the role of the centered subject, its potential either to exact critique or to offer a subjective path back to some lost authenticity. Also, to the extent that his work reflects on the experience of the filmmaker, it seems to resort to the modernist reliance on the subjectivity of the artist. In Wenders's case, however, it is more the filmmaking experience and the film vision generated as a part of that process that were often incorporated into the filmic text. In fact, this commitment to an evolutionary unfolding of the film almost as a by-product of the filmmaking experience defined in part the trilogy of road movies in the mid-1970s that first established Wenders's reputation as a *Filmautor*, both in Germany and abroad. In their self-referentiality and self-reflexivity, virtually all of his films can be read as allegories of their own making—especially *Kings of the Road*, *The American Friend*, *The State of Things*, and his diary films and documentaries. Thus with respect to both the diegetic and the authorial subject, Wenders lies once again somewhere between, and moving away from, European film art and the classical American idiom.

Other aspects of his work seem to identify him as a postmodernist filmmaker. Indeed, the situation of the New German directors, particularly of those who belong to the second wave which emerged during the late 1960s and early 1970s, had them adopting strategies typical of postmodernism. As they frequently took up American genres and styles that could appeal to the movie public of their generation, they were faced not only with the question of how to transform them so as to create "German" cinema, but also with the task of working within a dominant film language while producing a critique of that language itself. Thus even before New German Cinema had come of age, these directors found themselves engaged in a postmodernist method of combining popular and aesthetically innovative art forms to generate opposition to the dominant culture from within. Wenders has stated that as a student at the Munich Academy of Film and Television he had not only to discover a directing style of his own, but to invent for himself the whole art of directing.[30] If it is true, as Andreas Huyssen writes, that "postmodernism always has been in search of tradition while pretending to be innovation,"[31] then Wenders's conspicuous rhetoric of starting out of a cinematic no-man's-land might also be seen as an attempt to situate himself in a postmodernist setting, one free of that duality of cultures in which he grew up and evolved as a filmmaker.

Texts By and About Wenders

The idea for this anthology grew out of a need to bring together in one place both recent scholarship on Wim Wenders and writings by him not yet available in English. Although Wenders is arguably the leading European filmmaker of the last two decades, he has not received as much attention by scholars either in the United States or in Europe as some of his colleagues who also had their beginnings in New German Cinema. This is true even though his work, probably more than that of any other European director, reflects the tension between the European auteur tradition and the increasing dominance of the American media industry. Moreover, his films place this tension within the context of the unique relation to American pop culture and Hollywood cinema experienced by his postwar generation in the Federal Republic. This volume serves as an introduction to the central concerns of his cinema, while it also situates his work within German film history and the contemporary debates about film and media theory.

There exist certain recurring themes and tensions in Wenders's work that are central to the contemporary discussions surrounding postmodernism: his position between German and American culture, and between European auteurism and Hollywood studio production; the tension within German cinema between filmmaking as active intervention in life and films that invite the viewer to see openly and without coercion; the tension between authentic representation and simulation; the loss of traditional national and individual identities and the eclipse of a centered subject in film narrative; and the tension we identify as the most central and comprehensive one within Wenders's films and essays—that between image and narrative. Our introductory remarks have traced the history of these issues in his works, showing how closely they are tied to his youth in the Federal Republic and his development as filmmaker within the course of New German Cinema.

The various materials gathered in this anthology are united by their common focus on the concerns outlined above. The section "Documents" gathers materials in which Wenders himself addresses these issues. These texts chronicle important shifts and continuities in his work over the last fifteen years. The first two are from 1982, a pivotal year for Wenders's filmmaking. They document his loss of confidence in film images and his subsequent resolve to find a new, more viable relation between images and narrative. "Impossible Stories," an address at a summer film colloquium in Livorno, appears here in a new translation. The voice-over to his short *Reverse Angle*, a diary film made in New York for French television, is published here for the first time in its original English version. The last three essays stem from a later time (1991–92) and present his belief that film is now going through a period of technological transition that will have as dramatic an effect on cinema as sound did in the 1920s. In two short talks, "I'm at Home Nowhere" and "High Definition," he takes a fairly optimistic stance toward the latest developments in image technology. In "Talking about Germany" he discusses these developments in the context of the new unified Germany. Assuming a potentially controversial position, Wenders once again takes up in this speech the question of identity, arguing that a salvation from the proliferation of (American) mass-media images rests with (the German) language.

Our "Excerpts from Interviews with Wenders"—consisting of texts from the mid-1970s up to a 1994 interview with one of the editors in which he responds to the disappointing reception of his feature film *Faraway, So Close!*—offers his own informal and at times quite personal perspective on the central tensions that inform his films and writings. We have grouped them according to thematic categories in the hope that this arrangement will enhance their value as collaborative research material for both students and film scholars. They represent Wenders's most direct and insightful comments on the theoretical concerns that are central to the essays in this volume. Most of these excerpts are from interviews that were conducted in German and which until now have not been available in English translation.

The second half of the book presents nine essays by American and European scholars that explore individual films or aspects of Wenders's work. While differing significantly in methodology and scope, they share the concern of tracing and theorizing the many twists and turns that the relationship between image and narrative in his films has taken amidst the changes in contemporary European and American history, film history, cultural production, media technology, and aesthetics. These individual essays are also unified by their explicit or implicit attempt to situate Wenders's work, or at least certain aspects of it, within the debate about modernism and postmodernism.

In the first contribution, Richard McCormick addresses the question of literary adaptation in Wenders's collaboration with Peter Handke, as he focuses on the tension and affinity between film and literature in the broader political and cultural context of post-1968 West Germany. In

McCormick's discussion of *Wrong Move*, part of a more comprehensive study of feminist and postmodern tendencies, the film emerges as a postmodern mixing of high art and popular culture that reflects the complex interactions of writing, politics, specularity, and filmmaking in the early 1970s. Setting off Wenders's film from Handke's screenplay in terms of their "postrevolutionary" responses to German history, McCormick scrutinizes in each case the positioning of the writer within his respective literary and cinematic contexts of New Subjectivity and New German Cinema. He concludes that the film results in a substantially different political casting of the writer from that found in Handke's screenplay.

Timothy Corrigan's essay "German Friends and Narrative Murder" focuses on some of Wenders's American role models, namely, his ersatz Hollywood fathers John Ford and Nicholas Ray. Engaging *The American Friend* and *Lightning over Water* (the documentary about Nicholas Ray's dying of cancer), as well as Handke's America novel *Short Letter, Long Farewell*, Corrigan shows how Wenders's films rewrite traditional oedipal narratives by turning the desire to kill into "a conversation between Oedipus and his father." He argues that it is film's ability to depict the father-son relationship between directors in corporeal terms that subverts the traditional fetishization of the father's "body" in the anonymous narrative medium of film.

In his essay "Postmodern Culture and Film Narrative," Roger Cook investigates Wenders's shift in aesthetic strategies in the early 1980s. Tracing the roots of this (re)turn to narrative back to Wenders's earliest experiences with American cinema and pop culture, Cook argues that this shift occurs when the paradigmatic change to postmodern culture alters those models of reception that had informed Wenders's first contact with America. Reading *Paris, Texas* as a "coming to terms" with these developments in American culture, Cook maintains that Wenders confronts the ineffectiveness of his filmic approach in the film itself. He charts how the film situates the newest version of Wenders's alienated male protagonist within postmodern culture and, in doing so, brings the central (and centered) male figure typical of Wenders's films into question. He concludes that in his attempt to position the subject differently, Wenders is not abandoning all belief in the "authenticity" of experience but rather is searching for resilient narrative structures that can restore links to both individual and collective (past) experience.

The impact and anxiety of influence is taken up again by Nora Alter, who discusses Wenders's relation to Japanese director Yasujiro Ozu, Wenders's "only master." As Wenders repeatedly underscored, he turned to Ozu as a role model for his own development as an artist. Unlike his admiration for American directors whose work he had known long before Ozu's, this relationship seemingly lacks the overtones of oedipalization, colonization, and subversion. As Alter shows in her reading of *Tokyo-Ga*, the homage to the Japanese director is a hybrid work that stands at the juncture of modernist nostalgia and postmodernist cynicism, for it combines the topical study of Tokyo and Japan with disillusioned and sometimes paradoxical reflections on the production, meaning, and consumption of images.

In a second contribution, this one focusing on *Wings of Desire*, Cook suggests that after a period of filmmaking in America, Wenders's films became disengaged from the complex of American influences and oedipal associations. Applying theoretical film concepts that derive from Lacan, Cook examines how the film engages the viewing subject in the filmic discourse in a manner that supplants more conventional forms of viewer identification. As a film that works through those aesthetic issues confronting Wenders at the time, *Wings of Desire* involves the spectator both in an affirmative narrative infused with desire and, at the same time, in an analysis of narrative. In Cook's account, the film explores parallels between the investment of individual desire in narrative and the structuring of collective desire in national history, even while its own narrative evokes the German desire for an alternative national history.

Norbert Grob's reading of *Until the End of the World* critically assesses Wenders's taking leave of the aesthetics of leisure that informed much of his previous work. No longer based on slow, attentive, and faithful recordings of the everyday and without the straying and curious gaze of his earlier films, this postmodern mixture of genre, topics, and plots focuses—and thus narrows—its attention on the act of seeing itself, but blurs its vision in the process. Wenders's travelers turn into the very tourists he once detested for their "evil gaze."

The importance of the notion of gender in the films and writings of Wim Wenders is explored by Gerd Gemünden. His analysis of the conspicuous concern with male protagonists and male genres presents them as a problematic feature of most of Wenders's work, which, even while addressed primarily to audiences who are willing to identify with a male point of view, deconstructs traditional concepts of masculinity. Furthermore, questions of gender are shown to inform Wenders's approach to American popular culture, narrative, and the logic of representation. In doing so, they display the paradoxes typical of the postmodern condition. Most significantly, the exclusion of women has an aesthetic counterpart in Wenders's refusal to tell stories. However, the turn from narrative renders the protagonist susceptible to the lure of the unchained image as it proliferates in postmodern culture.

Alice Kuzniar also situates Wenders's aesthetics within the postmodern. Refuting Lacanian readings of Wenders and much of the psychoanalytic film theory based on his work, "Wenders's Windshields" engages Jean Baudrillard's theory of simulation in a study of the windshields and mirrors of Wenders's road movies. As Kuzniar shows through her analysis of their multiple devices of reflection, reproduction, and simulation (including acting), Wenders's lonely protagonists are not alienated or disenchanted characters but in postmodern fashion interface with their worlds through the window/mirror/screen. In her assessment of these male loners, Kuzniar observes that they do not display the hostility toward the hyperproduction of images that one often finds in Wenders's writings and "essay" films. Both Gemünden and Kuzniar contend that the indulgence in a free flow of images distinguishes Wenders's protagonists from the specifically male (Gemünden), alienated (Kuzniar) subject of narrative. And both pose the question of how Wenders counteracts the flip side to this fascination with images, that is, the postmodern tyranny of the screen(ed) image.

In the final essay, Thomas Elsaesser identifies the tension between the moviegoer and the moviemaker as central for the cinema of Wim Wenders. He traces Wenders's development from a spectator to a filmmaker making films about characters who position themselves as spectators of themselves and of life—a strategy that informs the most important aspects of Wenders's oeuvre: the interminable love-hate relationship with Hollywood; the formal-aesthetic issue of story versus image; and his political agenda of filmmaking. Dissecting the many paradoxes of Wenders's strategies of reflection and identification, Elsaesser explains how Wenders's anti-American tales make him the favorite European director in the United States.

Notes

1. "[Rock music] was for me the only alternative to Beethoven (and I'm really exaggerating here) because I was very insecure then about all culture that was offered to me, because I thought it was all fascism, pure fascism; and the only thing I was secure with from the beginning and felt had nothing to do with fascism was rock music"; Jan Dawson, "An Interview with Wim Wenders," *Wim Wenders*, trans. Carla Wartenberg (New York: Zoetrope, 1976) 12.

2. Dawson 9.

3. Dawson 13.

4. Timothy Corrigan, *New German Film: The Displaced Image*, (Austin: Texas UP, 1983) 10–11.

5. Wim Wenders, *Emotion Pictures: Reflections on the Cinema*, trans. Sean Whiteside and Michael Hofmann (London: Faber and Faber, 1989) 37.

6. Wenders 37.

7. Christian Braad Thomsen, "Five Interviews with Rainer Werner Fassbinder," *Fassbinder*, ed. Tony Rayns (London: BFI, 1976) 83.

8. See Anton Kaes, *From "Hitler" to "Heimat": The Return of History as Film* (Cambridge: Harvard UP, 1989) 75–76.

9. Timothy Corrigan, "Producing Herzog: From a Body of Images," *The Films of Werner Herzog: Between Mirage and History*, ed. Timothy Corrigan (New York: Methuen, 1986) 7.

10. Michael Rutschky, *Erfahrungshunger: Ein Essay über die Siebziger Jahre* (Cologne: Kiepenheuer and Wietsch, 1982).

11. Michael Dost, Florian Hopf, and Alexander Kluge, *Filmwirtschaft in der BRD und in Europa: Götterdämmerung in Raten* (Munich: Hanser, 1973) 129.

12. Taja Gut, "Unterwegs: Zur Filmkunst Wim Wenders,'" an interview with Wenders in *Individualität* 19 (1988): 35.

13. Thomas Elsaesser, *New German Cinema: A History* (New Brunswick, NJ: Rutgers UP, 1989) 5.

14. One should be cautious here not to equate the aesthetics of Fassbinder and Syberberg with the "protopolitical" aesthetic strategies characteristic of high modernism. This is Jameson's term for the high modernist attempts to transform the world through aesthetic innovation, substituting cultural politics for politics proper. In the films of even the most avant-garde New German directors, aesthetic innovation almost inevitably went hand in hand with sociohistorical criticism.

15. See Eric Rentschler, *West German Film in the Course of Time: Reflections on the Twenty Years since Oberhausen* (Bedford Hills, NY: Redgrave, 1984) 64.

16. Corrigan, "Producing Herzog" 6.

17. Elsaesser 208.

18. Wenders 49.

19. Rentschler 174.

20. Siegfried Kracauer, *Theory of Film: The Redemption of Physical Reality* (Oxford: Oxford UP, 1960).

21. Wenders vii.

22. From a 1957 *Cahiers du cinéma* interview with Anthony Mann; quoted in Wenders 6.

23. Wenders 7.

24. Wenders 38.

25. When Wenders first overlooked *Summer in the City* as a feature film it was in the context of his successful application to receive Film Subsidy funding for *The Goalie's Anxiety at the Penalty Kick* as a first feature film.

26. Dawson 9.

27. Wenders 24.

28. Wenders 24.

29. Wenders 25.

30. Rainer Nolden, "Wim Wenders: Ein Drehbuch zu Schreiben, das ist die Hölle," an interview with Wenders in *Die Welt* June 20, 1988. Wenders says that this was generally true of the New German directors, and he mentions Herzog and Fassbinder as examples. He refers to Schlöndorff, who had worked as an assistant with Louis Malle, as an exception to the rule. One could also include as an exception Kluge, who had not actually worked as an assistant but had been present as an observer during the making of Fritz Lang's final films at the CCC Studio in Berlin.

31. Andreas Huyssen, *After the Great Divide: Modernism, Mass Culture, Postmodernism* (Bloomington: Indiana UP, 1987) 170.

Documents

Impossible Stories

The only English equivalent of "erzählen" is the composite expression "to tell stories." And that is the crux of my problem here: You have invited someone to speak to you on narration who has always had nothing but problems with stories.

Let me go back to the very beginning. I was a painter, interested only in space: landscapes and cities. I became a filmmaker when I realized that I was not getting anywhere as a painter. The paintings lacked something, as did the act of painting. It would have been too easy simply to say that they lacked life; rather I realized that they lacked a concept, the notion of time. Thus when I began making films I thought of myself as a painter of spatial images who was searching for temporality. It never occurred to me that the missing element was "storytelling." I must have been quite naive. I thought making films would be easy. As a painter I thought that if I saw something I would be able to depict it as well; and I also thought that a storyteller (not that I was one anyway) simply had to listen to something first and then tell it. For me, making a film meant simply linking all those things together. That was a misconception—but before I can explain that, there is something else I have to talk about.

My stories always start from images. When I began working on my first film I was only interested in "landscape portraits." My very first film, *Silver City*, consisted of ten shots, each three minutes long—that was the length of a 16mm reel used for daylight shooting. Each shot was of a cityscape. The camera remained in one place, and nothing happened. Basically, these shots were like the watercolor paintings I had been doing before, only

This talk was first delivered in French at a colloquium on narrative techniques in Livorno, Italy, in 1982. Reprinted with permission from *The Logic of Images: Essays and Conversations by Wim Wenders*, translated by Michael Hofmann (London: Faber and Faber Ltd., 1991).

this time they were recorded on film. However, one shot was different: it was of an empty landscape with railroad tracks; the camera was placed right next to the tracks. I knew when the train would go by. I started shooting two minutes before the train arrived, and everything seemed to be exactly as it had been in all the other shots in the film: a deserted landscape. But then two minutes later someone ran into the picture from the right, passed by close to the camera, jumped over the tracks, and disappeared on the left. And just as he left the frame the train roared into the shot from the right, in an even more startling fashion than the strange man before. (Because there was no sound track—the film was only set to music—you could not hear the train coming.) In this tiny bit of "action"—a man crossing the tracks just before the train passes through—all of a sudden a "story" begins: What's wrong with the man? Is he being followed? Did he want to commit suicide? Why is he in such a hurry? And so on and so forth. The stillness of the "landscape with train" was interrupted. I think at this very moment I became a storyteller. And from that moment on all my difficulties began as well, because for the first time, at a set that I myself had arranged, something happened.

The problems became manifold very quickly, when I realized during the editing of the ten shots that after this scene in which a man recklessly crosses the tracks, people would expect something to happen in all subsequent shots. Thus for the first time I had to consider how to put shots together, that is, how to deal with dramaturgy. That was the end of my naive notion that I could simply string together a series of motionless shots without any connection. The connection created by the editing, or by the mere act of assembling shots—arranging and combining them in sequence—was already the first step toward narrative. People would see even the slightest connection between these images as an attempt to tell a story. But that was not what I wanted. I only wanted to combine time and space; nevertheless, from that moment on I was forced into telling stories. From then on and until this very day, there exists for me an opposition between images and stories, as if they were working against each other, though without totally excluding each other. To be sure, images have always interested me more; and the fact that they start telling a story as soon as they have been combined is still a problem for me today.

My stories always begin with places, cities, landscapes, or roads. For me a map is like a script. When I look at a city, for example, I begin asking myself what all could take place there; the same thing happens with a building, like in my hotel room here in Livorno: I look out the window, it's raining hard, and a car stops in front of the hotel. Someone gets out and takes a look around. Then the person walks down the street without an umbrella, in spite of the rain. Immediately a story begins to take shape in my head: Where is this person going? What kind of street is he turning into?

Of course, stories can also begin in different ways. The following happened to me recently: I am sitting alone in a hotel lobby, waiting to be picked up by someone I don't know. A woman comes in, looking herself for someone she doesn't know. She comes up to me and asks: "Are you Mr. So-and-so?" and I almost said yes! Just because I'm fascinated by the idea that I could actually experience the beginning of a story or a film. A story can actually begin with a dramatic event such as this one, but usually I come up with stories as a result of contemplative moments when I am looking at landscapes, houses, roads, and pictures.

Writers seem to come up with stories because of the logical connections inherent in narration—in the sense that every word tends to belong to a sentence and sentences tend to belong to a coherent whole; a writer does not have to force either the words into a sentence or the sentences into a story. There seems to be a kind of inevitability in the way stories come to be told. In films—at least in my films, for there are of course different ways of going about it—the images do not necessarily lead to something else; they stand on their own. I believe that an image is more self-contained, while words strive to form a coherence, that is, to be part of a story. For me, images do not automatically have this tendency to form part of a story. If they are to function like words and sentences, they have to be "forced" to do so; that is, they have to be manipulated.

My thesis, then, is that for me as a filmmaker, telling stories always means that you are forcing images into something. At times this manipulation develops into an artistic way of telling stories, but not necessarily. Often enough, the result is only abused images.

I do not like the manipulation required to force all the images of a film into one story; it is dangerous for the images because it has the tendency to drain them of their "life." For me, the relationship between stories and images is like the story of a vampire who tries to suck the blood out of images. Images are quite sensitive, like snails that pull back into their shells when you touch their feelers. They don't want to work like a horse, they don't want to carry and transport anything: neither a message, nor a meaning; neither a purpose, nor a moral. But that's exactly what stories want from them.

So far, everything seems to speak against stories, as though they were the enemy. But of course stories are also very exciting; they are powerful and important for mankind—as if they were giving people something that they deeply desire, something more than entertainment or distraction or suspense. What people want primarily is that there be a certain coherence. Stories give people the feeling that there is meaning, that behind the inscrutable disarray of all phenomena there is a hidden order in which everything has its place. This order is what people desire more than anything else; I would almost say that the notion of order or of stories is connected to the concept of God. Stories are a substitute for God. Or vice versa.

Personally (and hence my problems with stories), I believe more in chaos, in the inexplicable complexity of all those things around me. Basically, I think that individual situations are not related to each other, and the experiences in my life seem to consist only of such isolated situations; I have never been involved in a story with a beginning and an end. For someone who tells stories this is an outright sin, but I have to confess that in my whole life I have not experienced a single story. I actually think that stories deceive; or more precisely, by definition stories are fabrications. Nevertheless, they are extremely important for our survival. Their contrived structure helps us to overcome our worst fears: that there is no God, that we are nothing but tiny oscillating particles with perception and consciousness, but lost in a universe that remains beyond our conception. By creating coherence and meaning, stories make life bearable and allay our fears. That is why children like to hear stories before they fall asleep. That is why the Bible is one long storybook, and why stories should always have a happy ending.

Of course the stories in my films give order to the images. Without the stories, images that interest me would easily become lost and susceptible to all kinds of arbitrariness.

For this reason, film stories are something like travel routes. A map is the most exciting thing in the world for me; when I see a map I immediately feel restless, especially when it is a map of a country or city where I have never been before. I look at all the different names and want to know what they refer to—the streets of a city, the cities of a country. When I look at a map it eventually turns into an allegory of life itself. I can only bear to look at maps if I try to chart a path and to follow it through the city or country. Stories do just that: they provide orientation in an unknown territory, where otherwise you would travel to a thousand different places without ever getting anywhere.

What kind of stories are told in my films? They can be divided into two different groups; I make a sharp distinction between them because they belong to two totally different systems or traditions. What is more, I alternated between the two categories, except for a single film, *The Scarlet Letter*, and that one was a mistake.

The first group (A) consists of all the black-and-white films, except for *Lightning over Water*, which does not belong to either one of the traditions (I am not sure whether it is even a film at all, and that's why I am excluding it). The other group (B) consists of all the color films, all of which are based on published novels. Each film in group A, on the other hand, is based on an idea of mine—"idea" is a loose term here that includes dreams, daydreams, and experiences. All the films in group A were more or less made without a script, while the others followed a script very closely. The A films have a loose structure, while the B films all have a tightly knit dramatic structure. The A films were filmed in chronological sequence; each one evolved for the most part from a single known element, the situation with which the story begins. The B films followed the more traditional method of nonchronological, piecemeal filming whereby production concerns determined the sequencing. With the A films I never knew beforehand how they would end; I always knew the ending of the B films from the outset.

Basically, all the films of group A operate in a very open system, and those of group B in a very closed one. Both represent not only different forms of filmmaking, but also different approaches, different attitudes: openness on the one hand, discipline on the other. I did not discover or analyze the themes of the A films until I started shooting. The themes of the B films were known from the beginning in each case, and I then had to discover what was wrong or right about them. The A films developed from the inside out, the B films the other way around. A story had to be found for the A films, while one had to be forgotten for the B films.

The fact that (with the exception of the one mistake mentioned above) the A and B films were constantly alternating indicates that each film was reacting to the previous one—and precisely that indicates my dilemma.

I always made an A film because the previous film followed too many rules, so that I was not spontaneous enough and I lost interest in the characters. Also, I always felt that, along with the crew and the actors, I had to expose myself to a new situation. With the B films it was exactly the other way around: I made them because I could not stand how "subjective" the previous film was, and I had the need to work again with a firm structure, using the framework of a story. In the B films the actors played roles, they portrayed fictional characters who were different from themselves; in the A films they presented and interpreted themselves, or simply *were* themselves. With these films, my interest and work consisted in making my discoveries part of the film. For the B films, things had to be invented. It is becoming more and more obvious that you could call the one group "subjective" and the other "the search for objectivity." Of course, it is not quite that simple.

I would now like to turn to the question of how the A films began and what role the story played in them. The first film was titled *Summer in the City*; it tells of a man who has spent two years in prison. The first shot shows him coming out of prison and suddenly having to face life again. He tries to meet up with his old friends again and to reestablish old relationships, but he quickly realizes that nothing is the way it used to be. In the end he takes off to America. The second film in the A series, *Alice in the*

Cities, is about a man who is supposed to write a story about America. He is getting nowhere with it, and the film begins as he decides to return to Europe. By chance he meets a little girl, Alice, and her mother, and he agrees to take Alice back to her grandmother in Europe. But he does not know where she lives; all he has is a photograph of the house. The rest of the film consists of the search for this house.

A man tries to commit suicide—this is how *Kings of the Road* begins. By chance, another man happens to watch him, so he gives up on his kamikaze behavior. The second man has a truck. They decide to travel on together, again by pure chance. The film is about their travels and whether they have something to say to each other or not.

The last film of group A, *The State of Things*, is about a film crew that has to stop filming because the money has run out and the producer has disappeared. The crew does not know whether they will be able to finish shooting at all. The film is about this group of people who have lost their orientation and, in particular, about the director, who eventually returns to Hollywood to look for the producer.

All these films are about people who encounter unfamiliar situations on their journeys; they are all about seeing, about perceptions, and about people who suddenly have to see things differently.

In order to be as specific as possible, I would like to come back to *Kings of the Road*. How did it begin? One explanation would be that I had just completed *Wrong Move*—that it was a reaction to the film that preceded it. I felt that I needed to come up with a story in which I could investigate myself and my country; the previous film had been about Germany as well, but in a different way. This time it was to be a journey into unknown territory, unknown territory within myself, and in the middle of Germany. I knew what I wanted, but I did not know how to begin. Then everything began with a single image.

I was passing a truck on the autobahn; it was hot, and it was an old truck without air-conditioning. There were two men in the truck, and the driver had his leg hanging out the door to try to keep cool. This brief image, seen in the corner of my eye while passing the truck, made a strong impression on me. I happened to stop at the rest area where the truck also stopped. I went to the counter where the two men from the truck were standing. They did not exchange a word; it was as though they had nothing in common. You got the impression that they did not even know one another. I asked myself: What do these two men see? How do they see things on their travels through Germany?

At this time I was traveling a lot myself through Germany with my previous film, *Wrong Move*. As I traveled around I became aware of the situation of the rural movie theaters. I was fascinated by the theater interiors, the projection rooms, and the projectionists. Then I studied a map of Germany and noticed that there was one route through this country that I hardly knew at all. It ran along the border between the GDR and the FRG, in the very middle of Germany and yet right on its edge. And all at once I knew that I had everything I needed for my new film: a new route and the story of the two men who do not know each other. I was interested in what all might happen to them and between them. One of them would have a job with the movie theaters, and I knew where I could find these theaters: along the border.

Of course that is still not a story. All of the films in group A began with certain situations that I hoped would develop into a story. For this transformation to take place, one can apply the method of "daydreaming." What I mean is, stories always require a certain amount of control; that is, they know their destination and know how to get there, they have a beginning and an end. A daydream functions completely differently; it does not have this dramaturgical control. It has rather something like a subconscious guide who wants to move ahead, no matter where to; every dream is headed somewhere, but who can say where? Something in the subconscious knows where, but one can only find out by letting things take their course; and that's what I tried to do in all these films. The English word "drifting" expresses this very well. It is not the shortest path between two points, but rather a zigzag course. Perhaps a better word would be "meandering" because it implies a route but with detours.

A journey is an adventure through time and space. Adventure, time, and space—all three are important. Stories and journeys have them in common. A journey always entails curiosity for the unknown and creates expectations and heightened perceptions: on the road you begin to see things that you no longer see at home. To get back to *Kings of the Road*: after ten weeks of shooting we found ourselves still in the middle of the journey, although I had planned to finish the film by then. There was no money left to go on shooting, and yet we were still a long way from our destination. The problem was this: How should the journey end? Or: How could it be transformed into a story? At first I thought of an accident. Had the film been shot in America, it would have certainly ended with an accident. But thank God we were not in America and I had the freedom to proceed differently in order to get to the "truth of the story." So we broke off the filming and tried to drum up some money so that we could shoot for another five weeks. Of course there is the danger that a film of this genre could go on forever. The solution, finally, turned out to be that the two men would have to part ways and realize that it could not go on like this; they would have to change their lives. But before that there was another idea, another "detour": the two protagonists would search for their parents. I imagined that this would lead to a break in their relationship. So we filmed a long story of how the one visits his father, and another long story of how the other re-

Kamikaze (Hanns Zischler), suitcase in hand, is ready to resume his life at the end of *Kings of the Road* (1976).

turns to the place where he grew up with his mother. Unfortunately, this only improved their relationship so that after these two episodes we were even further from an ending than before. Suddenly and for the first time the two could talk to each other. We broke off the filming once again. It occurred to me that the film might end this way: the two begin to question what they had done before they met each other and eventually have doubts about their own goals. I imagined that the one traveling around to movie theaters begins to wonder whether it is worthwhile to try to help these rural movie theaters keep going; the other one resumes his professional work as a linguist and speech therapist for children. And in the end that is what we filmed.

The State of Things is also about stories. Of course, the figure of the director represents in certain aspects my personal dilemma: "Stories and life are mutually exclusive." That is his theory as a filmmaker. Later, though, when he goes to Hollywood he gets involved in one of those stories he never believed in, but one that actually kills him. Clearly, this is a paradox. And yet that is all that I would like to say about stories: they are one big impossible paradox. I reject stories completely, because for me they create lies, and nothing but lies; and the biggest lie is that they create a coherence where none exists. And yet we need these lies so much that it is totally pointless to fight them and to put together a sequence of images without a story—without the lie of a story. Stories are impossible, but it is impossible to live without them.

What a mess!

Reverse Angle: New York City, March 1982

"Another night, arriving at another airport and coming from yet another city: For the first time in his life he was sick and tired of traveling. All cities had become one. Somehow he kept thinking of a book that he must have read as a child. All he remembered from it was this feeling of being lost . . ."

That could be the beginning of another story or another film. Just cut to the close up. But it's not the way this one will work. This one doesn't have a story. What is it about then?

I hesitate to talk about myself. Okay, I'm a filmmaker, my films are even very personal; but never private. I was tempted, though, when I was asked if I'd make a sort of New York journal over a couple of weeks for French television. What made me want to do it in the end was the idea to take a camera myself and shoot something outside the context of a story. Just images.

One should think that after ten feature films I would regard this as my profession: to tell the stories through images. But strangely enough, I could never really believe that. Maybe because somehow the images always mattered more to me than the stories, or should I even say that often enough the "story" wasn't more than a pretext to find images. But images, too, aren't very reliable. From time to time, sometimes for weeks or even months, they seem to escape me. At least I don't see anything anymore that

This is the original text spoken by Wenders (in English) in his 1982 short film made for French television, *Reverse Angle*. It appeared in German translation in *Logik der Bilder*. Reprinted with permission from *The Logic of Images: Essays and Conversations by Wim Wenders*, translated by Michael Hofmann (London: Faber and Faber Ltd., 1991).

appears relevant and worth keeping. I totally lose the sense of conceiving images at all, and if I try, during such a time, they seem completely fortuitous, images without any form, because there is no look that could give them one. And the worst look that can happen: the point of view of a tourist.

And now too, without a story to tell, the images become interchangeable, arbitrary, and their objects in search of their lost form seem to be looking at me directly through the camera saying: "What do you want from us? Leave us alone!"

It means: another period of hostile images has started for me, and I'm running around in despair with my camera. No help to expect from the cinema. On the contrary, contemporary American films look more and more like their own trailers. So much here in America has this tendency to become its own publicity, leading to an inflation and invasion of mindless and despotic images. And television, as usual, the poison ivy of the eyes.

Finally, after days of blindness, it is two books that give me back sense and a liking of images—more peaceful ones, at least. A novel by Emanuel Bove—told very simply with a respect for details—and the paintings of Edward Hopper remind me that the camera, too, is capable of a description that lets things appear as they are. And with these newly found images, a new story sets in too: "She was sitting by the window, waiting. She looked at the sky and the park, just letting time go by . . ."

At the same time, another work with images is about to reach its end: the editing of *Hammett*, my first American picture, shot in Hollywood. There are three editors, working in three rooms, on three machines. The procedure is very different from the editing I've done before, less personal. I have the feeling that the story and the images don't belong to me. Here, the story and the images belong to the studio, to the producer.

One evening I appear on a talk show with Tony Richardson. Louis Malle is supposed to be there too, but he can't come. We talk, and we don't talk, of course, about the difference between European and American cinema.

The film that I made last year, during an eight-month interruption of *Hammett*, deals more precisely with this difference. The film is called *The State of Things*, and it ends in a mobile home going up and down Hollywood Boulevard, with a long dialogue between "the producer" and "the director" that leads to this song.

The producer of *Hammett*, Francis Ford Coppola, comes to New York for the very last days of editing. We have several previews in a screening room on Broadway with a random audience. Afterwards, there are long discussions about final changes and cuts.

In front of the house where I live in New York one can see the granite rock the city is built on. My next film, the next story, will deal with those rocks, too.

Working on the script I come across something the French painter Paul Cézanne said: "Everything is about to disappear. You've got to hurry up, if you still want to see things."

I hope it's not too late.

High
Definition

Good morning to all of you on this beautiful autumn day. The question of the day is: Can the dreams of artists and filmmakers be realized by High Definition Video?

My dreams and my nightmares are not only part of my life as a so-called artist, but also part of my life as a regular human being like all of you. So to define my position towards High Definition I have to place myself into the context of video in a broader sense. As you know, I am a filmmaker, so I hope you will not be disappointed that I am not going to do this from a technical point of view.

If I remember correctly from my school days, the word "video" is Latin. For several thousand years it meant "I see," and only for a very short period of time has it been the name for the electronic image. "Tele" is Latin, too; it means "far"; television is to see what is far away. Video—I see. As a filmmaker and photographer seeing is my business, my craft. And because I grew up with the photographic image, video (recording an electronic image) and television (sending or receiving an electronic image) had very little to offer in comparison to photography. In fact, in all honesty, video did not mean to me "I see," rather it meant "I don't see," or at least "I don't see well." Of course, video made cheaper and faster means of production possible, but these are qualities I do not trust very much. I prefer to see better instead of faster and cheaper. And especially these days when we are flooded constantly with images from all over, I would rather see less, but see well. To my mind, a few well-defined and precious, maybe even true images count more than plenty of mediocre ones. Thus my interest in High Definition was aroused by the claim expressed in the name

A lecture presented at the IECF roundtable discussion on "Can HDTV Make the Creators' Dreams Come True?" in Tokyo on November 5, 1990. Published here for the first time in the original English version.

itself. Thus far the two components, video on the one side and High Definition on the other, had been nothing but a paradox for me, one almost excluding the other.

During the past year I had the opportunity and the privilege—thanks to NHK and Sony—to work with High Definition and to use it to produce certain parts of my new film. I had the privilege to work inside NHK with their technicians and with my collaborator Sean Naughton, whom you will meet tomorrow, I think. The experience of this year has changed my vision of video. I am ready to believe now that the electronic medium can become an adequate tool for seeing and for enabling others to see. The electronic image is finally able to show an object appropriately—that is, without overlaying its so obvious and visible structure of four hundred or five hundred or however many lines onto the picture. Obviously a quantum leap has occurred that I assume will enable video and television to reach their full potential. Now they can finally do justice to the Latin origin of their names.

But, and this is what I really want to talk about, this "but" in capital letters: BUT is it enough if High Definition is technically able to see and to show us the world appropriately? I want to raise a few questions. I am not here to answer any of them, and I guess that is why we are all here, to raise questions and to discuss these issues. It is probably far too early for answers, anyway. High Definition is still in a rather experimental stage and only starting to become available to a wider public. So I am throwing a couple of questions at you, and I think for some of you who work much closer with television and video than me, some of my thoughts will be rather polemical.

For instance: I have always thought that it is one of the great cultural crimes of this century that video—the old conventional video—has replaced and largely destroyed its predecessor in the art of visual storytelling, the cinema. The electronic image has created its own language, a much simpler and cruder one than the organically grown, elegant language of cinema. Mainly for reasons of its own limitations—in definition, for instance —television has eliminated the beauty of the wide shot and replaced it with the paltry close-up. The "talking head" has become the mainstay of the electronic image. And mainly for reasons of competition between television stations, television has created faster editing rhythms and faster dramatic structures to keep audiences on a leash, thereby manipulating a whole generation, or maybe two by now, of children who grew up with television. The close affinity between television and advertisement has, in my opinion, also played a major role in shaping the language of television. In brief, the video culture has undermined and largely terminated the visual arts that preceded it. Movies nowadays already look like television for the most part, because their main exploitation comes afterwards on the small screen, and because their audiences have gotten used to television so much that they want movies to look like television.

So, I am not the first one to say that television has replaced cinema with something inferior; it has replaced it too fast, too greedily, and it was too badly equipped to replace it in the first place. If this is so, is the new High Definition electronic cinema just replacing the old electronic images with that same language, or will the High Definition cinema try to correct the harm and the injustice done to an old culture of images—the cinema? By replacing "Low Definition," High Definition has a historic chance to correct viewing habits and to discover once again a less terroristic, more friendly, in short, a more human vision. In the end "High Vision" will not be judged for its technical improvement—technology is always improving in every field anyway—High Vision will be judged at some time in the future for its moral improvement of vision. Do not misunderstand me, I am not the kind of moralist who believes we or anyone else will have much influence on what will eventually be shown on High Definition video and television. Of course, there will be High Definition porno, and no one is going to be able to prevent that. That is not what I am talking about. I am talking about how this new medium, as a rule, will satisfy the human need to see and to perceive the world, how it will entertain us and tell us stories.

In any case, I have high hopes that High Vision will be a less cynical language than its predecessor. And as a filmmaker I want to offer one piece of advice: the image makers and producers of High Definition should try to learn from a better source and a better tradition than from television. They should try to learn from the much more masterful and civilized language of cinema. High Definition is a very young culture; we are just witnessing its youth, actually its puberty. The best age to learn is when you are young. The older you get the more you get caught up in your bad habits. So I am hoping for a High Vision culture that does not develop bad habits right away. I am hoping, for instance, for the reestablishment of the wide shot and for aesthetic principles that are not just trying to exploit people's minds and eyes.

Another point I want to raise is the question of reality. This might turn out to be another moralistic issue. We all know how much the age of digital storage has changed the idea of "the original" and of "reality." Since I have been working now for a while on dream sequences at NHK, I know how much the electronic image, especially the digitally stored one, can be manipulated. That is nothing new, you all know that. The electronic image and especially the High Definition image is already by its very nature far removed from reality, a kind of abstraction of it. The single image, the single frame does not exist in the first place, and there is an enormous amount of technology between the eye that looks through the camera and the world in front of it. There is no longer a durable, tangible image. An enormous "loss of reality" occurs in the process between the recording of the electronic image and its reception. It is, therefore, no wonder that there is no more respect for reality in front of the television screen. This is again a very complex subject, and I am just mentioning it to get one thought across: High Vision could also use its gain in definition to counter this loss of reality. Loss of reality is a serious sickness of our civilization. It is a virus for which nobody has found the antidote, if anyone is even trying. It kills more life than any other virus.

High Vision, and this is the dream I have for it, could help sharpen our sense of reality; the nightmare of High Definition, on the contrary, would be that in the long run it would undermine even more any trust in the truth of images. High Definition is obviously the future of entertainment, of storytelling, of news reports; it is what our children and their children will be used to. In twenty years we will look back to the black-and-white sets of the sixties. Whether or not we will look at High Definition as something that truly improved our lives and our children's lives is in our hands right now. I am an optimist; there is a new language, and creative people all over the world should start working with it, making it their own and making it better—or even good in the first place. If the artists do not take this tool into their hands to help shape the new medium they will have no right later to complain if it does not correspond to their ideas.

I used High Definition because my new film dealt with dreams. I looked at almost all the dream sequences in the history of cinema, and I thought, none of them looks like dreams, they all look like movies. And while pondering what dreams could look like I stumbled onto the possibility of using High Vision technology. I was flabbergasted about the range of creative possibilities it offered. I was able to create an imagery—and we are not yet finished, we're still working on it—that no special effects could have produced. Some of our High Vision images have layers of up to a hundred elements, one on top of the other, which—as you probably know—is unthinkable in a movie; there would be no image left if you put ten duplicate negatives on top of each other. So, to come back to the original question: Can the dreams of artists and filmmakers be realized with High Definition? I could have spared you my whole speech, I could have just said: yes, it can. Thank you.

"I'm at Home Nowhere"

Friedrich Wilhelm Murnau was a great inventor of forms, a pioneer of storytelling, an artist of the image, one of the few great innovators of the seventh art form, the cinema. He was far ahead of his time, too far perhaps in order to endure this gap for very long. He lived his life as if he were a son of the second half of the twentieth century and not of the end of the nineteenth century. It is a great honor for me to receive the prize that carries his name. It is especially an honor to follow in the footsteps of Eric Rohmer, the first Murnau-prize recipient. I am grateful to the Murnau Society, the city of Bielefeld, and the association of Bielefeld banks.

A lot has changed in the cinema since the days when Murnau made films in Germany and America. The world has changed. And even if we cannot say that cinema changed the world, we can say that it contributed significantly to that change. Storytelling has changed, images have changed, the reception of images has changed, our way of experiencing the world has changed—to a degree, in fact, that would make Friedrich Wilhelm Murnau dizzy were he exposed to the wealth of images and the language of images that now confront us day to day, influencing, above all, those of us who are most open, the children.

Cinema is undergoing an upheaval. Therefore, I thought it appropriate to show a film tonight that in a way tried to take stock of cinema fifty years after Murnau's death. It is also not by coincidence that this is a black-and-white film and that the name of the director of the film within the film is Friedrich Munro. Nor is it a coincidence that the film begins in Europe, at Portugal's westernmost point, where Europe points its nose toward America, and that it ends with the death of the director in a street only an

This speech was given on March 17, 1991, upon acceptance of the Murnau Prize in Bielefeld, Murnau's hometown. It was followed by a screening of *The State of Things*.

hour by car from the place where Murnau met his death. In a telephone booth the evening before his death, Friedrich, the director, quotes a diary entry from F. W. Murnau: "I'm at home nowhere, in no house, in no country." Perhaps the view of cinema presented in *The State of Things* was too bleak; perhaps its point of view reflects too much the low point at which it was made. In the meantime, another ten years have passed and "the state of things" has long since changed again.

Cinema is going through a transition similar to the all-encompassing and revolutionary change from silent to sound film. The age of photography, of the photographic image, and thus of cinema itself, is coming to an end. At the end of this era, before entering the age of the digital-electronic image, cinema may be able to gather its forces one last time and do that for which it was invented: provide the people of the twentieth century with an image of themselves, both of their reality and their dreams. F. W. Murnau would be a great model for such an effort. He would certainly be the first to warn against a nostalgia that glorifies cinema and condemns the coming age of digital recording. He was a pioneer and he would still be one today. By definition, pioneers are optimists, and one can learn from them more about the future than about the past.

Today I don't see the future of cinema as bleak as I did in 1981 when *The State of Things* was made. Since then perspectives have opened up that were not conceivable at that time; or rather, the picture of the enemy has changed. We can no longer speak of the archenemy "television" and the devil "video"; instead, behind them a new ally and a new language of images is taking shape in the form of the high-definition, electronically mastered image. And then there will no longer be the "evil," overpowering American cinema and next to it the "poor" little national film productions in Germany, France, Italy, Spain, England, Poland, the Soviet Union— there will be an increasing awareness of "European Cinema" as a proud common language in all these countries, and hopefully an increasing awareness not only of this common language, but also of a truly European industry with its own institutions that can serve as a protecting roof and that can guarantee the survival of these small national industries. (For how long, is uncertain. Let us say: as long as possible, as long as cinema still exists.)

Such a great roof needs solid pillars and buttresses; for this reason, let us embrace Friedrich Wilhelm Plumpe, born in Bielefeld and also known as Friedrich Wilhelm Murnau, not so much as a "German" pioneer of film art as one of the great fathers of our European cinema.

Talking about Germany

Anybody who speaks necessarily speaks about him- or herself, be it only implicitly by the choice of words, the grammar, the pronunciation, or explicitly by stating a personal opinion, by speaking about one's own experiences, or even about oneself. I would like to do so quite explicitly. For me, "Talking about Germany" means talking about the German in me. I do not have much to say about "the Germans"; in fact, I do not even believe that "the Germans" exist.

My real name is not "Wim" Wenders, it is "Ernst Wilhelm" Wenders. I was conceived in the Eifel region during the last winter of the war and born in August 1945 in Düsseldorf on the Rhine as the son of the physician Dr. Heinrich Wenders and his wife, Martha. It was one week after the atomic bombs fell on Hiroshima and Nagasaki; it was the day of the Japanese surrender. I have always imagined that this must have been the newspaper headline on my birthday, to the extent that "we" already had newspapers again. When my father wanted to register me under the name "Wim," the town clerk told him that this was not a German name; thus my father had to agree to enter me into the family tree as "Wilhelm." I was given the middle name Ernst, after my godfather. But for some strange reason this name was entered first; as a consequence, I am often not even called Wilhelm, but rather simply referred to as "Ernst W.," for instance, whenever I enter the United States.

The first years of my life I spent in the house of my grandfather, the pharmacist Wilhelm Wenders, who owned the Pfalz Pharmacy on Kaiserwerther Street. The house survived the war, but almost everything around it had been destroyed. My first memories are of rubble. Heaps of rubble;

This speech was given at the Munich Kammerspiele, November 10, 1991.

chimneys pointing to the sky like fingers; a streetcar driving through hills of rubble. This, then, was my world; but as a child one accepts everything the way it is. Next we lived in Koblenz for four years, on the banks of the Mosel. That's where I began school at the Moselweiß Volksschule. Then we moved back to Düsseldorf, and I attended the Urdenbach Volksschule and then high school in Benrath. The boys high school had been relocated temporarily in the Benrath castle. Not long ago I was invited to the Élysée Palace, where I saw a painting of "my school" in President Mitterand's office. I proudly pointed to the windows of "my classroom," which at the time of the painting was still a part of the stables.

The last years of high school I spent in the Ruhr region, at the Freiherr-vom-Stein-Gymnasium in Oberhausen-Sterkrade. After my graduation I began studying medicine in Freiburg in Breisgau, but soon gave it up just as I would later give up the study of psychology, philosophy, and sociology. However, I did complete my studies at the Academy of Film and Television here in Munich, where I lived for ten years as a student, a film critic, and then eventually as a filmmaker. After that I spent seven years in the United States, coming away from this experience abroad with the knowledge that I am a German at heart and a European filmmaker. So I returned home, and since 1984 I have been living in Berlin, in the heart of the country about which I want to speak here today.

Why am I telling you my biography? Not because of me, you can be sure of that, but because I hope this rather German biography will provide me with an alibi to speak about Germany, as well as with the needed material.

But how do I speak about Germany? Sometimes I feel more like raging about Germany, or being ashamed of it; and I have even found myself boasting about Germany, or warning about it. But this way of talking is not of much use in this context; it is of little value when one addresses the "state" of Germany. So why am I standing in front of strangers and "speaking," when by definition I do something quite different, that is, make pictures, and when I cannot even speak without looking at my notes? Why, if not to discover something I am not aware of yet in this act of speaking and reflecting. Reflecting about what? About "Germany." The more I turn this word over and over again in my mouth, the less meaning it has and the more it becomes a purely geographic concept. But I am not referring to the map, which you all know well from the various shapes and roles this country has assumed over the course of time. Germany. It seems to me, if I may speak openly and freely, that this is something that does not even exist anymore. Or which at least does not yet exist again. It is, rather, a vacuum—perhaps not for you, but certainly for me. And that's the only reason I am standing here—to fill a vacuum, for myself. The occasion was appropriate, the task long overdue. What does "Germany" mean for me? I invite you to listen as I attempt to describe for myself this unknown country, to elucidate this strange word.

"Country." The *Father-land*, but also the *Mother-country*. The "faraway land," the "wide world." Actually, I have not been living in "a country" for a long time now. I am more on the road than at home; I travel all over the globe, even unto "the end of the world," if necessary. Each day the world is becoming a bit more like the proverbial village. What does "country" mean if there are no longer any borders, or if beyond the border everything looks the same? It is an anachronism, especially when a country thinks of itself as a nation, and even celebrates or fantasizes about its status as a nation—which is, in any case, a hopeless prospect. "We Germans" know this better than almost any other nation.

Recently Germany became *one country*—but does this mean that we are *a country*? And which country are we? I continue to see two—a rich one and a poor one. One that exists in 1991, and the other in a no-man's-time, not in a gray zone, but in a gray time, between times so to speak. It is rather fashionable to speak about jet lag and how to get over a nine- or twelve-hour time difference. Imagine a nine- to twelve-*year* time lag and the stupor you would feel.

How can we be surprised that there is so much hatred towards foreigners when the residents cannot even define their own country for themselves; when they do not know what their own place in this country is; when in their blind aggression they are not actually defending territory but rather fighting for inclusion in their own country? It seems to me that we are all foreigners here trying to settle an unknown country named Germany. This a bold thesis perhaps, but at least one that establishes a certain equality.

Fifteen years ago I made a film along the German-German border in the remote and desolate region at the edge of the military occupation zones. The two tired heroes sleep in an American army hut filled with the pinups and graffiti of American GIs. They get into a fight, and one of them, "Kamikaze," leaves at dawn, and the other, "King of the Road," wakes up alone, stumbles out of the hut, and stares through the fog at the frontier in front of him. What could he do, what gesture could he possibly make, now that nothing remained to be said? He screamed like Tarzan, a long, sad scream of the jungle. A little later "King of the Road" comes to a village and stops in front of a movie theater where he fixes the projectors, even though films are no longer shown there. The name of the theater, the name it had when we discovered it, was "The White Screen" [*Weiße Wand*]. That said it all, and we were able to end the film there.

When there is no country in sight anymore, does this other word or concept, "Heimat," continue to exist? Where do we experience better what homeland means than when we are abroad suffering from homesickness. I lived abroad for seven years in the United States. I wanted to become an American director, but I learned that it is not enough to live in America; one also has to live like an American, to act, think, and *speak* like an American. I was shocked, flabbergasted, the first time I was looking for a German word and could only think of the English word; it was a terrible feeling for me when I had to stop in the middle of a German sentence and ask, "Wie sagt man noch?" [Now how do you say that?], only to use the English word in the end. This was the moment of homesickness. I was about to lose something. It was not just one word or many words—which would be bad enough—but these words stood for something else, for my language. And with language I mean not just the words we use to express something—I know those words in the English, or rather the American language—but language as an attitude, a relation to the world, an "Einstellung." (This is a wonderfully precise word for a filmmaker, one that cannot be translated into another language: you film an "Einstellung," i.e., a shot; and you have a certain "Einstellung," i.e., an attitude or approach to the shot—the one does not exist without the other.) In my language there was no "It's nice to see you," no "Let's have lunch someday," and no "I'll call you later." When I said this in English, it was not "I" who was speaking. I was well on my way to becoming an American when the imminent danger that I would lose the German language showed me that these German words and this German grammar were a kind of framework inside me, something like an extension of the backbone into the brain. I would never really be able to say "I" or "me" or "moi," at least not without a certain *loss*. This is another precise word: *Ver-lust*, "to lose one's desire." I remember that just after this experience of *Verlust* I read a German book again, the first one after years of reading only books in English. It was a book by Peter Handke with the telling title *Slow Homecoming*; and with each sentence my own homecoming began to take on more concrete shape, a movement back into my own language, into my own relation to the world. Of course, it all had to do with the fact that I had lost interest in America, but that's another chapter, that doesn't belong here, *okay?*

Do you know where the expression "okay" comes from? For years I asked many Americans: "Why do you say 'okay'?" Sure, I understand KO, it comes from "knockout." But what does "okay" mean? Finally I found out from a trustworthy source. When the Model T was built by Mr. Ford and it became so incredibly popular that millions of them were being built, one had to devise the assembly line to produce the car quickly enough. The man at the end of the line made the final inspection and gave the final approval. At first he did this in his handwriting, but finally, because of the large number of cars, he had to use a stamp. And then he just stamped his approval on the first page of the title. The man was a German, of course; his name was Oskar Krause, O. K. . . . Okay?

Oskar Krause probably stayed in America; I did not, however. I came back. "Back" is in fact the wrong word—it seems more like I came "forward": forward into an unknown country, home to a familiar language. I realized that I live in this language, I thrive in it, and in this often bleak and dreary Germany it remains my only ray of hope.

I was never proud of this country, and I never wanted to stay here. Even as a child I always wanted to go somewhere else, and as soon as I was old enough to go I went to England, France, or Spain. Now I think that I was less attracted by what was foreign than I was repelled by what was around me. I found myself in the middle of the vacuum I described earlier: a strange barring of the past. You cannot fool a child into thinking that it cannot look back over its shoulder. But I grew up with the feeling that "we" should never look back. Behind us was a black hole, and everybody was staring into the future as if in a trance, busily working on the reconstruction of Germany, on the "miracle"—and, as I see it, this economic miracle was only possible through a gigantic act of repression. The enormous achievement was not the phoenix that rose out of the ashes, but rather the act of forgetting the ashes out of which it rose. A child cannot see through something like this, but the child that was me internalized this process and understood it later. As an adolescent during the 1950s I experienced this German act of repression as an absence of pleasure, of simple sensual pleasure. I don't mean to say that my parents had no sense of humor or were hostile towards pleasure; what I mean is that I grew up in a climate and an environment conditioned by the seriousness of life, a seriousness void of all joy. If it had not been for this climate, I would not have indulged so fervently in the imported pleasures that were available: American comics, American films, and American music. What they had in common was: they were fun, superficial, and they exuded pure presence. This feeling of living in the here and now and being satisfied with it was new to me. You can only live in the present if the past is an open book and the future an open field—this is what I learned from American cinema. Everything was "up-front" and "there" instead of shameful and concealed. My country was constrictive, theirs was wide open. I first discovered the horizon in American Westerns, which, even though they may have falsified American history, still knew how to tell stories rooted in history. I was an easy prey for these American myths, for I lived in a country without myths, a country that I saw as having neither stories nor history. The first books I devoured, when I was still barely able to read, books I read time and again, were Mark Twain's *Tom Sawyer* and *Huckleberry Finn*. Here too I found the same joy of life and devotion to the present. Huck Finn's Mississippi was much closer to me than the Rhine or the Mosel.

And then there were the Mickey Mouse comics. In this entertaining world of images and stories I found a regular school of life. I remember

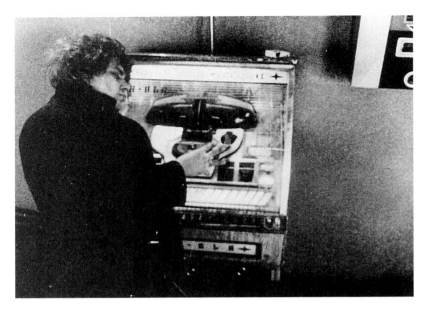

"Rock and roll saved my life"—the jukebox in the short *Alabama* (1968), with music by the Rolling Stones, Jimi Hendrix, Bob Dylan, and John Coltrane.

how once I was sick in bed for a while and my mother had to bring me the newest Mickey Mouse comic book when she went shopping. They must have been out of the latest issue, and my mother returned with a German comic, "Fix and Foxi." You cannot imagine how dull, boring, and empty it seemed to me! It followed the same formula of comic book stories, but it was so stupid, so arrogant, so obviously "made-for-children," without any irony, subtlety, or humor, that I started to hate this imitation, this falsification, this German aping of the American original. I am telling you all this to demonstrate how willing I was as a child to let myself be colonized by another country and let it show me what "pleasure," "ease," and "adventure" meant. There were German words for this, but they were empty, they had no correlates in actual experience.

I do not want to bore you with further details about Walt Disney, especially since it has taken on a quite different look today. I lived out my childhood dream of the "Promised Land," and now I know that Ducksville is in reality Los Angeles, and Uncle Scrooge is Donald Trump. The dreamland of my childhood has become a nightmare; the happy images have turned into images of violence and a form of entertainment that sells ease, pleasure, and immediacy to the highest bidder. This way of life that I missed so much *here* has become in the meantime a product over *there*, a form of advertisement. The landscapes of John Ford are now Marlboro

Country, the American Dream has become a marketing campaign. I came home in part because I could no longer stand Disneyland; the breath of "true images" no longer exists, only the bad odor of lying images.

Back to Germany, to a country that has its own history of images that lie. It is probably the first country in modern history that has been seduced in such a horrible fashion by false images and lies, so much so that after twelve years of dictatorship we have developed a deep mistrust of our own images and stories. I experienced this twice: once as a child when I was attracted to American images and stories, and again much later when there was a revival of picture making and storytelling in Germany. When we—if I may lump together the directors and authors of New German Cinema—started showing our first films, nobody wanted to see them. Only after this phenomenon of a new German film culture had been recognized abroad did we begin to gain an audience in Germany that was willing to look at images and stories made in Germany, in this cultural vacuum. Yet the relation between our images and foreign images continues to be absurd, be it in the movie theaters or on the television screen. Then and now identification is being imported; identity is not being produced from within, but rather brought in from the outside. Let me say, even at the risk of oversimplification, that just as during the postwar era and the time of the economic miracle, today we continue to work hard in Germany and produce economic goods for the whole world, only to import images and stories; we import a way of life, dreams, and myths. There is a flip side to this development as well: as the American economy declines its images dominate more and more the imagination of the peoples worldwide, exerting in some cases complete control. In which city in the world are they not showing, on this very day, November 10, 1991, in one or many of the cinemas in town, *Terminator 2*?

Still, I don't want to speak about American cinema, but rather about the vacuum that sucked the foreign images and stories into this country. Only in Japan have I experienced a similar vacuum, a similar sense that the self was being abandoned and obliterated. I don't want to draw comparisons either, because they always do injustice to both sides. Still, I want to tell how I came out of a subway in Tokyo and for a moment did not know where I was. On the building across from me there was written in gigantic blue neon letters: "Arbeit." I have to add that a few moments earlier I had taken some pictures in the subway of people who were sitting across from me, all of them asleep. I was the only person in a car full of sleeping people, and I thought, "They work too much." And here it was now: "Arbeit." Later I learned that this is the only German word that has become part of the Japanese language: "Arbeit-o." The building belonged to a publishing house that publishes the magazine *Arbeit*, a newspaper specializing in classified ads for help wanted or temporary employment. But I do not want to talk about Japan. I want to speak about a German vacuum—about the empty gazes in the supermarkets and the pedestrian zones, at the fast-food stands, at the tanning studios, in the video stores, in the sex shops, in the video arcades, in the discotheques, on the chartered flights. I am talking about the hordes of tourists stumbling through the world with their high-tech cameras and auto-focus camcorders, without ever arriving anywhere, without ever having been anywhere until they can look at their videos and photos at home in order to assure themselves afterwards that in fact "they were there," that they had experienced something, that they are alive. I am talking about a German way of life that is second-, third-, or even fourth-hand.

It is difficult today to experience something firsthand. Everywhere there are images, secondhand realities, and the images are proliferating at a breathtaking rate. Nothing stops them—no organization, no authority. A great many years ago, and for a long time, there was only one instance of each image—at first on walls and in caves, then on other backgrounds such as wood, or canvas, or on church walls. If you wanted to see these images you had to own them or go where they were located. Then came the printing of books and the distribution of drawings and copperplate engravings. Then came photography, a gigantic step that defined anew the relation between image, representation, and reality. But the negative still existed and hence the idea of an original, even if one could make as many reproductions as needed. For the first time, people could see other places without actually going there. Film only continued the logic of this development. The images started to move; they could not only describe situations but also tell stories. Then came television and the notion of participating "live" in an event that took place elsewhere. I remember how I sat for the first time in front of a television at the house of a friend whose parents did not share my parents' reservations about the "tube." Then came more channels, first via antenna, then via cable, and now via satellite. At first you could only watch one, today there are ten or twenty, and tomorrow there will be hundreds. Now there are also video recorders and cameras that enable everybody to create their own television. Add to that computers, video games, virtual reality, and, in the near future, digital recording, which will finally erase any notion of the original because even the one thousandth or one millionth copy will be identical with the original; and in the not-so-distant future it will no longer be possible to verify the truth content of an image. In short, images have distanced themselves more and more from reality and have hardly anything to do with it anymore. If you think back ten or twenty years, the rate of the expansion and inflation of images will make your head spin.

This is a global phenomenon, of course, but it is a particular catastrophe in Germany, a country that is highly susceptible to images and already almost totally engulfed in foreign images. Too many images cause a loss of reality—and this country that has had great difficulty securing an identity for itself needs, above all, to be grounded in reality.

Let me return to what brought me "home": that is, language, the German language. Even if the world of images is out of joint, and even if progress and technology foster the proliferation of images so that they are out of control and will get even more out of control in the future, there still exists another culture, a counterculture that has not changed and that will not change: the realm of storytelling, reading and writing, the word. I do not believe in much of what the Bible says, but I do believe fervently in this one maxim: "In the beginning was the Word." And I do not believe that it will one day read: "In the beginning was the Image." The word will remain. Of course, the word can be abused and manipulated. But in spite of all the commercial slogans, empty phrases, and yellow journalism, there will always be writers.

In this respect not much has changed from Homer and Plato down through Goethe and Kafka to the present day. As always there are those who sit down and write and others who sit down and read. No form of repression has ever been able to prevent this; no burning of books has ever stopped their circulation. My favorite scene in the history of film is the end of Truffaut's *Fahrenheit 451*. It is a science-fiction scene in a country where books have been banned and reading is a crime. The outcasts live in a tent city. Each of them *is* a book, that is, each of them has memorized a book that he or she passes on to someone of the next generation. In a long shot we see these "living books" as they walk around, each of them reciting a book in a different language. Then the voices all blend together into a kind of music, into a choir of humanity.

In Germany, too, the telling of stories has never ceased; but, unlike in the United States, images can no longer produce any identity here. Not even the most moving image of postwar German politics, Chancellor Willy Brandt genuflecting at the memorial of the Warsaw ghetto, has endured. In Germany images have been discredited once and for all. Only storytelling can have an impact here. There is a certain truth to the saying that this is a nation of "poets and thinkers."

Our *Heil*—some words such as this one have to be unearthed from under the rubble—our balm in this land of lost souls, is our German language. It is differentiated, precise, subtle, endearing, accurate, and nurturing at the same time. It is a rich language. It is the only wealth that we have in a country that believes itself to be rich when it is not. The German language is everything that our country no longer is, what it is not yet, and what it may never be. Perhaps you can accept this coming from a filmmaker.

Excerpts from Interviews with Wenders

WENDERS'S DEVELOPMENT AS FILMMAKER:
"THE CONCEPT OF STORY WAS FOREIGN TO ME."

JAN DAWSON: *Would you say that Ozu was a big influence on you?*

The only influence. Or at least the only master. Of course, the American cinema was important, and it still is. And our admiration for American cinema is still right, I think. Because the way of telling a story, the language of the American cinema, is still valuable. But the importance of Ozu for me—after *The Goalie*, I think—was to see that somebody whose cinema was also completely developed out of the American cinema, had managed nevertheless to change it into a completely personal vision. So Ozu was the one who helped me, and who showed me that it was possible to be colonized, or imperialized, in such a way that you really accepted the language. I mean, for me, there is no other language, no other film language than . . . I'm not even sure you can still call it an American one, but it was made in America at least.

DAWSON: *I'm not really sure I understand what people mean by film language, except that there's a conventional way of shooting a scene: and it's often conventional because it's the best way and the easiest way. And also the most expensive.*

There is certainly something like a best way of putting something. I really think there is. And it was in Ozu's films that I saw that there was a best way of shooting something; and still letting it have completely its own identity. That was my problem. I was very, very insecure about that. In *The Goalie*, every frame was already a conflict between my own vision and the fact that I appreciated the American one as the best. So that I had no confi-

60

dence in my kind of personal vision. What good is your own vision if you know that there's a (different) fine way of showing things.

DAWSON: *Do you see* Goalie, *then, as an American film, or at least as an attempt at one?*

I see *The Goalie* as a completely schizoid film, right in the middle of everything. Which was appropriate, really, because that's the situation of the main character, Bloch. It was my own situation, too. I wouldn't go so far as to call it schizoid, but I would describe it as being just on the way to having some identity. I can grasp it, if I see the film now. I can see now what I did unconsciously: and the mixture exactly reflects the situation of someone who has inherited something, like the American cinema, but doesn't have an American mind. I realized while I was shooting *The Goalie* that I wasn't an American director; that although I loved the American cinema's way of showing things, I wasn't able to re-create it, because I had a different grammar in my mind. That was the conflict, in every frame . . . that there were, in a way, two opposing grammars: one hidden, which I didn't yet know, and in which I didn't yet have any confidence; and one very obvious one. I think you can see it in the film.

DAWSON: *I don't like comparisons, but if we have to compare* The Goalie *with anything other than itself, I suppose the opening (the idea of the man walking away from the match) is closest to a Czech movie, because they have a good, absurdist tradition. As I remember it, the next 20 or 30 minutes are the American movie; and then the film enters this kind of no-man's-land. And this, for me, is one of the film's strengths: I didn't feel it as a conflict in each frame, but rather as a film about a change of direction. It took off for a no-man's-land, a dead-end frontier; and I think the conflicts strengthened the film.*

No. The conflict really took place in every frame. There's a scene I'm still very proud of, and that I like the most in the film; and it was a professional turning-point for me. We shot the film rather chronologically, so you can easily see how it developed. It's the scene where Bloch is traveling on the bus from Vienna to the border. It doesn't have very much importance in the film, it's a five-minute sequence, perhaps less: he's taken the bus, and the bus has stopped, and he's looking at this funny jukebox; and the train is accompanying the bus and it's getting dark . . . that's the scene where I felt, even while I was shooting it, that this was the way it was going to go on for me. There was some luck involved. I realized that this was my story, and I happened to find the right way of showing something. I lost this feeling again afterwards. Even at the border, there's still some Czech tradition, more in a comedy style: but I've always hated it. A tradition where things are used for amusement rather than because they exist in their own right.

* * *

TAJA GUT: *Long before you started making films yourself, you described your own films with astounding clarity in your film reviews—not so much in terms of content, but in the way you approach the image. I find it equally astonishing that right after 1968 you avoided all political jargon and developed instead something intuitive, perceptive, and caring that characterizes all your films. Where did you get the strength for these feelings in such times?*

That's precisely the question—at the time when I was right in the middle of all the political unrest, living in communes, at times with people who later turned radical and went underground. That was the point when I got out of that whole scene. I have often thought that many of these people had some great ideas, but that they wanted to realize them in a way that was completely masochistic. Many of them were ruined by their ideas because they had nothing to do with their feelings. I emerged from those times with an uneasy feeling.

After those days you had to start again from scratch, and the only possible starting point was your own actual and very private experiences. I had the feeling that only through these authentic and private experiences would I be able to communicate something that would have a more universal relevance. And on the other hand, the claim of the 1968 crowd that they were expressing a common message and speaking for everyone, that was an act of violence against themselves and against people in general.

That's why I began to make personal films, almost like diaries. My film reviews as well—that was during my time at the Munich Film Academy, when I also wrote reviews for *Filmkritik* and in a few cases for *Die Zeit*—only described personal experiences that I had with films, without trying to formulate a generally valid point of view about them. I think that my own films have developed almost logically from this method and even moral belief that one should talk only about one's own experiences. I still have a lot from that early point of view in me.

You also retain, of course, a lot of that which influenced you as a child—in my case, that I grew up in a Catholic family. Also that my father is a doctor and surgeon, a person almost obsessed with helping the people who came to see him. You cannot simply shake off the influence of such a model, of such a *Vor-Bild*.

GUT: *Was it always clear to you that you wanted to make films?*

Not at all. Quite to the contrary, I had already made three films, and not until the fourth, *Alice in the Cities*, did I stop and think: hey, maybe this is no accident, maybe there is a *path* here and something like a profession. Only when I made a film grounded in my own principles, namely, *Alice in the Cities*, did I suddenly realize that I could actually do it and that I had some things to tell in this language of film. But before that I was fully prepared to return either to writing or to take up painting again.

GUT: *You did some painting as well?*

I was actually a painter. Before I attended the Munich Film Academy I studied all kinds of things, most of it only halfheartedly. While I was studying medicine and philosophy I really didn't do anything but paint. In the end I decided to take up painting, and that was why I went to Paris. While I was there I began to go to the Cinémathèque almost daily—actually by chance, only because my apartment was so cold and the cheapest way to stay warm was to go the Cinémathèque, where a showing only cost one franc. But then it became almost a feverish passion. I often watched up to five or six films a day. It was a kind of crash course in film. And because there were so many films I began to take notes and write about them; it seemed so senseless that when the last film ended at midnight I couldn't remember what I had seen that afternoon. That led to my work as a critic.

GUT: *Rock music plays a significant role in all your films. You've emphasized several times that rock music saved your life (and the same is true for me).*

It's true, rock and roll shook a whole generation out of its isolation, and not only did it free it *from* something, but it also brought it *to* something—namely, to the realization of its own creativity. That was what was so fantastic about the rock and roll of the sixties, in particular the eruption of English rock—it opened people up to the pleasures and possibilities of their own imagination. Those British rock musicians whose music we grew up to, that second wave of rock that happened in my own generation— Chuck Berry, Elvis, and the other early rock stars were all before my time —they were people like me, art students and the like, who also had no real direction. And when they began to make music with so much force and electricity that it spread like wildfire, it ultimately led me to take my life into my own hands.

GUT: *Yes, the same thing happened to me. But later the whole thing became somewhat problematic. The whole mood of joy and awakening created by this music seemed so calculated and commercially exploited.*

Yes, of course. But I don't think that was so important. That's something we noticed later, and it didn't take anything away from the music. It was not until the seventies that the music was blatantly commercialized and as a listener you felt like you were being duped and strung along. Well, maybe I'm just naive, but I have always had the feeling that through the sixties this music had an energy that enabled it to rise above all the manipulations and doubts. *And* that rock and roll has always maintained, at least potentially, this power to move people and save lives, even now that it has become one of the largest industries. Of course, now one has to be much more selective.

GUT: *How do you see the relation between your life and your films? Are your films—among other things, of course—more a coming to terms with, or even a projection of, your own life?*

I think my films have always contained both elements, that is, experiences that I have had as well as projections into the future. They have been like throwing a stone and trying to get to where it landed. At the same time, they were steeped in my experiences and reflected the times in which they were made. Of course, I didn't use only autobiographical material, but also incorporated a lot of things from the lives of friends and people around me. I have always tried to learn something. From the very moment I realized that film is a tool I can work with and use to tell something—beginning with *Alice in the Cities*—from that moment on, in every film I wanted to focus on a certain subject and let that subject define itself in the making of the film.

That is, for me making a film involves solving the problem that the film poses, a problem that is itself not clearly defined when we start shooting. The film is then the path to understanding or learning something—or, as in *The State of Things*, to renouncing something. In reality, the film has always been a sort of program for shooting, a problem that needs to be clarified. The few times when I made a film that I had planned out beforehand it was a disaster. *The Scarlet Letter* and *Hammett* were flops because they were mapped out on the drawing board like a car. Filmmaking for me has always meant to start with an idea—and the film itself determined the task at hand, and not the drawing board. I have always approached filmmaking this way, right up to now, including also *Wings of Desire*.

* * *

JOCHEN BRUNOW: *What did the process of adaptation look like with* The Goalie's Anxiety at the Penalty Kick? *Was there an actual script?*

I had to write a script for the WDR (Westdeutscher Rundfunk) in order to finance the film. I did this in a very naive fashion. I remarked once in jest that every sentence in Peter Handke's novel read like the description of a shot, and then I took this comment literally. I divided the entire book into scenes. I marked each scene in the text of the novel and then split them up into individual shots. In this way I came up with a script that was probably truer to the novel than in any previous adaptation. Peter had to add some dialogue because there were gaps in the structure of the novel.

BRUNOW: *Did you follow your script when you shot the film?*

Yes, I followed it very precisely. I had to add some images, but I didn't alter the existing structure.

BRUNOW: *At that point in time, what role did screenplays have in your filmmaking?*

The script was basically new territory for me. *Summer in the City* had been done with a two- or three-page exposé. The shorts, too, were done without any script; there were only a few sketches of images. I came to filmmaking through images and as a painter. The concept of story was foreign to me, it was new territory. In those days, it was a process of gradually feeling out the filmmaking process, and for me the script was the strangest part of it. The restrictions caused by a script were still new to me, so at that time I didn't think of them as restrictions, but rather as an adventure. It wasn't until much later, with *Wrong Move*, that I developed a real freedom in working with a script.

BRUNOW: *That is, around 1974–75, after* Alice in the Cities. *The script for* Wrong Move *was again the result of a collaboration with Peter Handke.*

The plan to adapt *Wilhelm Meister's Apprenticeship* dates back to the time of *The Goalie*. Peter wrote the script by himself, and it consisted almost exclusively of dialogue. There were hardly any scene directions. My changes concerned only the route of the trip. I changed some places, but other than that I adhered strictly to the script. When I worked with Peter, I always took everything he handed me quite seriously—more so than with any other author I have collaborated with.

What a character says in a film is obviously a very important element. Here in Germany it has always been treated in an amateur fashion, or it has been considered to be of minor importance. I made a number of films for which I wrote the dialogue myself—*Alice in the Cities, Kings of the Road, The State of Things*—and I always thought they were lacking something. The dialogue was always the missing element. Sometimes I would think, okay, *Alice in the Cities* is basically all right. But with *Kings of the Road* I was sweating blood and tears so that the characters would just have something to say. On the one hand, having a text such as Peter's for *Wrong Move* was a great relief. It gives you the freedom to do other things. Knowing that what the characters say is taken care of frees up energy for working with the actors, the team, and the locations.

BRUNOW: *It seems to me the dialogue is for you the essential part of the script.*

Yes, the dialogue is very important, especially if there are several different characters. It is difficult to write a consistent dialogue for a particular role. It is a real art to have different characters speak differently in the same film, so that each character speaks his or her role appropriately. As a result of the *Autorenfilm*, one looks down on this skill. But the fact that there are no professionals in this area [in Germany, and in Europe in general—Eds.] often has a detrimental effect on the films.

BRUNOW: *It is directly due to the* Autorenfilm *that this profession no longer exists. The rise of the* Autorenfilm *led to the demise of this tradition.*

That's true, and I really regret it.

BRUNOW: *In* The State of Things *your alter ego, the German director Friedrich, has pretty bad things to say about screenplays, suggesting that they suck the life out of a film. He says that a story has too many rules, and that a film with a story has no room to breathe—it's a dead film.*

That position was a result of the situation at the time; I took this extreme position intentionally and worked through it in the film. Ultimately the film contradicts its own premises. What saves this improvised film in the end is that small bit of script and story, the director's meeting with the producer and their death—this little, actually contrived piece of fiction saved the film.

BRUNOW: *It sounds as if now you accept the necessity of stories and the structure of a script.*

Like I said, Friedrich was proven wrong. This element of fiction helped the film more than I ever thought possible. In order to be able to visualize and define the free space in the middle, you needs walls. After *The State of Things* I thought, "Now or never!" Either I learn from this film to reject its thesis about the impossibility of stories, or I have no real future as a filmmaker. That's why I tried to follow the script strictly in *Paris, Texas*. I wrote the script with Sam Shepard. Sam and I worked together up to the point where the father and son leave Los Angeles. Up to that point in the film all the dialogues and scenes closely follow the script, which was formulated in detail. The second part of *Paris, Texas*, on the other hand, was a fly-by-night experience. And you really notice it because it contrasts with the precise structure of the first part. However, there is a forward movement to the film that is maintained until the end, even when it loses at times some of its focus and structure—especially during the long scene with Travis and his wife in the peep show.

BRUNOW: The State of Things *has an inner structure that connects the individual elements and creates a kind of framework. In* Paris, Texas *there is only the external movement of the journey.*

That's an American tradition that Shepard brings to the film as writer.

BRUNOW: *With* Wings of Desire *you come full circle. As a collaboration with Peter Handke, it is based on a combination of literary sources and improvisation.*

It started with some fragments of a screenplay that I created in an attempt to structure the film as a whole. Then there were also ten texts by Peter Handke that we had worked out together at the beginning of the project. At the outset I described to Peter a skeletal story. This story had the potential to expand dramatically at any given moment because the angels could get involved in any imaginable situation. The problem with this story was not one of coming up with something, but rather of reducing the flow of ideas. Instead of writing a script, Peter wanted to work on it as if it were a play. The ten sections he wrote were like islands in the flood of ideas I had for the film. Shooting the film was like reaching one island, climbing onto firm ground, and then taking off swimming again. Richard Reitinger helped me with the scenes, but Peter's texts were the pillars that carried the film.

WENDERS'S METHOD OF MAKING FILMS:
"I PREFER MOVIES THAT ASK ME TO SEE."

IRA PANETH: *Making* Wings of Desire, *did you invent as you went along as you like to do?*

More than ever before. I was not all that conscious of it in the preparation, but as soon as we started shooting it became obvious how vast the possibilities of innovation were because of the invention of the guardian angel and the point of view it implied. So the shooting was very exciting. The camera being the eye of the angel was something altogether new for me, we could not really rely on anything we knew before. Every day we had to come up with new solutions. It felt like a first movie.

PANETH: *Visually the film is stunning, and I mean by this that it has a spaciousness and movement or motion to it that is different, rare in motion pictures. How did you work this out? Did you do a lot of shooting and edit it down?*

The problem of the film, if you can call it a problem, from the beginning was there were way too many ideas. Usually you're looking for ideas in a movie, you need them. This time the problem was to eliminate them. We shot way too much, a lot didn't end up in the movie. It was just endless what you could come up with because of the angels idea. The first version was five hours long.

We did shoot a lot of things in long takes. There was a lot of movement done in the camera and through camera movement, and not so much through editing. We didn't shoot as much as in *Paris, Texas* or *Hammett,* where we did more takes. We didn't have to do a lot over. Of course there are scenes that are rather intensive and that needed some sort of coverage, but even the coverage we did was not like the usual, where you do scenes from different points of view, more or less all over. Very often the choices of the point of view were made so the editing was really done before we shot, and we made some risky decisions—that a scene would only be covered from one point of view, and the continuation would be another point of view, and there was no overlapping footage. But it seemed right to take a lot of risks.

PANETH: *There were several things in* Wings of Desire *that seemed to indicate a nostalgia for storytelling: the line about the singer abandoned by mortal listeners and the link drawn between storytelling and childhood, among others. Is that something you feel?*

It's not really nostalgia, [storytelling] is almost this new discovery for me. It is one of the most reassuring things. It seems its very basis is that it reassures you that there is a sense to things. Like the fact that children want to hear stories when they go to sleep. I mean not so much that they want to know this or that, but that they want it as it gives them a security. The story creates a form and the form reassures them so that you can almost tell them any story—which you can actually do. So there is something very powerful in stories, something that gives you security and a sense of identity and meaning. And it seems to me that this sort of storytelling is disappearing a little bit. Because more and more we seem to be getting them from television and movies, and less and less through books. We're confronted with all these films and images and all that, so it seems that storytelling in that old sense, it's not becoming a lost art, but it's getting less important. And the stories we're being fed with mostly in television and film seem just to pretend being stories. Very often they try to act as if they were stories and are really just pure form, and behind there is just a lot of baloney and noise, especially in most of the films made for young people today that only seem to work if there's a lot of action and violence. That has almost replaced an old story structure, so in that sense you're right there is a nostalgia for stories, for real stories and for an epic feeling of a story.

PANETH: *I thought the handwriting at the beginning and the end and the library were wonderful gestures towards the written word.*

Yeah. When we were looking for a place in the city where the angels would live, would be at home, we looked for some time. Since angels are not really linked between people and God anymore we could not do a church, so we tried for another place. Then I remembered the ending of one of my favorite films, Truffaut's *Fahrenheit 451*, which is in this big open space, and there are all these people and everybody represents a book that they have learned by heart because books are persecuted and burned; and to me that was really a vision of paradise, with all these people walking around and sitting on benches in the park. I thought this is a heavenly place, a library, and then we found this big public library in Berlin, and it's really a wonderful place, with a lot of light, and built with a lot of respect for reading and books, and also so peaceful and quiet. There is also the whole memory and knowledge of mankind united there.

PANETH: *Have you found yourself encountering problems in terms of telling stories in film, since that became a focus of yours relatively recently?*

No. I believe very much in form of course, but also the form only seems to work if behind it there is a certain belief, so that the form is not just a hollow thing that you hope will do the job, but that the form has a certain necessity. So the problem is really to believe in the story. And then, of course, you have to believe in form too, because you can have a beautiful story to tell, but if you don't have the form to tell it with, it becomes also strangely meaningless.

PANETH: *You haven't encountered problems with narrative?*

Well, this one is not really representative because it is narrative in so many ways. And through the invention of the angels, and the fact that they can witness so much, that they can even listen to people's thoughts, so that you'd instantly be much more familiar than usual with every person since you could hear what he or she thinks. So there was a whole new range of entering into people's heads and into many different stories all the time. It was not really typical.

PANETH: *How do you conceive of the spectator and audience that you are making films for?*

I think I conceive of them as very important creative collaborators. And I have to explain that. If I look at the films I really like most, and if I look at myself as a spectator of other films, then I clearly favor movies that let me discover them. There is that sort of movie where you feel excited from the beginning because you realize that it is because you look at it that the movie really exists, and because you can put some strings together, and it is open to a lot of interpretation, and you have to sort of put in your own experiences or associations in order to make it work. I really don't like so much the sort of movie where it's all spread out and you really just sit there and it's poured over you and you have no choice: you see what they want you to see. I prefer movies that ask me to see. So in a way I'm trying to do the sort of movies that are for people that I presume to be like myself with other directors' movies. And as I travel a lot with my films and see them with different audiences in different countries, it's really amazing how much a film can change, and how much even between two audiences in the

69

same country; although I know it, I will see a different film.

* * *

RAINER NOLDEN: *For Alfred Hitchcock, writing the screenplay was the best part of work on a film; the actual shooting was just menial labor for him. What is the most important phase for you?*

The writing is hell for me. I hate it like the plague. I like best of all making the concrete preparations: driving around, looking for locations and people, creating the film not through writing, but rather through "experiencing it beforehand." Then I also like editing a lot. The shooting— no director can tell me that he likes that part of it. It can at times be quite interesting, but at the same time it's the pits. François Truffaut once said that after three or four weeks of shooting he always had one single wish: to get it over with and move on.

NOLDEN: *Is one part of it the fear that you might lose control of your own work because of the collaboration with others?*

Not because of the coworkers—on the contrary. The only person who I fear at times might let the film get out of control is me. Mainly because I have made all my films, with the exception of *Hammett*, using an open screenplay. I have always changed it a lot, at times even writing the script while shooting the film, as with *Kings of the Road* or *The State of Things* and *Nick's Movie*. Even in the case of *Paris, Texas* only the first half was written.

* * *

TAJA GUT: *Has working within the medium of film ever presented a problem for you? The illusion that there is actually no movement in it, but rather just individual images; the tremendous atomization of the individual images—from the countless shots, which usually go through several re-takes, to the cutting and editing. This incredible fragmentation, which applies to the actors as well, who can always only play a small part at a time. And on top of that the danger of manipulation—one can cut things out of film without any problem; the financial pressures; the extreme artificiality of the medium, the coercion film exerts on the act of viewing—*

Yes, that's true. Film is an act of violence, or threatens to become one at every stage of making a film. Let's begin at the end: when the film is finished, it becomes an act of violence in the moment it is shown, an act of violence insofar as the danger exists that it takes away the spectators' freedom to see something, dictating rather to them what they have to see. Without doubt that is a latent danger in all filmmaking. You can see this danger more readily in the special case of a commercial or a propaganda film, where everything is constructed so that the spectator sees *one* particular film and *one* particular message. In the extreme case it is indeed a form of severe manipulation, and manipulation is an act of violence.

There are, of course, films that present themselves to the spectator in such a way that the spectator has freedom, namely, a freedom to put the film together him- or herself or to decide in the end which film he or she wants to see. These are films that do not simply appear on the screen in front of the spectator like a given object, but rather give the spectator the freedom to interact with the film and to construct it according to one's own perspective. Such films do exist. And I am working to make my films like this, that is, that they first come together in the head of the spectator. That they do not always point their finger at something and say, "You will see this now and nothing else! and you have to understand it this way!" Instead, they take the finger away completely and present things for their own sake, so that, as in life itself, you can either look at something or not. That's difficult, because as soon as you begin to tell a story you restrict vision. And for that reason telling stories is a big problem for me, because it restricts and because it has the tendency to simplify things. And also to dominate blindly—both the spectators and the events that occur during the shooting.

And then you can point not only to the act of violence in the finished film, but also to the act of violence that takes place during the making of the film. The potential for manipulation is always there. For example, the manipulation when you shoot first the end of the film and then the beginning, and then the middle of the film at the very end, or the other way around. That means that when an actor comes to the set every day he or she actually makes only one small part of the film without knowing its significance within the context of the whole film, and thus has to jump around constantly in the story. That is also an act of violence. I try to avoid it where possible because I think it is an act of violence against myself as well. Except in rare cases, I always shoot my films chronologically. The actors come on the first day and we shoot the first shot, and on the last day the last shot. I can hardly work in any other manner. Now and then, when the reasons are compelling, I have to step out of this chronology. That in itself is usually painful enough, but at least you can sometimes arrange it so that the film as a whole doesn't lose its continuity.

GUT: *How is it possible to keep the idea of a film intact through all the processes of fragmentation involved in making it? In the case of writing or painting you always have everything in front of you, so that you can flip back in the text or look at the picture at every stage. You don't have a film, however, until at the very end after the editing.*

That's not true. At times I think that the work of a novelist is much more strongly subject to a particular formal conception than filmmaking.

Filmmaking is after all related to a craft where you can always—or at least in most cases—see on the next day what you have accomplished, in the form of the images on the screen. And a certain craftsmanship is involved; the director's work is shaped by various tangible elements: the framing of what the camera sees, the sequence of the images, the decision of what to include and to omit in the shot, the lighting, what the actors say. It's all closely related to a craft. Actors are craftsmen; they have learned a craft, at least in most cases. The cameraman is a craftsman, working with light is a craft. You find yourself in a situation surrounded by many different craftsmen, and you can check your work every day.

Of course, a director must have ahead of time an idea of what form all this will take, or always be ready to infuse all this craftwork with a formal conception. And at times I actually find this a less impressive accomplishment than what a writer achieves. Or what a composer who writes a symphony achieves. In those cases everything is much more fragmented and more difficult to bring into a form. You don't actually hear the symphony until it is performed. In filmmaking I have a piece of the film in my hand every day, I have people with whom I can discuss it, to whom I can convey something and who also continually have something to offer me. Every day I stand with the camera at some location that has something to offer, and I am always in touch with a reality, even bound to a reality, which always gives me something. There is always some landscape, some objects, birds fly through the sky, someone is standing in front of the camera, there are colors and forms—there is always something there. Because of that I always find the conceptual vision of a writer or composer much more amazing than that of a director.

GUT: *To get back to the act of violence. My question was actually aiming at something deeper: namely, that the film image in itself already creates a certain compulsion for the eye, apart from any content. As Kafka said, cinema disturbs seeing; films are iron window shutters.*

Film can certainly disturb seeing. It can make something visible, but it can also make something invisible. A film can actually cause one's eyes to close; many films don't do anything but this. You come out of them and for the next few days you are blind. Your eyes almost glued shut! And with other films, you come out and are more open to the world around you than ever before.

GUT: *I actually experience this quite strongly with your films—that I enjoy seeing again.*

In every film you see things for other people in a stand-in relationship. That's true. You have a great responsibility because of this. In this representative role you can put on blinders that affect other people. It is amazingly complex how a director performs for other people in a representative role. You not only see for them, but you also tell a story, let them listen to music. You experience all kinds of things with them. Film is quite a complex experience, whereby, of course, seeing plays a decisive role, but hearing as well; and feeling.

GUT: *The concept pair "stories-images" is a key one for you. You said somewhere that seeing is your profession and that stories are only a pretense for creating images. Why are images so important?*

What else? What else can you tell? Or how else can you depict life if not with images? That is, what can you use to create movement?—I am actually not a deductive person at all; I can't really make an assumption and then derive something from it—not at all. Actually I can only produce something if there is some movement. And then you can see where it is headed. And only in films, in working on a film with images, can you develop this path of movement toward something as a method. Probably in music as well. But I am really not very musical. I am much more of a visual person. First, I have a good memory for images; second, I can imagine them before they are there. I also like images. I don't get much out of it when someone tells me something, but when they show me something I can take it all in. In another age I probably would have become a painter, and I intended fully to become one; it's almost unbelievable that I had the good fortune to be able to make films.

GUT: *It says something about your work that at the beginning you had trouble interrupting the flow, cutting, so as not to show everything but just excerpts out of a flow of time.*

That's the problem you run into when you go from being a painter to being a filmmaker. My first films were just a continuation of painting, but using a camera. They were landscape paintings: the camera didn't move, nothing happened, no people moved through the image, there was no dramatic action at all—they were in actuality paintings, images stretched over a space of time. They were observing something, and they stopped when the film ran out. That seemed to me to be the only way to end a film. And then the idea of editing brought home to me the distinction between film and painting. Suddenly I discovered something completely different. It was a totally new way of thinking, another way of experiencing. And even when I got used to editing and also to the idea that it leads to a completely new language, one that becomes increasingly different from that of painting, I still attempted, like before, to maintain the proper relation to time, to do justice to time.

The framed image moving through time in *Same Player Shoots Again* (1967).

TELLING STORIES—WENDERS VERSUS HOLLYWOOD:
"A FRESH START IN FILM NARRATIVE, THAT'S MY GOAL."

WOLFRAM SCHÜTTE: *Which stories can in fact "no longer be told" today? For a good part of the controversy in* The State of Things *is about just that.*

It's significant that Friedrich was making a remake. It was also for me important to say that stories that are grounded only in other stories won't do—that is, they no longer should or can suffice!—stories that have as their reality only the reality of previous film stories. For some time now cinema has not been turning out much except remakes. That's why the question of the origin of stories in cinema is one of the most important. My film does not offer any suggestions, it does not say: this story is still possible and that one is not. But the fact that the producer and the director are shot is a clear signal that what links the two of them—this kind of cinema —won't do anymore.

SCHÜTTE: *Why is it that cinema no longer has any new stories to tell?*

Lotte Eisner once told me that Fritz Lang asked her, "Why do you bother to go to films anymore? You no longer see any new films; everything is only being told over and over again."

74

SCHÜTTE: *He himself did just that in his last films.*

Because that was the only way for him still to earn money in this profession. But since then the problem has become even more pronounced than Fritz Lang could have imagined. Once the film language of cinema had developed it became detached from its own origins and purpose—namely, to define reality and to create a definite form for representing the external world. This idea of cinema—for which it was, so to speak, originally "invented"—has completely vanished. As a result, this language of cinema only reflects back on itself.

SCHÜTTE: *But isn't one aspect of telling a story the desire to bring things together, to grab hold of fleeting impressions? Telling stories is not only providing meaning, but also giving order to things.*

That's right, and telling film stories is a way of evoking recognition and, by virtue of the form, giving order to a cacophony of impressions. The need for stories since Homer, whom I am now reading, is as well the need to discover a coherence in diverse impressions. Such a need exists because people experience very little coherence in their lives. Rather, the "impressions" keep growing in number at an inflationary rate. That's why I think the need for stories will continue to grow, because they have someone who narrates, someone who puts things in order and who introduces an idea: you gain a handle on your own life. That's what stories do: they re-affirm the individual's competency to determine one's own life.

SCHÜTTE: *But when I watch* The State of Things *I have sometimes the impression that you wanted to get away from "stories." The American cinema you liked so much was a cinema that told stories. Your film tries, almost literally, to come to grips with this. Do you want to return to a cinema of situations and associations, or to one like Kluge's?*

Well, that is the dilemma: that everything I want to tell is circumstantial, whether it is about cities or emotions or alienation. That everything I want to tell cannot be narrated without stories. This comes up in the film. Friedrich says, "There are no more stories," and then he is the one who becomes involved in a genuine story. *The State of Things*, because of the way that it originated, is itself an example of this. It was a fly-by-night film, it could have taken a different direction, could have made a different statement. I like it because it demonstrated to me the truth about "stories." The idea that cinema should have something to do with life and experiences (with my experiences as filmmaker as well as with the experiences of the spectators), this idea is inextricably connected to stories—the film made this clear to me. To my mind, films that give up on telling stories and only depict situations are not viable. Ultimately, stories are necessary to convey a message.

SCHÜTTE: *Is the story merely that thread that holds everything together?*

No, it is more than that; the story has a structure in itself. The story in *The State of Things* could have remained merely that thread; Friedrich could have left the producer again, who would have then continued to drive around the area in his motor home, thus leaving an open end. But if I had left it open like this with the narrative thread hanging in the air, then that would have also left open everything else I wanted to say. Because the story came to its conclusion (with the murder of the two main figures), everything else was defined in a clearer light. For this reason I feel that I have to take narrative structure seriously again, and also have to develop a dramatic language in order to be able to produce this "other" in narrative. I have been reading Homer for a couple of weeks, and I have not been disappointed in my hopes of learning from it something about the need for affirmative stories; why it is necessary to have a definite form in order to talk about things that are not connected by narrative.

SCHÜTTE: *But, I have to come back to this, didn't you in your films—for example, in* The State of Things *(not to mention earlier films)—talk about cinema and the traces it has left in your life, in your emotional being, and in your imagination?*

Up to now, yes. Now I would say that was a kind of ruse, an alibi so that I could present a story. The precondition for the narrative was that I always gave this alibi as a part of it. There were then always these signposts indicating that I know a language of cinema already exists, that this has already been done in film, and so on. I see all of that as something forced. It will change.

SCHÜTTE: *But isn't it important at that point where cinema as a tradition of representation and narrative is about to disappear, where it loses sight of its own history, to remind it of what it is, to preserve that tradition, and maybe even in a certain manner to remain true to it? Or do you think one should say: "That is all past now"? Should one set off in a completely new direction, into videos?*

One person has already taken that step—Godard. One should simply learn from his experience. Godard turned back again from that venture.

SCHÜTTE: *. . . although not completely . . .*

. . . not completely; he hasn't yet recovered from either the one or the other. He is probably more in a bind than those of us here in Germany. I have always paid careful attention to this tradition of cinema, and now in *The State of Things* I have even put myself on the spot. With the end of the film I have put myself in a position to follow through on my concept of what cinema should be today and in the future: namely, either demonstrate that narrative is possible again, or keep my mouth shut. And that is what I want to try in my next two films. I want to find a narrative cinema that avidly and with self-confidence establishes a connection between film art and life, and which no longer needs to reflect its own textuality in the narrative. So that one does not turn cinema over to the big spectacle films, but rather takes up the challenge confidently and tells stories—without regrets and without resorting to the wonderful film stories that once abounded in cinema. A fresh start in film narrative, that's my goal.

SCHÜTTE: *That seems to be what Peter Handke has in mind as well. But can one find a way back to such naïveté?*

That is, of course, the question. It won't take us back to a grand, mythlike narrative—to a depersonalized narrative. That was the great achievement of classical American cinema: that both in spite of and because of the studio system a collective narrative developed, instead of one based on the single voice (of the filmmaker). The collective narrative of cinema created all the myths that actually linked film narrative to the great traditions of the past. Neither European cinema nor auteur film has been able to achieve this. None of us here has been able to make such narrative films. Our stories have all been subjective stories. And now we have to realize that we can neither revive nor imitate this past narrative. Nor should we regret this. We are cut off from this past. Nevertheless, there still exists an enormous need for stories: like before, people still want to see coherence and meaning in things—and certainly not only in *Star Wars*, but rather also in stories that have significance for their own lives. We must learn not to lament the loss of this great resonant voice of the old cinema.

SCHÜTTE: *Television is full of stories everywhere you turn; but what makes cinema different is the free space, the gaps between the events and characters—that is, the things that appear for their own sake.*

There are an absurd number of rules for film narrative, but in spite of all these rules cinema has always had more space and freedom than television. Because of the reduction from the large screen to the television screen there are tighter rules in television. You can see this clearly when you watch movies on television. The free space is no longer visible on the small screen; for example, in the long shots of Westerns. The rules have to be drawn more tightly because the spectator's focus on the object is more restricted. In cinema there was always a wonderful sense of distance. But that's changing now too. In the new American films the spectator is "chained" to the screen in a way similar to television viewing. The free and open access keeps becoming more and more restricted.

SCHÜTTE: *Yes, I have the same impression. They are trying to fill up these free spaces in film, these gaps, with all kinds of attractions and stimuli, so that the spectator is never alone with himself in front of the screen.*

I always have the physical sensation of being tied to a rope—as if cables were running from the screen to each seat. Like dogs on a leash: this is the impression I often get at the movies today; and I can empathize with dogs who want to be freed from their leashes. The grand old cinema knew how to free people from their leashes. In a John Ford film, for example, the spectator was able to move together with the figures on the screen, enjoying the same freedom of movement—freed from one's leash. Television put these leashes back on, otherwise the people would be constantly changing channels.

* * *

KATHERINE DIECKMANN: Paris, Texas *is kind of a mystery, and seems to follow Peter Wollen's idea about Hitchcockian narratives being quest narratives, propelled by a search for an object or value. The film is specific to Nastassja Kinski and is centered on her practically from the start. With* The Goalie's Anxiety at the Penalty Kick, Wrong Move, American Friend, Kings of the Road, *there's no such locus and the films are most interested in disorientation. Structure is very apparent here.*

That's what made me like the story, the direction from the beginning —a very straight line. For once I was making a movie that wasn't meandering all over the place. That's what Sam Shepard brought to this movie of mine as an American writer: forward movement, which is very American in a way. I've always liked that movement and have always found myself incapable of doing it. Even with *American Friend,* I thought, "Great, we have this story by Patricia Highsmith, it's going to take us somewhere." But it never did. It went sideways, all over the place.

DIECKMANN: *You deliberately contrast the open desert with the populated, LA desert.*

Houston is more the opposite image to the desert in the beginning. With LA we tried to make it look like any Midwestern city—just nowhere. One thing about *Paris, Texas* from beginning to end—and this was true for each and every shot—was that we never thought of anything we'd seen before.

DIECKMANN: *That seems quite impossible.*

It's possible as an attitude. Of course there's a certain amount of imagery that has passed into the subconscious, and the very second you have a frame and you're shooting, either in the desert or in the city, it would be pretentious to say this is something that hasn't been done before. We always tried to see just what was there and find a way to show it that corre-sponded to what was in front of us, not some notion of what we were re-minded of. I'm talking about avoiding an attitude of quoting, and of knowing you're quoting something.

DIECKMANN: *What are the problems involved in trying to make "personal" films (your film diary projects, for instance, the one on Ozu) while staking your claim in the market?* Paris, Texas *has been hyped much more than your other films, what with the book, and because of Cannes.*

I fought hard to be in the position I'm in now. After the problems of the past few years, I got to the point where the only way out for me was to get a camera, walk down the street and just look at things. For one thing, the narrative has always been such a . . . romantic block, such a *problem.* I started out as a painter and some of that has survived in me. And I've al-ways thought that films—the very thing, movies—have been invented in the first place to witness the twentieth century. I've always been very at-tracted to documentaries, but have always thought that feature films are in a way the true documents of our time. Especially when they're outrageous fantasies, like, let's say, Hitchcock's *Vertigo.* If somebody 500 years from now happened to find *Vertigo,* they'd have a pretty clear notion of what America looked like in 1958. This is a very important component of film-making: even if a film is sheer fantasy—film is unique because no other form can do that—it's also a document of the time it was made. And I do like straight documentaries a lot. Though it's something of a lost form, be-cause television has taken over so much. But I think it's extremely healthy, a kind of therapy for anyone who tries to tell stories, to go out and have nothing to tell, no story, no fiction, and try to find the right way to represent something. I very much insist that this is part of my work.

* * *

GERD GEMÜNDEN: *It has been ten years since you made* Paris, Texas *and returned to Germany after having worked for many years in the United States. If you look back now from a distance at your stay abroad, how do you evaluate your experiences in the United States?*

Films like *Paris, Texas* or *Wings of Desire* certainly indicate the final stage of auterism; this kind of approach to filmmaking doesn't work any-more in Europe, because historically speaking it's an outdated way of mak-ing films. As a model it was first invented by Italian neorealism and the French nouvelle vague before it was picked up during the 1970s by West German filmmakers, who developed it further. This model now lacks power because it was premised on the single energy of one individual. This model has run its course, and you can see that in my own films too, even if *Paris, Texas* and *Wings of Desire* were some of the last successful auteur films.

Former angels in the rain—Damiel (Bruno Ganz) and Cassiel (Otto Sander) in *Faraway, So Close!* (1993).

GEMÜNDEN: *Let me turn to the moral aspect of your films. In your early films this moral aspect comes across as a certain respect for objects and the locations in which the characters move. It seems that you want to do justice to the things you show on the screen, and the films take their time in order to achieve this. In your last two feature films the moral aspect has been transposed from the level of form to the level of content. Many critics saw this as a lack of subtlety. One spoke of Wim Wenders as a moralist who is primarily concerned with delivering a message.*

The images can no longer carry the message. That's why I wanted to be more specific with *Faraway, So Close!* than with *Wings of Desire.* If I take the liberty to use the angels a second time and to continue their story, then I have to say something that too often remains unsaid.

GEMÜNDEN: *But the strength of your earlier films consisted in the fact that certain things remain unsaid.*

During the last ten years films have refrained from saying anything. With Antonioni, Truffaut, Bresson, there was always something that was being said. This hesitancy to say anything is a rather new phenomenon.

GEMÜNDEN: *But particularly these directors always showed more than they said.*

The hesitancy to say something rests on the inability to form an opinion. Everybody wants to stay out of things. But with the present situation, one cannot stay out of things. Today, films are evaluated exclusively by their entertainment value, and it bothered many people that *Faraway, So Close!* had a message, especially if they saw it as a Christian message.

THE AMERICAN ENTERTAINMENT INDUSTRY: "TELEVISION IS BECOMING UNBEARABLE—NAKED FASCISM."

REINHOLD RAUH: *In your films about music at the end of the sixties you used a lot of takes with long camera holds instead of synchronizing the cuts with the musical rhythm. Today's music films, that is, the videoclip, are made in exactly the opposite fashion. In your opinion, is there anything in these videoclips that is worth developing?*

There is certainly a possibility for a new aesthetics there. And at times you can even find a breathtakingly beautiful videoclip. You have to admit that some truly talented people are involved in making them. In one sense, it has become the field for experimentation, replacing for the most part the classical experimental genre, the short film. But the context in which they are shown, in which even the best videoclips appear—twenty-four hours a day on MTV, or wherever—is one of advertising. And this context, its commercial format, squelches the best talent. You can see this in America. They often don't even show the whole clip, but rather only excerpts from it. It has escalated to the point that the kids there can't even watch clips that last three or four minutes. The threshold for their concentration keeps sinking, so that they already can only watch for thirty seconds before they expect the next one to begin. It's a form of inflation, and the inflationary tendency has taken over the genre. Eventually it will lead to total disinterest.

The great thing about rock and roll, in my view, is that when you hear a piece of music over a period of time, in the summer or during the winter, you begin to form images in your own head that correspond to the music. It's like everyone creates their own videoclip for a song. That then becomes a kind of collective dream. In the case of the Beatles' songs, *Nowhere Man* or whatever, there existed a kind of worldwide videoclip, but only in the minds of the listeners. That was wonderful and creative. Today each song already comes with its own dream, so that you no longer create your own images for the songs. They are included in the package. And to my mind, that weakens rock and roll, destroying its suggestive power.

RAUH: *When you say "a worldwide videoclip," then you mean that each individual had his or her own set of images. You used a lot of rock* *music in your films, for example in* Alabama. *Wasn't that your own subjective set of images that the film presented?*

Yes, of course. But my films were also open, so that everyone had the opportunity and free room to generate their own set of film images. Videoclips are so-called "look-at-that" films, where you can only see what is happening in the film. There are some exceptions, some wonderful exceptions, where such openness exists. But when they appear in this twenty-four-hour rhythm along with two thousand others, one's eyes simply close up again. . . . There are some great videoclips, and I like watching them. But at the same time you become exhausted, and you realize that you get tired of the music you know from videoclips much faster than the music from the radio or albums. And that's really a shame.

RAUH: *When you use music in your new film, will you take into account the new form of reception produced by the contemporary music clip?*

I think you have to do the opposite out of a sense of responsibility. Take, for example, how Nick Cave appears in *Wings of Desire*, which in some ways is the opposite of any videoclip of Nick Cave that you might imagine. He appears in the same narrative framework as the epic events that make up the film story. And I plan to do the same in *Until the End of the World*, although I might use a videoclip there as a quotation. Or maybe I will have a scene in the film that takes the aesthetics of the videoclip ad absurdum.

RAUH: *Videoclips are above all a product of television. You have already expressed your opinion of American television, in* Alice in the Cities, *and then later in* Reverse Angle *and, particularly,* Chambre 666. *Soon German television will not be much different from the American, if it has not already reached that point. Is the situation hopeless in your opinion?*

I think for television in general—that is, for television that is broadcast globally by cable and satellite—there is little hope of rescuing it either aesthetically or morally. It's only getting worse. But because it is deteriorating, there will always be exceptions, some very good productions, but they will remain the exception. On the whole, I think television is becoming unbearable—naked fascism.

RAUH: *That sounds apocalyptic, like the "End of the World."*

Yes, that's the way it is. I think that in ten years television, with its fifty or sixty channels, will be exactly that—apocalyptic.

RAUH: *If you take that to its logical conclusion, then it would mean that due to the changes in consciousness, film as we now know it, particularly films like yours, would hardly have any more viewers.*

Yes, except for the fact that such developments always generate opposition. I am sure of that. As American films, or almost all films, look more and more like television, it is not surprising that independent filmmakers in America are beginning to gain a public by producing radically different kinds of films. For example, one could explain Jim Jarmusch's success with his blatantly reduced aesthetics with the fact that the mainstream films no longer reflect any aesthetics at all, that is, other than those of television. It's reached the point in America that all the film productions look like a Budweiser commercial—from the lighting to the editing and rhythm. Everything derives from commercials and the aesthetics of the videoclip. Films have become like eighty- or ninety-minute clips. That produces, of course, a natural form of resistance, where people are happy to see something different. And, in my opinion, the only guarantee that films will continue to exist is that the bulk of visual production will become catastrophically bad.

RAUH: *That sounds like Neil Postman. Only he argues that writing, literature, offers the way out of this demise.*

I agree completely. Literature, and possibly painting as well, will be the only fields that will preserve a form of subjectivity (*Innerlichkeit*).

* * *

ANDRÉ MÜLLER: *You were in Hollywood for four years. America was the land of your dreams, but the film you made there,* Hammett, *was not a success. Did this failure change you?*

I didn't take it as a failure; on the contrary, I was amazed that I had the stubborn determination to finish the thing although there were plenty of reasons to drop it. I know they won't let me make another film in Hollywood. But I don't care to anyway. You lose too much independence. It's terrible how they simply ignore so much talent and let it go to waste. It's not the artists, but rather a few agents and lawyers who make the decisions about the films. They swoop down on the masses of unemployed film people like flies around shit, taking what they need. The artists are just victims. Hollywood is the sleaziest industry you can imagine—a kind of contemporary Tower of Babel.

MÜLLER: *Does nothing remain from your American Dream?*

Oh no, I still get homesick when I think of a couple of places. But none of that original strong attraction is left. The worst thing about that country is its television, the way it presents itself in television. It's a monstrous creation, totally dehumanizing, you could say the very embodiment of evil.

MÜLLER: *Is television in Europe much better?*

Actually not! That's what makes me desperate. You come back out of this nightmare that you are fleeing—to France, for example—turn on the television, and suddenly you can't believe your eyes—first you see commercials everywhere, and then this idiotic, just plain stupid American entertainment programming. You are sitting in Paris, once the cultural capital of the world, and now everyone is imitating in a helplessly dumb fashion this American crap you've just escaped. In Italy it's the same thing, so you travel to Germany, the last bastion of hope, turn on the television in Düsseldorf or Munich, and what do you see? The Federal Republic as well has only this one wish—to belong to this great, terrible America and finally become the fifty-first state in the U.S.

MÜLLER: *Do you have an idea why it's like this?*

There are economic reasons. I'm convinced that eventually the most important industry for mankind, even more important than the defense industry, will be the entertainment industry. This infernal form of entertainment production will eventually trounce down all sense of cultural identity and every chance of self-determination. You can see this best in small American towns, where the people live their lives almost mindlessly, like in a science-fiction novel where the people have been administered drugs and are controlled like zombies. But this is true not only of America. It has spread and you can't stop it, either with warnings or actions.

MÜLLER: *Why don't you make a film that depicts this?*

That's what I'm doing; it will be my next film, *Until the End of the World*. There's a scene in it in Australia, about a people who have been destroyed, totally stripped of their culture—I'm talking about the aborigines. They live in huts that are almost completely empty, cooking over an open fire. But somewhere in the back of it there is a generator, and the only electrical devices are a television and a VCR with about fifteen to twenty videocassettes lying in the dust in front of it. This people possessed a wonderful culture with their own mythology—but it's all gone! I'm afraid that the same thing is going to happen to us in fifty years, unless there is a great worldwide cultural revolution that eliminates all television. That would be the first step.

* * *

GERD GEMÜNDEN: *In interviews, you have repeatedly warned of the stupefying effects of American film and television. The threat of the proliferation of images also informs* Until the End of the World—*the power of images can be addictive. The paradoxical situation for a filmmaker is that he or she has to show images in order to criticize them.*

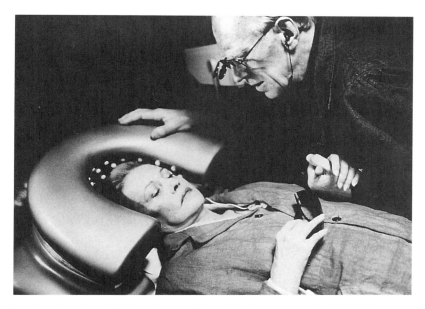

Seeing through technology—Edith (Jeanne Moreau) and Henry Farber (Max von Sydow) in *Until the End of the World* (1991).

That is certainly right. *Until the End of the World* has been shaken by the disease of images, but I don't think it has succumbed to it.

GEMÜNDEN: *But the cure for Claire, who is addicted to images, is found in writing, that is, in the story that Eugene writes about her; in the longer, yet unreleased version of the film, she and Sam are healed through painting. Is this not a problematic statement for a filmmaker?*

One can reproach me for this literarization. I see only one way to protect the images, to counteract the increasing prostitution of images, and that is through language. That's why I have put more emphasis on a concise use of language—already in *Wings of Desire*—in order to have language control the images and not just accompany them: language not only as dialogue, because that's something that you find in every film, but language as something above the images.

GEMÜNDEN: *Yet there seems to be an important difference between* Wings of Desire *and* Until the End of the World: *in the latter you have lost confidence in the images, and it now seems as if these images need to be protected. This is a long way from the trust in images that you showed in the long, almost banal shots of your short films, and in your fear of cutting (most notably in* Summer in the City *and* Kings of the Road*), and in your admiration for the movies of John Ford.*

85

▌ Documents

I no longer trust the narrative power of images, because the landscape around them has been undermined. The narrative force of images has disappeared to the same degree that their commercial force has increased. Today, images have to sell, not tell. Therefore we can no longer indulge in the narrative power of images as naively and innocently as we used to.

Sources

Brunow, Jochen. "Mauern und Zwischenräume: Ein Gespräche über das Schreiben von Drehbüchern." *Schreiben für den Film: Das Drehbuch als eine andere Art des Erzählens.* Ed. Jochen Brunow. Munich: Text and Kritik, 1991. 95–107.

Dawson, Jan. *Wim Wenders.* Trans. Carla Wartenberg. New York: Zoetrope, 1976.

Dieckmann, Katherine. "Wim Wenders: An Interview." *Film Quarterly* 38.2 (1984–85): 2–7.

Gemünden, Gerd. "I No Longer Trust the Narrative Power of Images: A Conversation with Wim Wenders." Unpublished interview, Berlin, March 1, 1994.

Gut, Taja. "Das Wahrnehmen einer Bewegung." *Individualität* 19 (1988): 31–50.

Müller, André. "Das Kino könnte der Engel sein." *Der Spiegel* 4 (1987): 230–38.

Nolden, Rainer. "Wim Wenders: Ein Drehbuch zu schreiben, das ist die Hölle." *Die Welt* June 20, 1988.

Paneth, Ira. "Wim and His Wings." *Film Quarterly* 42.1 (1988): 2–8.

Rauh, Reinhold. "Ein Gespräch mit Wim Wenders." *Wim Wenders und seine Filme.* Munich: Heyne, 1990. 237–64.

Schütte, Wolfram. "Abschied von der dröhnenden Stimme des alten Kinos: Aus einem Gespräch mit Wolfram Schütte." Wim Wenders, *Die Logik der Bilder: Essays und Gespräche.* Frankfurt am Main: Verlag der Autoren, 1988. 53–67. Originally appeared in *Frankfurter Rundschau* November 6, 1982: Feuilleton 3.

Arguments

The Writer in Film:
Wrong Move

> The ability to see and hear fades away when one has
> lost one's sense of self.
>
> —told to Philip Winter, protagonist
> in Wim Wenders's *Alice in the Cities*[1]

In his book on Wim Wenders, Peter Buchka asserts that all of Wenders's protagonists suffer from their inadequate perception of the world around them. They cannot really hear and see. They have lost their ability to perceive external reality, for they have lost their sense of self. Connected to these problems is the difficulty these characters have with language and self-expression.[2] If one looks at the Anglo-American popular culture of the late 1960s that was so influential upon Wenders, it is interesting to note a fictional character who could almost serve as an allegorical embodiment of what in Buchka's thesis is the typical Wenders character: the hero of The Who's rock opera *Tommy*, who literally cannot see or hear, who is called "deaf, dumb, and blind."

The juxtaposition of The Who and Wenders is not as far-fetched as it might seem. Alienation from the senses and from language—and the inadequate sense of self behind this alienation—is not typical merely of characters in Wenders's films. The concern with alienation from sense perception and experience, and the desperate attempt to overcome it, can be readily connected to what Michael Rutschky called *Erfahrungshunger*, or "hunger for experience," his term for the West German malaise of the 1970s. Nor is the phenomenon in question limited to West German culture during the

1970s—in the same decade, after all, Christopher Lasch labeled American society *The Culture of Narcissism*, maintaining that the contemporary American character was typified by a weak ego incapable of adequately distinguishing internal and external realities—an impoverished sense of both self and the world. This phenomenon can be characterized in less pathological terms by placing it in the context of "postmodernity": rather than speaking of weak egos, one might refer to the demise of the ideology of the "bourgeois individual subject." Related to this is anxiety about "loss of mastery," experienced not only by the individual but by the West in general.[3]

Postmodern culture has been characterized by its effacement of the old boundaries between high culture and mass or popular culture.[4] To return to popular culture, then, specifically to The Who (the group's very name capitalized on the identity crisis of its generation): how does the "deaf, dumb, and blind" Tommy find a way to express himself? Self-expression and self-realization come through mastery of pinball. One can see in this an apt metaphor for the attempt of youth in the 1960s to seek fulfillment in popular culture, having rejected both classical and modernist "high art" as equally institutionalized and elitist. This backlash against high culture certainly had its effect on Wenders, whose life was supposedly "saved by rock and roll."[5] Wenders's films highlight the trappings of American mass culture and technology in West Germany (with a specific emphasis on pinball machines, in fact).[6] They also reflect his ambivalence about them.

This is certainly true of Wenders's film *Wrong Move* (*Falsche Bewegung*, 1975), a revision of Peter Handke's screenplay of the same name (1973). This film is a unique reflection upon the interaction in West Germany during the mid-1970s of discourses about writing, politics, specularity, filmmaking, and history—political and literary history, both recent and more remote. The complexity of this interaction in *Wrong Move* makes it in turn a postmodernist text: it is, after all, a curious mixture of "high art" and mass culture—and in some ways what Linda Hutcheon calls a "historiographical metafiction" as well (i.e., a metafiction that is self-reflexive not just about fiction but about the representation of history as well).[7] A work of German literary classicism—Goethe's influential Bildungsroman *Wilhelm Meister's Apprenticeship* (1796), no less—is updated and adapted for the screen by Handke, and then filmed by Wenders, who rejected German high culture for rock and roll, pinball, and the movies. The first shot of this new Wilhelm Meister shows him playing an album by the Troggs and then putting his fist through the window. The tensions created in crossing boundaries of genre and media are paralleled by those created in the obvious historical contrast between the Germany depicted by Goethe and that in the film: *Wrong Move* follows its Wilhelm Meister through a West German landscape increasingly dominated by massive high-rise apartment complexes and shopping centers.

In order to analyze the film in terms of these overlapping contexts, I will first discuss Handke's script in light of its depiction of writing and its relation to New Subjectivity, a West German literary trend of the 1970s. Then I examine how Wenders's film depicts the travels of Wilhelm Meister, Handke's would-be writer, through West Germany in the 1970s.

Handke's Screenplay: Radical "Inwardness"?

"I am convinced of the power of poetic thought to dissolve abstractions and thus exert a powerful influence on the future." Handke spoke these words in 1973,[8] the same year he dates his script for *Wrong Move*.[9] According to Handke's formulation, writing's utopian potential transcends any merely "private" qualities associated with writing. In a statement made a few years later, Handke rejected any "abstract utopia" as a conscious or preconceived goal or strategy for his writing, maintaining that the utopian perspective arises *of itself* from the process of working with the realistic details he gathers from observation and experience. Such new perspectives open automatically from this process, providing solutions he had not planned: "The point of departure and the details must be realistic, completely realistic. When, however, new perspectives arise out of this, then I know that literature is simply superior to any other form of dealing with the world. And then I know—as dumb as it sounds—that it is needed. I have to have the feeling that other people need it, that it is useful literature, in the widest sense."[10]

The social character of literature is emphasized in this optimistic formulation of its potential; but its social and utopian character is guaranteed only by that which appears to be its radical privacy, for, as Handke said in the same interview in which he made the statement above, he believes "literature is only compelling when it penetrates the deepest levels of the self." Only through the most extreme subjectivity is intersubjectivity possible, he feels.[11] Such sentiments are somewhat reminiscent of Adorno: for example, the idea that literature is "most deeply bound to the social when it does not speak as a mouthpiece for society," or that a poem is understood only when the reader "perceives in its loneliness the voice of humanity."[12] In *Wrong Move*, at a crucial point in the film's discussion of poetry and politics, the old man suggests to Wilhelm that he should "become politically active and stop writing." The following exchange ensues:

Wilhelm: "But I had just realized—precisely *while* writing—that I couldn't formulate my needs in a political way. I found that up until then they had never been awakened by a politician, rather always exclusively by poets."

The old man: "What does the world care about your most personal needs?"

Wilhelm: "Everyone has his most personal needs, and those are the real ones. For me there are only most personal needs."

The old man: "But they are impossible to fulfill, in contrast to the needs with which politics occupies itself. Those personal needs can only be fulfilled through the illusion of poetry."

Wilhelm: "But that illusion implies the hope that they are capable of fulfillment—otherwise there wouldn't even be the illusion of it." (52)

In this long dialogue, Wilhelm declares that it is the poet and not the politician who inspires authentic social interaction, who manages to communicate by working at the level of his most personal needs, since these are "the real ones." The politician uses language that is unauthentic, impersonal, and reified, a co-opted, conformist language that alienates the individual and thus increases social isolation. Poetry is thus the only means to intersubjective communication, and in its glimmer, where the old man sees only hallucinatory illusion, Wilhelm sees the hope for a utopian future where those intensely subjective needs can be fulfilled, where the longing for individuality and community are not mutually exclusive. For Wilhelm does see the need for the sort of "political" community that is a synthesis of the two:

The old man: "Wilhelm, don't let yourself be led astray by your poetic feeling for the world."

Wilhelm: "If only both, the poetic and the political, could be one."

The old man: "That would be the end of longing—and the end of the world." (52)

Once again, the old man underscores the utopian nature of Wilhelm's vision; from his perspective, however, this is a warning. It is at this point in the text that he discloses his secret to Wilhelm: that he had presided over the murder of Jews in Vilna during the war (53). Later he will argue that an opposition to politics similar to that voiced by Wilhelm had, for the old man's generation, led ultimately to the "most terrible politics" (73). But Wilhelm is not interested in his advice; he will instead attempt to drown the old man (75).

The long discussion of poetry and politics must thus be seen in its textual context as somehow related to Germany's political past. One also cannot help but read it as almost a summary of arguments on the relation of literature and politics heard in West Germany between 1968 and the *Tendenzwende*, the tendential shift of 1973 and 1974 (a shift away from the politics of 1968). Some of the arguments of 1968, when literature was proclaimed dead, are echoed in the old man's suggestion to give up writing and become politically active. Wilhelm of course voices arguments connected to New Subjectivity: at a time when political activism seemed futile, literature seemed once again viable, and, in literature's greater suitability for the communication of authentic subjective experience, it was argued that literary endeavors were indeed political.[13] It is surely significant that allusions to this debate are found in Handke's script immediately before crimes of the German past are exposed; the debate in the script is to some extent haunted by that past.

At the end of the screenplay, Wilhelm stands alone on the *Zugspitze*, a peak in southern Bavaria. The implication is that the isolation he achieves there will enable him to write; the only sounds called for in Handke's script as Wilhelm stands there are those of a blizzard and the "noise of a typewriter . . . which gets stronger and stronger" (81). Wilhelm's mother, at the beginning of the script, had sent him away from Heide in northern Germany so that he could fulfill his dream of becoming a writer (9–11). He then wanders the length of West Germany, meanwhile being followed by various people whom he encounters by chance in the course of his travels. Not until he has wandered all the way to southern Bavaria does he find the isolation and distance from others he needs to write. It is interesting to compare the development of Handke's protagonist to that in Goethe's novel: "In contrast to Goethe's Wilhelm Meister, Handke's Wilhelm doesn't search for himself in confrontation with society, but rather by increasing his distance from it. The journey into the world becomes here an escape from the world."[14]

In an authentic fashion, Handke seems to argue, the individual subject can develop only through "the illusion of poetry," as the old man calls it. True self-realization comes through the process of writing, which is after all (according to Handke) "superior to any other form of dealing with the world."[15] For Wilhelm it is a manner of dealing with the world that requires being apart from it. Writing is a process of remembering in isolation. As he tells Therese, "When I am alone, I'll be able to remember, above all to remember you, and when I can remember again, I'll feel good and have the desire to write. As a process of remembering, I think, writing will finally become automatic" (77–78).

Only later, apart from her, will he be able to love her: "I know that later I'll love you very much, Therese" (78); living with her, he feels "als ob ich mich schwul zu mir selber verhalte"—that is, as if he felt homosexual desire for himself (77). This sort of self-obsession is actually a sign of alienation from the self, an alienation that in turn blocks him from experience of the world around him. To achieve contact with the people and things around him, he must struggle alone with his memories of them in the process of writing. Communion with the world through radical privacy— via the process of writing: here again this somewhat mystical paradox emerges. The alienated individual is forced to remove him- or herself from the world in order to regain subjective access to it, a phenomenon that is depicted in more radical terms in Handke's *Left-Handed Woman*.[16] This is a striking indictment of what Handke sees as the numbing alienation of modern life; as Eric Rentschler writes, this "critique of modernity" is of political significance insofar as it suggests the overwhelming power of "the forces that have imposed these limits on him [i.e., Handke] and other subjects who hunger for experience."[17]

This hunger is closely related to an emphasis on specularity, on what Rentschler calls "cinemorphic seeing."[18] There is a strong emphasis on visual perception in *Wrong Move*, given Wilhelm's concept of an "erotic gaze" (58); furthermore, Wilhelm's rejection of inspiration (*einfallen*) as the impetus for writing, in favor of the more empirical concept of observation (*auffallen*), the position he takes in his discussion with Bernhard on poetry (55–56), can also be easily related to the concern with visual experience on the part of the "specular subject."

But Wilhelm's trajectory away from social contact into isolation (where he will be able to write) seems at odds with the hunger for unmediated experience and with the passivity of purely visual experience. According to the screenplay, the film is supposed to end with a shot of Wilhelm dissolving into a shot of the *Zugspitze* in a blizzard (81): the visual image of white snow and gray sky, an image in danger of losing all contour, is coupled with the sound of a typewriter becoming ever louder. Visual experience is replaced by the whiteness of a blank page to be written upon; specularity is replaced by the solitary process of writing and remembering. For only in remembering does the visual truly open itself to experience; only through "afterimages" is the experience clear, as stated explicitly in the following passage, which, significantly, is supposed to appear as "writing over the image": "Sometimes I would stare in front of me, with the intention of not looking at anything in particular. Then I would close my eyes, and only with the afterimage that then appeared would I realize what had been before me. When I'm writing, too, I'll close my eyes and see with total clarity something that I had refused to notice with my eyes open" (61–62).

Writing is thus in a sense opposed to direct visual experience, which in and of itself remains inadequate and incomplete, much as social interaction does: just as Wilhelm will only be able to love Therese later, so will he only later grasp what he has seen. It is only writing that frees either interaction with his environment from alienation. When Therese criticizes him for overlooking a great deal in the world around him (32, 58), he admits that she is right. Buchka's thesis about Wenders's characters—that they cannot really hear or see—applies to Wilhelm in Handke's script as well.

In spite of his inability to see with much sensitivity, Wilhelm maintains that the process of remembering is more important than registering whatever visual impressions offer themselves (32). Later he formulates his concept of an "erotic gaze":

> Wilhelm: "I know that I don't have what is called a talent for observation, but I like to imagine that I have the capacity for a kind of erotic gaze. Suddenly something will catch my attention that I have always overlooked. Not only do I see it then, but simultaneously I get a feeling for it. That's what I mean by an erotic gaze. What I'm seeing is then no longer just an object being observed, but rather a very intimate part of myself as well. One used to call this seeing the essence of a phenomenon, I think. Something particular becomes a sign for the whole. I then write something that has not merely been observed, but something experienced. For this reason especially I want to be a writer." (58)

The erotic gaze is for Wilhelm something that overcomes him suddenly and changes what he observes—poorly—into something he experiences.[19] The mystical unity achieved between the perceived object and the perceiving subject in this experience is also closely related to writing; indeed, the experience sounds much like the descriptions of writing later in the text cited above—writing as a "process of remembering" that unites the subject with its alienated experience of itself and the world, ending the reified, objectified relation to both the self and others. The erotic gaze seems to effect the same unity, and indeed to be part of the process of writing. It is a gaze, in fact, that is supposed to occur only "with eyes closed": the "afterimages" he mentions in connection with his writing.

Thus for all the emphasis on specularity in Handke, there is in *Wrong Move* at any rate ambiguity as to which is more essential to the mystical experience: seeing or writing. Indeed, as I have argued, there is much evidence that seeing is definitely subordinated to writing. Although this primacy is less clear in Handke's next work, the novel *A Moment of True Feeling*, in *Wrong Move* it seems that only writing can make unmediated seeing possible; the erotic gaze is almost identical with the process of writing. Immediacy of experience paradoxically depends on the mediation of writing, which in turn is a process that transcends all mediation—and alienation.

Handke's script for *Wrong Move* implies a positive ending: the hero is finally able to write. In isolation the hero will transcend alienation, indeed history, since writing is the ground of transcendence, outside and beyond history.[20] There is no "diachronic longing" here—history is a violent distraction, as the hero's irritation with the old man illustrates.

Nonetheless, there is tension between the text's emphasis on writing and *Innerlichkeit*, or "inwardness," and its stress on the visual, especially because of its status as a film script. Furthermore, Handke's script was revised by Wenders in his filmic realization of *Wrong Move*, and the film treats writing—and Wilhelm, the would-be writer—in a distinctly different fashion; writing (and art in general) loses much of its idealistic aura and its insulation from history.

Wenders's Re-Vision: The Writer in Film

Instead of the snowstorm on the *Zugspitze* that Wilhelm had wanted to experience (77) and which we find at the end of Handke's script, Wenders's film ends with a shot of Wilhelm with his back to the camera, gazing off into the mountains. The sky is clear, and on the sound track we hear the voice of the narrator:

> I had told Therese I intended to stay in Germany because I knew too little to write about it. But it was only an excuse. I really wanted only to be alone, to be undisturbed in my torpor. I was waiting for some kind of experience, like a miracle, but the snowstorm never came. Why was I here instead of with the others? Why did I threaten the old man instead of letting him tell me more? I felt as if I had missed something, and I was still missing out—with every move I made.[21]

This is quite obviously a different ending. Wilhelm admits that his line about getting to know Germany (in the Handke script on p. 80) was merely an excuse to be alone; this isolation in turn is not any productive "process of remembering" but rather is described as "torpor." Wilhelm is filled with doubts about the choice he has made—not at all *fröhlich*, joyous, as in Handke's version (78); and, most importantly, there is no snowstorm —and no sound of typing.[22] The positive ending implied in Handke's script is totally inverted: Wilhelm does not succeed in becoming a writer, and his movement into isolation seems just as wrong as his other moves.

"I want to become a writer. But how is that possible without any interest in people?" (8). These lines at the beginning of the film, among the first to be heard as voice-over narration, indicate Wilhelm's social alienation. When one compares them to the lines in the voice-over at the end of the film—for example, "Why was I here, instead of with the others?"—it is clear that Wilhelm has changed little. By contrast, in Handke's version, his confident assertion to Therese—"I know that later I'll love you very much, Therese" (78)—implies that, near the end of his travels, he at least knows how to overcome his numbness. In the film he succeeds neither in acquiring desire for people nor in becoming a writer. Isolation will overcome neither his alienation from others nor his writing block.[23]

The only thing positive about the film's ending, indeed, is its implication that Wilhelm is beginning to gain the ironic distance on himself that the film has had from the beginning, in a way less evident in Handke's script. The film distances the spectator from its protagonist by the use throughout of voice-over narration. It is often used to report what in Handke's script are notes Wilhelm makes in his diary, which are supposed to be shown (e.g., pp. 8–9) or even superimposed over the image (e.g., p. 61). Wenders accomplishes two things in having them read over the sound track (in the first person) instead of merging them with the visual: first, he deemphasizes Wilhelm's writing, increasing the impression the viewer has that Wilhelm never succeeds in writing much, that his internal monologue rarely is externalized in writing;[24] and second, the distance between Wilhelm's internal perspective and the external, visual world is increased.

Mirroring his alienation, this gap between his perspective and the perspective of the camera is highlighted even when there is no voice-over. The camera distances the viewer from Wilhelm, but its perspective is not granted objectivity, as is clear from the opening shot of the film. Handke's script calls for opening the film with an establishing shot of the town's central square before showing Wilhelm in his room (7); instead, the film begins with a traveling aerial shot high above a town on a river, during which raindrops gather on the glass pane through which the camera films. Not only does this increase the contrast between the external world and the interior of Wilhelm's room, it increases the distance—literally—from which Wilhelm is filmed, and foregrounds the camera's perspective in doing so. For this is obviously no "objective" establishing shot but rather an acknowledgment of the camera's position; the raindrops on the glass, indeed, come very close to a direct foregrounding of the camera's lens. The position of the camera in the first shot is further specified in the second shot, where, from inside Wilhelm's window, the viewer sees a helicopter above the town. Bridging the two shots is the noise of the helicopter's engine, which replaces the opening music toward the end of the first shot.

The film's opening illustrates the distanced attitude that the film takes toward its protagonist, an attitude reflected in the filmmaker's admission of some personal dislike for the character.[25] This lack of sympathy is difficult to find in Handke's text; it is much harder to avoid seeing an identification between the text and the author, who seems to depict the protagonist's apparently negative traits as necessary to the existential position of the writer. It is the radical *Innerlichkeit* propagated in Handke's text that seems to be the object of criticism in Wenders's film. The split between Wilhelm and the world is not merely reproduced in the film, but depicted with irony.

The film has a somewhat surrealistic quality; its mood has been described as poetic and like a fairy tale.[26] This quality has doubtless to do with Handke's script and the fateful role chance plays in bringing a group together around Wilhelm and then dispersing it again. Chance events—of varying degrees of improbability—abound in the script. For instance, at the very beginning Wilhelm encounters the old man and Mignon on the train to Hamburg (17–18); after Wilhelm changes trains in Hamburg, they appear once again on the new train. The conductor on this train immediately assumes that Wilhelm is paying for these two uninvited companions, and Wilhelm good-naturedly acquiesces to this assumption (22). Then it becomes apparent that the conductor and the old man know each other from the war (23; see also 53). Such events continue, as for instance when, in the central episode of the script, Bernhard joins the group by chance (37) and then leads them, not to his uncle's house in the country, but by mistake to the house of the suicidal industrialist. The latter invites them in anyway: "I was just putting the rifle into my mouth, and as I heard the car, I waited, hoping it would stop" (41).

The film's depiction of this chain of improbabilities is filled with a humorous irony, a quality flaunting the "vraisemblable" of conventional narrative, the plausibility expected from a conventional realist film.[27] The improbability of the chance encounters is especially accentuated around the character of Bernhard, usually in a humorous way, as when Bernhard tells the others, "I think he isn't my uncle at all. And it isn't the right house, either. We are altogether in the wrong place, I'm afraid" (41). In context, it is a somewhat dark joke, and its evocation of the film's title makes it somehow emblematic.

Much of the humor can be explained in terms of the obvious discomfort of a protagonist "without interest in people" who nonetheless finds ever more people following him. This humor is part of Handke's story, for Wilhelm is a character who for most of the script is passive, pushed out of the house by his mother and diverted in his travels by the people who gather about him, including the would-be poet, Bernhard, who does manage to write poetry—which galls Wilhelm (44), even though he considers it bad poetry (56).

The group's dispersal takes place after the crucial walk in the hills near the industrialist's house (50–61); after the industrialist's suicide and Bernhard's unexplained departure from the group (61–62), however, chance plays a lesser role. It is Wilhelm who drives off the old man and decides to leave Therese. He begins to take control by actively opting to be alone. But here again, though Wenders follows the script so far, his changing of the ending mocks this increased decisiveness on Wilhelm's part, for he does not find the snowstorm, nor is he at all sure why he is there; no triumphal sound of typing leaves the viewer with the idea that his aimless motion is over. The subject in the film has his autonomy undermined throughout; isolation is no help.

As I have noted, there is a tension in Handke's text between seeing and writing, indeed between seeing and spoken as well as written language. In terms of the attraction she exerts upon Wilhelm, the seductive and silent character Mignon is an incarnation of this tension.[28] Wilhelm has his own sullen struggle with articulation. In the same diary entry at the beginning of the script in which he announces his lack of interest in people, he writes: "For two days I haven't spoken a word. I feel as if my tongue has disappeared from my mouth. But in my sleep I talk all night long, my mother says" (8).

Wilhelm, depicted as verbally uncommunicative and having difficulty writing, is thus peculiarly suited to being seduced by the silent Mignon, and in this he could stand for a whole generation disenchanted with verbal discourse and fixated on the immediacy of sensual experience—experience that often turned out to be a passive, hypnotic specularity as opposed to anything much more active. The verbal communication so problematic for Wilhelm is in turn that which characterizes Therese, the actress, who also finds Wilhelm unsuited to be a writer, and who in anger eventually strikes him with the sheet of paper upon which he has been typing.[29] She is also, however, the woman who desires him—and the woman whose bed he is seeking when he mistakenly finds Mignon.

The scene in which this incident occurs illustrates Wilhelm's inability to determine what he wants, his indecisiveness and passivity in the face of the desires of others. For in spite of the attraction Mignon can be said to exert upon him, the fact that he accepts her embrace has more to do with another "wrong move" than any active longing on his part. He is expecting Therese, who has insisted that he find her: "But I don't want to be left unsatisfied today" (44). Wilhelm embraces Mignon in the dark; discovering her identity, he slaps her, then caresses her, leaves the room, but, after leaning his head on the door, goes back to her (47).[30] The hero who speaks of his "erotic gaze" finds himself, when confronted with the erotic desires of others, stumbling blindly in the dark.[31] He also finds it easier to succumb in silence to Mignon's advances than to deal with Therese, a grown woman who articulates her desires openly and directly.

In the midst of Handke's allusions to language, nonverbal experience, the visual, and the erotic in his treatment of the characters Therese (the actress), Wilhelm (the writer), and the silent Mignon, some simpler psychosexual patterns can be noted. Although Wilhelm's initial contact with Therese is established by his gaze through the train window, as soon as she takes the initiative—by sending him a message—and he has to speak to her, the problems begin. By the end of the script he feels he must leave her, but he gives the silent (and much younger) Mignon the option of joining him. Her silence is seductive—and nonthreatening.[32]

Mignon's attraction as a character is obviously much stronger in the film than in the script, since only visually is the full effect of the silence Handke planned for her appreciable. Her presence has been seen as all the more provocative around the characters who voice the often long speeches of Handke's screenplay, which have been considered somewhat stilted and wordy. It is true that they are long, perhaps at times somewhat ponderous— certainly within the context of Wenders's work, with its generally laconic characters. But the tension between Wenders's camera and the scripted speeches is integral to the film: tension between the visual and the verbal was already built into Handke's script, as the character Mignon certainly demonstrates.

For Mignon functions as a site of seductive, nonverbal immediacy, an object of the erotic gaze to the extent that it is not completely subsumed by writing and thus *competes* with writing as an avenue to some sort of mystical transcendence. The tension between the silent Mignon and the language of the other characters, between the visual and the verbal, must also be seen in relation to the text's existence as a film script. It carries over into Wenders's film as well, but it is articulated differently.

There is a mystical immediacy attached to the visual both in Wilhelm's concept of the erotic gaze and in Handke's experimentation with the cinematic medium.[33] Handke's work is not lacking in self-reflexivity, of course, and his screenplay for *Wrong Move* is no exception. Wilhelm's concern with writing and his desire to write (46) are obviously central to the text, as are the intertextual allusions to Goethe and other writers: Wilhelm carries with him Eichendorff's *From the Life of a Ne'er-Do-Well* (*Aus dem Leben eines Taugenichts*, 1826) and Flaubert's *Sentimental Education* (*L'education sentimentale*, 1869) (12). Handke's idea of superimposing writing over the image is more cinematic; Wenders rejects it in this film but uses it in *Lightning over Water (Nick's Film)* (1980). This graphic representation of the materiality of writing also suggests writing on the film stock, but for Handke (logically enough) the emphasis here is clearly on writing.

What about Wenders's attitude to writing? As Buchka asserts, writing has played an important role in Wenders's work. His characters, experiencing difficulties with perception and verbal articulation, often attempt to overcome this alienation from the outer world—and inner self—by writing. But Buchka writes, "With *The Wrong Move*, the dream of finding one's identity exclusively through writing is exhausted."[34] Wenders's generally negative depiction of Wilhelm supports this assertion.

Beyond the mere depiction of writing, there is the question of writing as filmmaking. As mentioned above, in the opening shot of the film Wenders foregrounds his camera. As one critic asserts, Wenders is a filmmaker in whose films one notes "the clear presence of the camera within the images"; his films never remain exclusively bound to the narrative, but expose their own cinematic means of expression. "They inscribe the trace of their own discourse upon the stories."[35] He is thus a filmmaker for whom the notion of an "erotic gaze" might be somewhat problematic, in spite of his association with a cinema of "pure being as pure seeing."[36] A gaze that supposedly transcends mediation is rather close to the *illusion* of immediacy created in classic Hollywood cinema. Christian Metz (among others) defines that cinema in terms of the attempt to keep all evidence of cinematic discursivity (editing, camera work, etc.) as unnoticeable as possible so that the "story" seems to be a reality unfolding immediately before the spectator.[37]

In opposition to that type of cinema, Wenders's filmmaking could perhaps be called (to borrow from Roland Barthes) "writerly," although this invocation of the readerly/writerly dichotomy might appear to make Wenders much more of a modernist than he is.[38] Given Wenders's roots in Sensibilism (a movement of critics and directors centered in Munich in the late 1960s who were opposed to intellectual cinema and montage),[39] his love for the pro-filmic reality, and his consequent reticence about montage (at least in his earlier films), one would have to conclude that Wenders's style of *realism* (which I would compare in certain ways to Italian neorealism) is much too honest to efface the traces of its own construction. Precisely his respect for the pro-filmic reality seems to have compelled him to foreground his own intervention. It is this combination of self-reflexivity and narrative fiction, of neorealist and modernist influences, and his (ambivalent) interest in popular culture, that reveals the postmodern origins of Wenders's films.

Wrong Move, besides alluding to the traces of its own cinematic enunciation, also alludes to the historical situation of the cinema in West Germany, as Rentschler has observed.[40] He interprets Wenders's film as a critique of the radical *Innerlichkeit* bound up with the artist as depicted in Handke's script. Without a doubt, the precarious economic and political situation of the filmmaker in West Germany during the 1970s made an art as isolated as that to which Wilhelm seems to be drawn impossible, although the attraction was understandable. The film reflects a skepticism with regard to Wilhelm's solution to the problem of the artist in West Germany— and not merely because of the situation of the cinema there. Wilhelm's journey through Germany is changed in ways that make the historical and political background of the artist's dilemma there more evident than in the original screenplay.

▌ Richard W. McCormick

The Writer and German History

Wenders has said that it is impossible to make films in Germany without addressing the "hole" in German culture left by its misappropriation in the Third Reich.[41] In postwar West Germany that cultural vacuum was not addressed, but an attempt was made to "fill" it by the *Wirtschafts-wunder*, the "economic miracle" that created a new consumer culture. This meant goods and services, and international (mostly American) mass culture: Hollywood movies, television, and—especially for Wenders's generation—rock and roll. *Wrong Move* is an attempt to explore this cultural (and political) legacy, and the film's most postmodernist aspects are directly related to this historical investigation: it juxtaposes its allusions to Goethe and Eichendorff with the Bundesbahn and the autobahn (modern trains and expressways); flickering television sets with the industrialist's long, brooding speeches about alienation in Germany; Beethoven's melody to the "Ode to Joy" (whistled by Mignon and Therese) with the old man's disclosure of his war crimes in Vilna; and the scenic Rhine landscape of that sequence with the concrete monotony of Frankfurt-Hoechst, the location of Therese's suburban high-rise apartment.

Especially relevant to the film's critique of West German political and cultural history is a consideration of two of its elements: first, the journey Wilhelm makes through that nation; and second, the troublesome incarnation of the German past in the old man (called "Laertes" in the film credits) who accompanies Mignon and, uninvited, follows Wilhelm around.[42] Both are elements central to Handke's screenplay, but the first, the journey that structures the narrative, is altered in a significant way by Wenders.

In the original script, the film is supposed to open in Heide (7), from which point Wilhelm departs for Soest in Westphalia. He then travels with the group to the industrialist's house, and from there to Therese's apartment in Frankfurt-Höchst (63), only to end up alone on the *Zugspitze* in southern Bavaria (81). The film, on the other hand, opens with a shot of Glückstadt on the Elbe that emphasizes the extreme width of the river at its mouth. The Elbe is not just any river, but the one that symbolizes Germany's postwar division into two states.[43] The north-to-south journey through Germany in Handke's script is thus given a starting point that grazes, if ever so briefly and indirectly, the east-west rupture that was so much more a determining factor of postwar German political realities than the much older north-south split in German culture. This starting point is displayed before the viewer sees Wilhelm; it precedes the narrative and alludes to the political and historical situation that determines Wilhelm's journey to Bonn instead of, say, Berlin.

For in the film he travels to Bonn, and this is the major alteration that Wenders makes in Wilhelm's itinerary. The picturesque half-timbered buildings (*Fachwerkhäuser*) of Soest are replaced by the more prosaic Bonn, the "provisional" capital of the Federal Republic of Germany, the sleepy, midsized town chosen in 1949 as a temporary substitute for the metropolis east of the Elbe. The small-town eccentricities Handke sets in Soest (e.g., the man who screams, "Do you know what pain is?" [32]) have a political resonance entirely lacking in his version by being set in Bonn: "The first signs of public insanity and collective fear he encounters during a morning stroll do not transpire in an obscure corner of North Rhine–Westphalia; they take place in the capital of West Germany."[44]

It is also in Bonn that Wilhelm finally meets Therese and encounters Bernhard, two others with artistic aspirations. This meeting of would-be artists in the political capital of West Germany is also the prelude to a more significant confrontation about art and politics: the above-mentioned sequence in which, during the walk on the hills above the Rhine, Laertes and Wilhelm discuss poetry and politics, and Laertes reveals the secret of his past.[45] The latter, called "the old man" in Handke's script, is associated in both versions with bloodstains on the train seat that Wilhelm sees before the old man with the bloody nose actually appears. The stains are metonymic and metaphoric at the same time, with the latter function more pronounced in Handke's script, where the description "The seat across from him with the large brown spot" (17) evokes by naming the color brown the Nazi past the old man symbolizes. The blood on the white seat alludes most directly to the blood of Laertes's victims; it must also be seen in connection with the blood Wilhelm draws by putting his fist through the window, blood he then sucks (7).

In Wenders's film, the blood motif occurs one other time, at a point not in the original script: while the industrialist speaks of loneliness in Germany, he sticks a pen into his hand and draws blood, seemingly unaware that he is doing so. Wilhelm then uses this pen to write a diary entry, one of the few times in the film when he manages to write. Once again, the film places Wilhelm and his whole approach to writing in a negative light. Laertes (admittedly a rather improbable war criminal) bleeds out of guilt for the suffering he has caused others; the shedding of his own blood for others, albeit a few decades too late, is in contrast to Wilhelm, who impatiently tells the old man, "I have no feeling for the past" (28), and seems empowered to write by using the blood of another.

The old man as a symbol of the crimes of the Nazi past "haunts" Wilhelm, just as those crimes have continued to haunt Germany. The problem of postwar Germany has been the question of what to do about this legacy. One possible reading might be that Wilhelm's failure to kill Laertes symbolizes his inability to come to terms with politics, specifically, Germany's political past, an inability seen as another sign of his general narcissistic withdrawal, his passivity and lack of resolve.[46] However, I would suggest that, on the contrary, it is his desire to kill the man that demonstrates his inability to deal with the past; this desire exposes a violence beneath his withdrawal from politics, a violence that illuminates the nature of that withdrawal.

Wilhelm finalizes his plans to murder the old man while writing—writing something he thinks would be political: "I'm writing a story about a man who is a good-natured person and at the same time incapable of a sort of pity. I want to prove that good-naturedness and the lack of pity belong together. I believe it will be a political story. By the way, I think I'd enjoy taking a boat-ride. Where is that possible around here?" (72).

What one notices here is the obvious connection between the story he writes and his relation to the old man. There is, however, the odd problem of discerning whom he is writing about. Which one is basically good-natured but incapable of pity—the old man, who committed war crimes at Vilna, or Wilhelm, who has decided to drown the old man? Besides the obvious insight that Wilhelm seems caught in repeating (on a very small scale) the old man's crimes, it also seems that Wilhelm is trying to eliminate the man in order to destroy the memory of those crimes.

The burden of politics in Germany is its association with such crimes, and it is a burden that has more than once in the history of the Federal Republic vilified any type of politics beyond a supposedly value-free management of the economy. Disturbing that repression of the political—and the repression of historical memory—has proven to be a dangerous activity, one that invites violence. Wilhelm's alienation from politics, when disturbed in confrontation with the old man, brings about a desire for violence that in its knee-jerk, reflex-like nature betrays more a need to eliminate an obstacle to his narcissistic impassivity than any concern about justice for the old man's victims.

The old man has, after all, learned something from his experiences, and he is interested that Wilhelm should not repeat his mistakes. The latter finds the old man's advice and influence oppressive; in general Wilhelm would rather strike out in his impatience at the world he finds around him. The connection between his conflict with the old man and the problem of terrorism in West Germany after the demise of the student movement suggests itself rather clearly here. This is even clearer in another scene, during an exchange with Therese. During the walk in the hills, after the old man has disclosed his secret, Wilhelm explains to Therese his "erotic gaze" and his desire to become a writer. Therese expresses her irritation with the aimlessness of their situation in words that could easily apply to the quietism of which West Germany was so often accused:

Wilhelm (Rüdiger Vogler) gazes out from atop the Zugspitze in *Wrong Move* (1975).

> Therese: "Something has to happen, Wilhelm. Everything is so auto-
> matic, so finished, so sewed-up tight. I'm not enjoying this walk any-
> more. It seems like a postponement to me. We have to do something."
>
> Wilhelm, close-up: "Have you ever wanted to kill someone?" (58)

In the stultifying resignation of yet another failed German revolution, Wilhelm sees as the only action possible a despairing, individual act of violence. This type of political choice is more closely related to withdrawal into the "privacy" of art than is immediately apparent. The figure of Wilhelm embodies two "postrevolutionary" responses, both of which stem from resignation: terrorist violence and the withdrawal into aesthetics.

It is in this context, perhaps, that Wenders's film can be best distinguished from Handke's screenplay. For in the film, Wilhelm does not, after scaring off Laertes, go on into an isolation depicted as the solution to his writing block; instead he ends up on the *Zugspitze* with no blizzard, no sea of fog à la Caspar David Friedrich, only a merciless clarity that makes him doubt his move into isolation—and his inability to learn from Laertes. Wenders's film suggests that, in a "postrevolutionary" era, it is important not to succumb to the conformism of the dominant social order, as Handke's adaptation of *Wilhelm Meister* stresses, but that it is also all the more important to learn from history rather than withdraw from it or attempt to eliminate it. Wenders has spoken clearly of the artist's necessity to

105

confront the German past, that films cannot responsibly be made in Germany without addressing the "hole" in German culture left by fascism and the postwar repression of its memory. That is the vacuum into which Wilhelm apparently wants to escape. In Wenders's critique of that escape, one can also note a "postmodern" sensibility: there is no pure realm of human art separate from history, for politics and culture, like history and representation, are inseparable.[47]

Notes

This is a revised version of sections of my *Politics of the Self: Feminism and the Postmodern in West German Literature and Film* (Princeton: Princeton UP, 1991).

1. Cited in Peter Buchka, *Augen kann man nicht kaufen: Wim Wenders und seine Filme* (Munich: Hanser, 1983) 81. My translation (all subsequent translations in this article are mine).

2. Buchka 81.

3. Fredric Jameson has written of the "death of the subject," which he defines as the end of the "experience and the ideology of the unique self." This demise of the "bourgeois individual subject" can in turn be related to the rise of consumer capitalism and a postindustrial economy; Jameson, "Postmodernism and Consumer Society," *The Anti-Aesthetic: Essays on Postmodern Culture*, ed. Hal Foster (Port Townsend, WA: Bay Press, 1983) 115. Craig Owens, who viewed this crisis of the subject more positively than Jameson, called it a "loss of mastery," emphasizing especially the perceived erosion of *male* authority within Western societies; Owens, "The Discourse of the Others," in Foster, *The Anti-Aesthetic* 67.

4. Jameson 112.

5. Jan Dawson, *Wim Wenders,* trans. Carla Wartenberg (New York: Zoetrope, 1976) 11.

6. In Wenders's film adaptation of Handke's novel *The Goalie's Anxiety* (1971), for example, pinball machines form an important part of the settings through which the hero aimlessly wanders. Also, the title of one of his first experimental short films, *Same Player Shoots Again* (1967), is taken from a standard message flashed on a pinball machine.

7. The "historiographical metafiction" is an exemplary postmodern form, according to Linda Hutcheon; see her *A Poetics of Postmodernism: History, Theory, Fiction* (New York: Routledge, 1988) ix, 5–6, 105–23.

8. Peter Handke, "Die Geborgenheit unter der Schädeldecke" (Refuge under the skull), *Theater Heute* 14.12 (1973): 2.

9. Peter Handke, *Falsche Bewegung* (Frankfurt am Main: Suhrkamp, 1975) 81. All further references to this work appear in the text.

10. Heinz Ludwig Arnold, "Gespräch mit Peter Handke," *Text and Kritik* 24–24a (1976): 24.

11. Arnold 37.

12. Theodor W. Adorno, "Rede über Lyrik und Gesellschaft," *Noten zur Literatur*, vol. 1 (Frankfurt am Main: Suhrkamp, 1985) 75, 85.

13. See, for example, Jürgen Theobaldy, "Literaturkritik, astrologisch: Zu Jörg Drews' Aufsatz über Selbsterfahrung und Neue Subjektivität in der Lyrik," *Akzente* 24.2 (1977): 188–91.

14. Rainer Nägele and Renate Voris, *Peter Handke* (Munich: Beck, 1978) 105.

15. Arnold 24.

16. Handke's book *The Left-Handed Woman (Die linkshändige Frau)* appeared in 1976 (Frankfurt am Main: Suhrkamp), and the film (which he directed) in 1977.

17. Eric Rentschler, *West German Film in the Course of Time: Reflections on the Twenty Years since Oberhausen* (Bedford Hills, NY: Redgrave, 1984) 173.

18. Rentschler 172–73. See also Russell A. Berman's discussion of Werner Herzog's "cult of primal seeing" in "The Recipient as Spectator: West German Film and Poetry of the 1970s," *German Quarterly* 55.4 (1982): 499–511.

19. The word I have translated as "seeing the essence of a phenomenon" is *Wesenschau*, often translated as "phenomenology." Peter Pütz stresses the allusion here to Husserl; "'Schläft ein Lied in allen Dingen,'" *Peter Handke*, ed. Raimund Fellinger (Frankfurt am Main: Suhrkamp, 1985) 177.

20. Indeed, Handke's text seems to plead for artistic autonomy and to demonstrate that passion for purity which Peter Bürger finds typical of modernism; in *Postmoderne: Alltag, Allegorie und Avantgarde,* ed. Christa and Peter Bürger, (Frankfurt am Main: Suhrkamp, 1987) 10.

21. Quoted in Buchka 51. Buchka also prints a still from this last shot across from a copy of Caspar David Friedrich's painting *Wanderer über dem Nebelmeer* (Wanderer above a sea of mist) (ca. 1818) on pp. 52–3. The similarity between the two images was noted as early as May 23, 1975, in a review of the film by Frank Scurla in the *Saarbrücker Zeitung* ("Die Leiden des jungen Autors"); it certainly supports the connection Wenders himself makes between his films and German romanticism in the interview with Dawson (23).

22. In a review of the book in which this chapter first appeared, Frederick A. Lubich sees in the snowstorm an "ironic allusion to the snow chapter in Thomas Mann's *Zauberberg*"; rev. of McCormick, *Politics of the Self*, in *Journal of English and Germanic Philology* 92.2 (1933): 306. This observation is persuasive, although one might quibble that the snow chapter is already ironic in Thomas Mann. But what is interesting here is that there seems to be no irony in Handke's use of the snowstorm in his original script, whereas in Wenders's film the irony is clear.

23. On the comparison of Handke's screenplay to the film, Wenders himself said that he produced the final draft of the script (Dawson 4). See also Rentschler 178 and Kathe Geist, *The Cinema of Wim Wenders: From Paris, France to "Paris, Texas"* (Ann Arbor: U.M.I. Research P, 1988) 48. Geist provides information based on her own interview with Wenders that Handke did have a role in writing the final version of the script, but she nonetheless concludes that "Rentschler is probably right that the changed view of Wilhelm's isolationism from positive to negative is Wenders's contribution."

107

24. "His reflections, productions of an interior monologue, often appear as ones the writer has not put to paper"; Rentschler 175.

25. Cited in Kathe Geist, "Wenders in the Cities," *New German Filmmakers: From Oberhausen through the 1970s*, ed. Klaus Phillips (New York: Frederick Ungar, 1984) 395.

26. Manfred Mixner, *Peter Handke* (Kronberg: Athenäum, 1977) 215.

27. Christian Metz, cited in Timothy J. Corrigan's "The Realist Gesture in the Films of Wim Wenders: Hollywood and the New German Cinema," *Quarterly Review of Film Studies* 5 (1980): 210–11 and note 10, 215. The improbabilities in *Wrong Move* remind me in a way of Buñuel's *Phantome de la Liberté*, although the Buñuel film has a dreamlike structure that makes a point of undermining a cohesive plot.

28. Mignon was played by Nastassja Kinski in her first film role; she was fourteen years old when she signed the contract to play the part (Dawson 24).

29. Therese has her own struggle with reified language as an actress condemned to speak the words of others—and as a woman condemned to speak words written (mostly) by men (69–70). For a general discussion of the role of women in Wenders's films, see Geist, "Wenders in the Cities," and Kathe Geist, "Mothers and Children in the Films of Wim Wenders," *Gender and German Cinema: Feminist Interventions*, vol. 1, ed. Sandra Frieden et al. (Providence, RI: Berg, 1993) 11–22.

30. In the film he never even leaves the room; but, interestingly enough, after an indeterminable time lapse, *she* goes back to Laertes' room.

31. Siegfried Schober called him "this erotically blind one" in his review "Die Leiden des Wilhelm M.," *Der Spiegel* March 10, 1975: 134.

32. It is interesting to compare the "erotic gaze" of Wilhelm to Laura Mulvey's discussion of the "male gaze" in the ("classical") narrative cinema, where its function is to allow the male spectator to reclaim (infantile) feelings of omnipotence; Mulvey, "Visual Pleasure and Narrative Cinema," *Film Theory and Criticism*, ed. Gerald Mast and Marshall Cohen, 3rd ed. (New York: Oxford UP, 1985) 810. Wenders's film depicts Wilhelm's "look" as potent only for as long as it remains "cinemorphic" (passive), but when confronted with the actual woman on the other side of the train window, Wilhelm's impotence—narratively speaking and otherwise—is thematized.

33. See Nägele and Voris 100–02 on the theoretical and experiential conflicts within Handke's attitude toward film.

34. Buchka 82, 88.

35. Norbert Grob, *Die Formen des filmischen Blicks: Wenders—Die frühen Filme* (Munich: Filmland Presse, 1984) 99–100.

36. Thomas Elsaesser writes that the desire for "an experience of 'pure being as pure seeing'" is probably "best met by the films of Wim Wenders and Werner Herzog"; *New German Cinema: A History* (New Brunswick, NJ: Rutgers UP, 1989) 5.

37. Christian Metz, "Story/Discourse: Notes on Two Kinds of Voyeurism," *Movies and Methods*, vol. 2, ed. Bill Nichols (Berkeley: California UP, 1985) 543–49.

38. See Roland Barthes, *S/Z: An Essay* [1970], trans. Richard Miller (New York: Hill and Wang, 1974) 3–4.

39. On Sensibilism, see Rentschler 115 and Geist, *The Cinema of Wim Wenders* 14–17.

40. In Glückstadt, his hometown, Wilhelm rides on his bicycle past a cinema playing *Die Rückkehr der reitenden Leichen* (The return of the corpses on horseback); in Bonn he stands in front of a cinema playing Coppola's *The Conversation*; in Therese's apartment outside Frankfurt, Mignon and the old man watch Straub and Huillet's *Die Chronik der Anna Magdalena Bach* on television (in Handke's script they watch Dreyer's *Jeanne d'Arc* [70]); and, at a drive-in, Wilhelm, Therese, and Mignon watch Peter Lilienthal's *La Victoria*, about the situation in Chile. See Rentschler 177–78.

41. Dawson 7.

42. Laertes is, of course, the father of Odysseus, the wanderer. Wilhelm, the fatherless wanderer pushed out of the house by his mother, roams West Germany in search of an identity, finds Laertes, and sees in him a father figure he would like to kill—an appropriate reading for the intergenerational tensions in the film with regard to Germany's past.

43. The Elbe was actually the border between East and West Germany (a border Wenders used in his next film, *Kings of the Road*) for only a short stretch. But it was perceived as the border in common speech ("East of the Elbe") and indeed was the meeting place of American, Russian, and British troops at the end of World War II. It actually provided a water link between the two German states.

44. Rentschler 175.

45. This is also one of the most cinematically impressive sequences of the film, called a "marvel of figure groupings" by John L. Fell in his review "The Wrong Movement," *Film Quarterly* 32.2 (1978–79): 50. James Franklin describes it this way: "In a three-shot sequence . . . the main characters steadily but almost imperceptibly ascend a mountain"; *The New German Cinema: From Oberhausen to Hamburg* (Boston: Twayne, 1983) 143. See Wenders's description of it in Dawson 24. In my opinion, it is the very virtuosity of this shot that foregrounds it—the minimal editing combined with the camera's role in the choreography: staying anchored to no single person's movement, and not disguising its independence from the movement of the characters.

46. For example, Shelly Frisch, "The Disenchanted Image: From Goethe's *Wilhelm Meister* to Wenders's *Wrong Movement*," *Literature/Film Quarterly* 7.3 (1979): 213.

47. Hutcheon argues forcefully against the notion that postmodernism is ahistorical: "History is not made obsolete: it is, however, being rethought—as a human construct" (16).

German Friends and Narrative Murder: *Lightning over Water*

TIMOTHY J. CORRIGAN

> "If it's a question of murder,
> your mind jumps from one thing to another,"
> he had heard somebody say in a movie.[1]
> —*The Goalie's Anxiety at the Penalty Kick*

At the conclusion of Peter Handke's *Short Letter, Long Farewell*, the Austrian protagonist/narrator and the woman who had tracked him across the United States finally confront each other; the scene shifts to the California home of John Ford. Earlier in the novel, this aging, one-eyed moviemaker and his film *Young Mr. Lincoln* had already become a crucial, if ironic, image in the narrator's journey across America, as Ford's classically oedipal film came to represent for the narrator a utopian image of self "fully present in body and mind," where "not only the drunks, but also the actors playing the drunks, were listening intently to Lincoln."[2] Beginning with a search for a mysterious woman (an estranged wife), this 1972 novel turns the protagonist's hunt into a flight from the murderous plans of the same woman; and the two mirrored figures in this plot then arrive together at the home of a filmmaker whose holistic images of America have formed

From "German Friends and Narrative Murders: Lightning Over Water" by Timothy Corrigan in *Cinema Journal*, vol. 24.2, pp.9–18. By permission of the author and the University of Texas Press.

a backdrop for the narrator's own distanced and fragmented look at America. Like so many Handke novels, the metaphoric murder-mystery that structures *Short Letter, Long Farewell* becomes strangely twisted into a story about identities, images of self, and the violence of language; and the cinematic metaphors and references that permeate it underline a crisis of subjectivity whereby the central character struggles to locate his isolated self in a community of narrative images. If Handke's narrator is a lost and pursued son, Ford, as the emblem of a narrative community, becomes his guiding and mostly absent father with whom he ultimately finds shelter.

In the denouement, Ford talks aptly about stories and egos, summarizing the differences between his narratives of America and the tales of Europeans, such as the one Handke's protagonist has just acted out, by praising the American ability to surrender the selfhood that the European clings to. "We don't take our egos as seriously as you Europeans," Ford says. "We don't long to be alone: when a man's alone, he's contemptible; all he can do is poke around in himself, and when he hasn't anybody but himself to talk with, he dries up after the first word."[3] Here and throughout this conversation, Ford the father seems to decry the presence of any physical, egoistic self; and as he recalls the familial narrative of his films, he appears to vanish joyfully, like Oedipus, into them. The classic storyteller thus becomes an ironic conclusion to a murder-mystery about a prodigal and alienated son threatened by death. In Ford's larger-than-life status (as in narrative images), his symbolic son's violent path through the novel seems, ironically, like a perverse memory that threatens to dissipate before the filmmaker's yellow brick road of classical, patriarchal narrative. A moment of narrative and imagistic crisis, this bizarre tension of the conclusion approximates that found in other narratives created by Handke and his sometimes collaborator Wim Wenders, as it dramatizes what traditional narratives attempt to disguise: namely, how narratives (following that historically imposed law of the father that feminists have challenged in theory and practice) work to recuperate, legitimize, and distance the violence of self-consciousness (of the son); or, more in the spirit of this novel, how the narrative works to murder the self-conscious, recalcitrant, and violent reality of its subject, the son, while it develops into the selfless, already violated, and anonymous perspective of the father.[4]

Narrative Murders

Given the cinematic characters and their roles, the obvious comparisons one could make here between Handke's novel and Wenders's *Lightning over Water* are almost too easy. In both cases there is a nostalgic confrontation between the pseudo-autobiographical narrator and the man behind his cinematic memories. In this sense, the Handke novel becomes almost a paradigm of this and other Wenders films which, on many levels, enact a play between presence and absence in the form of a German consciousness engaged with the lost America of Hollywood.[5] Yet what may be more significant here is that in Handke's novel, as in Wenders's encounter with Nick Ray in *Lightning over Water*, the meeting with Ford follows a narrative course motivated by murder: in both the novel and the film, the narrative journey describes the plot of an inverted murder-mystery in which the victim and killer seem to shift roles, and from the beginning the presence of a potential murder pervades the protagonist's consciousness as an act that he has already metaphorically committed or one that he perfunctorily moves forward to perform. Structured around oedipal encounters, this detective-thriller quest becomes the reflection of the internal law of the narratives themselves, according to which they act out memory or meetings with the memory as the self-consuming displacement of a central violence.[6] Or, as the narrator of Handke's *A Sorrow beyond Dreams* describes the murderous horror of storytelling that would later haunt Wenders's *Lightning over Water*, "Narration is only an act of memory . . . it holds nothing in reserve for future use; it merely derives a little pleasure from states of dread by trying to formulate them as aptly as possible; from enjoyment of horror it produces enjoyment of memory."[7] The attraction and danger of these narrative murders, in short, is that they operate according to a pleasure principle.

Thus the narrative work of both Handke and Wenders develops around an actual or symbolic violence directed at a physical body, a body that is then rid of its physical presence as that violence transforms it into an image, a lost body, and a memory. Here the focus is a notion of the body as a field for language and narrative, and the systematic and metonymic appropriation of that body by this narrative language necessarily abstracts that figure as an *other body*: Kane attempting to manifest his lost Rosebud self in a collection of images, statues, and mother figures; the reporter searching through fragmented tales for the lost figure of Kane; and Welles creating his narrative out of the deadly impossibility of both. As the individual encounters a narrative and symbolic structure (anything from another individual to the Hollywood film industry), for Handke and Wenders this figure experiences a kind of mirror-stage schizophrenia in which he recognizes himself as dislocated from a former, usually more whole, self. This dislocation comes to represent the fragmentation and destruction of that former body; and memory, above all else, bears witness to this loss in its nostalgic efforts to retrieve—narratively—that lost unity. As handmaiden of memory, narrative becomes both the vehicle for describing and enacting the destruction of a once singular body *and* the classical means of retrieving it as an illusory and whole presence: narratives describe both the murder of the child's imaginary figure at narrative's symbolic hands *and* the absence of the already murdered father who is present only as the ghost and law of the narrative that must sacrifice his child. Dorothy dies into the narrative world of Oz; she matures only after her wizard father (absented most obviously through the gigantic image on the screen) sends her and her fragmented selves (a heart, a brain, and courage) through a series of symbolic deaths; finally understanding the power of the symbolic over the physical, she is admitted into narrative society as its wizard father vanishes into the heavens. In Julia Kristeva's words, narrative is based on "the third-person father," who is not "a particular dead body" but Death itself. "As long as a son pursues meaning in a story or through narratives, even if it eludes him, as long as he persists in his search he narrates in the name of Death for the father's corpses."[8]

Narrative murders follow an economics of exchange: the production of an absent body, narrative language, and images always plot the encounter between two figures, one dead in narrative and the other dying in its process. In this encounter the reality of the victim—or, more accurately, reality *as* victim—can only mutely testify to the other's tenuous but murderous art. Besides *Short Letter, Long Farewell*, several Handke novels address this action directly. In *The Goalie's Anxiety at the Penalty Kick*, the cinephile, Joseph Bloch, murders a girl just when "the pressure of words" drives him to think "up sentences about things instead of words for them, in belief that a story made up of such sentences would help him visualize things"; the novel *A Sorrow beyond Dreams* revolves explicitly around the work of writing death's form, transcribing a self-murdering mother as a "story about the nameless, about speechless moments of terror . . . in which extreme need to communicate coincides with extreme speechlessness."[9] Wenders's films are even more transparent in some ways. What is implicit in the narratives of films like *Wrong Move, Alice in the Cities*, and *Kings of the Road* moves to the foreground in *The American Friend*, the self-reflexive story of the disintegration of a craftsman's body, a body that becomes paradoxically both the product and the producer of the murders he commits. Here, an American friendship whose bond is the metaphoric union of murder and a cinematic language becomes the narrative frame and motive for the gradual collapse of the body;[10] as with Handke's protagonist/narrators, the narrative image itself thus becomes a self-conscious murderer whose linguistic crisis is witnessing the murder it commits, the cinematic image guiltily admitting its attempt to incorporate the physical figures that it necessarily makes absent.

The excitement a film like *The American Friend* provokes oddly resembles the kind of perverse pleasure that is associated with the viewing of snuff films. But in this case the violence becomes consciously displaced to the level of narrative language where murder appears first and foremost as an *erotic* violence sustained by the desire that propels both narrative language and the spectatorial gaze.[11] Especially in *The American Friend*, but in other Wenders films as well, the film presents, in an overdetermined form and material, an erotic play that inscribes a symbolic body over the annihilation of a real figure. Using this model as a prototype, film narrative becomes a version of necrophilia. From this perspective, *The Invasion of the Body Snatchers* is film's archetypal love story; and, in the commercial exploitation of the films of a dead actor, the violence behind Werner Herzog's *Fitzcarraldo*, or the actual killing of the cameraman in Patricio Guzmán's *The Battle of Chile*, the cinema unwittingly displays the central violence of its pleasure principle and the eros of its terroristic politics. Like Wenders's Tom Ripley, who buries himself in a series of Polaroid death masks, film narrative leaves a trail of corpses that, like memory itself, makes the images that replace them the object of its fetishistic excitement. Within the big sleep, which describes the narrative art of so many films, the oedipal logic of the narrative and the place of all those dead bodies is ultimately absorbed into the cinematic dreams they sustain and the sexual encounters they provoke.

Anti-Oedipus: *Lightning over Water*

If this is the common structure of the Handke/Wenders narratives, as they ironically comment on the common structure of classical narrative, what distinguishes and valorizes Wenders's *Lightning over Water* is precisely its attempt to confront, refuse, and overturn this structure (and not simply make it more self-reflexive).[12] Ostensibly the film blatantly recalls the narrative logic that *The American Friend* refines, and, to underline this, it begins with a replica shot from the Soho opening of the earlier film, using also the film-noir voice-over of Wenders returning to New York to see the dying Nick Ray. Like other Wenders films, the confrontation is the subjective one between a lost body and a consciousness attempting to retrieve it, specifically, the consciousness of Wenders the filmmaker engaging the body of Ray. But at this point the similarities end and the crucial differences begin. The boundaries of these differences are perhaps best suggested, on the one hand, by the regular accusation that the film exploits Ray, and, on the other, by the sentimental disguise of the same dying Ray in another film, Helpern and Gutman's *I'm a Stranger Here Myself*. The two are related, since what those negative criticisms and the alternative example suggest is that Wenders exposes and abuses Ray by not sufficiently disguising or deferring his death within the sentiment and craft of filmmaking, that is, by not having the art of the murder-mystery redeem the death of the physical figure as it does in *The Maltese Falcon*, *The Big Sleep*, or, for that matter, *The American Friend*.[13]

Yet this aesthetic failure is precisely the point. *Lightning over Water* is meant to confront directly that murderous displacement of the body that the image-play of the filmic narrative usually accomplishes, so that instead of an oedipal narrative as erotic murder, *Lightning over Water* becomes as anti-oedipal as it is anti-nostalgic: the son tells the tale of the father rather than the father overseeing the son's story—a reversal through which Wenders intends to preserve the lives and deaths of both. Whereas in *The American Friend* an American entrepreneur literally frames and so metaphorically strangles his German subject in a narrative machinery specifically associated with the machinery of film, in *Lightning over Water* that entrepreneur is now a German filmmaker whose hesitation and resistance to murder Ray with a narrative and imagistic gloss is the film's central crisis and distinction. In the first film, Ray as Derwatt is the archetypal dead father of the murderous art of film, his presence as an absence being the primary force behind the duplications and forgery that are in the film and finally which are the film. In the second film, Ray returns as Ray, a present father, authentically dying and petulantly confronting both the film of the son and the son himself as the representative of narrative's double murder.

In *Lightning over Water* Wenders thus confronts oedipal murders on two levels. On the one hand, he challenges and exposes the very structure of narrative as murder in order to preserve his own voice as son and Ray's physical presence as dying father. On the other hand, Wenders engages a more strictly historical bond, one that, according to Serge Daney, has made young European directors constantly produce and reproduce cinematic homages in order to keep the absence of their auteur fathers filmically present and alive.[14] As opposed to the Hitchcock of Truffaut or the Sirk of Fassbinder, in *Lightning over Water* Ray is not simply a cinematic presence but a dying body resisting its dramatic displacement within the film; and, as several shots suggest, Ray becomes more powerfully present in this capacity than as those images from his own film next to which he occasionally appears. Halfway through *Lightning over Water*, Ray offers Wenders a substitute scenario that closely resembles his metaphorically displaced role in *The American Friend*: the story is of a painter who needs both to make money and "to regain his own identity as fully as he can before he dies"; fatally ill with cancer, he would consequently steal and forge his own work. As the camera moves among Ray, Wenders, and Tom Farrell (the other, competing, son who sits at an editing table examining piles of film),[15] Wenders counters this narrative detour since he knows it would ultimately be a regressive retreat to the fetishized narrative of *The American Friend*: why make the detour of turning him into a painter, he asks bluntly, "Why isn't he you, and why isn't he making films instead of paintings? It's you, Nick. Why take the step away?" Ray, though, has the last word: "Then it has to be about you, too," he points out, since Wenders's (the son's) camera eye

How not to kill the father—Wim Wenders and Nicholas Ray in *Lightning over Water* (1980).

must be equally implicated in the tearing of the oedipal veil of the murder-mystery. About this role as camera and narrator, Wenders becomes even more explicit when, late in the film, he indicates to Ray his fears about the murder that film becomes; at this point, Ray's features have deteriorated further, and it is a videotape that displays the ravaged face. "I had this thing —this oedipal feeling," Wenders says, "that this film might kill you. . . . All the confusion and . . . the subconscious fear . . . led me to making images that I didn't like. . . . The film, whatever we did, looked very clean, pretty, . . . licked off. And I think that is a result of fear. That's what you do if you haven't made up your mind what you want to show. And then you try to show it beautiful."

In this last scene specifically and throughout the entire film, Wenders's use of video to counterpoint a cinematic image becomes a crucial textual measure of his work to distance *Lightning over Water* from *The American Friend*, to resist the textual murder that the latter describes. In the earlier film, the video images that occasionally mark the narrative become an analogue for the technological anonymity that Ripley represents, and their force as a representational vehicle culminates in that dramatic metro sequence, just after Jonathan's first murder: the series of video cameras that trace his flight are clearly no one's point of view, and in their blank, third-person representing of the murderer they graphically and hor-

116

rifically abstract the figure of Jonathan as a visual correlative to the bodily illness associated with his American friendship. In *Lightning over Water*, though, where video images are even more prominent (mainly through the ubiquitous camera of Tom Farrell), their position is more constructive and less deconstructive: video images function in this film neither as a deadly abstraction of the body nor as some sort of direct apprehension contrasting the film image; rather, here video describes, above all else, difference, graphically marking within frames differences in bodily scale and explicitly calling attention to the temporal changes separating the video image from a film image that normally reduces time to an immobile present.

At one point, for instance, Tom and Wenders watch a monitor with a talking head soliloquy by Ray, which Tom has taped weeks earlier. The film cuts between the film image of Wenders, Tom, and the video image of Ray (at one point strikingly isolating what appears as his completely disembodied head against a black backdrop). Wenders then reflects to himself on the terrifying representational gap that he both witnesses and participates in and which the video has made suddenly apparent: "I was very confused. Something was happening each time the camera was pointed at Nick, something that I had no control of. It was in the camera itself, looking at Nick through the viewfinder. Like a very precise instrument, the camera showed clearly and mercilessly that time was running out." As a summary of the film's central motif, here Wenders's film both records and describes the murder it commits, and the narrative murder, always a function of time and memory, turns on itself, much like Handke's novel, as a critical act through which exposition becomes an exposing; and, by means of the video and other self-reflexive devices, *Lightning over Water* is thus able to witness its tendency to kill, a witnessing that operates according to a visual dynamics whose differences ultimately create a real space for the reprieve of the victim, for the dying body of Ray.

Bertolucci consequently comes close to the heart of this film when he remarks how it works specifically to refashion the egocentrism and subsequent loneliness that Handke's John Ford found so destructive to European artists in their roles as fatherless sons.[16] In Wenders's film, Bertolucci remarks, "Loneliness is not just that of a killer out of a thriller who would find out, by one of these poetic licenses only allowed B films, that his client and his victim are one and the same person." In *Lightning over Water*, rather, Wenders looks directly at "his cursed father/master—an identification that is also an exorcism."[17] Put another way, Wenders as surrogate narrator is not just a killer but also the detective searching through his own plot like the character in Borges's "Garden of Forking Paths"; and his discovery of the coincidence of his client and victim is the discovery that to carry out his narrative commission is literally to arrest his own action as murderer. If consummating love by telling one's story means murdering the father, "if to love is to survive paternal meaning,"[18] here Wenders instead offers a voice and a place to the father whereby they can both claim the vitality of their differences and the possibility of a love not based on the eros of death and the absence of the father. Wenders identifies with that father as victim rather than as a displaced lover, an identification most tellingly presented in a scene loosely adapted from *King Lear* and one that not surprisingly echoes the bind of Oedipus: as Wenders watches, Ronee Blakley (Wenders's wife at the time) comforts the sick Ray; their conversation ends, however, with Ray acknowledging his lying to his wife (perhaps an oblique reference to the small fictions that support the family narrative); and as Ray confesses, an exposing of himself, the scene immediately changes to Wenders, the son, storyteller, and silent substitute in the father's hospital bed. Ray ironically emerges here, as an allegory for the entire film, through and beyond the drama of his role as father/auteur: he emerges as dying father made into the role of auteur, and in the mutual admission of this double status he assumes what most filmic fathers miss—substance and presence.

In *The American Friend*, the cinematic eros of the detective murder-mystery provides Wenders with a narrative and oedipal paradigm for mistaken identities and fictional oppositions and, at the same time, with a paradigm of his own relationships with the auteurs who were his cinematic forefathers. But in *Lightning over Water* both those paradigms are confronted, leaving only a singular auteur living in a dying body, showing a father sharing his death bed (not his marriage bed) with his son, and ultimately recording an old lover rejecting the murderous narrative that he has bequeathed and which always embodies his relationship to his son. The auteur/client escapes his role as the victim of his son's narrative, while the killer/son/detective discovers the method of his own murder. This son then returns with this evidence to the client he would kill, not to save his life but to preserve his death from the eros of the oedipal displacement that usually mutes and replaces that death. Indeed, many specific shots in *Lightning over Water* could be used to corroborate this argument, but the most dramatic and incisive is without doubt the final shot of Ray: while he looks directly into the camera, Wenders's offscreen voice tells him to "say cut"; Ray retorts "You say cut"; they then banter back and forth about whether or not to say "cut"; and Ray's last living action on film is a contradictory exclamation into the eye of the camera, "Don't cut, CUT." In this single shot, Ray thus demands and acquires from the son the contradictory reality that the medium forces a filmmaker to live and die by, the reality of an individual whose life is necessarily bound to the murderous game of narrative cinema. In Serge Daney's words, "This is a game which no one wins," but here "it is a game which saves the film from voyeurism or necrophilia pure and simple," as Ray and the camera literally see each other on such immediate and exclusive terms that the spectator is deprived of all the eros of death.[19]

What *Lightning over Water* witnesses, therefore, is a conversation between Oedipus and his father, a conversation that film alone has the ability to enact adequately in the actual corporeal terms that are the foundation of the relationship, a conversation that for once allows the son to speak for himself and to look directly at the physical reality of the father/auteur. The funeral barge and wake that end this film are not consequently for Ray but for the machinery and celluloid mounted on the barge and representing the means by which that auteur/father traditionally remains present as a ghostly narrative absence: to paraphrase the conversation of the crew on the barge, Ray's last directorial assertion is to claim his actual death as the end of the film; and what that crew threatens to cremate, as one of them holds a match in the image, is not Ray's body but the anonymity of a narrative medium that has historically fetishized the body in order to make murderous stories of the son.

That anonymity is precisely what Handke's histrionic John Ford hailed as the principle behind the nostalgic stories of his films, a principle with which he protects America as if it were the absent member of a conversation. And when the German friends before him at the end of that novel recount their own inverted narrative of murder and discovery across the imagistic body of America, Ford can only ask in amazement if it is *really* true. But there the amazement is that of the auteur at the inversion of his own narrative art; in *Lightning over Water* the amazement should be that of the spectator at the auteur's accession to his dying body and the son's refusal to be the story of that death. This is indeed an oedipal homecoming, the resurrection of a Kafkaesque figure, Wenders at Colonus. In Bertolucci's words, "Sam Spade realizes he's shooting something never before shot—what Proust called, in his last words, 'the boundless frivolity of people about to die.'"[20]

Notes

1. Peter Handke, *The Goalie's Anxiety at the Penalty Kick*, trans. Michael Roloff (New York: Farrar, Straus, and Giroux, 1974) 100–01.

2. Peter Handke. *Short Letter, Long Farewell*, trans. Ralph Manheim (New York: Farrar, Straus, and Giroux, 1974) 114–15. The oedipal configuration of Ford's *Young Mr. Lincoln* is discussed in the well-known essay written by the editors of *Cahiers du cinéma*, "John Ford's *Young Mr. Lincoln*," in *Movies and Methods*, ed. Bill Nicols (Berkeley: U of California P, 1976) 493–529.

3. Handke, *Short Letter* 161.

4. This historical dominance of an oedipal narrative is, of course, what many feminists have attempted to dismantle or reject.

5. See Timothy Corrigan, *New German Film: The Displaced Image* (Austin: U of Texas P, 1983); and Eric Rentschler, "American Friends and New German Cinema: Patterns of Reception," *New German Critique* 24–25 (1981–82): 7–35.

6. This idea figures largely in psychoanalytic theory and especially in Stephan Heath's *Questions of Cinema* (Bloomington: Indiana UP, 1981).

7. Peter Handke, *A Sorrow beyond Dreams*, trans. Ralph Manheim, in *Three by Peter Handke* (New York: Avon, 1977) 295.

8. Julia Kristeva, "The Father, Love, and Banishment," *Desire in Language: A Semiotic Approach to Literature and Art*, ed. Leon S. Roudiez (New York: Columbia UP, 1980) 150–51.

9. Handke, *The Goalie's Anxiety at the Penalty Kick* 17; *A Sorrow beyond Dreams* 265.

10. The film describes the odd pact that develops between the American entrepreneur Ripley and the Swiss-German craftsman Jonathan, when Ripley discovers that Jonathan may have an incurable disease and then involves him in a series of murders. Throughout the film there is an ambiguity as to whether Jonathan is actually deteriorating or whether the mafia simply manufactures the sickness as a hoax to entrap him. Textually and allegorically, the film equates both the friendship and the illness with the codes, technology, and ubiquitous presence of Hollywood images.

11. See Christian Metz, *The Imaginary Signifier* (Bloomington: Indiana UP, 1982); or, for a less theoretical discussion, see William Rothman, *Hitchcock: The Murderous Gaze* (Cambridge: Harvard UP, 1982).

12. Several short discussions or reviews of the film have appeared, such as Kathe Geist, *"Lightning over Water," Film Quarterly* 35.2 (1981–82): 46–51; Richard Combs, *"Lightning over Water," Sight and Sound* 50.2 (1981): 96–97; and Ron Burnett, "Wim Wenders, Nicholas Ray, and *Lightning over Water*," *Ciné-Tracts* 13 (1981): 11–14. There is also Jon Jost's account of the film, "Wrong Move," *Sight and Sound* 50.2 (1981): 94–96.

13. In *The Big Sleep*, for example, the actual logic of the murders and the presence of the dead body that motivates the narrative search are never confronted. In both cases, the plot refocuses those questions in terms of Bogart and Bacall, making the excitement and romance of the narrative hunt dominate the actual horror that instigates it.

14. "Wim's Movie," *Cahiers du cinéma* 318 (1980): 15–16.

15. See Tom Farrell, "Nick Ray's German Friend: Wim Wenders," *Wide Angle* 5.4 (1983): 60–67.

16. Note the common description of New German directors as a generation of filmmakers divided from their true forefathers (Lang, Murau, etc.) by World War II and its aftermath.

17. Bernardo Bertolucci, "The Boundless Frivolity of People about to Die," in Wim Wenders and Chris Sievernich, *Nick's Film: Lightning over Water* (Frankfurt am Main: Zweitausendeins, 1981) 5.

18. Kristeva 150.

19. Daney 17.

20. Bertolucci 5.

Postmodern Culture and Film Narrative: *Paris, Texas* and Beyond

ROGER F. COOK

In the last few years, Wim Wenders has become a name mentioned with increasing frequency in the discussion of postmodern cinema. Those critics who have applied the postmodern tag to Wenders's work often grant that there is an ambivalence in his films between modernist and postmodernist aesthetic strategies.[1] This ambivalence surfaces in films from all periods of his filmmaking, but it has a distinctly different character beginning in the early 1980s. While his earlier films combine elements of popular culture and modernist film art more freely, this mixture becomes more highly charged with critical reflection after *The State of Things*.[2] Although popular culture remains an integral part of his cinematic discourse, his films begin to issue as well a dire warning about the growing threat the media industry poses to (post)modern society.

Certainly this critique is not new to his films. From the flickering television set in the New Jersey motel room in *Alice in the Cities* to the Polaroid snapshots in *The American Friend*, his films in the 1970s often portrayed the proliferation of (re)produced images in a critical light. However, due in large part to his first direct experiences with Hollywood filmmaking (*Hammett*, 1982), the consequences of the ever more pervasive visual media began to hit close to home. With the autobiographical documentary and feature films of 1982, *Reverse Angle* and *The State of Things*, both made before the *Hammett* project was completed, he first focused on the specific threat to film images. In *Paris, Texas* the critique of the American media

121

industry that had surfaced throughout his films in the 1970s and become a central theme in *The State of Things* expands to encompass the totality of images and signs that make up "America." Also, in the long prose poem "The American Dream," written shortly after he had finished shooting *Paris, Texas*, Wenders reflected on his gradual disillusionment with America. Looking back on the shock effect that American culture, and in particular American television, had on him during his first visit to the United States in 1973, he describes his euphoria during the first day in New York City, while he still believed that he would now experience the "America" that had fueled his dreams. But it lasted only that day, until he returned to the hotel in the evening, "turned on the television / And discovered America," a media-induced culture that had "reduced / all images to the same level of artificiality and calculated effect."[3] These early impressions foreshadow an awareness of the postmodern deterioration of images that was already forming in him but which did not come to fruition until after the *Hammett* experience.

Still, as his criticism of the colonizing American culture industry becomes more deliberate, Wenders does not dismiss all its products out of hand and continues to incorporate various forms of popular culture into his films. He still includes rock music and elements of Hollywood cinema in his films, not just as part of a postmodern parody of superficial culture but rather as popular art forms that still speak forcefully to the needs and desires of his spectators. However, as a result of his waning faith in the autonomy of the image and in the ability of alternative culture to resist the colonizing forces of the dominant media industry, he began to search for oppositional strategies for his feature films. After *The State of Things* Wenders attempted to structure his films tightly around a central narrative in a way that he had in the past either intentionally avoided (*Alice in the Cities*, *Kings of the Road*, and *The State of Things*) or at least gravitated away from even when he had a scripted story to follow (*Wrong Move* and *The American Friend*). He portrays 1982 as a pivotal year in his filmmaking. Citing *The State of Things* as cinematic evidence for his new thesis, he came to the conclusion that films can deconstruct the dominance of media-vision only by constructing narrative contexts that envelop images in a new web of meaning: "I want to find a narrative cinema that avidly and with self-confidence establishes a connection between film art and life, and which no longer needs to reflect its own textuality in the narrative. . . . A fresh start in film narrative, that's my goal."[4] But as his resolve to develop a new film narrative took shape, it was accompanied by a more pessimistic view of the public's ability to resist the forces of the media industry. In fact, it was this growing concern that precipitated his new approach to narrative. In *Reverse Angle* he warned that the objective power of the camera —that is, "to describe things in a vigilant manner, so that they can appear in the proper light: the way they are"—is diminishing.[5] And if the spectator had acquired a predominantly media-induced way of seeing, the strategy of inviting the audience along on the filmmaker's journey through Germany (*Wrong Move, Kings of the Road*) and/or America (*Alice in the Cities*) would no longer work. The final voice-over of *Reverse Angle*, a quotation from Paul Cézanne followed by Wenders's terse comment, reveals just how bad Wenders thought the situation was: "'Everything is about to disappear. You've got to hurry up, if you still want to see things.' I hope it's not too late."

What results from the crisis of the early eighties is a cinema that combines more traditional narrative control with a strong critique of post-modern culture. Some critics argue that such films often lapse into pastiche, thus sacrificing their potential to provide a viable alternative to Hollywood cinema. Richard Kearney lumps *Paris, Texas* together with films by Martin Scorsese, Robert Altman, and Francis Ford Coppola as postmodern "film critique(s) of the American Dream" that are unable to create an alternative cinematic vision.[6] I would suggest a less dismissive approach to Wenders's more recent films, one that includes among other considerations the specific historical and autobiographical context of his postmodern critique of culture. Examining *Paris, Texas* in some detail and taking occasional examples from his subsequent films, this essay evaluates Wenders's strategies for combining postmodernist critique and narrative with the express goal of establishing "a connection between film art and life."

Retiring the Alienated Hero

Paris, Texas is particularly well suited for such a study. As he avowed once in an interview, Wenders turned to Sam Shepard as a writer who could provide a forward-moving script that would help him overcome his ingrained aversion to narrative stricture. Equally important, of course, he had in Shepard a writer whose plays about the contemporary American West expose the reduction of national and individual identities to empty images. In the film Wenders develops his own strategies for isolating and attacking the high-tech economic complexes that threaten myth, history, and even experience itself. He establishes a duality of two worlds in America, contrasting a "hyperreal" postmodern culture with what Jean Baudrillard has termed the "archaic envelope" of place, object, and myth.[7] The latter, the one introduced in the opening sequence of Travis on foot in Devil's Graveyard near Big Bend, Texas, is part of the American West that abounds in a past of mythical proportions. It is a world of individual style, where the person is carved in the likeness of the land, both psychologically and physically. We first see Travis crossing the desert in a long shot reminiscent of John Ford. The camera cuts to a lean hawk perched on rocks, and then to a close-up of Travis that highlights the striking similarity in features between these two creatures of the desert. The other world first enters the film, appropriately enough, via cable hookup. After the local doctor in the antiquated Terlingua Medical Clinic asks the operator for a phone number in Los Angeles, the camera cuts to a shot of Walt outside his workplace in Glendale with a cordless phone in his hand. The shot is from a low angle, with the modern rectangular building of the studio rising behind him. Here the correspondence between the building and the square features of Dean Stockwell's face are, if not as striking, at least as poignant thematically. The modern biotechnical design of the building—it resembles a magnified computer chip—represents the other extreme from the adobe hut in the desert clinic. In the most obvious allusion to "simulacrum" (Baudrillard's term for the condition where "simulation envelops the whole edifice of representation"),[8] Wenders shot the scene not with an actual building in the background, but rather in front of a cardboard cutout which when first seen from the low-angle shot appears to be a multistory building.

Wenders films the journey back to California as a gradual return from the habitat of the Texas desert to the cybernetic environment of Burbank. The sequence of locations is at times out of order geographically, but the shift in relationship between man and his environment is consistent. Walt's conversation with the tequila-swigging local doctor in Big Bend takes place at a lunchroom table and booth, displaced onto a roofed patio with only a mobile home and the desert landscape in the background. The progression from the desolate motel in Marathon, Texas, to the El Rancho Motel and Railsback Diner in Fort Stockton, to the Astroburger in Four Corners, California, and eventually onto the Los Angeles freeways, tracks Travis's reentry into contemporary mainstream society. The path is rough, and full integration never occurs. Twice he runs away from Walt and tries to continue his trek through the Texas desert. Later he insists on searching through row after row of seemingly identical rental cars to find the same one they had had before: "We need the same car, Walt. How are we going to go in another car?" While Walt and the rental clerk search for the car with the same license number, Travis recalls its more intrinsic characteristics: "It's got a bump on the hood." When he later prepares for his trip back to Texas, he rejects the generic rental car in favor of one that projects his own times and character: a trail-worn 1958 Ranchero. This difference in sensibilities recalls Baudrillard's theories about the effects of the postmodern environment of electronic communication interfaces and simulated screen realities. He suggests that on the highway "the vehicle now becomes a kind of capsule," with "the surrounding landscape unfolding like a televised screen." For Travis the car remains what, according to Baudrillard, it had been before the age of simulacrum—"an object of psychological sanctuary," a live-in extension of the personality and not merely a "vehicle and vector."[9]

Dean Stockwell and Harry Dean Stanton on the set of *Paris, Texas* (1984).

Travis's struggle to defy a non-naturalist high-tech world peaks in the search for Jane in Houston. First, he and Hunter, armed with their toy walkie-talkies (as opposed to Walt's more sophisticated cordless telephone), take on the spatial, cold surfaces of the downtown drive-in bank with its four wings of multiple drive-through automatic tellers. When they locate Jane and follow her to the peep-show joint, one sees the seedy underside to the clean-surfaced environments of a post-gender cybernetic existence. The peep-show also demonstrates how pervasively lived human relations are informed by the viewer-screen mode of experience. The scene illustrates Baudrillard's claim that space has become an absolute and that we relate to the events and bodies located in it, including even the extension of one's own body, as if they were simulations on a screen.[10] Travis sees Jane in a simulated setting, imitating the movements of her own body, while the peep-show participants, although close enough to touch each other, must speak through wires to communicate. Even here, in this underworld realm to which sexual drives have been diverted, "screen" images (i.e., present actions that are simulated as screen images) and electrically transmitted voices replace direct sight and sound.

Yet into this dismal world of simulated experience enters the rebel cowboy from the days of the genuine West. He returns their son to his rightful mother and then drives off into the sunrise. Having rolled into the hostile environment and faced the worst that contemporary American culture has to offer, he can now return self-assured to his natural hideaway. Narrative has reestablished itself and meaning resurfaces, at least within the confines of the diegesis, and the belief lives on that experience, depth, and desire can withstand simulation, surface, and function. Or does the film story deceive us, and its hero? Do the images reveal that the happy ending is an illusion that exists only to placate our obsolete desires? In the final scene the frame betrays the limitations of the story. From the top level of the parking garage, Travis looks up to view the emotional reunion through the hotel window. His visual eavesdropping simulates television viewing, while the camera angle from within the hotel room offers a commentary on the larger cultural role of screen images. As Jane and Hunter come together and embrace, a television is situated prominently in the middle of the frame. This television is itself framed within a matrix of lighted office windows from the nearby high-rise, which appear like a bank of monitors in a television control room. We see them through the same window that Travis is watching from below. This complex network of screenings, itself framed within the modern high-rise landscape of downtown Houston, makes it clear in what kind of world Travis unknowingly leaves them behind. The high-tech design environment will either reduce the relationship between Jane and Hunter to a clichéd and even electronically simulated version of itself, or the residue of genuine needs and desires will be diverted into archaic or possibly perverted offshoots such as the peep show. The last shot in the film adds the final touch to the ironic dismantling of the cowboy myth. The camera cuts from Travis's smile in the car to a shot out of the back of the car that shows the Houston skyline framed against the reddish sky. On a large lighted billboard in the right center of the frame we read "Together We Make It Happen—Republic Bank." The bank's billboard appropriates in no uncertain terms the narrative truth of the film story for its own cold-surface world of electronic interchange. In the postmodern world, the story is stripped of myth and desire. Narrative remains as an empty shell that the biotechnically structured corporate complex can assimilate into its public-relations discourse.

In drawing these connections between Wenders's representation of a hyperreal, technologically reproduced culture and postmodernist theories of simulacrum, it is easy to read Wenders's critique of contemporary American culture as postmodern skepticism about signification per se. Kearney seems to conclude as much when he cites *Paris, Texas* as a prototypical example of the postmodern film that portrays "a totalizing system of false imitations."[11] But such a reading looks past the specific national and cultural context of his critique. Wenders's most radical assertions about the empty signifier came in "The American Dream," but he never suggests even there that a referential relationship between signs and the real no longer exists, or that the sign never had any reference outside its own signifying system. Rather, he describes the cultural identity produced by the American entertainment and media industry. His main focus is on that image of America which had appealed to him in his youth and attracted him to Hollywood in 1978. He concludes that the "American Dream" is now just another media cliché that substitutes for life in America:

> Whatever the "American Dream" once was,
> no one dreams it any more.
> Now it is only dreamed for us
> by the advertising industry.
> An enormous billboard stretches
> across the whole country.
> As more and more of the poor and entrapped
> stand in its shadow,
> it proclaims freedom and prosperity that much more loudly.[12]

Thus Wenders's critique is not one that necessarily assumes an unalterable breach between signs and the real, but rather is aimed at a particular form of cultural production. Still, it suggests a postmodern condition that renders obsolete the heroic will of man in modernity. The individual who can forge his own identity in a life story whose meaning is in turn anchored in a master narrative seems to be a relic of the past. This crisis leads Wenders to question the male characters who had been at the center of his films. His heroes were typically male outsiders wandering aimlessly, less in search of direction than defiantly convinced that none is to be found. His films often ended at the point where they find hope *ex negativo*, by rejecting their isolation as individualistic loner-heroes. At the end of *Wrong Move* Wilhelm appears to be questioning his isolation as he looks out from the *Zugspitze* on a clear day. Wenders's version of the last scene implies that the solitary writing of the autonomous individual, which the ending to Handke's screenplay offers as an only alternative, provides in fact no solutions.[13] At the end of *Alice in the Cities* and *Kings of the Road* the protagonists have come as well to the awareness that inclusion and involvement are preferable to the isolation and resignation in which we find them at the beginning of the film.

On one level these films revolve around the protagonist's search for identity, but they also raise the question of whether any kind of authentic narrative is still possible. Despite the male protagonist's failure to find a place for his anachronistic identity in the paved, screened, and reflective surfaces of a high-tech cultural landscape, *Paris, Texas* ends with the sense of a new beginning. Despite all the postmodern trappings of the final scene in the hotel room, there is a feeling of hope and a new beginning in Jane and Hunter's embrace. As Wenders later explained, this final scene constituted for him the end of a long odyssey and, at the same time, the possibility for new stories to begin: "This scene had for me a liberating effect: there was a feeling which I knew would have consequences for my next film, no matter which film it was. (The last shot as Travis leaves: I let him disappear in my own way, and all my previous male characters went with him. They have all taken up residence in a retirement home on the outskirts of Paris, Texas.)"[14] His response to the crisis of identity and representation is neither a reversion to modernism nor a resignation that gives up on the individual subject caught in a world of simulation. Although the film offers no preview of the adjustments needed, it does suggest that any path back from simulacrum and surface textuality will depend on the intuitive responses of a centered subject. The lone cowboy Travis fails to find a way through the surface reality of empty signs and sterile environments, but the end of the film still holds out hope for a new positioning of the subject, one that can adapt to the external vacuity of a postmodern environment.

Cultural History, Narrative, and Identity

Rather than trying to develop a radically new narrative form, Wenders addresses the need for viable film stories thematically in the stories themselves. Reflecting on the making of *Wings of Desire* in a 1988 interview, he confirms this approach, asserting that content is the key to an alternative narrative cinema:

> I think that at one point in time cinema invented its narrative mode and that there is really very little improvement needed in it. Where improvement is needed and where one should and must devote all the energy inventing, or rather discovering, something is in the kind of stories films tell—that is, not so much how you tell stories, but rather *what* you have to tell. . . . No matter what comes of it, I will always try to narrate in this classical film language—which I value so highly —something useful, and, I hope, every once in a while, something new as well.[15]

Although one might question to what extent the feature films from *Paris, Texas* on employ a "classical film language," in their narratives they not only engage the emotive powers of Hollywood cinema but also show them to be an essential element of corrective postmodernist narrative. In one way or another the films stories in *Paris, Texas, Wings of Desire, Until the End of the World*, and *Faraway, So Close!* all champion narrative's potential to sustain both individual and cultural identity.

However, *Paris, Texas* suggests that the clinging to past myths and identities exemplified by Travis inhibits the narrative from moving forward to new networks of collective identities. As the first step in Wenders's effort to develop a new kind of narrative, it also shows just how difficult it was for him to free himself from his traditional pattern. The entire film is needed to extract the alienated male hero from the central subject position of the narrative. The central problem in *Paris, Texas* is the erosion of psychic depth in the postmodern age. Travis's loss of identity is attributed to a culture that reproduces images with increasing autonomy, irrespective of its own history. For the protagonist the result is the dissolution of memory into isolated signifiers. All that remains of Travis's identity are two tattered photos, both of which document the failure of memory and the loss of identity. The photomat strip of Travis, Jane, and Hunter pictures a family that no longer exists. Only after the super-8 home movie restores certain memories for Travis and Hunter do they set off to Texas to piece the family back together again. In their new lives this past has become for all three just one more facet of a simulated reality that effaces those memories and identities structured around their nuclear family relationships. Hunter, after viewing the home movie, declares that that was not his mother but only a fictional representation of her: "That's only her in a movie . . . a long time ago . . . 'in a galaxy far, far away.'" Jane has traded in her previous life that ended with their marriage for a simulated existence in the peep show. She reveals unknowingly to Travis her loss of identity: "I just don't think I'm the one you want to talk to." And Travis, who had sought to erase all memory and identity in the Texas desert, has to have Walt's Mexican cleaning lady coach him on how to become the "father" once again.

The clearest sign of both Travis's loss of identity and the resilient bonds that draw him back to it is the second photo, the one of Paris, Texas. It shows only a barren, vacant lot, in the middle of nowhere, with a "for sale" sign on it. When he first shows the photo to Walt, he is unable to remember why he purchased the land. Only at a later stage of their trip to California does he recall the reason: his mother had once told him that she first made love with his father in Paris, Texas. Before vanishing into the desert landscape, his parting grasp at some last connection to his past life and identity had been to purchase this piece of land where perhaps he had been conceived. The photo reveals, on the one hand, the arbitrary origins in which his identity is "grounded." On the other hand, it demonstrates that even though his as well as all human origins are unaccountable, the identity that arises out of them is nevertheless indelible. No matter how commodified (as indicated by the "for sale" sign in the photo) and stretched the umbilical cord between the individual subject and its early structures of identity might become, there remains a residue of memory and desire that binds them together. In his faith in narrative and its emotive powers to break through simulated reality, Wenders depends on the diachronic dimension of experience sustained by memory and desire. *Paris, Texas* seems to suggest that the individual's psychic roots back to an emotional center will survive any cultural shift toward simulacrum.

On the level of cultural identity, the film exhibits a similar faith in cinema's ability to restore a diachronic connection to the past. The film's images and narrative work together to revive twentieth-century landscapes of the American West that are already in danger of becoming archaic. In this case, the sterile referents of a simulated culture are the contemporary architectural and advertising landmarks stretched along America's highways. On the journey from Texas to the Los Angeles suburbs we see a kind of archaeological exhibition of institutions and establishments from different decades of the twentieth century. As Travis and Walt move from the desert landscapes of Devil's Graveyard near Big Bend, Texas, toward the arteries and networks of contemporary American freeway and airport civilization, they pass through time layers of past culture. Outmoded relics of the twentieth century lie almost like layered sediments of past culture, in danger of being buried behind a surface reality of postmodern facades, pavements, and images. The cardboard cutout of Walt's office building serves as an emblem for the sterile surfaces of the contemporary architectural environment. In postmodern film, shots of older diners, motels, drive-ins, and the like help create the nostalgia mode of what Fredric Jameson has termed "retro" culture.[16] These films reconstruct past styles in such a way as to revel in the disconnectedness of stylistic images and past experience. The perspective Wenders offers of this past in *Paris, Texas* counters this nostalgic fascination with style. The layering not only of past styles but even of the very buildings and artifacts, which themselves exist on the margins of contemporary America, restores a historical dimension not only to the styles but also to those experiences linked to them.[17] But perhaps more importantly, these artifacts from recent periods of American history are linked via the film story to Travis's need to keep moments of his own past alive in the present as part of a living, narrated history. In this way, the narrative invests them with a psychic force and dispels the disinterested "retro" reception.

In *Wings of Desire*, Wenders tackles this same theme from a different angle. The story of the angel's "descent" into human existence revolves around the nostalgia that moves Damiel from desire to action, and from the narrative that is needed to effect the assumption of identity.[18] Throughout the first part of the film, narrative is fragmented into the snippets of inner monologue overheard by the wandering angels. A sustained narrative develops only in the second half, when Damiel becomes human and assumes a life story with his own past. The key vibrant element is not, however, some kind of authentic lived experience as opposed to inauthentic or simulated experience in a (post)modern society. The film validates childhood memories in a way that confirms that the real only takes on meaning through a system of signs. Thus the longing for stories in *Wings of Desire* is not a nostalgia for a past era of simpler and truer values: Damiel, the male half of the two lovers who are longing for a life story, has no actual past! It is rather a desire for stories that avow their own fictionality even as they pave the way to future experience.

This revived, alternative link to the past does not constitute any kind of direct access to experience or history outside of representation. Still, for Wenders, childhood memories charged with desire entail a relationship between representation and reality that is qualitatively different from that found in those empty narrative shells recycled in television and cinema. The forward movement of the story in *Wings of Desire* depends on a continual return to a *level* of experience that one had as a child. Wenders inscribes the film within the Handke poem that is itself inscribed within the refrain "When the child was a child." The distinction the poem creates is not between an authentic lived experience and the representation of that experience, but rather between clichéd images of childhood and a poetic expression of the feeling that accompanies childhood memories. The images of the poem are more than just individual memories of childhood experiences; they signify the vibrant power these memories possess: "When the child was a child, it threw a stick into the tree like a lance, and it still vibrates there today." Handke's poem describes and creates an *epic* feeling that infuses stories with the power to sustain memory and construct an identity anchored in past experience.

German Roots in Classical American Cinema

Long before Wenders resolved to return to such an epic form of narrative, there was a film scene that, through one simple action, expressed for him this relationship to past experience. In Nicholas Ray's film *The Lusty Men*, when Jeff McCloud (Robert Mitchum) returns after many years to the ranch house where he had spent his youth, the first thing he does is crawl underneath it and pull out from a hiding place a box containing a few coins, a rusty revolver, and a rodeo program. In an often cited film quotation in *Kings of the Road*, Bruno returns to his childhood home on the island in the Rhine and pulls out from under the porch an old box of comic books. In both cases the objects themselves are not important, but rather they act as vehicles for those elemental *structures of desire* that form during youth and then resurface in various manifestations throughout life.

Wenders's faith in the life-sustaining power of such narrative moments charged with desire has its own psychic history, one mediated through cinema. In his youth the grand stories of classical American cinema dominated the movie programs and met certain psychic needs in the suspect cultural climate of the Federal Republic. His generation was saddled with a postwar culture that opted for the illusory choice of a totally new beginning, the Zero Hour of May 1945, rather than a painful process of coming to terms with its past (*Vergangenheitsbewältigung*). Thus the scene from *The Lusty Men* mentioned above had more significance for his filmmaking than just its influence on his film language. It represents his faith in cinema's ability to create myths such as those that filled the cultural void of his youth. His filmic homage to Nicholas Ray—later extended to feature length in *Lightning over Water*, which includes the original ranch house scene from *The Lusty Men*—also foretokens the stance he would take when the postmodern proliferation of images threatened this power of cinema. Indeed, there is a direct correspondence between the cultural climate in the first two decades of the Federal Republic and the threat of simulacrum in postmodern society. In both cases a rupture between the present and the past lies at the heart of the crisis. In the aftermath of Nazi Germany Wenders's generation had foreclosed on its psychic investment in its cultural traditions and its national identity. In the age of the empty signifier all forms of representation are hard pressed to break through the totalizing dynamic toward simulacrum and establish a diachronic link to past experience.

Thus what is at risk in Travis's crisis is not only the individualistic male hero of the American West, but also Wenders's own grounding in classical Hollywood cinema. The self-styled loner of Wenders's road movies is a throwback to the films he viewed during his youth and to the myths that inspired, above all, the American Dream—myths created by the big-screen narrative style of classical cinema. A simulated media culture that has lost contact with such myths and figures would threaten the roots of Wenders's own cinematic vision. In "The American Dream" Wenders reflected retrospectively on his gradual discovery of this dynamic that threatened his relationship to cinema. One particularly telling incident involved a cultural icon that was charged with his early libidinal attraction to America. In the early 1970s, before his first visit to America, he happened upon a newly opened Holiday Inn in Holland with the trademark green-and-yellow neon sign in front of it. He stopped, climbed out of his car, and approached the sign, which he knew from American films and postcards and which now stood in front of him like "an American landmark [*Wahrzeichen*], / a monument for the expectations of 'America.' . . . It surpassed its function in such a way / that the excess brought joy."[19] He relates this incident as an example of how the surface quality of the image had exerted its seductive force on him and attracted him to America's self-projected image of itself. His firsthand experiences in the United States disclosed the vacuity beyond the neon lights and television screens and eventually tempered his fascination with America's images.

But it was not until later, when the effect of the empty signifier in postmodern cinema hit closer to home, that Wenders began to search for alternative narrative strategies. The lure of the empty signifier generates a postmodern form of nostalgia that is qualitatively different from the emotional link to the past that lies at the heart of Wenders's films. Baudrillard argues that when "the transition from signs which dissimulate something to signs which dissimulate that there is nothing" occurs, a kind of proliferation of myths of origins and signs of reality takes place as a counterreaction to the loss of the signifier.[20] And when the reality principle grasps at last straws to counteract the loss, this only accelerates the play of signs and sustains simulation. In cinema this detached play of signifiers creates the form of film nostalgia described by Jameson. As intertexuality becomes "a built-in feature of the aesthetic effect," filmic representations of "pastness" become the trademark of postmodern films.[21] Stylistic referents for periods such as the 1950s in America are recycled, so that the nostalgia is no longer a desire to experience history through some reconstructed understanding of the times, but rather a longing to feel an *already existing* nostalgia for the past.

The nostalgia for stories that fuels Wenders's narratives is then something directly opposed to the postmodern retro-nostalgia. It reflects the need for a deeper link to the past instead of just an impassive interest in a revolving network of already existing stories and styles. When asked about the nostalgia for storytelling expressed in *Wings of Desire*, Wenders responded that the longing for stories is growing because of the vacuous films being produced by Hollywood. He asserts that they have the structure of stories but lack any grounding in lived experience—they lack "an epic feeling of a story."[22] The distinction here is not between fiction and reality, just as Damiel is an angel who assumes a human past he never actually lived. It is rather the distinction between empty referents and psychical structures of identity, a distinction that has its roots at one and the same time in Wenders's childhood, in classical American cinema, and in a historical juncture that stripped Germany of its cultural identity. Not only did Wenders, like Damiel, find an ersatz (cultural) past, but his grounding in this past remains his guiding vision as filmmaker: "I perceive the history of film as a very peaceful domain, where one can cast anchor in complete confidence. A place where one is in good hands, in good company."[23] If one is inclined to share Wenders's belief that the diachronic relation to the past is a resilient one that will survive the postmodern (hyper)free play of signs, then there is no better evidence to be offered than the filmmaker's own life story. Across a complex and shifting network of displacements, his origins in a "classical film language" have not only remained intact, but in doing so they have helped sustain the system of representation that bears them.

Notes

1. David Caldwell and Paul W. Rea claim that *Wings of Desire* displays the main traits of postmodernist works of art but does not efface central oppositions and dualities, as is usually the case in postmodernist film. They argue that in doing this it keeps alive the tension between modernism and postmodernism; "Handke's and Wenders's *Wings of Desire:* Transcending Postmodernism," *German Quarterly* 64.1 (1991): 46–54. David Harvey includes *Wings of Desire* in his treatment of postmodern films, but he too sees an ambivalence, arguing that the first half of the film is postmodern but that the second half reverts to the "modernist spirit"; *The Conditions of Postmodernity* (London: Blackwell, 1989) 320.

2. In an analysis of postmodern tendencies in *Wrong Move*, Richard McCormick writes that "it is this combination of self-reflexivity and narrative fiction, . . . and his (ambivalent) interest in popular culture that reveals the postmodern origins of Wenders's films"; *Politics of the Self: Feminism and the Postmodern in West German Literature and Film* (Princeton: Princeton UP, 1991) 167. (An essay version of McCormick's reading is included in this volume.)

3. Wim Wenders, "Der Amerikanische Traum," *Emotion Pictures: Essays und Filmkritiken* (Frankfurt am Main: Verlag der Autoren, 1986): 151–52. (Translations are my own.)

4. Wolfram Schütte, "Abschied von der dröhnenden Stimme des alten Kinos," an interview with Wenders in *Frankfurter Rundschau* November 6, 1982: Feuilleton 3. For other statements by Wenders about his new stance on narrative, see in this volume the film text of *Reverse Angle*, the 1982 talk "Impossible Stories," and the interview excerpts in the third section of "Texts and Contexts" (which includes this passage from the Schütte interview).

5. Wim Wenders, "Reverse Angle: New York City, March 1982," *Logik der Bilder: Essays und Gespräche*, ed. Michael Töteberg (Frankfurt am Main: Verlag der Autoren, 1988) 33. The film's original script in English is included in this volume. It appeared in *Logik der Bilder* in German translation.

6. Richard Kearney, *The Wake of Imagination: Toward a Postmodern Culture* (Minneapolis: U of Minnesota P, 1988) 322. For a more moderate position on Wenders's postmodernist strategies, see Nora Alter's essay in this volume. She argues that his manipulation of images oscillates between modernist critique and postmodern cynicism.

7. Jean Baudrillard, "The Ecstasy of Communication," *The Anti-Aesthetic: Essays on Postmodern Culture*, ed. Hal Foster (Port Townsend, WA: Bay Press, 1983) 129.

8. Jean Baudrillard, "Simulacra and Simulations," *Selected Writings*, ed. Mark Poster (Stanford: Stanford UP, 1988) 170.

9. Baudrillard, "Ecstasy" 127.

10. Baudrillard, "Ecstasy" 128ff.

11. Kearney 322.

12. Wenders, "Der Amerikanische Traum" 165.

13. Eric Rentschler first pointed out that Wenders changed the end in Handke's sceenplay, giving the film a much more negative view of Wilhelm's withdrawal

into his subjective world; *West German Film in the Course of Time: Reflections on the Twenty Years since Oberhausen* (Bedford Hills, NY: Redgrave, 1984) 178. One should not mistake this skepticism about solitary subjective writing to be a sign that Wenders lost faith in literature's power to give meaning. To the contrary, from *Wings of Desire* on, his films show literature to be the most "viable antidote to visual overstimulation," as Alice Kuzniar says in her essay in this volume. Gemünden, Grob, and Alter also discuss the hope these later films place in literature.

14. Wenders, "Le souffle de l'ange," *Logik der Bilder* (Frankfurt am Main: Verlag der Autoren, 1988) 134. *Le souffle de l'ange* was originally published as a special issue, edited by Wenders, of *Cahiers du cinéma* 400 (1987): 67–70. Published in German in *Logik der Bilder*. (Translation is my own.)

15. Friedrich Frey, "Über das Verfertigen eines Films beim Drehen: Wim Wenders unterhält sich mit Friedrich Frey," *Frankfurter Rundschau* September 10, 1988.

16. Fredric Jameson, "Postmodernism, or The Cultural Logic of Late Capitalism," *New Left Review* 146 (1984): 66–67.

17. This analysis, including the archaelogical metaphor of a layered past, is indebted to Jim Collins's distinction between these opposing attitudes toward the past. He offers *Blade Runner* as an example of the first type of film, which presents a "layering" of past styles and epochs, as opposed to the "retro" style of films like *Body Heat* and *Raiders of the Lost Ark*, films Jameson used as examples in his depiction of the nostalgia mode of postmodernist cinema; *Uncommon Cultures: Popular Culture and Post-Modernism* (New York: Routledge, 1989) 132–34.

18. See my essay on *Wings of Desire* in this volume.

19. Wenders, "Der Amerikanische Traum" 151.

20. Baudrillard, "Simulacra and Simulations" 170.

21. Jameson 66–67.

22. Ira Paneth, "Wim and His Wings," an interview with Wenders in *Film Quarterly* 42.1 (1988): 6. Compare also how Wenders describes this state of things in "Der Amerikanische Traum"; for example, "No one knows how one should live. / There are no examples, no guidance. / The images offered in television and cinema / do not provide any help. They only add to the disorientation / because they have no relevance for reality. / Americans have lost every sense / that there could be a connection between life and the images of television and movies— / every recollection that at one time there was a connection" (156).

23. Frey, "Über das Verfertigen eines Films beim Drehen."

Documentary as Simulacrum: *Tokyo-Ga*

NORA M. ALTER

> The author has never, in any sense, photographed Japan. Rather, he has done the opposite: Japan has starred him with any number of "flashes"; or, better still, Japan has afforded him a situation of writing. This situation is the very one in which a certain disturbance of the person occurs, a subversion of earlier readings, a shock of meaning lacerated, extenuated to the point of its irreplaceable void, without the object's ever ceasing to be significant, desirable.
>
> —Roland Barthes[1]

Interspersed among the better-known and lucrative feature films of Wim Wenders are his lesser-known documentary—or, more precisely, "essay" —films, which he also calls "diary" films. These designations denote a genre or medium that highlights, simultaneously, both the fictional aspect of feature films, their pretense to reality, and also the more or less surreptitious and unfulfillable desire of documentary to *be* reality.[2] They create, so to speak, the documentary as simulacrum—a "simulacrum" with a dual, (im)possible problematic: a copy of a copy without original; and, paradoxically, a copy of an original without copy. To (re)produce both documentaries ("images," in Wenders's diction) and features ("narratives") is of course by no means unique to Wenders among New German (or other) filmmakers; for example, Rainer Werner Fassbinder and Werner Herzog engage in both practices, sometimes in a single film. But no director has stated as bluntly as Wenders that his essay or diary films *are* his film theory.[3] Grasping Wenders's film theory, therefore, demands grasping his style of "quasi-documentaries."

One could trace this theory back to the 1979 Hamburg Declaration of German filmmakers, which had called for an end to the artificial separation of "the feature film from the documentary,—experienced filmmakers from newcomers,—films that reflect on the medium (in a practical way as experiments) from the narrative and commercial film."[4] Furthermore, Siegfried Kracauer's "two basic tendencies" of all cinema, to be "realistic" and "formative,"[5] can now be found equally in documentaries and in feature films. And thus according to Kracauer's theory, the binary distinction between these two genre has been considerably blurred. In fact, as Fredric Jameson notes, the very notion of "genre," along with all its attendant internal and external distinctions, is an obsolete modernist concept that, under postmodern cultural and economic conditions, has been replaced by "medium" and especially "media," that is, by concepts that include specific material technologies and social institutions as well as more strictly aesthetic values grounded in literature.[6] Incidentally, Jameson's additional claim that, in contrast to film, which is essentially modernist, video, TV, HDTV, and MTV are more properly postmodernist has been strongly supported by Wenders.

At any rate, throughout his career Wenders has expended a significant amount of energy and resources on producing essay films, often alternating between a feature-length film and a shorter essay film that functions for him like a sketch used by painters.[7] The 1977 feature *The American Friend* was followed by the 1980 essay *Lightning over Water*; the 1982 feature *Hammett* by both the mixed-genre *The State of Things* and the essay *Reverse Angle* in the same year; the 1984 feature *Paris, Texas* by the 1985 essay *Tokyo-Ga*; the 1987 feature *Wings of Desire* by the 1989 essay *Notebooks on Cities and Clothes*, which in turn was followed by the features *Until the End of the World* in 1991 and, in 1993, *Faraway, So Close!*

I shall focus here on *Tokyo-Ga*, in part because, by Wenders's own admission, it comes at a certain crisis point in his directing career, and also because it is informed by a nexus of intersecting problems that have haunted him, and film history in general. Actually, *Tokyo-Ga* was filmed in Tokyo in 1983 after *Hammett* (and Wenders's problems with Hollywood and Coppola, as depicted in *Reverse Angle*), but it was edited and produced in 1985 after his last American film, *Paris, Texas*. In turn, *Tokyo-Ga* inspired in his next feature film, *Wings of Desire*, the use of voice-over narration: "If I hadn't made *Tokyo-Ga* after *Paris, Texas*, then I wouldn't have dared to do that thing with voices in *Wings of Desire*."[8] More generally, at

the time of *Tokyo-Ga* Wenders stops looking so obsessively and almost exclusively to America and Hollywood and turns back to Europe, and more
specifically to Germany, for his own identity and for the locus of his films.
It is somewhat surprising that this return to the Old World also entangled
him (as it has so many European intellectuals from Oscar Wilde to Roland
Barthes) in things "Japanese."

Tokyo-Ga is a hybrid work that combines at least three themes: an
homage to Japanese director Yasujiro Ozu; a topical study of Tokyo and
Japan; and a rather disillusioned and sometimes paradoxical reflection on
the production, meaning, and consumption of images, on the general nature
of film, and on what has been for Wenders its greatest adversary—TV,
MTV, and video. Wenders's reflection is paradoxical because the production of images is obviously at the very core of his own commitment to the
cinema, and hence the critique of that production undermines his own art
and profession. But Wenders is also frustrated because his ideological
perspective on images, and hence his critique of them, is still steeped in
modernism, close to a Herzogian rejection of the naive dynamism of the
industrial age, whereas his own inclination as an artist and his own use of
images are definitely marked by the less nostalgic, more cynical Klugean
ironies and fragmentations of postmodernism. *Tokyo-Ga* stands at the interface of these conflicting and perhaps ultimately irreconcilable concerns,
combining and expressing them in often complex configurations that simultaneously resist critical narration and yet require it.

(Re)searching Ozu

The whole of Japan is a pure invention.

There is no such country, there are no such people.

—Oscar Wilde[9]

The first subject of *Tokyo-Ga* is Yasujiro Ozu (1903–63), arguably
the most distinguished and certainly most prolific Japanese filmmaker.
Wenders, who was born on the day of Japanese capitulation in World War
II, shoots his film in Tokyo in 1983, on the twentieth anniversary of Ozu's
death. To make a film about another filmmaker is by no means new territory for Wenders: his 1980 essay film *Lightning over Water* recorded the
final days of Nicholas Ray; and both Ray and Samuel Fuller figured prominently in *The American Friend*. Ozu was dead in 1983, Ray was dying in
1980; are these only coincidental deaths?[10] Pier Paolo Pasolini writes that
"so long as we live, we have no meaning. . . . Death effects an instantaneous montage of our lives."[11] Pasolini's "postmodern" take on death, however, stands in opposition to the more "modernist" take of Walter Benjamin, who related death to narrative rather than montage: "Death is the

sanction of everything that the storyteller can tell. He has borrowed his authority from death. In other words, it is natural history to which his stories refer back. . . . [T]he 'meaning' of his [a character's] life is revealed only in his death."[12] Wenders oscillates between these two positions: montage (or, more exactly, pastiche) and narrative. And Youssef Ishaghpour has noted that *Tokyo-Ga* "is a funereal commemoration" with technological means and, as such, Wenders's "Eastern" complement to the "Western" version informing *Lightning over Water.*[13]

The (re)search for Ozu takes Wenders not only to "real" Tokyo and its periphery but also to the Tokyo of Ozu's films, with a stress on the evocation of both the artist's role as mediator between the city and its filmic images, and the city's role as mediator between these images and the imagined identity of the artist. Wenders shot the footage for *Tokyo-Ga* during the 1983 Japanese-German Film Week, with the intention to film a "diary" one week in duration. He ended up staying a fortnight, but after the editing two years later the film shows (approximately) seven "days" in and around Tokyo. This temporal lag—between an initial empirical or realistic search and a more interventionist and formalistic research—is emblematic for all of *Tokyo-Ga.* For, similarly, Wenders initially arrives in Tokyo to try to recapture the city that was the topic of Ozu's films; but, in so doing —like the anthropologist who changes what he or she sets out to investigate—he initiates a long process by which cinema aestheticizes, distorts, or at least appropriates (another's) reality. In fact, from the very beginning Wenders calls into question the validity of his project, admitting (in the manner of Susan Sontag) that if he had not looked at Tokyo through the lens of his own camera, he might have remembered it better.[14] It may be noted that the entire problem of first recording and then editing an experience—be it real or imagined—and rendering it visible in the form of an image will be further explored in *Until the End of the World* (1991), where our most subjective imaginary—namely, dreams—is recorded while we sleep and then transposed technovisually so that it can be objectified, manipulated, and, theoretically at least, made available to universal vision.

The first (and crucial) step was the choice of Ozu as the focal point of *Tokyo-Ga.* Ozu was not a personal acquaintance of Wenders's, as were Fuller and Ray. Wenders discovered Ozu's films relatively late, during a trip to New York City in 1973. Yet Ozu represents one of the most important filmmakers for Wenders, perhaps, by his own admission, *the* most important. It was from him that Wenders learned "that refusing to explain things was right and that you could explain them well enough by just showing them."[15] Another key to this overdetermined fascination is found in the underlying theme of most of Ozu's films: the urban filmic landscape in general and Tokyo in particular.[16] The same landscape, with "the same simple stories, of the same people, in the same city of Tokyo,"[17] will draw

Wenders back to Tokyo a few years later in his 1989 *Notebooks on Cities and Clothes*. In addition, it was surely significant for Wenders that, chronologically, Ozu's fifty-four films—some black and white, and finally some in color—encapsulated most of the *formal* and *technical* evolution of cinema. For in that sense, Ozu *is* cinema metonymically if not literally, and exploring his art becomes an exploration of previous visual technology—an archaeology of its past and its basic potential.[18]

Precisely because of this long career without breaks, Ozu has come to be seen as the "father" of Japanese cinema, or even as the "father" of cinema *tout court*. As a paternal figure, he could certainly provide a continuity of cinematic practice (which was so notably lacking) in post–World War II Germany.[19] But then in the sensitive post-Nazi era, latching onto a figure of a Japanese "father" had its own ideological problematics. The jury on Ozu's own ideological commitments is still out.[20] It is then disturbing that nowhere in *Tokyo-Ga*, nor elsewhere, does Wenders raise the question of Ozu's politics, let alone answer it.[21] This failure could be seen by leftists as *Tokyo-Ga*'s "symptomatic silence," its "determinate absence."[22] For most viewers, this silence will simply manifest Wenders's overall tendency to give elusive (not to say evasive) responses to questions, his implementation of Ozu's teaching that it is preferable to "explain" things by "just showing them." But it is doubtful that *Tokyo-Ga* even attempts to *show* any negative aspect of fascist patriarchy and its complex afterlife.

The film's *formal* and *aesthetic* statements are much clearer. It is particularly interesting that Ozu's use of a 50mm camera lens to shoot all his films led directly to Wenders's experiments with different lenses, notably, shooting the same street in Shinjuku that often appears in Ozu's films. First shot with Wenders's standard 35mm lens, the street looks uncannily strange, even though that lens most closely approximates the "normal" visual field of the unaided human eye. Then Wenders refilms the street with Ozu's 50mm lens with straight telephoto effect, and the same street bursts into special life, even though the lens distorts "normal" vision by further reducing the field of depth to an almost "photographical" two-dimensional plane. But that new and vital image, Wenders sadly notes, is neither the street's nor really his own: it belongs to Ozu. As Peter Beicken and Phillip Kolker suggest, "The son—by the act of changing a lens—becomes the father. . . . Wenders finds a father, seems almost to see from behind his eyes, but realizes that, finally, the patriarch's images are not his own."[23] But one can push this interpretation further by asking: What exactly is happening technically at such filmic moments? Objectively, Wenders does appropriate and then discard the image produced by Ozu's "eye," replacing it with "his own."[24] To that extent he seems to fall within the Bloomian category of "epigonal misprision" (i.e, creative [mis]appropriation) known as "daemonization," whereby the "later poet opens himself to what he believes to be a power in the parent poem that does not belong to the parent proper, but to a range of being just beyond that of the precursor."[25] By a similar act of (re-)creative misprision, the epigone Wenders starts *Tokyo-Ga* with the credits and opening footage of Ozu's *Tokyo Story*, then inserts the footage of his own *Tokyo-Ga*, and finally splices back to the end of *Tokyo Story* before giving his own credits.

Ozu's mastery of his own cinematographic style brought him to a level of formal perfection that eventually generated a new fashion in filmmaking, one especially influential in Japan (but also on Peter Handke and Wenders himself). Now Wenders, in his own film, is looking in turn for a personal form that would somehow break with fashion and yet would also succeed, like Ozu's films, in showing both the continuity and the transformation of postmodern society. In a 1973 interview, just after having discovered Ozu in New York, Wenders explains that "the importance of Ozu for me . . . was to see that somebody whose cinema was also completely developed out of the American cinema, had managed nevertheless to change it into a completely personal vision. So Ozu was the one who helped me, and who showed me that it was possible to be colonised, or imperialised, in such a way that you really accepted the language."[26] Ozu, like Wenders, had no choice but to operate under the ambiguous sign of Hollywood influence, and yet he was able to carve out for himself an original film language appropriate for Japan. Wenders, long plagued by anxiety resulting from the continuing American presence in Germany, understood the anxiety felt by the Japanese occupied by the Americans. He formulated it most laconically and notoriously in *Kings of the Road* (1976): "The Yanks have colonized our subconscious." Or, as he explained in an interview that same year, "The American army was still here, and it still is. . . . But the fact that U.S. imperialism was so effective over here was highly favoured by Germany's own difficulties with their past. One way forgetting it, and one way of repression, was to accept the American imperialism."[27] But *Tokyo-Ga* is no longer a modernist product. Expressing the postmodern spirit of "liberation" from Hollywood, it is supposed to be a kind of Trojan horse in the belly of late capitalist technoculture. But who or what will spring forth from it fully armed is never made clear—not in any of Wenders's films, and not in his other modes of theoretical reflection.

Images/Simulacra/Hyperreality

The real is not that which can be reproduced,

but that which is always already reproduced. The hyperreal.

—Jean Baudrillard[28]

Through Ozu, *Tokyo-Ga* targets the modern city of Tokyo and modern civilization "everywhere." Ozu's films, as recaptured by Wenders, show the transformation of life in Japan, within the filmic iris as it were, from preindustrial to modern society, with an ensuing deterioration of the traditional family.[29] In *Tokyo-Ga*, Wenders explicitly subscribes to the derived proposition that the decline of national consciousness and identity is necessarily linked to, and coterminous with, the dissolution of the nuclear family. This proposition leads to the second subtext of *Tokyo-Ga*: its discourse on image production and reproduction.

As recorded by Wenders's camera, the most significant sequences seem at first glance to involve an overall loss of essence, a loss of something like the possibility of an unmediated vision or meaning. They show a world dominated by mass-media images, artificial signs of an alienated hyperreality. In this sense, *Tokyo-Ga* seeks not merely to document and/or construct the surface consciousness of a ritualized Japan, but also to problematize the very distinction between document and construction (which the Hamburg manifesto and Kracauer's film theory tried to transcend).

On his first edited "day," Wenders shows the Pachinko parlors, an apocalyptic picture of sets of pinball machines. Rows of Japanese men lose themselves in an endless game as if to escape their reality (or rather move from one reality into another) by a process of prosthetic self-reification, transforming themselves into tiny mobile spheres. In contrast to Vegas slot machines, winning at the Pachinkos is not the primary goal. Wenders's voice-over observes that Pachinkos first appeared after World War II, "when the Japanese people had a national trauma to forget" (*Tokyo-Ga*). They imitated and yet differed from American pinball machines. Pachinko, like Ozu, thus both remained caught up in the hegemony of Hollywood and yet somehow produced its own identity and style. We may also recall here young Wenders's own well-known fascination with pinball machines introduced by the conquering GIs, together with their films during their initial colonization of the German national unconscious. At this juncture the intuition of a symbolic triad begins to take shape in our vision of Wenders's vision: the defeated Japan and Germany, but also the victorious United States, completing the set of the three dominant industrialized postwar powers. The paradoxical Pachinko, as noted by Barthes, evokes the problematic of film as read by Wenders—they both are "a collective *and* solitary game."[30]

During the third "day" of *Tokyo-Ga* (let us skip momentarily over "day" two), most of Wenders's filming takes place in a five-tiered driving range where Japanese men, for hours on end, hit hundreds upon hundreds of golf balls. It does not matter where the balls go, or even if they are actually hit. It is the ritual performative gesture of swinging the golf club that counts, the mediatized image of doing the right or rather the fashionable thing. Wenders notes that in some of Ozu's later films there are similarly ironic comments on golf and its transformation into pure form, as the goal to get the ball into the hole has been forgotten. Golf, traditionally a competitive sport, has been metamorphized, both by the Japanese themselves and by Wenders's vision, into a self-referential set of visual gestures, a zen or satori, as it were. Once again the "original" Western model has been transformed into something uncannily all too familiar and yet radically different and "other."

On the fourth "day," Wenders films the manufacture of wax reproductions of restaurant dishes. These expensive simulacra of food are displayed in the windows of restaurants as a sort of concrete menu where one can appreciate perfectly formed sandwiches, salads, spaghetti noodles, and so forth. They are consumed visually though not otherwise—a particularly ironic commentary on the relation of vision to more primary bodily functions and needs. The skill of creating fake food apparently has become a highly technical and lucrative craft, even an art. In the surprisingly low-tech, pre-Fordist factory, Wenders is allowed to film the entire quasi-artisanal production process, with one notable exception: namely, the lunch break when real fast food is brought in and consumed. Thus the only live moment of restoration—that is, biological incorporation—eludes the eye of the camera. In a sense, of course, this manufacturing of seductive, deceptive, simulacrum dishes is not dissimilar from filmmaking. The creation of fake food starts with real food that is fixed with artful means, just as real life is artfully fixed on celluloid when it becomes cinematic images. It is as if the materialist-modernist slogan *man ist, was man ißt* (one is what one eats) has become a postmodern—but still materialist—*man ist, was man sieht* (one is what one sees).[31] All this has little to do with morals, as in Brecht's "zuerst kommt das Fressen, dann die Moral" (first eating, then morality). Wenders's essay film only records pastiched simulacra of simulacra, in a time-space continuum where reality is always already hyperreal.

"Day" five (following a conversation with Herzog and an aborted trip to the Japanese version of Disney World, arguably *the* icon of all simulacra) takes Wenders to a public park on a rainy Sunday afternoon. The park is invaded by groups of Japanese teenagers gathering around loud boom boxes. Each group is dressed in costumes corresponding to the specific musical style. In one corner the young people play music of the "rebellious" 1950s (Elvis), in another Blondie of the 1970s, in another rock of the 1960s, and so on. This is fashion as aural-visual simulation. Everybody attempts to reproduce the images—the signs and subcultural "style"—of borrowed models, mainly American or, more accurately, *seemingly* American.[32] What is thus produced is a form of cultural "history" or a simulation of "history." For the Japanese students, who go to the park without parental consent, this activity constitutes an apparent form of rebellion, but a rebellion that is sheer form; and their music is pure style, like Pachinko, the driving range, perhaps even film itself. That formalizing process, to be true, may also be mirroring the American model, since in the United States the same music, once a sign of rebellion, also ended up being co-opted and commodified—if it, too, was not already always a more or less unwillingly agent of that very commodification and co-option.[33]

One could ask here the old question raised by all art: How much is reality, and how much artifice ("Is it live or is it Memorex")? Or, more generally, how new was Ozu's cinematographic art, and how original is Wenders's own film? How "new" was New German Cinema? Was it ever substantially different from tradition? Are we supposed to see all of the modern world, whether filmed or not—Japan, Germany, and the United States—as *merely* derived spectacle or simulation, a Baudrillardian or Debordian nihilistic universe, a "televisual" projection? Wenders's *Tokyo-Ga* surely reflects a basic fascination with spectacles in a society where mass-produced images, disseminated as commodities, lose their connection to reality and become consumed and valued only for their sake *as* images. And yet, at the same time, Wenders the filmmaker (who never reflects very hard in his films on commodification in economic terms)[34] himself contributes to this multiplication of images and feeds off them, *incorporates* them in various senses of the word. Whether Wenders's critique of spectacularization reflects adequately on this semiparasitical relation is an important but unresolved question in *Tokyo-Ga*.

So much for Tokyo and Japan, and, beyond them, the modern world. We may take their images at their face value as images of reality; that is, we believe that—however aestheticized, spectacularized, and distorted—they reflect or express a real Tokyo and evoke a real world. But one could as well argue that Wenders's sequences are not "true" images of Tokyo, that they are *only* arbitrarily selected and ideologically reedited images without any basic regard for reality, that they are *only* attractive spectacles to entertain viewers. This is but one of several points where *Tokyo-Ga* opens up onto its third main theme: namely, a reflection on the nature of film and its images. The problem of *reality* is thus left unresolved, displaced by the obsessive self-reflexivity of the *medium*.

Production Values

What counts is that the mobile camera is like a

general equivalent of all the means of locomotion that it shows or that it

makes use of—aeroplane, car, boat, bicycle, foot, metro.

—Gilles Deleuze[35]

Wenders's still partly mimetic problematic is rooted in his initial decision to give his film about Ozu the form of a documentary.[36] Unlike his 1980 *Lightning over Water,* which he wanted to be a "movie without any rules," a documentary is supposed to be governed by rules of realism and verisimilitude. Logically, then, Wenders subtitles *Tokyo-Ga* a "filmed diary" intended "just to take a look without wanting to prove anything"—a traditional claim for realistic objectivity. In the same spirit, *Tokyo-Ga* includes several obviously "objective documents": actual sequences from Ozu's *Tokyo Story* (1953); black-and-white photographs of Ozu at work with his crew; and four interviews in contemporary Tokyo. Two of these are with Western filmmakers Werner Herzog and Chris Marker, and two are with Japanese closely associated with Ozu: actor Ryu and cameraman Atsuta. These documentary images serve to persuade viewers—by metonymy—of the documentary veracity of all of *Tokyo-Ga*: *If* what they show is true, *then* true also must be the remainder of Wenders's images of Tokyo and his vision of the postmodern world. In that sense, one might be tempted to say, the logic of *Tokyo-Ga* does illustrate and update cinema's old, perennial capacity to record reality by answering positively the question of the Real: we do (and should) believe what we see on the screen.

At the same time, however, with a perversely iconoclastic (not to say iconophobic) pleasure, Wenders multiplies references to the misleading nature of *all* cinematographic statements: Japanese, German, American, and other. From this metafilmic perspective, *Tokyo-Ga* must be viewed as a film about films rather than a film about reality—a filmic practice both defined and confined by cinematographic illusion.[37] Not only does it open and close with the scenes of Ozu's *Tokyo Story,*[38] but also inserted, on the television in Wenders's hotel room, is a clip from the final scene of John Ford's *She Wore a Yellow Ribbon.* The images of the ongoing larger film, here Wenders's own Tokyo, may offer an illusion of *the* "real" Tokyo, but they also reflect the illusory-cum-real images of Ozu's cinematographic Tokyo onto which Wenders grafts his own parallel discourse. For instance, each of Ozu's films includes a picture of a train presented as an allegory of modernity.[39] Wenders opens his documentary with a traditional shot of a train excerpted from Ozu's *Tokyo Story,* then matches it with his own shot of a contemporary bullet train. And all throughout *Tokyo-Ga* images of trains and subways travel across the screen. To be sure, for Wenders, the function of the train as the allegory of mechanized modernity, and the seemingly irrevocable alteration of the quality of life, is not limited specifically to Japan; it is a universal sign of modernism. His Tokyo represents merely yet another hyperreal instance of what is always already occurring globally. In this sense, like Mike Davis's Los Angeles, it is an imaginary archaeological site of the future.[40] But it is also a self-consciously imaginary construction in the present: "faraway, so close." He could say with Barthes, "I can . . . —though in no way claiming to represent or to analyze

145

reality itself (these being the major gestures of Western discourse)—isolate somewhere in the world (*faraway*) a certain number of features (a term employed in linguistics), and out of these features deliberately form a system. It is this system which I shall call: Japan."[41] For in postmodernity national boundaries tend to lose their materiality, becoming simulacra.

And no doubt the train, the quintessential *modern* form of transport, may also have appealed to Wenders, and before him to Ozu, because the simultaneously integrating and fragmenting impact of train travel on territorial and national identity is remarkably similar to a comparable impact of international cinema. Railways in the nineteenth century, as Wolfgang Schivelbusch notes, abolished traditional notions of space, destroyed boundaries, and reconfigured the "here and now." At the same time (a thesis later developed in Virilio's *The Lost Dimension*),[42] "when spatial distance is no longer experienced, the difference between original and reproduction diminishes."[43] The same disorientation and/or transformation may result from filmic experiences that collapse spatial dimensions even faster than the images of reality viewed through the windows of a moving train—like frames of a film. Asked why there are so many trains in his films, Wenders responds: "Ozu has trains in almost all of his films too. . . . The locomotive with all of its wheels simply belongs to the cinema. It's a piece of machinery like the cine-camera. They are both products of the nineteenth century, the mechanical age."[44] Thus Wenders's film offers a more adequate film "theory" in that sense than do his rather disjointed attempts at theorizing.

On "day" two, Wenders has a long sequence of the Tokyo metro where he focuses on the train windows as they go by, looking exactly like celluloid frames—each window an individual frame. This is a striking illustration of Deleuze's thesis in *Cinema 1*, that—in a certain kind of cinema, exemplified by Wenders—there is a direct link or "translation" between a film frame and the view from the window of a moving vehicle: "One might conceive of a series of means of translation (train, car, aeroplane . . .) and, in parallel, a series of means of expression (diagram, photo, cinema). The camera would then appear as an exchanger or, rather, as a generalized equivalent of movements of translation."[45] In any case, just as Ozu showed in his films the deterioration of Japanese culture in the age of the train, so Wenders records a similar continuous deterioration but with an increasing pessimism and the concomitant nostalgia. His Japan of the 1980s is informed at one and the same time by the most striking display of high tech and by the persistence of premodern tradition—not to say also by the most traditional vision of ritualized modern society.

In the same spirit of double allusion (and allusiveness), the train in the framing shots refers not only to modernity, that is, a real outside world, but also to the train in the first film by the Lumière brothers. It refers further to the analogous visual experience provided by the view from the moving windows, or rather—by a further play on reality versus art—by the very consciously composed *image* of that train, filmed and edited at an angle rather than head-on. Reference could also be made to Wenders's *The American Friend* (1977), with its own train sequence and its allusions to Hitchcock's *Strangers on a Train* (1951), or to Wenders's film about a modern Wilhelm Meister, *Wrong Move* (1975), in which a train is the primary means of transport and modern/postmodern *Bildung*.

All these explicit or implicit allusions clearly position *Tokyo-Ga* within the tradition of a self-referential cinematographic aesthetic practice. Wenders is aware, in his own words (which could have been Harold Bloom's), that "in the instant when one puts a camera on a tripod and looks through it, three generations of filmmakers, or indeed four, have already done so."[46] Each time, one enters willy-nilly into the technohistory of film. As Bill Nichols remarks in his theory of documentary, "The documentary effect, as it were, turns us back toward the historical dimension and the challenge of praxis with a forcefulness borne of the text's almost tangible bond to that which it also represents *as though* for the first time."[47] It is in the site of precisely this *"as though"* that Wenders's (re)produces his images.[48]

Nichols also argues that "documentary operates in the crease between the life as lived and the life as narrativized."[49] As Pasolini implied, between lived experience and its narrative there always stands edited montage or pastiche. And so we must see *Tokyo-Ga*: a filmed narrative pastiche that is to test the truth of another filmed narrative. They both refer to the same rather jaded reality: Tokyo. The very title *Tokyo-Ga* can mean something like "Tokyo, *nicht wahr?*" or "Oh, Tokyo, right?" The very act of filming present-day Tokyo shifts it into the past.[50] By the same token, the future drops out of the postmodern temporal flow in and of Wenders's films.

What, then, is the narrative backdrop in *Tokyo-Ga*, and what symptomatic images and technologies does it adopt? Wenders's stated purpose was to see whether he "could still detect any traces of the time, whether there was anything left of that work, images or even people, or if too much had changed in Tokyo and in Japan in the twenty years since Ozu's death."[51] At this level, he is searching for evidence of an assumed true statement about (or image of) Tokyo—a reality that is created, however, by the artful work not only of his own or Ozu's making, but of a camera and its edited trace. For Wenders's visual memory of Tokyo is assembled largely from frozen images from the "text" of Ozu's films. One is reminded here of Raymond Bellour's theory that, in film, the use of nonmoving images opens up a space for reflection not only on the movies but on the act of viewing the movie: "By creating distance and another time, the photograph allows me to think in the cinema. It allows me to think the film as well as the very fact of being in the cinema. In short, the presence of the photograph allows me to cathect more freely what I see. It helps me (a little) to close my eyes though they keep on being open."[52] And Bellour notes that the use of still photographs is a constitutive feature not only of essay films but also of essay videos because it is a way of allowing "the image to think" in order to stave off death.[53] In a similar spirit, one of Wenders's recurring shots in *Tokyo-Ga* shows Japanese who take photographs and videos of one another—an image of generalized image taking that appears to be truthful precisely *because* it is so obviously artificial. And, toward the end of the film, like viewers of a striptease, we finally get to see Ozu himself, after first being shown his grave. This revealing image is accessed through a series of black-and-white photographs that show the master shooting and directing films, including *Tokyo Story*.

On the other hand, there are also striking images that appear more spontaneous than artful, and in that sense more "realistic." Actually, however, it is only the single image of a small protesting boy who is gently but irresistibly dragged by his mother in a subway station that provides Wenders with a feeling that he is somehow "really" in touch with (a) true—albeit resisting—reality. This is one of the few shots taken by Wenders from a high mobile angle and not from Ozu's low and intimate angle, one of the few sequences that are emblematic of his own style, his own signature as it were. In that sense, the image of the child in *Tokyo-Ga* becomes an allegory for all of his own work, even for (film) history: being propelled, protesting, into an uncertain future or "adulthood." And what will this technocultural "adulthood" be? What will be its death? For Wenders, as we will see, that end will come with TV, MTV, and video. At one point in *Tokyo-Ga* Wenders seems to suggest, however, that cinema ended already with Ozu's death in 1963! But where does this leave Wenders and his own filmic corpus?

A basic paradox that underlies *Tokyo-Ga*—and all of Wenders's essay films more generally—is that, as a documentary, it seeks a goal that cannot be reached, and yet must be sought—an objective truth about a reality that is always subjectively perceived and thus always elusive. In search of a more or less postromantic closure, Wenders's visit to Ozu's grave allegorizes that paradox: on the gravestone he finds no name, only the Chinese character *mu*, which means "emptiness" or "nothingness." "We are nothing," the romantic poet Hölderlin had written in *Hyperion* (a text known to Wenders),[54] "what we seek is everything." This lack of closure, inscribed on the opaque black rock of Ozu's headstone under the guise of closure, understandably troubles Wenders. For him, his voice-over says, nothingness *cannot* exist; only reality can exist and be perceived, recorded, and edited into a film. One can never film nothingness but only suggest it, as it were, by a real reference to an absence and/or by an artificial reference to a presence. Wenders's search for Ozu takes him to such a suggestion of determinate absence: a gravestone inscription that is real but refers to a nothingness that cannot, by definition, be represented. Alternatively, all cinema's search for reality is figured by images that may in some sense be real, and can be artistically striking, but can only always suggest a reality without any objective reliability or possibility of realization. In that sense *Tokyo-Ga* displays a particularly deep tension that underlies all of Wenders's recent films, both essay and feature: a tension between images of a porous reality that can only be hinted at on the one hand, and images of a clearly artistic representation of reality that seems omnipresent on the other. Thus, for Wenders, the very distinction between image and narrative, between feature and essay film, also becomes—or theoretically ought to become—porous, threatening to collapse completely. It is here that, as Jameson noted, under conditions of postmodernity genre is superseded by media, and modernist film by postmodern video and television. We are further reminded that a constitutive feature of essay film is its incorporation of other media, including photography and even video. In the case of Wenders, the "empirical" distinction between feature and essay becomes "hermeneutic": we could have a "feature" viewing of an "essay" film, and, vice versa, an "essay" viewing of a "feature." *Tokyo-Ga* is as much (about) the one as (about) the other.

This complexity underlies even the most "documentary" features of the film, that is, the interviews that are expected to document reality by recording an authentic human voice and presence. The first is with Chishu Ryu, an actor who played in most of Ozu's films. Strangely enough, Ryu almost always acted out characters much older than he was. He describes himself as being a blank page, a tabula rasa—almost like Ozu's gravestone —that was completely empty until Ozu filled it with his instructions and made it into an artificial construction. Ryu's filmed testimony, supposed to assist the search for truth, implies, paradoxically, that while filmed statements always involve misrecognition because of their artificial nature, the author of that deception, at least for Ryu, is the greatest *realist* filmmaker himself. Indeed, Ozu remade his studio in his own image and re-created reality with an especially painstaking mix of authentic and artificial elements.

Of course, this sequence also evokes Wenders himself shooting and editing *Tokyo-Ga*, including his presence in the film as voice-over (we also see his hands on occasion) that has an obvious suturing function as a kind of master narrative. The issue of Wenders's painstaking (and apparently painful) editing—editing that he never refers to as a vital part of Ozu's filmmaking process—is raised only in his later recollections. He notes that *Tokyo-Ga* "made me realize that editing a documentary is a much more complicated business than editing a feature film. . . . The editing took

149

months; it got out of all proportion to the filming."[55] Here Wenders is trying to problematize his own relationship to the problem of representation by alluding to his own (not Ozu's) pastiche technique, even while still keeping to the surface of the "real" world. He must thus *resist* the "rare image" advocated by Herzog and, playfully, select any such an image less in terms of risk, as Herzog also demands, than in terms of *resistance*—as displayed by the little boy gently dragged by his mother off-frame into an undecided, nondiegetic future.

The second interview, on "day" five, is with Werner Herzog and may be viewed as emblematic for post–New German Cinema's aesthetic and even political perspectives. The two filmmakers meet for a conversation atop the Tokyo Tower, a simulacrum of the Eiffel Tower.[56] Herzog complains that there are no longer any "pure and clear and transparent images" left to film in Tokyo, nor, for that matter, in our familiar modern world.[57] His only chance as a filmmaker, he insists, would be to join the space shuttle, go into a war zone, or climb to the top of a mountain and see something *really* new.[58] For Herzog, not only theoretically but in the actual shooting of films, pure images must entail extreme risk even to the point of death (and at least one actor has died during the shooting of his films). But, even as Herzog decries the lack of images in Tokyo, Wenders's camera begins to pan surreptitiously over the various images that Tokyo supplies for his own film, their apparent interest—even if only qua simulacra—thus clearly putting the lie to Herzog's fret, which now seems naive, nostalgic, modernist, or even premodern. At first glance, we seem to have a "Mexican standoff" between two of the giants of New German Cinema: Herzog, who represents a "cinema of purity" and finds virtually *no* more real images to film; and Wenders, who represents a "cinema of immersion" and finds—if anything—*too many* images of too many cultures in which to revel. Yet we are also seeing Wenders struggling less with Herzog himself than with a certain "Herzog effect": namely, Wenders's *own* continuing search for modernist and premodernist authenticity even in a resolutely postmodernist condition (mistrustful of "master narratives," *all* narratives even). And he must continually problematize this very search, to the point of killing it off again and again.

The Herzog interview is immediately followed, on "day" six, by a very fleeting encounter with French documentarist and self-described "essayist" Chris Marker. This easily overlooked "interview" takes place in a bar bearing the name of one of Marker's best-known films, *La jetée* (1962)—a "feature" film consisting almost entirely of still photographs and already asking a basic question taken up three decades later in *Until the End of the World*: namely, whether the unconscious can be captured in a photographic image. Marker had considerable influence on the practitioners of German essay films with, among others, his *Sans soleil* (1982). Wenders himself, at the beginning of *Tokyo-Ga*, alludes to Marker's remark a year earlier in *Sans soleil*: "I remember, I remember a January in Tokyo, or rather I remember the images I filmed in January in Tokyo. They have replaced my memories, they are my memories. I wonder how people remember who don't film, who don't photograph, who don't use tape recorders."[59] Wenders's version in *Tokyo-Ga* is: "I no longer have the slightest recollection. I recollect nothing whatsoever. I know I was in Tokyo. I know it was in the Spring of 1983. I know. I had a camera with me and I did some filming. I have the pictures, they have become my memory. But I think to myself: if you'd gone there without a camera, you would remember more."[60] Of course, like *Tokyo-Ga*, *Sans soleil* was in part an effort to capture the essence of Japan, where Marker was momentarily expatriated, as well as an attempt to problematize that very effort. It could be claimed that Marker's presence in *Tokyo-Ga* shows, and even explains, why Wenders grants him a privileged access to a Tokyo that he himself does not enjoy. It might even be said that *Tokyo-Ga* is not only an explicit tribute to Ozu as feature filmmaker and narrator, but an implicit tribute to the photographer, essayist, and imagemaker Marker. Marker, however, like the workers eating their lunch in the wax food factory, does not allow himself to be photographed, except for a shot of one eye. It is the monocular eye of artists working in two-dimensionality, contrasted with binocular "natural" vision.

The last—and most technically oriented—interview presents on "day" seven Yuharu Atsuta, Ozu's cameraman. It was Atsuta who, under Ozu's guidance, simplified the technique of visual expression by shooting only with a 50mm-lens camera fixed at the eye level of someone sitting on the floor or even lower. He recalls that Ozu objected vehemently against the use of any different lens or position, convinced that it was this shooting technique that enabled him to get images that were both epistemologically or ontologically "true" and formally and technically "flawless"—in other words, images that disclosed a deeper order in a "chaotic" world out of order and joint. Actually, of course, Atsuta implies that Ozu's vision of reality only *appeared* truthful, that its perfection resulted from a particular filming style, that is, precisely from artifice. Wenders plays with lenses and agrees. Shooting techniques, he implies, are always a personal matter although already always impersonal at the same time. They are historical and technological, but also a matter of an individual, sometimes idiosyncratic personality that projects its vision on actors and cameramen.

Atsuta's interview finally leads to a further questioning of the nature of filmed reality: yes, there are real streets in Tokyo; and yes, they must be filmed to keep cinema alive; but the filmed images of these streets reflect as much art as reality. This is an obviously self-reflecting (but also onanistic, solipsistic, or cannibalistic) notion of cinema as an art that feeds on itself. This nostalgic self-reflection, no doubt, explains Wenders's admiration for the craftsmanship of the great film auteurs, especially Ozu, who had a stop-watch and tripod specially constructed for his personal use. Wenders also at one point looks through the original handwritten screenplay of one of Ozu's films. Of course, he cannot comprehend what is written in Japanese, but it impresses him as an authentic document. Yet pervading the film is the fear that somehow all this past authentic world is being threatened and irrevocably changed. As Wenders's extensive, framing quotation from *Tokyo Story* reveals, one can actually hear Ozu's obtrusive stopwatch on the sound track, a reminder of time moving inexorably forward, but also a denial of realistic verisimilitude. Indeed, this aural (not visual) generates an almost Brechtian "alienation effect" evoking "epic cinema." But, as so often happens in Wenders's films, it is the viewer who is required to make such connections.

Television as Adversary

Television [is] the poison ivy of the eyes.

—*Reverse Angle*

You try to fly but you cannot fly

You try to hide but I'm by your side

You run from me, run from me, run from me . . .

I am the adversary, I am the adversary,

I am the adversary . . .

I grow and grow and grow

Between ideals and fact,

Between the thought and the act.

—Crime and the City Solution[61]

As we approach the twenty-first century, Japan is undoubtedly one of the wealthiest (and, at least on the surface, most stable) countries in the world. As such, it offers fascinating features: soaring real-estate values, alleged buyup and sellout of art, intensive education and recreation programs, a fully socialized and integrated workforce, various models for getting rich quickly, and masses of Japanese tourists who circulate everywhere, as ubiquitous as the Japanese products that dominate the world marketplace, workplace, recreation sites, and homes: computers, televisions, cameras, video recorders, and so on. Through vertical and horizontal integration, media industries like Sony and Panasonic develop not only technological means for the production and reproduction of images but also networks that control and determine their distribution and consumption. The total picture (cliché or not) is indeed fascinating, but it also may be found threatening for art

The ubiquitous television in Wenders's first feature film, *Summer in the City* (1970).

(and not only art). Japan may epitomize postmodern civilization, but not all aspects of that civilization are met with approval, at least not by Wenders.

If there is one feature of this cultural logic that Wenders has particularly disliked, even feared, at least in the past, it is television—the great adversary. "In principle, I believe that television is unbearable—it is naked fascism [der nackte Faschismus]."[62] Of course, television has been viewed for a very long time as the competitor and eventual killer of cinema—and that may explain Wenders's ire. In 1960, Kracauer's *Theory of Film* still could offer the pious wish that film would hold its own against the television challenge[63]—but a lot has flowed down the fiber-optic current since then. And television itself has evolved and developed new features: MTV or CNN define quantitatively and qualitatively a different medium from the old CBS or NBC and interpellate quite different subject formations. Thus, while he conceded in 1989 that "the great thing" about rock and roll is that it can create in listeners a "collective dream," Wenders complained that, with the advent of MTV, "today each song is already supplied with the dream, so that one can no longer supply it with images. They already come with it."[64]

No wonder, then, that television, like medieval evil, is omnipresent (not only visibly, but also invisibly as "mood") in *Tokyo-Ga*: in the form of commercials in the backdrop, in shop windows along the streets, in Wenders's hotel room, in taxicabs, and so forth. In fact, television has been increasingly intruding into Wenders's other films, insinuating its supposedly malevolent, totalitarian, fascist presence into every nook and cranny of everyday life and becoming the second nature of (hyper)reality. However, some of Wenders's more recent work takes a somewhat more benevolent view of video. For example, in *Notebooks on Cities and Clothes* Wenders goes into detail about the advantages of video over film. He made music videos in 1993 for the Irish rock group U2. It is even possible to receive *Until the End of the World* and *Faraway, So Close!* as "MTV"—in fact, the sound track to the former has had greater commercial success than the film. Nonetheless, given the sheer strength of Wenders's earlier hostility against television, one suspects that he will always oscillate back and forth on the subject, never really escaping from the negativism. For televised images are proliferating globally, and, says Wenders's voice-over, "every shitty television set has become the center of the world."[65]

Among the three great Western powers, *Tokyo-Ga* points only to two, Japan and the United States, linking them in an unholy alliance. Wenders explicitly claims that, although it is the Japanese who build the most and best television sets, these sets primarily show American images, and that it is these images that become "the center of the world." Yet it must be noted that Wenders himself narrates *Tokyo-Ga* in English, and American English at that. And no mention is made (either in the film or in the credits) of the Japanese interpreter for the interviews. On the one hand Wenders admits he knows no Japanese; on the other it is only his disembodied voice that mediates what is being said to non-Japanese audiences. Is Wenders himself participating in a baneful linguistic hegemony, or is he trying to gain power over that hegemony by appropriating its language as his own?[66] His suturing voice-over is extremely controlling and authorial; and, though he may want to "show" something without "explaining" anything, this voice undermines the alleged innocence of his film.

It seems that, for Wenders, film can always offer something that television cannot. In the Rauh interview of 1989, just before German reunification, Wenders's vision of the future of cinema is linked directly to the future of an integrated common European market. He sees a united Europe where cinema would be as much its cultural flagbearer as television is for Japan and America: "Film is in fact a vanguard for the European idea of 1992. It is today the case that films are coming out of different European countries and being made by colleagues and means from three, four different nations, in which they are also being seen . . . and even as form, as language, film is the only trans-European culture [übereuropäische Kultur] that we have today."[67] Wenders, as a defender of *Kultur*, turns (his) cinema into a modernist project for European unity and *Gemeinschaft*. He thus undertakes this project in earnest (and at great financial cost) immediately after *Tokyo-Ga* with *Wings of Desire* and *Until the End of the World*.[68]

The problem here is how to reconcile Wenders's filmic project (as we have seen it stated both explicitly and implicitly in his films, interviews, and essays) with his most recent ideological twist after the reunification of the two Germanies under capitalist hegemony. As he returns again to "Germany," literally and figuratively, like so many other German intellectuals across the political spectrum, he states in his 1991 "Talking about Germany" that "our balm in this land of lost souls . . . is our German language [unser Heil in diesem zur Zeit so heillosen Land ist unsere deutsche Sprache]. It is differentiated, precise, subtle, endearing, accurate, and nurturing at the same time. It is a rich language. It is the only wealth that we have in a country that believes itself to be rich when it is not. The German language is everything that our country no longer is, what it is not yet, and what it may never be."[69]

Reading these lines, and between them, one has the impression of hearing the (West) German National Anthem as sound track; after all, its original lyrics were written in the middle of the last century at a time when the German language in a significant sense *was* the German nation. But, more disturbing, at least for some, may be that Wenders seems also dangerously close here to the cliché (audible from popular and mass culture to Heidegger and beyond) that Germans (and by extension the again-expanding German nation) are especially blessed with *die heilige deutsche Sprache*. The specific terms with which Wenders buys into this claim are very close to his own earlier description of Ozu's images, the trace of which he is trying to record (to "show," not "explain") in *Tokyo-Ga*—those most privileged of images he had described as "true, valid, and useful." Now it seems that his *cosmopolitan and internationalist filmic* project is being supplemented, if not replaced, perhaps only momentarily, by a project that is specifically *national*, *linguistic*, and (in *Faraway, So Close!*) *Christian*.

Small surprise, then, that Wenders had earlier, in that crucial year 1989 to be exact, justified film, in good part, by linking it to the high culture of literature and painting, claiming that "literature, and perhaps also painting, is likely the only thing that can save something like inwardness."[70] Only by alluding to representing this interiority, this "inner experience" (as Dilthey, even Bataille, might say), can Wenders's films momentarily define their own limits and place their vision both personally and historically. Wenders himself came to filmmaking through painting, and this idea of a painted image being more original than film seems to have haunted him ever since.[71]

At several points in his films, Wenders celebrates Polaroid technology precisely because here, too, there is no negative, only an "original."

Similarly, in *Notebooks on Cities and Clothes*, he suggests that digital imaging may provide the only "true" images of the future, again precisely because there is no "original." And, significantly, *Notebooks on Cities and Clothes* was shot in both 35mm and in the adversary video.[72] Here he seems, at least, to begin making his reluctant concession to the twenty-first century. No longer was television for Wenders so symptomatic of the "decline," as he had put it, of the West and of the world.

Although there is in *Tokyo-Ga* ample evidence of Wenders's hostility toward television and video, I argue that his fascination with the world of the simulacrum and the power of audiovisual media to replicate (if not "redeem") reality belies this antipathy, forcing him to confront all techno-cultural forms, including now High Definition Television.[73] This inquisitiveness reaches a kind of apex in *Until the End of the World* but retreats in *Faraway, So Close!*, where Wenders again becomes skeptical about new technologies and their social impact, in part because of his aversion to all forms of pornography. Nonetheless, *Tokyo-Ga* confirms the general thesis that it is in his essay films, primarily, that Wenders struggles to work through the various "crises"—not only in his own work but in the postmodern condition.

Notes

I am grateful to Anton Kaes and Eric Rentschler for their helpful comments on an earlier draft of this essay, as well as to Loris Morella for first bringing the film to my attention.

1. Roland Barthes, *Empire of Signs* [1970], trans. Richard Howard (New York: Hill and Wang, 1982) 4.

2. The term "essay film" has a complicated history. It resurfaced in the 1980s in discussions of Chris Marker's film focused on Japan, *Sans soleil* (1982), but its origins were earlier. In 1940 German avant-garde filmmaker Hans Richter (who had collaborated with both Eisenstein and the French Surrealists) used the term *Filmessay* to describe the need to expand documentary in order to film "problems, thoughts, even ideas" and to break away from the "redepiction of external phenomena" and "chronological sequence." In a seminal 1948 manifesto entitled "The Birth of a New Avant-Garde: The Camera as Fountain Pen," Alexandre Astruc called upon filmmakers to inscribe their celluloid with written texts, or "essays," so as to push the medium beyond imagined audiovisual limits. Typically, the essay film has taken a middle position between "feature" and "documentary," but also, in the ideal case, pushes both media in new and unexpected directions. Another feature of the essay film is its intense self-reflexive aspect: not only is the director's presence typically included and problematized (e.g., as "diary"), but also the entire medium itself. This strategy commonly includes the more or less uneasy incorporation into the essay film of other media: for example, photography, painting, drawing, and video, as well

as writing. Practitioners of the essay film include Wenders, Marker, Jean-Luc Godard, Harun Farocki, Hartmut Bitomsky, Derek Jarman, Jean-Marie Straub and Daniele Huillet, and Valie Export. For a useful introduction to the essay film, including basic texts by Richter and Astruc, see Christa Blümlinger and Constantin Wulff, eds., *Schreiben Bilder Sprechen: Texte zum essayistischen Film* (Vienna: Sonderzahl, 1992). See further the special issue of *Augen-Blick* 10 (1991), ed. Hanno Möbius, "Versuche über den Essayfilm."

3. Reinhold Rauh, "Ein Gespräch mit Wim Wenders," *Wim Wenders und seine Filme* (Munich: Wilhelm Heyne Verlag, 1990) 253. This interview was conducted in 1989.

4. "The Hamburg Declaration" [1979], in *West German Filmmakers on Film: Visions and Voices*, ed. Eric Rentschler (New York: Holmes and Meier, 1988) 4.

5. Siegfried Kracauer, *Theory of Film: The Redemption of Physical Reality* (London: Oxford UP, 1960) 30–37.

6. Fredric Jameson, *Postmodernism, or The Cultural Logic of Late Capitalism* (Durham, NC: Duke UP, 1991) 67.

7. Wenders freely admits how much fine art influences his filmmaking and how initially he came to filmmaking through his own painting. For example, he referred in 1989 to his early films as "paintings, but not with paints and canvas, but rather with a camera. I modelled myself more on painters than directors"; Wenders, "Die Wahrheit der Bilder" [1989], *The Act of Seeing: Texte und Gespräche* (Frankfurt am Main: Verlag der Autoren, 1992) 57. He also continues to photograph, as well to produce what he calls "electronic paintings," which include reproductions of images of "memories" and "dreams" depicted in *Until the End of the World*.

8. Rauh 248. (My translation.)

9. Oscar Wilde, "The Decay of Lying: An Observation," *Intentions* (London: Methuen, 1909) 45.

10. It is interesting that no mention is made by Wenders of Fassbinder's death in June 1982, especially as his death is commonly viewed as marking the end of New German Cinema.

11. Pier Paolo Pasolini, "Observations on the Sequence Shot" [1967], *Heretical Empiricism*, ed. Louise K. Barnett and Ben Lawton (Bloomington: Indiana UP, 1988) 236–37.

12. Walter Benjamin, "The Storyteller" [1936], *Illuminations*, trans. Harry Zohn (Great Britain: Fontana, 1973) 94–100.

13. Youssef Ishaghpour, *Cinéma contemporain: De ce côté du miroir* (Paris: Éditions de la Différence, 1986) 167—in the chapter "L'état des choses: Wenders: *Hammett, L'état des choses, Tokyo Ga*" (157–78).

14. See Susan Sontag, *On Photography* (New York: Doubleday/Anchor, 1977), which critics have quipped might have been more accurately titled *Against Photography*.

15. Jan Dawson, "An Interview with Wim Wenders," *Wim Wenders*, trans. Carla Wartenberg (New York: Zoetrope, 1976) 10. This interview was conducted in 1976.

16. Later, in *Tokyo-Ga*, Wenders asserts in a conversation with Herzog that it is in the "chaos" of Tokyo that he seeks his images.

17. See also Wenders, "Tokyo-Ga," *The Logic of Images*, trans. Michael Hofmann (London: Faber and Faber, 1991) 60. This text, which apparently served as a draft script for the film, does not always correspond exactly to the voice-over in the final version. When the film voice-over is cited, it will be noted in the main body of the text as *Tokyo-Ga*; when the written text is cited, the reference will be given in the notes. While the difference between these two texts is undoubtedly significant in other contexts, it is not necessary to take account of it here.

18. For Ozu's influence on Wenders see Kathe Geist, "West Looks East: The Influence of Yasujiro Ozu on Wim Wenders and Peter Handke," *Art Journal* 43.3 (1983): 234–39. Geist wrote her piece before Wenders made *Tokyo-Ga*.

19. This explains perhaps why Wenders turned, at least initially, to American auteurs such as Samuel Fuller and Nicholas Ray. (At one point in his career, Wenders had imagined Fritz Lang as a kind of father figure.) By instructive contrast, Fassbinder found a major source of inspiration in Douglas Sirk (or Detlef Sierck, as he was known in Germany before his emigration).

20. It is not clear what Ozu's political position was during World War II. He was sent to Singapore to make propaganda films for the Japanese regime (in 1942 his film *There Once Was a Father* won a prize for the best propaganda film). Ozu later became a soldier and eventually landed in an Allied POW camp. For contrasting views of Ozu's relationship to Japanese fascism, see Joan Mellon, *The Waves at Genji's Door: Japan through Its Cinema* (New York: Pantheon, 1976); and David Bordwell, *Ozu and the Poetics of Cinema* (Princeton: Princeton UP, 1988), esp. 282–95.

21. See in this regard Jameson's incisive critique of Wenders for not having followed through on his postmodern pretentions, and having instead ended up leading viewers "into a fantasmagoria of the perceptual fragmented present no less sombre and insulated than the classical solipsism and anomie reserved for the traditional individualistic centered subject." *The Geopolitical Aesthetic: Cinema and Space in the World System* (Bloomington: Indiana UP, 1992) 166–67.

22. These terms are (loosely) derived from Louis Althusser and Étienne Balibar, *Reading Capital*, trans. Ben Brewster (London: New Left Books, 1977) 13–40; and Althusser, *Lenin and Philosophy and Other Essays*, trans. Ben Brewster (New York: Monthly Review Press, 1971) 229–42.

23. Robert Phillip Kolker and Peter Beicken, *The Films of Wim Wenders: Cinema as Vision and Desire* (Cambridge: Cambridge UP, 1993) 89. See especially ch. 1, "The Boy with the Movie Camera: Biography, Historical Background, Student Films."

24. Wenders in his later film *Until the End of the World* "appropriates" both Ozu's main actor, Chishu Ryu, and that same Shinjuku street shot.

25. Harold Bloom, *The Anxiety of Influence* (London: Oxford UP, 1973) 15. Bloom's six categories are never completely distinct, and in Wenders's relationship to Ozu one finds contaminating evidence, say, of "Tessera" (comple-

tion of the work of the precursor) as well as of "Kenosis" (discontinuity with the precursor).

26. Dawson 8.

27. Dawson 7.

28. Jean Baudrillard, *Simulations*, trans. Paul Foss, Paul Patton, and Philip Beitchman (New York: Semiotext[e], 1983) 146.

29. This transition in Japan roughly parallels German industrialization, which, in the European context, came significantly later than in England and France. The resulting shock was recorded by many Japanese intellectuals who in the 1920s traveled and studied in Germany (where they had gone precisely because of this perceived parallel) and then returned to find a Japan they hardly recognized as it became torn between "Western" and "Eastern" values. This crisis cut across ideological lines: some were Marxists, some became Heideggerians. I am indebted to Geoff Waite for this information as well as for the upcoming Tatsumi reference on Japanese cyberpunk.

30. Barthes 27; my emphasis.

31. This moment in *Tokyo-Ga* seems to confirm a thesis about postmodernism developed by Japanese media critic Takayuki Tatsumi. Discussing the cyberpunk novels of William Gibson, Tatsumi describes what he calls "the postmodern paradox" as a situation in which "the perceiver literally becomes the perceived." He goes on to give this example: "Gibson's Chiba City may have sprung from his misperception of Japan, but it was this misperception that encouraged Japanese readers to correctly perceive the nature of postmodernist Japan. In short, the moment we perceive cyberpunk stories which misperceive Japan, we are already perceived correctly by cyberpunk." Takayuki Tatsumi, "The Japanese Reflection of Mirror Shades," *Storming the Reality Studio: A Casebook of Cyberpunk and Postmodern Science Fiction*, ed. Larry McCaffery (Durham, NC: Duke UP, 1991) 372.

32. In the park Wenders finds a group of people who "don't let the rain stop them from *being an American*" (*Tokyo-Ga*). The humor of this scene, at least for some viewers, depends on the debatable assumption (which also seems to be Wenders's) that the young Japanese are merely "imitating" things American; in fact, however, they are (also) appropriating American images (among others) of what Dick Hebdige called "counter-hegemonic style"; see *Subculture: The Meaning of Style* (London: Methuen, 1979). For some of the cultural-political implications of style in this sense see Greil Marcus, *Lipstick Traces: A Secret History of the Twentieth Century* (London: Secker and Warburg, 1989, and Cambridge: Harvard UP, 1990); and Jon Savage, *England's Dreaming: Anarchy, Sex Pistols, Punk Rock, and Beyond* (New York: St. Martins, 1992).

33. For a relevant discussion of the way carnival can function socially—often simultaneously—as rebellion and co-option, see Peter Stallybrass and Allon White, *The Politics and Poetics of Transgression* (Ithaca: Cornell UP, 1986), esp. the Introduction.

34. Compare, for example, Guy Debord's famous 1960s definition of spectacle as "capital accumulated until it becomes image." *La societé du spectacle* (Paris: Buchet-Castel, 1967), thesis 34. (The text is not paginated.)

35. Gilles Deleuze, *Cinema 1: The Movement Image* [1983], trans. Hugh Tomlinson and Barbara Habberjam (Minneapolis: U of Minnesota P, 1986) 22.
36. Rauh 248.
37. I am reminded here of Jameson's thesis that "in the postmodern, autoreferentiality can be initially detected in the way in which culture acts out its own commodification." *The Geopolitical Aesthetic* 5.
38. It should be noted that Wenders is hardly alone in his fascination with *Tokyo Story*. David Bordwell and Kristin Thompson note that it "was the first Ozu film to make a considerable impression in the West." Also interesting, in the light of Wenders's disruptive narrative technique in *Tokyo-Ga*, is Bordwell and Thompson's thesis that "instead of making narrative events the central organizing principle, Ozu tends to decenter narrative slightly. Spatial and temporal structures come forward and create their own interest. Sometimes we learn of important narrative events only indirectly; an ellipsis occurs at a crucial moment"; see *Film Art: An Introduction*, 3rd ed. (New York: McGraw-Hill, 1990) 329. Alluding again to the "determinate absence" of Ozu's wartime past and political ideology, perhaps one might say that this problematic *is* present in *Tokyo-Ga* after all—but only, paradoxically enough, indirectly through its ellipsis.
39. This allegorical connection has been pointed out often by, among others, Walter Benjamin in his *Das Passagen-Werk* [1934–1940], ed. Rolf Tiedemann (Frankfurt am Main: Suhrkamp, 1982); and Francis D. Klingender in his *Art and the Industrial Revolution* [1947], ed. and rev. Arthur Elton (Frogmore: Paladin, 1975); as well as earlier and filmically, say, by Dziga Vertov in his *Man with a Movie Camera* (1929), or by Walter Ruttmann in *Berlin, Sinfonie der Großstadt* (1927).
40. See Mike Davis, *City of Quartz: Excavating the Future in Los Angeles* (London: Verso, 1990).
41. Barthes 3.
42. See Paul Virilio, *The Lost Dimension* [1984], trans. Daniel Moschenberg (New York: Semiotext[e], 1991).
43. Wolfgang Schivelbusch, "Railroad Space and Railroad Time," *New German Critique* 14 (1978) 35.
44. Wenders, "Film Thieves" [1982], *The Logic of Images* 35.
45. Deleuze 4–5.
46. Rauh 255.
47. Bill Nichols, "Questions of Magnitude," *Documentary and the Mass Media*, ed. John Corner (London: Edward Arnold, 1986) 111.
48. On the aesthetic and political role in the cinema and elsewhere of the "as if," see Slavoj Žižek's discussions of the theories of Octave Mannoni in *For They Know Not What They Do: Enjoyment as a Political Factor* (London: Verso, 1991) 245–53.
49. "It, like the historical fiction, presents the question of how to figure the body, the structure, or present the person situated in history within a text situated as narrative"; Nichols 114.
50. The "narrator transforms the present into the past"; Pasolini 235.
51. "Tokyo-Ga" 60.

52. Raymond Bellour as cited by Stojan Pelko in "Punctum Caecum, or, Of Insight and Blindness," *Everything You Always Wanted to Know about Lacan . . . But Were Afraid to Ask Hitchcock*, ed. Slavoj Žižek (New York: Verso, 1992) 107.

53. Raymond Bellour, "Zwischen Sehen und Verstehen" [1990], in Blümlinger and Wulff 63.

54. Wenders, "Das Wahrnehmen einer Bewegung" [1988], *The Act of Seeing* 47.

55. Wenders, "Le souffle de l'ange" [1987], *The Logic of Images* 107.

56. There have been a number of meetings or encounters between Herzog and Wenders: in 1976 in Düsseldorf and in the collective essay film *Chambre 666*, and so on; indeed, these rituals have become almost filmic ritual.

57. Herzog describes the search for images in aesthetic, optical, and metaphysical terms (purity, clarity, transparency), while Wenders uses terms that are epistemological and pragmatic. Thus, speaking of Ozu, he writes: "Never before or since has the cinema been so close to its true purpose: to give an image of man in the twentieth century, *a true, valid and useful image*, in which he can not only recognize himself, but from which he can learn as well" ("Tokyo-Ga" 60). Apparently Herzog did not much like this moment in *Tokyo-Ga*. Wenders discards Herzog's type of image already in his 1975 *Wrong Move*. At the end of the film, the main protagonist goes to the top of a mountain, expecting a storm or a moving aesthetic experience—but, as his voice-over says, nothing happens.

58. Herzog seems to have at least partially realized his dream during the 1991 Gulf War when, in his *Lektionen in Finsternis*, he filmed the war-ravaged Near East against the sound track of classical, including Wagnerian, music.

59. Also cited in Anton Kaes, "History and Film: Public Memory in the Age of Electronic Dissemination," *Framing the Past: The Historiography of German Cinema and Television*, ed. Bruce A. Murray and Christopher J. Wickham (Carbondale: Southern Illinois P, 1992) 317.

60. "Tokyo-Ga" 60–61.

61. Crime and the City Solution, "The Adversary," on the motion picture sound track of *Until the End of the World*, 1991 Warner Brothers Records Inc., 9 26 707–4.

62. Rauh 240.

63. Kracauer 166–67.

64. Rauh 238. Ironically, Wenders's diatribe against MTV, and by extension the "new" television in general, is informed by the same traditionalist arguments that defenders of literature have used to attack cinema since its inception for ostensibly murdering imagination.

65. It is ironic, therefore, that after all the credits of *Tokyo-Ga* are over, those of Ozu and those of Wenders, the last words that appear on the screen are "Commissioned by Westdeutscher Rundfunk."

66. Wenders's English-language voice-over has become something of a signature in his essay films. We hear it also in *Lightning over Water, Reverse Angle*, and *Notebooks on Clothes and Cities*. Therefore, it comes as a surprise to hear Wenders's contemplative voice in his native German in *Report from Hollywood* (1982), directed by Edward Lachman.

67. Rauh 260. Wenders might well be simultaneously interested in (given the great importance for him of popular music) and distressed by (given his self-depiction as a "filmmaker" in opposition to MTV) Jacques Attali's thesis that it is music (today presumably including MTV), above all other media, that has the most right to claim to be the "herald" of future culture and political economy; *Noise: The Political Economy of Music* [1977], trans. Brian Massumi (Minnesota: U of Minnesota P, 1985).

68. In *Until the End of the World* Wenders visits all the countries that figured in his earlier films. But he also moves beyond Europe and the United States to the Australian outback. A certain primitivism is thus added into the pot.

69. Wenders, *The Act of Seeing* 198. In English translation in this volume.

70. Rauh 241.

71. "But for a filmmaker, Vermeer is the only painter there is. He's really the only one who gives you the idea that his paintings could start moving. He'd be the ultimate cameraman, the ultimate top-notch cameraman. Ozu's are the only film images I can think of on a level with Vermeer's painting" (Dawson 23). In *Until the End of the World* Wenders at one point re-creates a Vermeer painting when Claire captures the image of the daughter and granddaughter. For important discussions of the problematic relationship between film and painting (though not about Wenders specifically), see the anthology *Cinéma et peinture: Approches*, ed. Raymond Bellour (Paris: Presses Universitaires de France, 1990).

72. It is true that he had attempted to mix the two media in *Lightning over Water*; however, the end result was technologically cruder, and one is not sure to what degree financial constraints may have dictated the use of video. In any case, it was not yet integrated into his filmic theory and practice.

73. See Wenders, "High Definition" [Tokyo, 1990], *The Act of Seeing* 94–99. In English translation in this volume.

Angels, Fiction, and History in Berlin: *Wings of Desire*

ROGER F. COOK

As in the case of *The State of Things* (1982), the idea for *Wings of Desire* originated while Wenders was working on another film. In 1981 the pause came in the midst of Wenders's most frustrating experiences with the American film industry: between the two shootings of *Hammett*. Drawing from his own immediate experiences as a European filmmaker in Hollywood, he addresses in *The State of Things* the difficulty the director and filmwriter face in maintaining their personal artistic vision when working within the system of profit-oriented Hollywood film production. The German director Friedrich Munro and the scriptwriter Dennis run up against the Hollywood producer's attempts to control the final film product before the filmmaking even begins. In Wenders's own experience making *Hammett*, the producer Francis Ford Coppola experimented with a computerized video version of the complete film (as did the producer in *The State of Things*) that was to serve as a model for the shooting. The attempt ended with the script, and almost the computer as well, flying out the window.[1]

Wings of Desire is not, of course, about the filmmaking process, but the lessons Wenders learned in America help explain its unique composition. Wenders has stated that in making *The State of Things* he worked

Originally published in *The Germanic Review* 46.1 (Winter 1991):34–47. Reprinted with permission of the Helen Dwight Reid Educational Foundation. Published by Heldref Publications, 1319 18th Street N.W., Washington, DC 20036-1802. Copyright 1991.

through his conviction that each film should reflect its own place within a certain tradition of filmmaking. He became less concerned with critical self-reflexivity and more intent on making films that through the strength of their story and narrative form work against the grain of contemporary dominant cinema.[2] In his work on *Hammett* Wenders learned that in order to make such films the filmmaker needed to oppose the forces of the film industry at every stage of the project. The intensive negotiations and preparations during the production work for *Hammett* predetermined too rigidly what the film would be and how the director should shoot it. Coppola, acting on behalf of Orion Studios, radically altered the script by Tom Pope so that it better conformed to the conventional Hollywood detective genre. Yet Wenders knew that his experiences with Coppola were only the tip of an ominous iceberg. The American film industry was becoming almost exclusively interested in existing or "prefabricated" story lines that are already known to the public and which would fill both the audience's expectations and the network of mainstream commercial movie theaters throughout the country.[3]

The lesson Wenders learned from the making of *Hammett* concerns, however, not only interference by the producer and the studio. He came away with the conviction that the original concept for the film should remain open so that during the filmmaking the director can discover and incorporate into the film new images and ways of seeing. Perhaps more so than in his other films, Wenders remained true to this principle—which he later referred to as his "Arbeitsmethode" for the film[4]—in the making of *Wings of Desire*. Certainly in his road movies of the 1970s, particularly *Alice in the Cities* and *Kings of the Road*, he left himself considerable leeway for the shooting of individual scenes. But with his new resolve to tell stories, it became more difficult to balance the advantages of an open, evolutionary filmmaking method against the need to plan the narrative.

The inspiration for *Wings of Desire* came in 1985 when Wenders returned to Berlin to work on the long-standing film project *Until the End of the World*. As it became obvious that the preparations for this film would take up to another two years, after a gap of already three years since his last filming, Wenders felt the need to get behind the camera again. After living outside Germany for most of ten years, he returned with open eyes and aroused curiosity.[5] Sensing the importance of Berlin both as a bridge to the past and as a pivotal city for peaceful coexistence in the world,[6] he arrived at the idea for the film: angels living in Berlin preserve the memory and even presence of Germany's history, while helping the inhabitants bear the burden of their nation's past.

Realizing that an effective poetic language would be essential for the angels' speech, he turned to Peter Handke for a script. Handke agreed to write a number of dialogues based on the story, on the conditions that the film would evolve extemporaneously ("ein Film, 'den man aus dem Ärmel schüttelt'")[7] and that he would not have to come up with a complete script. This offer fell neatly into place with Wenders's approach to the film. As Wenders began planning out a succession of scenes, Handke worked on the dialogues and sent them on as he completed them. By the time he began receiving the scripts, Wenders was far along in his preparations for the shooting. He soon realized that because of the separate input the film was in danger of becoming too amorphous. Acknowledging that Handke's dialogues followed a single concept more consistently than his own arrangement of shots and scenes, Wenders let them serve as the guiding light ("Leuchtturm")[8] as the film evolved. Each evening he met with his coworkers, often late into the night, to work out the details for the next day's shooting, and only occasionally as far ahead as the following day.

Given this course of inception, it comes as no surprise that the final product departs in some ways from the original concept. In his work notes or "Treatment" for the film, Wenders wrote that if he had to give a preliminary summary of the story, it would go something like this: "God, angered by mankind's inability to learn from the past, was about to leave humanity on its own in 1945, some of the angels intervened, pleading that mankind should have one more chance to redeem itself. Angered by this intervention, God banished these angels from heaven, exiling them to the desolation of Berlin in 1945. There they were doomed only to observe the follies of human existence, unable to intervene in the course of events."[9] However, in the film this woeful plight of the angels in Berlin does not dominate the story in the way that the original sketch suggests. Although *Wings of Desire* does not offer a cheerful portrait of the city or its inhabitants, it is also neither depressing nor pessimistic. Quite to the contrary, it generates pleasure and gives, as the English title suggests, wings to desire.

Due, I think, to both this open form of filmmaking as well as to his commitment to narrative, *Wings of Desire* became much more than the film Wenders originally had in mind. From a love story set in a Berlin inhabited by fallen angels, it evolved into a film that investigates the role narrative plays in the formation both of individual identity and of the national identity of psychically scarred Germany. Moreover, the film suggests that contemporary cinema needs a new form of epic narrative in order to participate in this process of identity formation.

In my analysis of the film, I will first chart how the film's aesthetic strategies and, in particular, the techniques employed to create the angels' point of view situate the viewing subject within the filmic discourse differently from dominant cinema. Then I will argue that Wenders incorporates into the story of Damiel and Marion his conviction that, within a sea of textuality, narrative provides the individual a lifeline to authentic needs and desires. *Wings of Desire* offers such a narrative, one that is to give wings to desire in the spectator while at the same time involving the audience in an analysis of desire in cinematic narrative. In the final section I will show how Wenders's call for a new narrative relates to the city of Berlin and the German history it embodies. In this connection the film speaks not just to problems of recent German history, but to the concept of historical perspective itself.

Suture and the Desire for Narrative

Using the concept of "suture," film theory explains narrative closure not just in terms of the film and its formal construction but rather as a process of drawing in and enclosing the viewing subject in the film's textual system. The filmic concept stems from Lacan's account of how in the individual psyche a coherent, unified subject is "sutured" within a symbolic order structured by desire and governed by language. By applying this basic operation of identity formation to the cinematic apparatus, psychoanalytic approaches to cinema have provided insight into the emotional and psychological processes that motivate the spectator's investment in a narrative. Beginning with Jean-Pierre Oudart's article "La suture,"[10] the writers associated with *Cahiers du cinéma* introduced suture into film theory. In the mid-1970s the concept began to play a major role in the theoretical discussions in Britain and North America, with the result that psychoanalytic studies of the viewing subject have proliferated. In my reading of *Wings of Desire* I borrow from several theoreticians of suture, including some who have been at odds with each other concerning the scope and consequence of this concept.

Although my reading of *Wings of Desire* certainly owes much to the French scholars, claims I make concerning Wenders's film run counter to the original polemical thrust of their work. For them, suture denotes the operation by which cinema encloses the subject in an ideology. Their analysis bears upon dominant or classical Hollywood cinema, and they restrict the scope of suture to the ideological effacement of the cinematic code. They are reductive as well with respect to the semiotic system of suturing, positing at times the shot/reverse-shot system or point-of-view cutting as *the* fundamental cinematic articulation of suture. Other French film theoreticians who complement a general semiotics of cinema with Lacanian notions of the subject and signification, such as Christian Metz and Jean-Louis Baudry, have avoided such a rigid application of suture to the cinematic apparatus, arriving nevertheless at the even more pessimistic conclusion that cinema itself functions as a support and instrument of ideology.[11]

Anglo-American film scholars have expanded on these psychoanalytic theories of cinema without sharing their negative assessment of the basic cinematic apparatus.[12] However, such challenges to the original French position on cinema and ideology have pertained for the most part only to films that resist closure and foreground lack and alienation. Thomas Elsaesser's 1980 article on Fassbinder is an important example of such criticism in the area of German cinema. Focusing on Fassbinder but also claiming relevance for New German Cinema in general (mentioning by name Herzog, Wenders, Syberberg, and Kluge), Elsaesser responds to the more radical conclusions drawn by Baudry and Metz. He rejects their implication that "the cinema is indeed an 'invention without a future' because it systematically ties the spectator to a regressive state, in an endless circuit of substitution and fetishization."[13]

Nevertheless, both suture and narrative closure of any kind have remained ideologically suspect. *Wings of Desire* provides an excellent opportunity to reexamine the bias that, in the wake of Oudart and his successors, persists against identification and narrative (closure). In the discussion of suture, the emphasis has been on those processes of identification that position the viewing subject within the filmic discourse so as to conceal enunciation. For this reason, theoreticians of suture have focused heavily on classical editing strategies. The term itself is particularly well suited to dominant cinematic narrative because the filmmaker, at least in most productions of dominant cinema, stitches together a series of partial disclosures with the intention of concealing their discontinuity and disjunctures. The camera is unable to disclose the desired perspectives on the story without cutting and splicing, but classical editing techniques also intentionally limit the camera's potential to "see." The constant breaks in the camera's vision produce a sense of deprivation and stir a longing in the spectator to see more, to have more disclosed. The subject, made aware of its inadequacy, seeks a secure position in the filmic discourse that conceals the lack.[14]

As the basic operation of subject formation in the individual, suture is always occurring in the viewing subject and thus, in some manner, within the cinematic apparatus that envelops the spectator.[15] However, I propose to show that the textual system in *Wings of Desire* sets the conditions for suture differently than do narrative films of dominant cinema. Not only is the investment of desire motivated less by lack and anxiety, but when narrative closure occurs the sutured subject maintains more autonomy from any invisible, transcendental Other that controls the power of enunciation.

As is usually the case in Wenders's films, in *Wings of Desire* the camera follows, at least during the black-and-white part of the film, the protagonist, and in this case both the main figure, Damiel, and, to a lesser extent, his companion angel, Cassiel. Because the protagonists are angels, Wenders had to establish a radically new point of view for the camera, one unique not only to his own work but to cinematic narrative in general. Locating the camera as the eye of an angel presented constant challenges during the shooting and resulted in innovative solutions, particularly in terms of the camera movement, which was to give the illusion of unlimited movement through space and time.[16] It also altered dramatically the emotional interaction between the spectator and the film. Instead of intentionally arousing anxiety, the film puts the spectator at ease. In part, the camera's consistent look from the point of view of the angels creates this effect, but Wenders has maintained that even more important than all the camera movement was the effort to create a benevolent look ("einen liebevollen Blick") for the eye of the camera.[17]

On another level, the angels' point of view limits the system of interdiegetic looks in a way that enhances the viewing subject's sense of security. The initial shot/reverse-shot sequence occurs with Damiel, complete with wings, standing on the tower of the Gedächtniskirche. From his perspective we see a young girl below who has stopped in the middle of the crowded crosswalk and is looking up at him while the adults go about their business without seeing him. This shot and the subsequent ones of the two girls on the bus and the child on the airplane establish that the protagonist is invisible except to children and angels. The unthreatened and nonthreatening looks the children direct at the angels, many of them directly into the camera, mirror the benevolence in the look of the angels. The limited visibility of the angels exposes the viewing subject, who has assumed Damiel's point of view, only to such harmless looks, providing shelter from the often critical or even malicious looks of mature humans. Moreover, after this first shot/reverse shot that establishes the visibility of the observer angels, Wenders avoids point-of-view cutting for the black-and-white part of the film in which Damiel remains an angel.

The technical measures needed to establish the camera as the eye of the angels contribute to the spectator's feeling of security, while also creating a unique relationship between the viewing subject and the transcendental point of view that unifies the images into a "film." Baudry argues that the relationship between the camera and the subject determines the nature of the transcendental self,[18] that illusory unity in a filmic discourse that constitutes the spectator as a coherent "subject" in its own image. In dominant cinema the cuts between different points of view are pieced together so as to generate an "ideal *picture*"[19] of the film as reality. In *Wings of Desire* Wenders shot predominantly from a single point of view, employing long takes and extensive camera movement to establish the narrative space normally achieved by editing together different point-of-view shots. The very nature of the angelic point of view already implies the transcendental position that in dominant cinematic discourse must be sutured out of successive moments of primary and secondary identification (the basic two-step shot/reverse-shot sequencing in point-of-view cutting). From the beginning the spectator identifies primarily[20] with the transcendental point of view secured for him or her, assuming at times a perspective identical to Damiel's, at other times one similarly defined but independent of his. The moment of lack, the knowledge that the camera perspective implies an "Absent One" who must appear in the frame (e.g., in the reverse shot) and fill in for the absence, is thus minimalized in *Wings of Desire*.

Although the beginning scenes clearly align the spectator with Damiel's point of view, the film offers at the same time a degree of freedom to go along with this identification. With the aid of Henri Alekan, the octogenarian cinematographer who cut his teeth in the 1920s working with Eugene Schüfftan, Wenders produces a free-floating camera, a modern version of the "unchained camera" ("entfesselte Kamera") introduced by F. W. Murnau.[21] In the sequence that begins in the airplane, Wenders utilizes the mobile camera to establish the angelic point of view of the protagonist. From the aisle of the airplane approaching Berlin, the camera assumes Damiel's point of view as he turns away from the passengers to look out the window of the plane. After an aerial shot of Berlin, the camera frees itself from the confines of the plane, moves through the clouds, passes the radio tower looming over Berlin, picking up a few seconds of the broadcast as it passes, and descends across the freeway toward the adjoining apartment buildings. The illusion of no physical limitations clearly identifies the camera lens with the vision of angels. As the camera moves freely through the walls of the apartments, the motion remains fluid and seamless, even when the rooms are obviously not next to each other. Throughout the film the camera moves with the spatial—both vertical and horizontal—and temporal freedom of the ethereal angels. It ascends effortlessly onto Victoria's winged shoulder atop the *Siegessäule* and on into the skies above Berlin; it travels back in time with Damiel and Cassiel to view the prehistoric Berlin landscape; and it transverses the physical, but also psychic, barrier that splits apart the divided *Hauptstadt* of the German nation. The conscious assumption of the angels' point of view reduces the need for successive, complementary shots. In fact, the elated feeling gained in the most fluid moments of the unchained camera recall Oudart's equation of the initial shot, prior to the awareness of the restricting frame lines, with "the field of *jouissance*."[22] Particularly the initial sequences of the angels' movements give the sense that such frame lines do not exist or are continually receding from the look of the spectator.

Yet even if the Absent One loses its power over the viewing subject, other dominant forms of secondary identification take hold and provide positions of representational unity. British and American theoreticians, building on the work of the French, have stressed how narrative closes over the lack and inadequacies that surface in the sutured viewing subject.[23] Kaja Silverman describes how the gaze of the spectator tends to link itself to the gaze of a fictional character who promises more control over the fragmented series of images. Typically, one or more fictional characters within the diegesis are endowed with the controlling and enunciating powers of the Other outside the fiction, so as to provide an anchor for the spectator's point of view and, also potentially, to conceal the enunciating moment outside the film. Usually when the spectator seeks out a figure in the diegesis with enunciatory, controlling powers for a "stand-in" relationship, he or she relinquishes to some extent the authority to organize and structure the film images into a story.[24]

In *Wings of Desire* the viewing subject clearly situates itself parallel to Damiel and Cassiel. The angels lack, however, precisely that power of authorship and enunciation that characterizes the typical stand-in point of view. In the first dialogue between Damiel and Cassiel they pull out their notebooks and exchange recent observations on out-of-the-ordinary yet uneventful occurrences in Berlin: "When the train pulled into the Zoo subway station, the conductor called out 'Fireland' instead of the name of the station. . . . A woman passing by who closed up her umbrella while it was raining and let herself get wet. . . . A pupil who described to his teacher how a fern grows out of the earth, and the astonished teacher . . ."[25] Because these simple events are defamiliarized—that is, they stand alone outside of their normal context in everyday existence—each points to a whole life story of epic proportions that lies behind it. But the angels can only observe and record them as isolated incidents and are unable to place them in a larger narrative context in which they would gain a particular significance. As angels, they are endowed with a universal vision of human existence in the present and back into the past, but they lack a past of their own and thus any individual investment in the future. They can neither write history nor tell stories. While Damiel, who is beginning to feel the pull of existence, bemoans this, Cassiel accepts it as their place in the world:

> Damiel: It's so wonderful just to live a spiritual existence and from day to day to attest for all eternity to that which is purely spiritual in people—but sometimes my eternal existence becomes too much for me. (19)

> Cassiel: To remain alone! To let things happen! To remain earnest! We can be wild only to the extent that we remain earnest and unconditioned ["unbedingt ernst"]. To do nothing else but observe, collect, testify, authenticate, preserve! To remain spirit! To remain apart! To remain in words! (21)

They exist detached from mankind without any stake in what happens ("unbedingt"). Nor can they influence human life ("To let things happen!"), except for their ability to offer a modicum of consolation. Fixed in this form of existence, they lack in every sense the controlling voice and power of the author.

As long as the camera maintains strictly the angels' point of view, the viewing subject retains a certain amount of autonomy from the narrativization process. *Wings of Desire* fosters this sense of autonomy in the spectator by delaying narrative closure until the viewing subjects have begun to relish their maneuverability and depend on their own faculty for creating stories. Because the primary forms of identification discussed above quell the anxious urgency to be sutured within a closed narrative, the spectator can revel in the fragmentary, open scenes as the camera moves through Berlin picking up seemingly arbitrary scenes out of everyday life as well as snippets of interior monologue. Nevertheless, the spectator tends to become irritated as this free-floating position, without anchor in a controlling narrative, persists. This does indeed occur, I think, in the first third of the film. The spectator conditioned by dominant cinema becomes restless, impatient for the narrative control to assert itself. In this way, the film arouses in the viewing subject a desire for narrative, which it then foregrounds in the story of Damiel's entry into human existence. Thus, with respect to the spectator's expectations and desires, the sense of autonomy from narrative is an illusion from the beginning.

Also, the impression during the early part of the film that there is no controlling narrative unifying the various scenes and images is deceptive. For as soon as Damiel senses the urge to experience physical existence, his look loses its objective distance and the film story begins to unfold—before we as spectators are aware of it. Marion, despite her affinities to Damiel, appears first as just another figure encountered by chance in the wanderings through Berlin. Her long interior monologue, which begins with her on the trapeze and continues until the climactic color image in the trailer, reveals how interlocked she and Damiel are by their desires. In this first encounter her thoughts suggest the leitmotiv refrain, "When the child was a child," which at the beginning of the film Damiel had already repeated several times in voice-over: "When the child was a child, I wanted to live on an island. A woman alone, sovereign, alone" (44). But only much later, during the dream sequence, does she speak a complete stanza of the voice-over poem. Throughout the initial sequence with Marion, desires build in Damiel and subconsciously in the spectator as well. The camera remains objective, with both Damiel and Marion included in most of the shots, until she begins to take off her costume. Damiel, who in the foreground of the frame has had his back to her, turns while the camera moves in to assume his subjective point of view and looks down over her bare shoulder. First the one hand comes into view, stroking along her neck and shoulder; then the camera turns with Damiel's look to view the left hand holding the stone that he has picked up in her trailer and is now turning over repeatedly in his hand, as if trying to come to a decision. Both these actions recall his first conversation with Cassiel in the Kudamm automobile showroom, where he had expressed his longing to experience the sensation of weight or to be moved by the graceful form of a neckline. During this sequence Marion's interior voice echoes Damiel's desire as it has been captured in the camera: "I only have to be ready, and every man in the world will gaze at me. Longing. Longing for a wave of love that rises up in me" (49). Damiel's hand pulls back out of the frame, and the camera retreats to a full shot of Marion sitting on the bed. For a few seconds the image turns to color, not only signaling Damiel's arousal to sensuality but also arousing the same longing in the spectator.

This first scene with Marion serves to extend the identification with the angelic perspective to the realm of desire. The significance of this scene for the film story becomes evident once one has seen the entire film, but in the course of the initial viewing Damiel's desire remains apart from any narrative scenario. Wenders has asserted that "in a way she [Marion] is the leading character, as she is the only human being in it from the beginning."[26] Based on my viewing of the film, I doubt whether Marion assumes for the spectator, at least consciously, such a central role in the narrative until much later. Apparently, this is due less to Wenders's intentions than to the way the film's structure evolved during the shooting. Even after Marion's voice-over expression of intimate fears and desires, the spectator remains uncertain whether Marion will play a more involved role in the film or will remain just another one of those figures whose paths chance to cross with that of the angels. After the trailer scene, the film returns to its fascination with the diverse observations from the angels' point of view. A long sequence of wanderings through East and West Berlin follows the scene in the trailer. The dying motorcyclist, the old narrator reading in the library and seeking the Potsdamer Platz, the prostitute on the street, the chauffeured drive through Berlin of both the present and 1945, the extended sequence with Peter Falk on location—all intervene before Damiel takes his angel companion Cassiel with him to the afternoon circus performance. Another such long sequence occurs before he then returns for the third encounter with Marion at the evening performance.

While Damiel slowly moves toward his decision "to leap into the stream," the desire for a narrative wells up in the spectator. The trailer scene aligns the erotic desire for Marion not only with Damiel's longing to enter the physical realm, but also with the spectator's need to become invested emotionally in a fictional world. This occurs even while the desire for a narrative is growing. For just as Damiel's quest for Marion had begun long before he becomes flesh and blood, so the spectator becomes firmly engaged in a cinematic story line before the film shifts permanently to color and assumes a linear narrative structure. Still, the fragments of dialogue and interior monologue encountered haphazardly in the extraneous wanderings through Berlin reinforce a more autonomous involvement in the narrative development. Because these texts stand alone, outside of any unifying narrative context, the spectator gains some freedom from the cognitive impulse to explain the significance of every shot or spoken text in the film. At one point it becomes impossible to fit all the text fragments into a comprehensive whole that provides each of its parts with a specific, clearly deducible significance.

Although they are apparently only coincidentally encountered verbal acts, the conversations, the overheard thoughts, or the passages read in the library spur the spectator—even in the fleeting moment before the next text —to start piecing together the story of each "extra." These repeated beginnings activate the audience's participation in constructing the narrative. As in other Wenders movies, particularly the purer road movies like *Alice in the Cities* and *Kings of the Road*, the spectator must complete the film by adding personal experiences and associations. Wenders has stated that this is the kind of movie he himself likes and the kind he wants to make: "I really don't like so much the sort of movie where it's all spread out and you really just sit there and it's poured over you and you have no choice: you see what they want you to see."[27] In a fashion similar to his road movies, the spectator experiences along with the protagonist(s) and creates the film from a never identical, but always comparable, point of view. However, because in *Wings of Desire* the camera becomes the eyes (and ears) of an angel, the visual and verbal texts flow by at a speed that does not allow the spectator even to pick up all of them, much less to form out of them one big story. Nor do the angels produce a narrative out of the stream of history, for this is not *their* domain but that of humans. Eventually the spectator must give in, not to prepackaged cinematic narrative of the type Wenders abhors, but rather to the flow itself. The spectator who does not become frustrated by this overload is compelled to sit back and let the words flow past, content with picking up those lyrical fragments that strike up a meaningful chord. In this manner the film generates between itself and the spectator a relaxed relationship, but one charged with needs, those expressed by the downtrodden Berliners and shared in a personal way by the spectator, and with the growing desire, in Damiel and in the spectator, to be anchored in a story.

The choice of individual texts within the flow of voice-over seems arbitrary, at least with respect to their function for the overall narrative structure. But on another level these texts reflect on Wenders's aesthetic strategies in a quite intricate manner. Above all, we detect the filmmaker's intentions in the thoughts of Homer, the mournful old Berliner who represents the archetypal epic narrator. In the first scene in the library, Damiel strolls through the aisles, overhearing the silent reading of seventeen quite varied texts, until he encounters Homer climbing the stairs. As the aged storyteller pauses to catch his breath on the landing, we hear his thoughts:

173

"My listeners have in time become readers, and they no longer sit together in a circle, but rather individually, and one knows nothing about the other" (30). His lamentation reflects not his own desire for gratification but rather the needs of the readers. Only in the library do we see angels other than Damiel and Cassiel, and here they are numerous, all actively consoling the isolated readers. On one hand, this peaceful temple for the preservation of books and the solace of reading, the modern and bright Berlin public library, serves as a home and refuge for the angels. Wenders indicated that the idea for the library scenes stemmed from the end of Truffaut's *Fahrenheit 451*, where the preservers of knowledge and culture wander through an idyllic park, each reciting a book while committing it to memory.[28] Although the library setting provides a refuge for the angels, Homer's words suggest that the relationship in our contemporary world between reader and text is deficient with regard to individual needs and desires. The readers sit isolated from each other, and the texts they read are fragments of an ever-expanding body of knowledge that overwhelms the individual and thwarts attempts to find a larger meaning in our existence.

For Wenders, film has become the contemporary medium for a narrative that can create new myths. Homer, who complains in a later scene that as the archetypal epic narrator he has been stripped of his voice, regains his important role in the film. Ironically, however, he is no longer the narrative voice itself, but rather he speaks the self-referential commentary on the need for a new narrative form. In his thoughts on the landing Homer reassures himself that an age-old narrative still strikes up of its own accord out of the depths, with the narrator functioning only as its mouthpiece, not its creator. He describes such a text as "a liturgy for which no one has to be initiated into the meaning of the words and sentences" (31). This describes how the film and the narrative it envisions differ from the discursive practice encountered in the library. There the reader steeped in conventional hermeneutical methods struggles to grasp the meaning of the text, to place it in relation to a world of meaning that lies outside it. The concrete or poetical presence of the text is abandoned for the world behind it. In keeping with Homer's account, *Wings of Desire* itself comprises a liturgy of freely flowing images and texts whose rhapsodical enchantment eases the ingrained resolve to get at what the film means. Also, texts have at times a similar effect on figures within the diegesis. At one point Damiel actually performs a liturgy that leads the inner voice of a dying motorcyclist away from his fear of death and into a stream of isolated experiences, phrases, or concepts:

As I was going up the mountain and sun came out of the fog in the valley
The fire on the edge of the cow pasture

174

The potatoes in the ashes
The boathouse far away on the lake
The far East
The high North
The Wild West. (52–53)

This liturgy stills the fear of death by restoring in some way contact to an authentic, almost primordial level of existence.

The thrust of the film is not, however, simply to defamiliarize in this way everyday experiences. Rather, both the film story and the voice-over comments suggest repeatedly that a narrative context is necessary to impart meaning to isolated moments of existence. Although motivated by different pasts, both Damiel and Marion are searching for a life story or individual vision that can sustain them. The key to their dual quest, and thus to the film itself, lies in their ability to form out of their experiences a life story that accommodates their own needs and desires. The first step to such an authentic, unappropriated narrative entails taking language and images out of their predominant contexts and stripping them of the significance they usually carry. The film itself performs this function for the spectator as well, in that throughout the first half and more of the film we see everything through the eyes of the angels, who only observe and record from a standpoint outside the world of human interests. In order to actually give flight to their desires, Damiel and Marion must take the second step and regroup the defamiliarized fragments of their existence into their individual life stories and, within the context of their love story, into a shared life story as well. Thus the main film story of Damiel's "fall" raises the question of the integral role narrative plays in human existence, while the filmic creation of the angels' point of view involves the spectator in both the desire for a narrative context and the contextual freedom for beginning anew.

Narrative and the Textuality of Desire

The desire for narrative generated in the first half of *Wings of Desire* has its roots in Wenders's experiences as a filmmaker. During his work in America Wenders came to the conclusion that a new narrative cinema must establish itself against the growing dominance of industry-produced films. In 1982, while finishing up the last editing on *Hammett*, he addressed this problem in *Reverse Angle*, a short film made for French television. Including shots from American television, typical advertising images, and some scenes of the editing work on *Hammett*, he documents how predominantly media-produced images and perspectives increasingly dominate not only the filmmaker but the public vision itself. He explains how this awareness led to a fundamental change in his own filmmaking. No longer able to trust images to stand on their own, he had to find stories that through the strength of their constructed (narrative) context give the film images a new meaning over and against the dominant, media-induced way of seeing them.

At that time he remained skeptical about the potential of narrative cinema. He felt that neither European cinema nor the auteur filmmaker has been able to produce more than isolated subjective stories, whereas the need has become greater for an alternative collective filmmaking in opposition to Hollywood. For Wenders, the great classical American cinema of the past had created a form of collective narrative capable of creating life-sustaining myths. He felt that in response to a Hollywood now under the control of a self-propagating media industry, filmmakers would have to work toward a new collective cinema with roots in both authentic individual experience and the age-old traditions of epic narrative. Already in 1982, well before he had conceived of *Wings of Desire*, Wenders had begun to focus on Homer and his epic narrative as a model for the role stories would play in his future films: "Telling film stories is a way of evoking recollection and, by virtue of the form, bringing an order to the cacophony of impressions. The need for stories since Homer, whom I am now reading, is as well the need to hear that one can discover a coherence in diverse impressions. Such a need exists because people actually experience very little coherence in their lives."[29] In the same interview, he asserted the commitment to narrative filmmaking that led first to *Paris, Texas* and then to *Wings of Desire*: "I want to develop a narrative cinema which avidly and with self-confidence establishes a connection between film art and life. . . . So that one does not simply turn over cinema to the big spectacle films, rather takes up the challenge confidently and tells stories—without regrets or without resort to the wonderful film stories that once abounded in cinema. A fresh start in film narrative, that's my goal."

Wings of Desire does indeed envelop the spectator in a unifying context, but in the course of this narrativization it also opens up to scrutiny the discursive act of narrative closure. The central story itself, Damiel's abandonment of his spiritual existence as angel and his entry into the stream of history, represents allegorically the role narrative plays for Wenders. When Damiel becomes flesh and blood the film begins to resemble a typical romance. The love story that has Damiel and Marion searching for each other stands as a diegesis of its own within the film. The wandering continues but becomes twofold, taking on purpose and direction. Even Marion, who, as she confides to Peter Falk, "knows nothing" about the man she is seeking, begins as well to move unswervingly toward the dramatic rendezvous. The spectator, whose look in the first part of the film had coincided with that of Damiel's in a more freely associative way, now becomes involved in a more conventional process of suture. Nonetheless, the viewing subject, conditioned by the autonomous stand-in position assumed up to this point, acts not out of anxiety but rather is moved by shared desires. The change to color stock enhances the sensual pleasure and the identification with the characters' desires, at the same time signaling that the film has begun to conform more to the structures of conventional linear narrative. The evolving narrative reflects itself as cinematic love story at every step, without becoming self-parody, even when the climactic scene—from the lavishly decorated barroom, including a bucket of champagne on the bar, to Marion's passionately red dress and matching lipstick—says to the spectator at every turn, "This is a romantic scene in a movie." Thus the film both draws attention to the way desire is generated in cinema and also induces the spectator to take the investment of desire seriously.

The film also, even after it has become a romantic narrative, eschews the male-female roles of the conventional love story. Marion's voice-overs give the audience access to her innermost subjectivity and dispel the mystique that typically shrouds the female inner world. When the circus packs up and leaves we see Marion, in obvious juxtaposition to the fictional persona of the beautiful trapeze artist, as an ordinary person in unassuming dress. Particularly in the scene with Peter Falk at the *Wurst* stand she comes across neither as a circus beauty nor as a movie star, but rather as demystified woman, as an individual in a common, everyday context. Damiel as well, even at the height of the romantic fiction, never falls into the role of the typical male lead in a romance. Even though his search for Marion is his only goal once he becomes human, Damiel does not act like the love-struck male obsessed with a woman. Although the "bewitched" male of a love story often has difficulty functioning normally or even loses his hold on reality, Damiel remains wide awake to the world, eager to perceive and experience as much as he can with his newly gained senses. Nor is this the story of a fallen angel, one seduced out of a pure spiritual world into the realm of the senses. Even on the morning after they have consummated their love, Damiel's choice stands as the gateway to an inspiring and rewarding journey. The negativity embodied by the woman in the male-female relationship, which often exists as subtext even in the love story with happy ending, does not appear in *Wings of Desire* at all.

The departure from conventional patterns of romance corresponds to the object of desire that motivates both Marion and Damiel. She exhibits the same desire that leads Damiel to cast his lot with mankind. At the end of the closing-night party at the circus, she expresses her resolve to keep alive a guiding narrative informed by her own desires: "Simply to be able to say, as I am now: 'I am joyful.' I have a story ["Geschichte" = story or history]! And I will continue to have one!" (110). She utters these words in response to an internal crisis spawned by the closing of the circus and the loss of the fictional role of the beautiful woman on the flying trapeze. Her identity crisis peaks as she sits at her dressing table in front of the three-paneled mirror before her final performance. There she asserts, "Sometimes the only thing that matters: to be beautiful, and nothing else" (98). In a wording that recalls an enduring figure of the German screen, the self-contained femme fatale of *The Blue Angel*,[30] Marion reveals how the fictional persona of the trapeze artist provides an anchor for her desires and needs. It is Marion's longing for her own self-sustaining story that attracts Damiel to her and ultimately inspires him to become human. When Damiel first encountered her she had just lost the fictive role of angel that had enabled her to share such desires with the circus spectators.

The love story climaxes in Marion's speech to Damiel, the moment Wenders has called "the climax of the whole film."[31] Her words, and just the act of the woman speaking them in this context, not only break with the patterns of male-female speech in dominant cinema[32] but also counteract more familiar processes of suture that might have begun. Although during the first half of the film Wenders had secured an alternative space for the viewing subject, as the spectator gets drawn into the love story conventional patterns of identification begin to form. After Damiel becomes human the narrative provides a sheltered, invisible, and more familiar position within the diegesis, one that effaces the affirmative, active, and self-aware viewing subject generated earlier. The encounter in the barroom undoes this conventional suture dramatically. The camera reflects the gaze of the spectator back at the intercinematic system of gazes and desires at work both within and outside the diegesis. During Marion's final monologue the camera catches in successive close-ups of the lovers' faces the intense gaze into the other's eyes. In direct violation of a cardinal rule of classical cinema, the gaze as well as the words of the final two speeches are directed simultaneously at the other and at the spectator. Their eyes do not look past the lens into the eyes of the other next to the camera, but rather directly into the camera. As the spectator is situated alternately in the place of the man and the woman, the viewing subject becomes acutely aware of the look focused on it. The invisibility granted the viewing subject via suture in Hollywood cinema is destroyed.[33]

As the one who at the climactic moment in the love story puts the significance of their relationship into words, Marion takes control of her life (story) and becomes at the same time the figure in the diegesis endowed with the powers of authorial enunciation. During the successive close-ups her words comment on how cinema draws the spectator into its sphere: "Not only the whole city, the whole world is taking part in our decision at this moment. The two of us are now more than just two. We embody something. We are standing in the world arena, and the whole arena is full of people who want the same thing we do. We are conducting play for everyone!" (162). Her words here provide insight into the relationship at that very moment between the spectator and the fictional figures in *Wings of Desire*. Just as Marion and Damiel are gazing into the eyes of the other who signifies their desire, we the spectators gaze at the film and find our look and our desire mirrored by the camera. No longer are just the two intradiegetic players involved in the play; rather, the reciprocal close-ups create a triad of looks that includes the audience. Also, the locus for the scene, "the world arena" as Marion calls it, extends outside the narrative or intradiegetic space and encompasses all those who view the film (and is not restricted to just those in the theater at that moment). It is a space in between the narrative projected on the screen and the physical presence of the audience, and one charged with the desires of both the fictional film figures and the spectators in the theater.

What Marion, Damiel, and the spectator share is the need for a life-sustaining fiction. Marion's struggle for identity reflects this need, but it is also at the very heart of the main event in the film story—Damiel's crossover into mankind. When Cassiel, after his jaunt together with Damiel back into history, asks whether he really intends to become human, Damiel replies: "Yes. Going to secure a past, a story of my own" (84). In the context of the film story we understand that because of his belated birth he must invent a background for himself. But in the larger thematic context, this refers to the personal need for one's own life history as well as to the fictionality involved in any version of history. Life as a human differs from the free-floating spiritual existence of the angels not only because of its grounding in a specific concrete physical past, but also because our vision or story of that past is what motivates our decisions and shapes our future. When Damiel enters history, the story of his past begins to determine his life, even if it is a purely fictional creation. For this reason, I do not agree with Wenders's remark in an interview that Peter Falk's reference to his grandmother was completely out of place.[34] The references to a grandmother who logically cannot exist do not disturb the spectator in the least, not because the entire story suspends realistic expectations, but rather because human existence would dictate that he create his own life story with a past.

Yet Damiel does not pursue a life story of his own only in order to complement his physical existence. Rather, from the very beginning it is his desire to live in the state of human fictionality/textuality that leads him to "leap into the stream" of physical existence. He does not succumb to the lure of sensual pleasures; rather, he is attracted to the stream of images in the human world of representations. As Damiel proclaims in the final monologue, spoken while Marion performs the figure of the siren on the rope above him, their desire has conceived not a mortal child, but an immortal collective image: "The image that we have conceived will accompany me into death" (167). When Damiel chose to step into the stream of time, to

Angels in a BMW showroom on the Kudamm—Damiel (Bruno Ganz) and Cassiel (Otto Sander) in *Wings of Desire* (1987).

sacrifice total consciousness and gain the unconscious, he chose this alternative despite Cassiel's warnings that none of it will be true. He chose to live in a fiction of words and images, a sea of narrative that compensates for the loss of the child's unconscious existence in the world of the senses. And even here we see the film reflecting that it is not a real state of childhood that fuels this desire, but rather an already compensatory conception of childhood. The film itself is inscribed within a written text whose refrain, "When the child was a child," points to this, in Freud's term, "belated" (*nachträglich*) relation to past experience. Damiel embraced, in full intellectual awareness, a fictional world of the senses—not the actual sensual pleasure itself, but that imaginary realm that had enticed him to trade in his angel's wings for wings of desire. With his eyes glazed over from fantasizing, sitting together with Cassiel in the BMW convertible, he put it this way: "It is not that I would like to conceive a child or plant a tree, but wouldn't it really be something to come home after a long day and, just like Philip Marlowe, feed the cat" (20).

When Cassiel warns that none of it will be true, he does not mean just that our plans and hopes often remain unfulfilled. In contrast to the objective, uninvolved point of view of the angels, our vision of the past is also a fiction informed by our needs, desires, anxieties, and hopes for the future. Moreover, this vision is mediated through a collective textuality of

180

words, images, and emotions. As Damiel becomes human, those impulses that awakened desires in him will find their expression only in this collective medium of representations. The allusion to Philip Marlowe calls attention to one such—and for Wenders a particularly significant—cultural sphere that mediates our desires and fears. Classical Hollywood film had exerted a particularly strong influence on the young Wenders and inspired his work as filmmaker. It carried for him a myth-forming power that he would, only after his filmmaking experiences in America, be able to put in perspective for his own filmmaking. This power of epic, mythical narrative reveals itself when Damiel is moved to give up his existence outside of the physical world by the single, seemingly insignificant image of Philip Marlowe feeding his cat. Damiel embraces the human capability of representing experience in a fictional, constructed context, even while knowing that this is the human condition per se, and that at the end of his life he "will have lived within" a fictional account that never coincides with the "facts" of one's existence.

Epic Narrative and History

At the end of the film, Wenders clearly situates *Wings of Desire* as a new beginning of narrative epic in cinema. While we view Cassiel perched on the shoulder of the angel Victoria atop the *Siegessäule*, Homer declares in voice-over the great need for the epic narrator in the (post)modern age: "Name for me those men and women and children who will be searching for me—the narrator and minstrel who sets a tone for them—because they need me more than anything else in the world" (169). The film closes with the words "Fortsetzung folgt" ("the continuation will follow") superimposed over the sky above Berlin, while we hear in voice-over "nous sommes embarqués" ("we have embarked"). Wenders ascribes this momentous role to *Wings of Desire* primarily with respect to the cinema industry. He is mounting a response to what he sees as a mass-media industry that threatens to engulf all narrative within a medium of images and words appropriated for advertising and commercial ventures. But the story of Berlin, of *Der Himmel über Berlin* ("The Sky over Berlin")[35] that unites a divided city and people, also promises a new beginning in the continuing search for a national identity. The film invites the spectator, at what seems to be a most inopportune time, to join in an epic-making beginning of an alternative, yet affirmative, filmic discourse. I say inopportune because of the growing call in the Federal Republic for a relativized, if not totally revisionist, formulation of German history. In this context one might argue that the filmmakers are indulging in a somewhat naive and possibly dangerous form of mythmaking, particularly since the film fails to investigate in any specific way the role Berlin has played in recent German history. And when one considers that its call for the beginning of a radically new form of cinema comes twenty-five years after Oberhausen and the founding of a New German Cinema that has employed various narrative forms and filmic strategies to examine the German past critically, then the suspicion grows.

However, when one compares the historical perspective presented in *Wings of Desire* with some of those that emerged after Ronald Reagan's ill-advised visit to Bitburg in May 1985, one finds an oppositional model to recently relativized accounts of German history. Although the Bitburg incident was instrumental in awakening again—or, in the case of some Holocaust survivors, for the first time—the voices of remembrance, it signaled as well a new outcry for a German patriotism that has freed itself from the past. The Historians' Debate that broke out in the summer of the following year shifted the discussion to a more intellectual and somewhat less accessible arena for the larger public. Thus the positive effect of raising anew the question of history was not as widely disseminated, while the efforts to relativize the past gained ground. Although some might object to this oversimplified account that lumps these two episodes together, I would suggest that the textual system in *Wings of Desire* brings out problematic aspects of both these attempts to revise recent German history. Even while recognizing the historical significance and potential legacy of Richard Weizsäcker's May 8 speech to the Bundestag, I would still argue that the upshot of the whole affair was to restrict remembrance rather than foster it.[36] The enactment of the *Ausschwitzlügegesetz* (federal laws making it a federal offense to claim that the Holocaust did not occur) looks, to this observer's eye, suspiciously like lawmakers washing their hands of the whole matter. This scenario, together with the obvious political opportunism involved in the affair, could help explain the curious overreaction to Philip Jenninger's speech to the Bundestag on the fiftieth anniversary of the Kristallnacht pogrom. In any case, it is clear that German lawmakers were readily willing to follow Reagan's lead when he said—in rejecting Helmut Kohl's initial proposal of a visit to a concentration camp—that he was in favor of "putting that history behind [him]."[37]

In one way, *Wings of Desire* fits the pattern of these quests in the 1980s for a viable German identity. The film proclaims to be, at least in some sense, a new Zero Hour forty years after the Nazi era ended. During the chaos of the immediate postwar years, many of the questions of Germany's past, and with them an answer to the question of its identity, were tabled for the sake of reconstruction. Just as the term *Vergangenheitsbewältigung* ("coming to grips with the past") came to signify that exactly the opposite had happened, the festering identity crisis was symptomatic of the way the German nation had suppressed memories of its past. Reagan and the Bitburg incident offered a new Zero Hour, one that would not only put away the Nazi past but also grant the concessions to remembrance that allowed the Federal Republic to become prosperous so quickly. Again the cornerstone of the new, psychosocially more secure—and politically rededicated to the Atlantic alliance—Federal Republic was to be exclusion of the past rather than remembrance.

When Wenders situates *Wings of Desire* as the beginning of a new form of cinematic narrative, this carries with it certain national implications. That is, it claims to respond in some way to the nation's need to face the future with restored self-confidence. In his original notes on the film, Wenders remarked that after a long absence from Germany he could and would want to relearn what it means to be German only in the city of Berlin.[38] He felt that over a twenty-year period his most enlightening experiences of "Germany" occurred during his visits to Berlin, because only there does Germany's history pervade everyday life both physically and emotionally. In the Federal Republic, on the other hand, he sensed almost exclusively the absence or denial of the past. Thus even though Wenders's main concern was to film a story—and specifically a love story—in and about Berlin, *Wings of Desire* would include this history if it held true to its setting.

The scarred city of Berlin that one sees in *Wings of Desire* remains the symbol of German national identity. In the early sequences of the film we often see the ugly, scarred side of the city—for example, areas around the Wall near the Anhalterbahnhof and Potsdamer Platz, or stretches along the autobahn and S-Bahn. These are shot almost exclusively from camera perspectives that accentuate the more desolate side of these locations. Even more pregnant with history than the physical scars is the emotional state of the inhabitants, most of whom are lost in thought about the isolation or misery in their lives. The presence of the angels offers indeed little comfort and consolation to this city rent asunder. Other scenes, most notably the BMW showroom on the Kudamm, make it clear that prosperity is not lacking. The problem remains the inability to form a positive and alternative story of Germany that incorporates rather than excludes the bad and ugly past. And at the same time, the film suggests that the historical tradition that led to the Third Reich continues to exert its influence. In their jaunt back into time, Cassiel and Damiel even recall the beginning (the prehistoric "Zero Hour") of a militant human history: "When he [the first man who was attacked by his fellow men] fled, another history began—the history of wars. It continues even today" (84). The Zero Hour of 1945, the *Götterdämmerung* of the Nazis, obviously did not signal the last act in this long chapter of history, nor did it lead to a new beginning. Recent claims by a leading member of the Bonn government seem to bear out that much more of a link remains between the Federal Republic and the tradition of aggressive German nationalism than one previously would have admitted. Theo Waigel, head of the Christian-Socialist Union party and minister of the

183

interior, revived the "German" claim to lands east of the Oder-Neiße line and, in doing so, asserted that the concept of a German Reich had not necessarily been laid to rest with the defeat of the Nazis.

As he wanders through the desolate Potsdamer Platz seeking in vain the vibrant city square he remembers from pre-Nazi Berlin, Homer bemoans the failure of mankind to strike up a new, alternative form of epic narrative: "But no one has been able to strike up an epic of peace. What is it about peace, that in the long run it fails to impassion and that it does not lend itself to narrative? Should I give up now? If I give up, then mankind will lose its storyteller. And when mankind has lost its storyteller, it will also have lost its childhood" (57). This is the role the film sets for itself as a new beginning in narrative, epic cinema. The film depicts as well the past in all its horror. Homer declares the need for an epic of peace as he leafs through a book of photographs by August Sander entitled *Menschen des 20. Jahrhunderts*. Wenders sets counterpoint to Homer's thoughts stills from the book that show survivors of a bombing attack on Berlin identifying loved ones and acquaintances from among the rows of victims. We see a close-up of a baby and then one of two young children lying next to each other, all victims of the bombing. The epic of war, the traditional form that Homer longs to replace, is itself never addressed or described in the film. But these images stand in for it in its absence and evoke vivid memories of the recent German version of the epic warrior's tale. They recall the Nazi vision of the final victory, the thousand-year Reich, and, of course, the accompanying myth of the *Götterdämmerung* that is reflected in real human terms by the 1945 photographs. *Wings of Desire* builds out of these psychic and physical ruins a new story of Berlin and its epic past, one that strives to enthuse through a desire for peace.

In one of the seemingly arbitrary texts overheard in the library, we find a key to the historical perspective needed for such an alternative epic. As Damiel passes the second reader, we hear, "In 1921 Walter Benjamin bought Paul Klee's watercolor 'Angelus Novus' (ill. 34). Up until his flight from Paris in June 1940, it hung in his various offices. In his last work, 'Theses on the Philosophy of History' (1940), he interpreted the painting as an allegory of mankind's look back into history" (23). Although Wenders could not expect the typical spectator to catch the significance of this passage, if even take note of it at all, it has particular significance for the question of historical perspective on the past of both a nation and an individual. Benjamin's interpretation of the painting describes precisely the perspective granted the angels in *Wings of Desire*:

> A Klee painting named "Angelus Novus" shows an angel looking as though he is about to move away from something he is fixedly contemplating. His eyes are staring, his mouth is open, his wings are

spread. This is how one pictures the angel of history. His face is turned toward the past. Where we perceive a chain of events, he sees one single catastrophe which keeps piling wreckage upon wreckage and hurls it in front of his feet. The angel would like to stay, awaken the dead, and make whole what has been smashed. But a storm is blowing from Paradise; it has got caught in his wings with such violence that the angel can no longer close them. This storm irresistibly propels him into the future to which his back is turned, while the pile of debris before him grows skyward. This storm is what we call progress.[39]

The angels in *Wings of Desire*, as in Benjamin's account of the "Angelus Novus," are not able to alter the course of history; they only observe and verify it as they accompany it into the future with a painful countenance. They too would like to alleviate suffering in both the present and the past, but, as we see when Cassiel fails to deter the young man from jumping off the Europa-Center, they can only watch the human tragedy as it unfolds. They can move back along an infinite time continuum, viewing past moments as if they were in the present. They have in this way a greater potential to see and preserve the past. But in another sense their perspective is more limited than human vision, for as they move into the future simultaneously with man they can only look back in time. They lack the embeddedness in the present that is the crux of human history and which always implies a particular vision of the future.

In "Theses on the Philosophy of History," Benjamin distinguished between exactly these opposing perspectives on history: "History is the subject of a structure whose site is not homogeneous, empty time, but time filled by the presence of the now [*Jetztzeit*]."[40] Accordingly, the present is not an empty point of transition, such as the fictional point of view of the angels in *Wings of Desire*, but rather an active force that constructs out of past experience as needed a picture for the future, a vision that accompanies and forges the future as we repeatedly, in continuously revised form, invoke it in the present. In contrast to the common enlightenment model of history as a continuous line of progress, Benjamin proposes the "tiger leap into the past" back to a particular moment or period of history that can serve the needs of the present. Taking as an example the image of ancient Rome propagated during the French Revolution, Benjamin describes the actual historical continuum as a succession of fashions, each of which finds somewhere in the past the form that best fulfills the needs for the present.[41]

As pessimistic as Benjamin's description of the "Angelus Novus" seems, and as negative as the film's depiction of Berlin's reconstruction since 1945 may be, *Wings of Desire* is a film imbued with a spirit of hope for new beginnings. One finds similar hope in Benjamin's essay. Although written in one of mankind's darkest hours, and when Benjamin was facing his own impending doom at the hands of conquering evil forces, "Theses on the Philosophy of History" reaches an optimistic conclusion. Offering his last theses on a central question that had concerned him throughout his entire life,[42] he argues that the correction of this fundamental misconception in man's view of history holds the potential for ending the errant path of human "progress." The story of the angel who becomes man represents allegorically the shift in historical perspective that offers hope. When Damiel in the first conversation with Cassiel expresses the longing "To be able to say 'now' and 'now,' and not like always 'forever' and 'in eternity'" (20), this echoes Benjamin's position on the role of history. The conception of an even time continuum extending back into time has veritable meaning only for fictional beings like the angels. The free-floating camera in the first part of the film, with its arbitrarily recording eyes and ears that could move freely back into time, would be the ideal vehicle for the historian steeped in nineteenth-century positivistic historicism. When Damiel becomes human he can no longer function as a pure recorder of history. Tied to the present with all its personal and collective concerns, he possesses a more restricted and biased point of view, but, along with it, the basis for generating change. While the constructed point of view of the angels represents this idealized view of history, Damiel's decision to give it up suggests that hope for mankind lies in other forms of representation. As an angel of peace in a city that lives from day to day with the scars and consequences of the warrior epic, Damiel brings the needed impulse for a new epic whose heroes are, as Homer declares, "no longer the warriors and kings" (56).

As a film that exudes affirmation and the hope for new beginnings, *Wings of Desire* faces stiff opposition from that section of the German scholarly community that holds stubbornly to a modernist tradition of negativity and alienation. Some of the initial criticism I heard expressed by fellow Germanists in America complains that the film does not deal directly with thorny issues of Germany's recent past. It is not surprising to hear such objections coming from the area of German studies in America that in examining the cultural texts of the Federal Republic, particularly in film studies, has so often focused on the representation of Nazi and post-1945 history. But as I have argued here, Wenders does not ignore the issues of Berlin's past. Rather, he integrates them into a new aesthetic vision that answers to one overriding question: How can Germany *live with* that past? In this regard, Wenders's film fits quite well the description Andreas Huyssen has given for an aesthetics that goes beyond modernism but flies in the face of the convenient postmodern adage "anything goes": "The point is not to eliminate the productive tension between the political and the aesthetic, between history and the text, between engagement and the mission of art. The point is to heighten that tension, even to rediscover it and to bring it back into focus in the arts as well as criticism."[43] Such a tension exists no more strongly than in a work of art that seriously attempts to revive a form of German epic, while reflecting at every turn the constant danger it entails; in a work that attempts to raise out of the severest ruins of the age-old warrior myth a new myth-forming epic narrative.

Notes

This essay was first published in *Germanic Review*, Special Issue: German Film (Winter 1991).

1. Wim Wenders, *Le souffle de l'ange*, Special Issue of *Cahiers du cinéma* (Frankfurt: Filmverlag der Autoren, 1988) 30–36. First published in *Cahiers du cinéma* 400 (October 1987): 67–70. German translation in Wim Wenders, *Die Logik der Bilder: Essays und Gespräche*, ed. Michael Töteberg (Frankfurt am Main: Verlag der Autoren, 1988) 110–38. In English translation in *The Logic of Images*, trans. Michael Hofmann (London: Faber and Faber, 1991).

2. Wolfram Schütte, "Abschied von der dröhnenden Stimme des alten Kinos: Aus einem Gespräch mit Wim Wenders," *Frankfurter Rundschau* November 6, 1982: Feuilleton 3.

3. Wenders addressed this problem in a short film he made for French television during the two shootings of *Hammett: Reverse Angle*, dir. Wim Wenders, Road Movies, 1982. He also comments on this issue in a more freely associative way in the long prose-poem "Der Amerikanische Traum," in *Emotion Pictures: Essays und Filmkritiken, 1968–1984* (Frankfurt am Main: Suhrkamp, 1984) 139–70. See particularly pp. 156–57, 161–62.

4. Wenders, *Logik der Bilder* 98.

5. Wenders, *Logik der Bilder* 133–34.

6. For Wenders's remarks on Berlin as a locus of German history and a seedbed for world peace, see Wenders, *Logik der Bilder* 93–98; and Ira Paneth, "Wim and His Wings," *Film Quarterly* 42.1 (1988): 4.

7. Wenders, *Logik der Bilder* 98.

8. Uwe Künzel, *Wim Wenders: Ein Filmbuch*, 3rd rev. ed. (Freiburg im Breisgau: Dreisam, 1989) 213.

9. This is an abbreviated translation of Wenders's account in "Erste Beschreibung eines recht unbeschreiblichen Filmes: Aus dem ersten Treatment zu *Der Himmel über Berlin*" in Wenders, *Logik der Bilder* 99.

10. Jean Pierre Oudart, "La suture," *Cahiers du cinéma* 211 and 212 (April and May 1969); Oudart's article appeared in English translation as "Cinema and Suture," *Screen* 18.4 (1977–78): 35–47; see also Daniel Dayan's article that introduced Oudart's work to English readers: "The Tutor-Code of Classical Cinema," *Film Quarterly* 28.1 (1974): 22–31.

11. Christian Metz, *The Imaginary Signifier: Psychoanalysis and the Cinema*, trans. Celia Britton, Annwyl Williams, Ben Brewster, and Alfred Guzzetti (Bloomington: Indiana UP, 1982). Two important works by Baudry in translation are Jean-Louis Baudry, "Ideological Effects of the Basic Cinematographic Apparatus," *Film Quarterly* 28.2 (1974–75): 39–47; and "The Apparatus:

Metapsychological Approaches to the Impression of Reality in the Cinema," *Camera Obscura* 1 (1976): 104–28. Both of these articles, as well as several other writings I cite, are contained in the collection *Narrative, Apparatus, Ideology: A Film Theory Reader*, ed. Philip Rosen (New York: Columbia UP, 1986).

12. Initial responses to Oudart and Dayan include William Rothmann, "Against the System of Suture," *Film Quarterly* 29.1 (1975): 45–50; Stephen Heath, "On Screen, in Frame: Film and Ideology," *Quarterly Review of Film Studies* 1.3 (1976): 251–65; Colin MacCabe, "Theory and Film: Principles of Realism and Pleasure," *Screen* 17.3 (1976): 7–27; and Heath, "Notes on Suture," *Screen* 18.4 (1977–78): 48–76. Later writings that have influenced my use of the concept of suture will be documented later in context.

13. Thomas Elsaesser, "Primary Identification and the Historical Subject: Fassbinder and Germany," *Narrative, Apparatus, Ideology: A Film Theory Reader*, ed. Philip Rosen (New York: Columbia UP, 1986) 537. First appeared in *Ciné-Tracts* 11 (1980): 43–52.

14. Kaja Silverman describes suture in a similar vein in *The Subject of Semiotics* (Oxford: Oxford UP, 1983) 201–06.

15. In his response to Oudart and Jacques-Alain Miller in *Screen*, Stephen Heath makes this point: "To say that the system of suture is a particular logic, a writing, is not, however, to say that cinema could be articulated as discourse outside of any suture"; "Notes on Suture" 68. One should add to Heath's statement that to say that the system of suture (in cinema) is "a particular logic, a writing," is not to say that it includes only one form of writing. That is, it would be a mistake, one I think Oudart makes, to place the "logic" of suture in cinema on the same plane with the general logic of the signifier described by Miller, for the system of suture in cinema includes numerous variables that structure and alter the "sutured" discourse.

16. Wenders talks about the camera movement in the interview with Paneth 5.

17. Künzel 214–15.

18. Baudry, "Ideological Effects" 45–46.

19. Stephen Heath, "Narrative Space," *Screen* 17.3 (1976): 95.

20. The distinction between primary and secondary identification used here stems from Lacan's account of subject formation in the infant. Baudry applies the distinction to the way the viewing subject identifies with the image in cinema ("Ideological Effects" 46), and Metz discusses it in more detail (54–56). In their theories, primary identification refers to an identification attached to the image itself, whereas in the secondary phase identification shifts to the transcendental subject that stages the succession of film images. Neither they nor subsequent critics who speak of primary processes of identification would apply this term to the identification with a specific point of view created by the camera or the narrative space of the film. But because of the close correspondence of the angels' point of view with the camera in *Wings of Desire*, it is, I think, appropriate to make the correspondence between the two stages of subject formation and the points of view assumed by the viewing subject.

21. For an account of how Murnau and his cameraman Karl Freund used the "entfesselte Kamera" in making *The Last Laugh*, see Lotte H. Eisner, *Murnau* (Berkeley: U of California P, 1973) 62–67.

22. Oudart, "Cinema and Suture" 41.

23. Heath, "Narrative Space"; MacCabe, "Theory and Film"; and Kaja Silverman in her chapter "Suture" in *The Subject of Semiotics*.

24. Silverman, *The Subject of Semiotics* 204–06 and 231–32.

25. Wim Wenders and Peter Handke, *Der Himmel über Berlin: Ein Filmbuch* (Frankfurt am Main: Suhrkamp, 1987) 19. The translations are my own. Hereafter cited in the text.

26. Paneth 5.

27. Paneth 7.

28. Paneth 6.

29. Schütte, "Abschied."

30. The German phrase at the end of this statement, "und sonst gar nichts," harks back unmistakably to the refrain of the famous cabaret song sung by Marlene Dietrich in *The Blue Angel*: "Ich bin von Kopf bis Fuß auf Liebe eingestellt—und sonst gar nichts." ("From my head down to my toes, I'm attuned to love—and nothing else.")

31. Paneth 5.

32. From Silverman's work on the limitations placed on the female voice in dominant cinema, we can see how Marion's speech is transgressive both formally as well as in content: "Classical cinema projects these differences at the formal as well as the thematic level. Not only does the male subject occupy positions of authority within the diegesis, but occasionally he also speaks extra-diegetically, from the privileged place of the Other. The female subject, on the contrary, is excluded from positions of discursive authority both inside and outside the diegesis; she is confined not only to safe places *within* the story (to positions, that is, which come within the eventual range of male vision or audition), but to the place *of* the story." Kaja Silverman, "Dis-Embodying the Female Voice," *Re-Vision: Essays in Feminist Film Criticism*, ed. Mary Ann Doane et al., The American Film Institute Monograph, series 3 (Frederick, MD: University Publications of America, 1984) 132.

33. These two extended looks into the camera also obstruct identification with that look (usually of the male lead) that dominates and coerces the (often female) other in the diegesis. In the close-up of Damiel, he smiles benignly into the camera, not at the object of his desire, but at its source. Marion's speech disrupts conventional patterns of male dominance (see note 32) even more abruptly than the look into the camera. On the other hand, earlier scenes, particularly the voyeuristic moments in the trailer, tend to place the female subject in subordination to the male gaze in questionable contexts.

34. Friedrich Frey, "Über das Verfertigen eines Filmes beim Drehen: Wim Wenders unterhält sich mit Frierich Frey über Ankerwerfen, '68, Parallelproduzieren, Engel, Städtisches, u.a.," *Frankfurter Rundschau* September 10, 1988.

35. This is the original German title of the film; the German word "Himmel" can mean either sky or heaven.

36. An example of how von Weizsäcker's speech surfaces in discussions of German national identity is the 1987 edition of *Meet Germany*, a booklet published by the "private, non-partisan German organization" *Atlantik-Brücke*. In an article entitled "The Perennial German Question—Is There a German Answer?" the historian Michael Stürmer, one of the central figures in the Historians' Debate, talks about the "tremendous impact" of and "resounding response" to von Weizsäcker's speech, explaining that "the President sought to restore the country's self-confidence, thereby making it possible for Germans to face the future while not ignoring the past." Following the article are some excerpts from the speech under the title "There Can Be No Reconciliation without Remembrance." Yet nowhere in Stürmer's article is there any mention of Reagan's visit to Bitburg, which took place just days before Weiszäcker's address to the Bundestag. *Meet Germany*, 19th rev. ed. (Hamburg: Atlantik-Brücke, 1987) 48–51.

37. Geoffrey H. Hartman, ed., *Bitburg in Moral and Political Perspective* (Bloomington: Indiana UP, 1986) xiii.

38. Wenders, *Logik der Bilder* 94.

39. Walter Benjamin, "Theses on the Philosophy of History," *Illuminations*, ed. Hannah Arendt, trans. Harry Zohn (New York: Schocken, 1969) 259–60.

40. Benjamin 263.

41. Benjamin goes on to place materialistic conditions for "the tiger leap into the past" that could bring about revolutionary change: "This jump, however, takes place in an arena where the ruling class gives the commands. The same leap in the open air of history is the dialectical one, which is how Marx understood the revolution" (263). Although Wenders does not share Benjamin's Marxist ideology, the optimism shared by *Wings of Desire* and "Theses on the Philosophy of History" stems from the shift in the view of history.

42. See "Anmerkungen der Herausgeber" in Walter Benjamin, *Gesammelte Schriften* 1.3, eds. Rolf Tiedemann and Hermann Schweppenhäuser (Frankfurt am Main: Suhrkamp, 1974) 1223–27.

43. Andreas Huyssen, "Mapping the Postmodern," *New German Critique* 33 (1984): 52.

"Life Sneaks out of Stories": Until the End of the World

NORBERT GROB

To See What There Is to See

"Ideal forms are ailing. . . . The things that are portrayed too realistically don't stand the test of life."[1] Ernst Bloch's observation from *Spuren* may serve well as a motto for Wenders's narrative style. Even in later works such as *Paris, Texas* and *Wings of Desire*, with their daring and complex design, the story leaves space for that which lies far away, off center, and out of focus. The assumption in these films is that straightforward dialogues and a clear thesis cannot capture what really goes on in people, and in the world in general. Each diagnosis needs to leave room for other indicators; the wound has to be examined, but so do the smaller symptoms surrounding it. Or to put it differently, only the byways, the detours, and the roads less traveled are leading anywhere, because the main highways are battered, worn out, and lead to dead ends. From its beginnings, the cinema of Wim Wenders has always tried to turn the viewer's eye toward those things that are peripheral to the main track but which nevertheless aim at the center. To quote Bloch again, "Things on the margin are beginning to play an increasingly important role. We should pay attention to the little things, look into them more closely. The curious and the strange often tells us the most. Certain things can only be expressed in such stories, and not in a lofty, epic style."[2]

If the work of a film director can be characterized by one essential trademark, for Wenders this would be the open form, the gaps, the lack of

191

closure. His films defy both baroque abundance and classical fullness. The stories of these films—which often seem skeletal—subsist on these gaps: the free-roaming gaze, the loose transitions, the empty images. It is essential to these films that they do not aim at capturing the essence of things. Rather, Wenders's accomplishment consists in portraying the unaccomplished and the mundane. The *objet trouvé* is ubiquitous in his films, as if it were the result of pure observation. The camera clings to staged arrangements as if it were discovering incidental scenes. In other words, the films show a work of fiction and pretend to have merely found it, thus seducing the viewer to miss the deception. However, the aesthetic strategies of these seductions are clearly marked. We are shown, for example, how the length of a shot changes our perception; because our perception is focused on the surface of things, we are led to understand how any aesthetic of the redemption of physical reality remains in fact an illusion. It is therefore only a matter of point of view whether the world shown to us appears as part of a larger context or whether it speaks exclusively on its own behalf.

The stories in Wenders's films build a framework, but without obliterating the conditions and the constituents of the narrative. Amidst the stylistic elements that make up the work as a whole, each single element retains its individual part in the construction of the whole: we can still see the place behind the location, the people behind the characters, the events behind the plot, the furnishings behind the set design, the real objects behind the props. These films do not try to prove anything. The filmic text is simultaneously both discourse and dialogue; and on the level of its composition, the film presents a (point of) view, simply showing what is evident without presenting evidence.

The stories do not propel the films forward; they merely prevent them from falling apart. It is rather the detours, the subplots, and the wrong tracks that predominate and create space for the unexpected. The frame that the camera imposes on the images does not restrict our look but rather enhances it. Linking seemingly random events to an intelligible reality, the camera discovers, and therefore creates, something new. By virtue of their visionary concept, Wenders's films uncover relations that otherwise would remain invisible. Because the images remain receptive to the unexpected, they acquire a different timbre, as they do in the films of Jean Renoir and Roberto Rossellini. The characters appear more distant and at the same time more authentic, even if they take the liberty of expanding their roles through improvisation. As a result, Wenders's films make a certain surface reality manifest, and this in turn gives them their depth: suddenly we can see the coldness that pervades people and things, and the melancholy of the heroes who move around in it; the emptiness of the world, its sad banality, and its lost beauty.

Wenders's early dreams have their source in the epic films of John Ford, and throughout the seventies and eighties Wenders realized this dream in his own work. These films, writes Wenders, contain stories that are not "trying to suck all the blood from an image;"[3] they contain "faces that are never forced into anything," "landscapes that aren't just backgrounds," "pictures that [do not] block your vision," and "sounds that [do not] stifle your senses."[4] In June 1970, while still working on his first feature, *Summer in the City*, Wenders published a brief text about the rock poet Van Morrison. It was neither a portrait nor a review, but instead a literary fantasy about the sensual experiences evoked by his songs. In the text Wenders reminisces about films in order to describe Morrison's music, at the same time expressing his feelings about the music in order to get at his concept of cinema. He writes about "moments in films that are suddenly so unexpectedly direct and overwhelmingly concrete that you hold your breath, or sit up, or put your hand over your mouth."[5] These plain and yet mysterious moments evoke the utopian element of cinema. In these moments, openly visual experiences lead to an awareness of something invisible, and that which usually can be grasped suddenly slips beyond reach. As Wenders goes on to explain, Morrison's songs "[give you] for extended periods . . . a feeling and a notion what films could be like: a perception that does not always jump blindly at meanings and assertions, but rather lets your senses extend further and further. Where something really becomes indescribable."[6] Claiming that Morrison's songs express pure sensuality without any direct meaning (an oversimplification in any case), Wenders calls on this music to help him reflect on the utopian potential of cinema. It is an evocation that points toward the secret miracles of cinema: how it can produce the unimaginable out of concrete presentations, the indescribable out of objective description, that which is unsaid out of direct statements. In this understanding of such *true* moments one finds an important early credo for Wenders's cinema—or even more, the conception of cinema manifested in his first films.

As this early text makes clear, Wenders wants to capture and retain reality at a moment when it is not yet explained and interpreted, when it still radiates a distinct notion about its condition. Near the beginning of *Alice in the Cities*, we watch Philip Winter (Rüdiger Vogler) approach New York by train. Behind the bars of a metal bridge we recognize the Manhattan skyline, the Hudson River, and the sky above and behind the houses. The view of the camera remains fixed, but the movement of the train, indicated by the metal bars of the bridge passing by, creates the illusion of a moving camera. The steel bars and the skyline form a single *Einstellung*, that is, one shot but also one coherent view of the world. A location has been filmed from an unusual point of view without elevating its object into a metaphor for something else—Manhattan is what it is. But presented as a slice of reality seen from a unique perspective, the shot also conveys something else. It also says that life in Manhattan is a life behind bars, crammed into houses that reach out of their enclosed streets into the sky above. The shot shows all this without any particular emphasis or explanation. In this way, it creates an image "suddenly so unexpectedly direct and overwhelmingly concrete" that it strikes like lightning, and we are suddenly moved "by an object as event and not as substance."[7]

The focus is always on small, quite unimportant things that turn out to be the most important and noteworthy. Wenders commented on *Wings of Desire* that he wanted to make "something that's physical and concrete as tangible as possible. Well, there is the angel who is an expert in human affairs, but he does not know anything physical, he has no experience. And suddenly, he experiences everything on a very sensual level. That's what films always want to do: relate sensual experiences, yet they are so poorly equipped to do it. Through this angel we can suddenly say: there's nothing more beautiful than this cup of coffee; or you lick your blood and there is no greater joy."[8]

For Wenders, cinema is a window to the world where the images stop moving and become salient; they neither allude to nor give meaning to anything. As I have said, Wenders is interested in showing what is evident, not in presenting evidence. His goal is to extend the act of seeing so that the viewer too can discover what there is left to discover in the world. According to Wenders, the cinema fascinates through its attention to details that describe things the way they *are*. Its aesthetics are premised on making something visible that otherwise would remain concealed—even though everything is *seemingly* visible on the surface. Wenders's images make things visible without manipulating them; that which is real is not engulfed by the fiction, but rather retains its own special quality. Individual elements seem like fragments or excerpts, and yet they never hint at a larger whole. Wenders offers, instead of reconstructions, glimpses of particular moments; instead of arranged locations, we see the continuity of real space. Looking at his films, therefore, is never an act of mere observation but always a sensual discovering, a way of seeing that he first admired in the work of Yasujiro Ozu, "[whose films] were actually and continually about life, and in which people, things, cities and landscapes all revealed themselves."[9]

In Jean-Luc Godard's essayistic film *Pierrot le fou*, we find this adage: "Poetic language grows out of ruins." The destruction of the commonplace is necessary to create the unique. Wenders begins beyond the commonplace and also beyond that which has long been destroyed. Denying the distinction between poetic and explanatory discourse, Wenders integrates his reflections on form directly into the narrative. Obviously the straightforward narrative has to make room for sketches and experiments; the gaps between the fragments create a productive tension where each small episode derives its meaning only through its relation to others. Wenders is after the minute and mysterious changes in form and tone—he tries to create a feeling of expanse, the atmosphere of dusk, shadows with transparent backgrounds. In the films of John Ford, Howard Hawks, and Raoul Walsh, Wenders saw that the viewer needs room for imagination, and that the more effective fiction is the deeper it can penetrate the productive imagination of its audience. And from his European colleagues—above all Luis Buñuel, Jacques Rivette, and Andrei Tarkovsky—Wenders learned how to use stories, thoughts, and songs more freely. In their films the viewer is not just a passive recipient but becomes an active agent entangled in a narrative web. The viewer finds him- or herself in the role of the narrator or the protagonist, carrying through to conclusion the process the images had set in motion.

Wenders began with small exercises, short films that probed the relation between observation and movement and studied how images change depending on whether the camera or the object moves or remains fixed. In 1970 he began making feature films. His protagonists became involved in more complex stories; the dramaturgy took on new dimensions, and the ellipses became more daring. The formal elements as a whole became more varied, even though the objectively observing camera remained the central axis.

On a horizontal plane, one finds a conventional division of Wenders's work into three phases. In the early phase (until *Kings of the Road* [1976]), Wenders is in search of his own style, which he achieves with *Alice in the Cities* (1974). In the second phase (1976 to 1984), he experiments with more conventional narratives in Germany (*The American Friend* [1977]) and Hollywood (*Hammett* [1982]). These experiments and experiences find their filmic expression in *The State of Things* (1982) and *Paris, Texas* (1984), the latter thematically tied to the earlier films, although its style and plot already transcend them. A third phase begins with *Wings of Desire* (1987)—new heroes, new stories, new experiments.

On a vertical plane, one could structure his films according to the kind of cinema they represent, that is, films that set out to explore versus those that want to entertain. On the one hand, Wenders makes "open" films —films about people who resist the closure of narrative. In films such as *Summer in the City, Alice in the Cities, Wrong Move, Kings of the Road, Lightning over Water, The State of Things, Paris, Texas, Wings of Desire*, and *Until the End of the World*, a curious camera explores the world through which the protagonists move. On the other hand, there are the entertaining films that are primarily interested in telling a story, where the characters and the camera are subordinated to the plot: *The Goalie's Anxiety at the Penalty Kick, The Scarlet Letter, The American Friend*, and *Hammett*. This kind of cinema is characterized by genre conventions and the pleasure derived from changing, extending, and subverting them. Even if Wenders is not so much concerned with retelling the same story in different versions, even if he is less interested in finding new nuances than in creating new designs, he still adheres to the main principle of genre film; that is, he arouses the emotions of his audience whenever possible. For Wenders there is no contradiction between open films that set out to explore or to discover and films that involve the audience emotionally through entertaining and suspenseful stories.

Wenders has commented about these two kinds of cinema in *The State of Things*, itself a reflection on the potential and limits of cinema. Toward the end of the film, the Hollywood producer Gordon and the protagonist, Friedrich Munro, a European director, become involved in an argument. Gordon says, "The same old story, I keep telling you. Without a story you're dead. You can't build a movie without a story. Have you ever tried building a house without walls? It's the same. You can't build a house without walls. A movie's got to have walls, Friedrich." "Why walls?" replies Friedrich. "The space between the characters can carry the load."

By now Wenders knows that he has to tell stories in order to convey what really matters. But that is only one part of the story. The other part is that he still takes images very seriously. In *Reverse Angle* he confesses that he is perhaps using stories only as a pretext for making films, and it is precisely this tension that gives his films their attraction and energy. As he noted in his essay "Impossible Stories," "I totally reject stories, because for me they only bring out lies, nothing but lies, and the biggest lie is that they show coherence where there is none. Then again, our need for these lies is so consuming that it's completely pointless to fight them. . . . Stories are impossible, but it's impossible to live without them."[10]

Wenders's counterstrategy, to the extent that he is able to adhere to it, is to avoid excessive fragmentation. His style is bent on strengthening the filmic atmosphere exuded by the people, the things, and the spaces between them. Most importantly, he tries to give the impression of temporal and spacial continuity, as if the gaps between individual shots were hardly any bigger than those gaps in human perception caused by the batting of an eye. Yet at the same time, the flow of the narrative is interrupted time and again by extensive looks that lose themselves in observations; time and again, the inner and outer experiences of the protagonists take precedence over the story. These ruptures indicate the kind of scruples Wenders has about imposing a linear order. The desire for storytelling and the deep mistrust in stories—these are just two sides of the same coin.

With Images against Images: *Until the End of the World*

For more than twenty years, Wenders's utopian vision has been to make a film like "the way you sometimes open our eyes. Just looking, not trying to prove anything."[11] His visual metaphor for this act of filming has been the observing and pensive woman at the window (a variation of Edward Hopper's painting *Morning in a City*).[12] In his 1993 feature film, *Until the End of the World*, only a trace of this desire remains. The images of the Australian desert around which the film is organized, and which Wenders had discovered for himself fourteen years earlier, reflect a curious and awe-inspiring look at the barren, jagged, and exotic landscape, as if one could not grasp what the camera is preserving on film. Even the protagonists appear transformed; nothing compels them to take action. They even shrug their shoulders in amazing indifference about a nuclear catastrophe.

In *Until the End of the World* Wenders tries his hand at the cinema of illusion, of simulation and affected emotions. The film starts out as if Wenders wants to outdo Terence Young and his cinema of imitation and posturing. It seems that indeed "everything has changed," as Robert declared in his farewell note in *Kings of the Road*. First of all, *Until the End of the World* is about a fictional catastrophe in which a falling nuclear satellite threatens the entire world. Second, there is a love story between a woman, Claire Tourneur, who enters into the adventurous life of a man, Trevor McPhee as he calls himself at first, only to change later to Sam Farber. And the film is also a journey around the world by way of the diverse genres of the cinema: the eccentric and decadent ambience of Federico Fellini in Venice; a detective thriller in Lisbon; a political satire in Moscow; a slapstick comedy in Tokyo; the world of Yasujiro Ozu in the Japanese mountains; a crime story in San Francisco; and finally a science-fiction thriller in the Australian desert. Multiple emotions and fantasies come into play, as well as complex and confusing plots and subplots that lead to ever more involved feelings and fantasies.

Roland Barthes once said that love at first sight is like "hypnosis"[13]—it arouses, electrifies, transforms, stirs, and numbs us. This is precisely the condition Wenders has attempted to create on the screen. A woman follows a man—or, in Wenders's own words, Penelope does not stay home to await the return of Odysseus but rather chases after him to show him that her feelings for him are also his feelings for her. A woman and a man, somewhere in Lyon, in 1999, next to a video telephone. He says there is something in his eye. She replies that she can't find anything and adds, "You have sad eyes." He replies, "I'm not a sad man." As he walks away, she follows him with her eyes for a long time. A short time later he appears again and pleads with her to help him, whereupon she takes off with him in her car. That's how the whole shebang gets started. A dance around the

The Penelope who does not want to stay home—Claire (Solveig Dommartin) in *Until the End of the World* (1991).

world begins: Venice, Lyon, Paris, Berlin, Lisbon, Moscow, Beijing, Tokyo, San Francisco, Australia. But apart from the carnivalesque love scenes in Lisbon, it is hard to believe that Claire and Trevor really experience the feelings they pretend to have for each other. Hence the chase around the world deteriorates into a curious whim. Especially Claire's exaggerated postures ridicule the feelings she is supposedly experiencing, so that we understand why Trevor deceives her and tries to get rid of her. It is all too obvious that nothing clicks. A love story without visible emotions is like a wet firecracker, a complete counterfeit that can only hope for a tolerant viewer.

At an early point in his career, Wenders claimed that telling a story was always in part an act of deluding, while the images on the other hand contained the potential for truth. With *Until the End of the World* he presents a film where the story consistently and openly manipulates the truth of the images. And the link between the two? Wenders's own comment on storytelling in *The State of Things*: "Life sneaks out of stories—they are dead."

Neither Claire nor Trevor cares very much whether the place they are visiting is different from the ones they have already seen. At one point Claire stands at the Russian-Chinese border and watches dejectedly as a truck in which she believes Trevor is traveling vanishes into the night, along with the red taillights of the train from which she has just disembarked. As she watches them disappear, her look is concerned only with the story, and nothing else. In this state of mind, she turns to the camera in a simulated pose reminiscent of Greta Garbo in *Anna Karenina*. This woman is the exact opposite of the genuine traveler, as described by Paul Bowles: that is, someone who searches for diversity as well as for the human element that brings out the differences among people. It is perhaps at this point that Wenders's failure becomes most obvious. From the very beginning he was concerned with the redemption of physical reality; now that for the first time he has the chance to investigate this reality more comprehensively, his special awareness of the state of things fails him. He sends his protagonists off on their journey like tourists—and no one knows better than Wenders what this means: "The worst look that can happen: the point of view of a tourist."[14]

Until the End of the World begins and ends in space, spanning the years from 1999 to 2001. The act of seeing and the moral issue of producing images—which have been one of Wenders's central concerns all along—now become the central subject of a film. *Until the End of the World* is a film about a journey around the world in which a man equipped with a special camera shoots images that will enable his blind mother to see. Not only does the special camera record what lies in front of it, it also captures the very act of seeing, that is, the brain activity of the cameraman who is shooting the images. This "subjective picture" is then transferred to the brain of the blind person—it is a recording of both an act of seeing and an act of remembering, because the cameraman has to remember his own images at the moment of their transmission. After the experiment finally succeeds, a witness to the process comments, "Only miracles make sense."

When the protagonists finally come to rest in the Australian desert, the film story begins to reflect on the effect images have on us: What do they reveal? What do they conceal? What do they do *with* us? When Edith, Farber's blind mother, "sees," that is, perceives visual impulses, for the first time, she is amazed by the colors, movements, and forms—and then covers her eyes with her hands. This gesture—which recalls similar gestures by Dimmesdale (Lou Castel) in *The Scarlet Letter* and Derwatt (Nicholas Ray) in *The American Friend* (who also remarked: "Take care of [your eye]. A new one is hard to get.")—expresses a fascination with the mystery of seeing. It is as if that which is self-understood is also beyond comprehension. As Wenders once commented, "What I find fascinating about seeing is that, in contrast to thinking, it can be free of opinions about things. . . . In the act of seeing you can find an orientation [*Einstellung*] to another person, to an object, to the world, which is without any predilection. The more beautiful word for seeing is perceiving [*wahrnehmen*], because it contains the word true [*wahr*]. The act of seeing contains potential

199

truth. . . . Seeing is an immersion *in* the world."[15] For Edith, this immersion in the world is at first fascinating and overwhelming, but soon the experience transforms her; she becomes more silent, withdrawn, and depressed. The act of seeing, which was supposed to move her closer to the world, now distances her from her memory and her imagination—seeing is no solution. Before her death, she offers her final verdict: "The world is not okay."

The most daring endeavor Wenders undertakes in the first part of the film goes beyond all science fiction—it is the attempt to capture images of the world as such. The journey around the world is informed by the desire to replace the eyes of the blind mother; this raises the question, How can the world *as such* be photographed at all? Wenders circumvents this problem by only showing the creation of images indirectly, focusing rather on the various intertwining subplots that arise. Consequently, the journey around the world remains an enigma at first. A woman meets a man and gives him a ride in her car. On the way he steals some of the money she is supposed to bring to Paris to the bank robbers; this in turn ignites the chase —"I simply want the money back." But every time she catches up with him she offers him help, while the money is hardly ever mentioned. Trevor has problems understanding this altruistic behavior: "Three countries in three days, just to have breakfast with me?" Even though Claire offers reasons why she keeps giving chase, her relentless pursuit seems to be little more than a whim.

Other elements further complicate this story about money, love, and the wondrous new camera. Claire hires a detective, a visual joke that adds little more than a somewhat distorted slant to the film; bounty hunters, CIA agents, KGB officials, and Japanese gangsters all join the dance around the globe, as do an English novelist and a French thief. This bizarre play of opposing interests, vicious intrigues, and ambivalent obsessions feels like a postmodern homage to film noir: lots of money is at stake; science is pitted against politics; cases of false identities abound; everyone is out to con everyone else. But then Wenders smooths out the conflicts and tones down the drama, abandoning entire subplots. Somehow, it is not all as bad as it might at first seem—and somehow, that is the worst part of all.

What one sees of the world in the midst of this wild chase is full of ambiguity—on one hand a vision of future culture, and at the same time an homage to previous styles of cinema. We are hurried from one place to the next without the individual cities ever developing a clear profile. One has to read this as a pessimistic premonition. Beijing looks like the Paris and Berlin of today. Paris and Berlin resemble the Los Angeles of Ridley Scott's *Blade Runner*. Only Lisbon has retained a certain urban charm; the streetcars still move at a leisurely pace, and one can get on and off as one pleases (shown filmically as a cross between Hitchcock's *39 Steps* and

Buñuel's *La ilusión viaja en tranvía*). Tokyo, however, is pure madness (its chaos resembles the remake of a Marx brothers comedy), and San Francisco has become a gangster town where even the criminals fear for their lives (it exudes the nervous energy of a city in a John Cassavetes thriller). In Wenders's darkest prognosis, there are no longer any differences in individual mentalities. People have become the same everywhere; their lives are interchangeable, their thoughts are standardized. Only the crazy outsiders such as the French thieves, the old people in the Japanese mountains, and the Australian aborigines hold out promise for another, more sensitive age.

John Berger has noted that every film is "a shuttle service between different places and times."[16] In this respect, *Until the End of the World* offers a wide range of diverse hopes and fears. What will the world look like in 1999? In Venice people are speeding on motorboats down the Canale Grande. Onboard computers operate automobiles. Video telephones are everywhere. The Boeing 747-400 jet is still a part of the Lufthansa fleet, but now as a shuttle plane. In Paris the Eiffel Tower continues to be the central landmark, and *Libération* continues its publication. Small video cameras with built-in monitors have become as convenient as pocket cameras, and everybody has one. The Hotel Adlon has been rebuilt in Berlin, where a blue neon sign, "Bauknecht," shines above the skyline. Laptop computers convert spoken words into writing. The movement of every individual around the globe can be traced via credit cards and electronic IDs. Red flags are still waving in Moscow. With a simple photo, a computer can establish a person's identity. Cars clog the streets of Beijing; a stone monument of a tank reminds us of the bygone revolution. In Tokyo, people sleep in lockers hardly bigger than a coffin. Only in the Japanese mountains and the Australian desert does everything remain as it has been for centuries: windy, quiet, and unpopulated.

Wenders makes it clear to the viewer that, to some extent, we have to take leave of the world as we know it. This unavoidable farewell is indeed the central experience of our time. To quote John Berger again, "Our century is the century of involuntary travel" and of "disappearance."[17] Perhaps this is why, according to Berger, "cinema provides this century's most appropriate way of telling stories." In fact, the title of one of Berger's short stories may serve as his definition for cinema as well: "Every Time We Say Good-Bye."

In *Until the End of the World* Wenders uses for the first time a narrator who structures and unifies the different strands in the story. Previously his voice-overs had been more of a compensation for the film's limited script, as in *Summer in the City*, or provided an inner commentary, as in the case of Wilhelm's voice in *Wrong Move*. The narrator-character Eugene Fitzpatrick, Claire's former boyfriend, structures the story from an authorial perspective. He also contributes significantly to the film's self-reflective stance about the proliferation of images. Only late in the film do we realize that the entire film story is in fact a novel Eugene is writing about the experiences of his former girlfriend, whom he still loves. This is important insofar as the film takes a significant turn after Edith's death. Ravaged by grief and disappointment about his invention, Henry Farber, Sam's father, turns his computerized camera into a device for recording the brain activity of one's dreams, with the terrifying result that all who experiment with it become addicted to their dream images. Claire and Sam become apathetic junkies, unable to respond to the other's love and concerned only that their pocket monitors keep reproducing their recorded dreams. As these scenes make unmistakably clear, the further the proliferation of images progresses and the more thoroughly these images dominate our experience, the less autonomy people will have in their access to images.

Clearly, this is the climax of Wenders's pessimism: the visionary filmmaker warns what dangers exist in the unrestricted production of images. The words of the narrator sum up Wenders's own bleak findings: only words can save us from the endless flow of unshaped images—provided these words record events precisely, while still leaving room for the free play of imagination. At the end of *Until the End of the World*, the narrator writes his novel about Claire's adventure, which she then reads in order to be healed. There can be little doubt about the thesis of the film: only words can save us from an addiction to endlessly proliferating images.

From its beginnings, the cinema of Wim Wenders has tried to evoke the invisible and to show the melancholy vision behind it. The images of his cinema conjured up our reality so that we could see its second face, its true and actual character. The most important achievement in his films has been the delicate balance between that which was shown and that which was not shown. By omitting the center, Wenders stimulated the active imagination of his audience. Even in *Until the End of the World*, he refrains at least initially from trying to show the world as a whole—a mental picture that no images are able to reproduce. Later, however, he proceeds to do something that his experience as filmmaker should have forbidden him: he produces the recorded and addictive dreams visually by means of electronically produced color visions. This gives the impression that he is trying to create a visual elixir that parallels the intoxicating effects of alcohol or heroin. Needless to say, he fails.

Writing about Heinz Goldberg's *Paganini* with Conrad Veidt, Béla Balázs described how the demonic violin player is able to enchant the prison guards with his music and still "every ounce of resistance." Even "the crowd outside, charmed by his music, opens a path for the fiddler and his fiddle."[18] This magic and demonic play of the violin only worked because it was a silent film. As Balázs commented: "How great a virtuoso would have been required to play the violin in a sound film in order to achieve this? A merely visible, inaudible music, existing only in the imagination of the spectator, could have such a magic effect. The effect of music actually played would depend on the public's musical sensibility and taste, a quantity susceptible to innumerable variations. But to make it credible that the music did actually cast a spell on the prison guards, it would have to have a like effect on the whole audience."[19] This expresses *in nuce* Wenders's dilemma.

There can be no doubt that Wenders knows full well what he is doing. And he knows the cinema better than any other contemporary German filmmaker. Thus it seems even more incomprehensible that he attempts to cast his own spell against the bewitching excess of images. With the same purpose in mind, he has been experimenting for a long time with High Definition Television (HDTV), "where even after the hundredth generation and after one hundred manipulations, the image is as clear as the original."[20] But it seems that because of his involvement in these technical aspects Wenders has lost touch with his own cinematic precepts. He fails to distinguish between what should be made visible and open to scrutiny, and what should be left up to the subjective imagination of his audience. He has reified dreams, investing them with a visual mystical power. In doing so, he distorts the true force of the dream world in cinema, overlooking the fact that film is the medium par excellence for endowing dreams with their own fertile power. To quote John Berger one last time, "Great films are always revealed dreams."[21]

Translated by the editors

Notes

1. Ernst Bloch, *Spuren* (Frankurt am Main: Suhrkamp, 1985) 55.
2. Bloch 16.
3. Wim Wenders, "Impossible Stories" (reprinted in this volume). First published in German as "Unmögliche Geschichten," *Die Logik der Bilder*, ed. Michael Töteberg (Frankfurt am Main: Verlag der Autoren, 1988).
4. Wim Wenders, *Emotion Pictures: Reflections on the Cinema*, trans. Sean Whiteside in association with Michael Hofmann (London and Boston: Faber and Faber, 1986) 49. Slight changes have occasionally been made to the translation.
5. Wenders, *Emotion Pictures* 52.
6. Wenders, *Emotion Pictures* 53ff.
7. Roland Barthes, *The Empire of Signs* [1970], trans. Richard Howard (New York: Hill and Wang, 1982) 57.
8. Wim Wenders, quoted in Norbert Grob, "Alle Helden sind Engel," *Die Zeit* October 30, 1987.

9. Wim Wenders, *The Logic of Images: Essays and Conversations*, trans. Michael Hofmann (London and Boston: Faber and Faber, 1991) 63.

10. Wenders, "Impossible Stories" (reprinted in this volume).

11. Wenders, *The Logic of Images* 61.

12. Cf. Wenders's drawing for his first film review for the Munich journal *Filmkritik* (February 1969). Reprinted in the catalogue for the exhibition at the Frankfurt Film Museum, 1988.

13. Roland Barthes, "Fragmente einer Sprache der Liebe," *Fragmente* (Frankfurt am Main: Suhrkamp, 1986) 129.

14. From the voice over of *Reverse Angle* (reprinted in this volume).

15. "Interview mit Peter W. Jansen," Frieda Grafe, et al., *Wim Wenders* (Munich: Hanser, 1992) 68.

16. John Berger, "Was ist ein Film? Every time we say goodbye," *Lettre International* (Spring 1991): 63

17. Berger, "Was ist ein Film?" 61.

18. Béla Balázs, *Theory of Film*, trans. Edith Bone (London: Dennis Dobson, 1953) 200.

19. Balázs, *Theory of Film* 200ff.

20. "Interview mit Peter W. Jansen" 83.

21. Berger, "Was ist ein Film?" 63.

Oedi-pal Travels: Gender in the Cinema of Wim Wenders

GERD GEMÜNDEN

"Jeder Mann ist ein Abenteuer (die Frauen schauen zu)" (Every man is an adventure [the women look on]): thus reads the poster advertising Wim Wenders's 1976 film *Kings of the Road*.[1] The story is that of the chance encounter of two men drifting along the German-German border and their tenuous and temporary bond, which is severed when the two part company after a few days of communal travel. Male protagonists and male stories are at the center of virtually all of Wenders's feature films (with the exception of *The Scarlet Letter*, a film from which the director now distances himself) and even most of his shorts and documentaries. The conspicuous absence of women may mislead us to believe that gender is not an issue in the cinematic universe of Wenders—it is. In this essay I want to explore the relation between Wim and women by focusing on how gender issues structure his approach to American mass culture, to narrative, and to the logic of the image as the three areas that lie at the center of his filmmaking and his essayistic and theoretical work.

American Mass Culture: Between Lifesaver and Fatal Attraction

Like the works of no other recent German director, the films of Wim Wenders foreground the pivotal role American mass media and popular culture play in shaping the political, social, and psychological identity of the postwar generation of Germans. Many of his films employ American

205

genres such as the road movie and the thriller or elements from film noir, featuring as a constant ingredient the mostly diegetic use of American and British pop music and an abundance of mass-media icons such as pinball machines, billboards, Coke bottles, and the ubiquitous jukebox. Typically, Wenders's protagonists are heavily Americanized young men whose native language is German and whose identities are shaped in decisive yet contradictory terms by the American way of life. Through these films, Wenders's aesthetics emerge under the sign of a love-hate relationship that vacillates between an admiration for the Hollywood cinema of the fifties, with its technological proficiency, and a rejection of its economic and ideological status. While Wenders's position is by no means unique among German intellectuals, writers, or filmmakers of the immediate postwar generation— the names of Rainer Werner Fassbinder and Klaus Lemke or Rolf Dieter Brinkmann and Peter Handke come to mind—few of his contemporaries succeed in achieving the high level of self-reflexivity and ambiguity that informs all his work and which serves to undermine any solely celebratory or condemning stance.

Although Wenders's cultural schizophrenia has been well documented,[2] critics have paid little attention to the fact that in his films America and its mass culture appear as gendered constructs.[3] If one looks at Wenders's own statements about America, the United States seems to be portrayed as a kind of ersatz father, that is, as an alternative to a German fatherland tainted by a fascist past and unacceptable to the rebellious son. In an oft-quoted passage from a review of Joachim Fest's *Hitler—A Career*, Wenders notes, "I don't think that any other country has had such a loss of faith in its own images, stories and myths as we have. . . . There are good reasons for this distrust, for never before and in no other country have images and language been treated with such a complete lack of conscience as here; never before and in no other place have they been degraded to impart nothing but lies."[4] Elsewhere he states, "[Rock music] was for me the only alternative to Beethoven . . . because I was very insecure then about all culture that was offered to me, because I thought it was all fascism, pure fascism; and the only thing I was secure with from the beginning and felt had nothing to do with fascism was rock music."[5] While this characterization is admittedly exaggerated, the fact remains that Wenders and his generation were socialized into perceiving the mythic rather than the ideological propensities of the English-speaking world.[6] The heroes of the films of John Ford, Howard Hawks, and Nicholas Ray provided German adolescents with a much desired new mythology and served as models for European apprentices like Godard, Truffaut, and Wenders. Before becoming a filmmaker himself, Wenders reviewed the films of Ford and Ray (among many others) for *Filmkritik* and *Süddeutsche Zeitung*, praising them in a peculiar prose of positivistic description and paraphrase, while intentionally imitating in his style the surface quality that he perceived to be their aesthetic forte.[7] Writing about Ford, Wenders marveled at "the friendliness, the care, the thoroughness, the seriousness, the peace, the humanity . . . those faces that are never forced into anything; those landscapes that aren't just backgrounds, those stories which, even if they are funny, are never foolish; those actors who are always playing different versions of themselves."[8] Together with Nicholas Ray, who also stars in *The American Friend*, Wenders made *Lightning over Water*, an experimental documentary about their friendship and Ray's dying of cancer.[9] Clearly, this turn to U.S. filmmakers of an older generation is an attempt to rid himself of a cultural legacy that he repudiates yet dares not fully confront; like many of his characters, Wenders tries to escape the oedipal triangle rather than act it out, turning it into an oedi-pal relationship.

One should be cautioned, however, against seeing Wenders's attraction to American directors simply in terms of the father-son relationship that I've tenuously outlined so far. Wenders, for one, rejects any reading of his admiration for Ford or Ray as the search for an ersatz father.[10] What is more important, his films themselves invalidate the association of American cinema with typically male activities and characteristics. In Wenders's films, rock music, billboards, the ever-present jukebox and pinball machine, and cinema itself are almost always associated with the female. In three of his films the girlfriend or woman in whom the protagonist is interested works in a movie theater.[11] (These are *The Goalie's Anxiety at the Penalty Kick, Wrong Move*, and *Kings of the Road*, but one may as well add Jane, the peep-show artist of *Paris, Texas* to the list, for hers is the most sophisticated form of spectacle.) In *The Goalie's Anxiety at the Penalty Kick* we see Bloch playing the jukebox while escaping to the Hungarian border after committing a murder in Vienna. The song playing on the jukebox is "Gloria," the name of his female victim who worked at the cinema. Philip, the journalist of *Alice in the Cities*, does not know how to deal with seven-year-old Alice, yet he is willing to accept his responsibilities after a visit to a Chuck Berry concert. Whereas previously he had turned Alice over to the police, he now takes her back to conclude the search for her mother. "King of the road" Bruno Winter compensates for his inability to relate to women ("I always felt lonely inside a woman—lonely to the bone")[12] with a truck replete with portable record player, jukebox, movie stills, and projection machines. The house of the androgynous Tom Ripley —he kisses his friends and confesses his attraction to Jonathan Zimmerman —displays a Canada Dry neon sign, a pool table, and a Wurlitzer jukebox. Their friendship is latently homoerotic, with Ripley assuming the role of the seducer who lures Jonathan away from wife and child into a life of instability and adventure.[13] It would be easy to continue the list. In all these cases, mass culture serves as a replacement for women; the imaginary femininity of mass culture leads to the real exclusion of women on the level of narrative. Thus Wenders's imaginary America emerges not so much, as is often asserted, as the land of the spiritual ersatz father who is free of a tainted Nazi past, but as the mother figure.

This depiction of mass culture positions Wenders within a modernist tradition of the late nineteenth century, when "mass culture [became] associated with women while real, authentic culture remain[ed] the prerogative of men."[14] While Wenders's films can be seen as continuing this modernist tradition of gendering mass culture, they do deviate from it in significant and complex ways, placing them more within a postmodern sensibility. Like much of postmodern art, Wenders's films and their "heroes" are not obsessed with the anxiety of influence that defines high modernist art's volatile relationship with everyday life, but, on the contrary, are infatuated with mass culture and its icons. Instead of the misogynist and masculinist undertones typical of modernism, the lure of mass culture is portrayed sympathetically, a welcome remedy or, in Wenders's own words, a "lifesaver."[15] It is through mass culture and (its) technological reproduction that the male protagonists first make contact. After Robert's involuntary swim in the Elbe, Bruno and Robert quite literally "warm up" to each other when Bruno offers Robert a blanket and plays the song "The More I See You, The More I Want You" on the portable record player in his cab. Later in the film, they loudly accompany the tune "Just Like Eddy," a ritualistic act that marks the high point of their friendship. Travis, the estranged father in *Paris, Texas*, first meets with the sympathy of his son, Hunter, when together they watch a home movie showing scenes of earlier happy family life. I have already mentioned the transformative power of a Chuck Berry concert on Philip Winter. However, the attraction with such a feminized America bears serious consequences for Wenders's respective protagonists: Bruno Winter, the thoroughly Americanized movie-equipment repairman, remains a loner in his moving/movie truck, although the film's ending suggests that everything must, and indeed will, change. Jonathan Zimmermann's dangerous liaison with Tom Ripley turns into a fatal attraction when Zimmermann's dealings with his American friend lead him into the hands of the Mafia and to his early death. In *The State of Things*, Friedrich Munro, the German director of the Hollywood-produced film *The Survivors*, dies when loan sharks catch up with him and the producer, Gordon, in Los Angeles.

In all these cases, mass culture and Americanization—employed by Wenders as two virtually synonymous terms—are overdetermined concepts that connote complex processes of political, cultural, and sexual repression and displacement in the young Americanized male protagonists. The scenes of Robert and Bruno relating to each other best when lip-synching rock music reveal their inability to verbalize conflict, namely, the conflicts be-

A friendship formed by rock and roll—Bruno (Rüdiger Vogler) and Robert (Hanns Zischler) in *Kings of the Road* (1976).

tween each other, between them and their parents, and between them and women. Their singing along to records acknowledges a common childhood of displaced rebelliousness; instead of confronting the father, these German youths embrace the escape offered by rock music:

> Whenever I'm sad
> Whenever I'm blue
> Whenever my troubles are heavy
> Beneath the stars
> I play my guitar
> Just like Eddy.[16]

The relation of gender to mass culture pertains not only to the way in which Wenders's protagonists associate icons of mass culture with the female. In terms of spectatorship, mass culture has traditionally been considered to ascribe its user—or better, consumer—a passive, uncritical, and complacent position, traits usually associated with the female.[17] Bruno and Robert (as well as Philip Winter, Joseph Bloch, and Friedrich Munro) are prime examples of the hypersensitive, hesitant, and insecure males—in Germany labeled with the derogatory term *Softie*—who are caught up in narcissistic introspection and struggle with their masculine roles. Travis, the inept father and husband of *Paris, Texas,* has to learn from his son and the Mexican maid what a responsible male looks like, checking his so

209

acquired image and ego in the mirror. Unlike Wenders's other male protagonists, he does finally confront his wife, Jane, but the peep-show setting provides his monologue with the protection of invisibility and a voice estranged by the intercom system. His deeds accomplished, Travis flees the scene and rides into the Houston sunrise as a billboard sign ironically comments, "Together we make it happen."[18]

However one may choose to evaluate Wenders's preoccupation with mass culture, its association with masculinity is conspicuous in postwar German culture. An abundance of male postwar German artists have focused on America (writers from Wolfgang Koeppen, Max Frisch, and Martin Walser to Peter Handke, Gerhart Roth, and Rolf Dieter Brinkmann, and filmmakers such as Werner Schroeter, Edgar Reitz, Rainer Werner Fassbinder, Werner Herzog, and, more recently, Percy Adlon), while very few women deal with this subject (Marianne Rosenbaum in her *Peppermint Peace* and Monika Treut in *Virgin Machine* and *My Father Is Coming* seem to be the exceptions that confirm the rule). This suggests that the very problem of Americanization is one of *male* identity and that American culture has mapped itself in very complex ways over specifically male approaches to questions of German history, nationality, and identity.

Male Fantasies, Male Narratives

Clearly, women stand in the way of Wenders's narratives, which typically begin with a disoriented young man emotionally at a loss, often because he has left his wife (Robert Lander in *Kings of the Road*, Travis in *Paris, Texas*), is about to do so (Jonathan Zimmermann in *The American Friend*), or is trying to shake her off (as Philip is trying with young Alice in *Alice in the Cities*, and, in a different vein, Bloch, who murders his one-night stand in Vienna). Much of each film is then spent with the protagonist coming to terms with his problematic relationship to women, often in connection with some form of male bonding and performed as a search for the mother (*Alice in the Cities* and *Paris, Texas*). Love in Wenders's films is always the impossibility of love between a man and a woman, displaced onto mass culture, and analyzed by a male buddy, an oedi-pal.[19]

To be sure, Wenders's films are *Männerfilme*—the poster of *Kings of the Road* provocatively states, "Wenn Männer unterwegs sind, kommt was ins Rollen" ("When men are on the road, things are bound to happen")—they are films by a man, about men and male topics. Yet these films foreground this male-centeredness as problematic and, in fact, have been interpreted this way by German feminists, as we see in the following interview with Helke Sander and Margarethe von Trotta:

[Helke Sander:] "Maybe men should altogether refrain from using women as the projection of their own problems. They should deal with themselves. Women in films are always signs for something else. Wim Wenders has resisted that in his *Kings of the Road* by leaving them out altogether.

[von Trotta:] "I agree. I don't understand the reproach that women are excluded. I think it is only logical if he says: 'I know better how to speak about men because that's where my own experiences are.' "[20]

Although Wenders's cinema (like Hollywood) does not avail the female viewer a position, it still deviates from dominant cinema because it renders forms of masculine identification problematic. Wenders's employment of the road movie, which, like its cousin, the Western, is traditionally considered a male domain, proves this point. Clearly, his road movies subvert the Hollywood convention where women are excluded and relegated to the role of an object in the drama of male desire and conflict; while the focus is still on men, the issue becomes the male protagonists' uneasiness with women.[21]

The problem of the exclusion of women on the level of narrative has also to be seen as part of Wenders's *general* problem with narrative, and even his refusal to tell stories. His early short *Same Player Shoots Again* (1967) consists of five times repeating the same shot of the limping legs of a man holding a gun, each shot tinted in different black-and-white film stock—a structure that imitates, as the title explains, the five plays the pinball machine allows per game. The short *Silver City* (1968) is strung together from ten three-minute static shots of an immobile camera and depicts mundane and banal scenes of the Munich cityscape. The relation between image and story is generally perceived by Wenders as a threat to the image, which is constantly being molded and manipulated in order for a story to take place, "a vampire who tries to suck the blood out of the image."[22] This tension between showing and telling dominates not only the early shorts but virtually all of Wenders's feature films, especially *The Goalie's Anxiety at the Penalty Kick, Wrong Move, Kings of the Road* (the story of a friendship between a projectionist and a psycholinguist), and *Alice in the Cities* (where the protagonist cannot write about America but obsessively takes pictures).

No film deals with this subject more self-consciously than *The State of Things*. Made at a moment of personal crisis and marking a turning point in Wenders's career, this film examines self-critically the state of stories and the relation of women to narrative. In many ways the film summarizes familiar stylistic elements and (non)narrative patterns of Wenders's previous oeuvre and, of course, his own biography as filmmaker. The German director Friedrich Munro is a representative of non-Hollywood filmmaking;

his black-and-white science-fiction film *The Survivors*, as well as the first half of *The State of Things* itself, is poor on plot and suspense and rich on incident and atmosphere, "infusing a Hollywood genre with modern music, slow pacing, a poetic camera, and a tendency towards silence."[23] The depiction of the stranded crew idle at a hotel in Portugal, which takes up the first hour of the film, only hints at a general story line, while individual relationships remain vague and inconclusive. Sketches of character portrayals are interspersed with exquisitely framed shots of the Portugal seacoast and the desolate hotel, creating a mood of stagnation and suffocation. Although the last part of the film, with its faster pace, rock music, urban landscape, and road-movie sequences, is in many ways the antithesis of the Portugal scenes, it is only the other—that is, American—side of the Wenders trademark. As with most of his films, we find familiar forms of plotting men and male plots and frustrated attempts at heterosexual interaction. Looking for Gordon in the jungle of Hollywood, Friedrich turns into the Fordian searcher that *The State of Things* time and again alludes to; after Gordon tells Friedrich that he loves him, they find their communal death. The search for the absent father(s) encounters only traces they left behind: the billboard at the Nuart Cinema announcing the John Ford film, the memorial star of Fritz Lang on Hollywood Boulevard, the Murnau quote that Friedrich leaves on somebody's answering machine.[24]

What distinguishes *The State of Things* from earlier projects, however, is the analytical and self-critical rigor with which Wenders scrutinizes the obsessions and aporias of his own filmmaking. Friedrich explains to his crew that "stories only exist in stories, whereas life goes by in the course of time without the need to turn out stories"; his own skepticism toward original narratives leads him to do a remake of Allan Dwan's *The Most Dangerous Man Alive*. But the film's end proves him wrong: when he and Gordon are shot by the loan sharks, Friedrich is indeed experiencing what only a few hours earlier Gordon had called "the biggest story in the world," that is, death.

Likewise, women again have no part in the narrative; while there are several actresses among the crew in Portugal, the story does not develop until after Friedrich leaves his lover Kate and his other "dependents" to search for Gordon. This exclusion from the picture—that is, from *The State of Things* and from actual photographs—is questioned by Friedrich's lover. One evening Kate[25] looks through Polaroids and comments into her dictaphone:

> What's really interesting are these Polaroids that Julia made. Here Friedrich is perfectly framed and I am only half in the picture. Here is a beautiful framing job of Friedrich, looking very dapper, and I'm not visible at all. And Mark right in the middle of the picture with Anna

totally out of the shot, just her head remains. Dennis and Robert couldn't be more beautifully framed—they have plenty of space all around, even the curtains look good here. Whereas Joan only seems to have her entire body in the photograph because Dennis is on one side of her and Joe is on the other side of her; and of course Julia had to get both of these men, so Joan wins by default.

As the child of a director and an actress, Julia has internalized the dominant aesthetics of photography and filmmaking that marginalizes women; what triggers Kate's comments is her surprise to see these aesthetics permeate the ways of seeing of her presumably still innocent daughter—especially since these Polaroids taken during dinner are free of the artistic framing and grouping of the film production and thus attest more authentically to the spontaneous perception of the photographer.

The Logic of the Image: Between Manipulation and Seduction

Wenders's refusal to tell stories and the concomitant value placed on pure visual representation resurface in his oeuvre in the form of a self-conscious preoccupation with the image and its modes of technological reproduction. Virtually every Wenders film revolves around the question of the status of the image—from the early short *Alabama: 2000 Light Years*, an allegory on the death of the camera, to the philosophical reflections on video and film in the 1989 documentary *Notebooks on Clothes and Cities*, and, more recently, to his feature *Until the End of the World*, a monumental science-fiction road movie about the invention of a contraption that can make the blind see. All his films thematize more or less explicitly the defense and preservation of pure and transparent images vis-á-vis a multiplicity of threats to the image. These threats seem to fall into three categories: first, a threat to the image by the story, which deprives the image of its autonomy by forcing it into the service of an imposed narrative logic; second, a manipulation of the image that exploits it for specific ideological purposes (embodied, according to Wenders, by contemporary Hollywood films, television, and MTV); and third, a proliferation of images that uproots the autonomy of the pure image, severs it from its referent, and seduces the viewer into a world of simulacra. The second part of my essay has already described the relation of image to narrative; I will now focus on the threat of manipulation and the threat of seduction—both notions that, with their connotations of the feminine, again foreground the importance of gender in understanding Wenders's cinematic universe.

In *Alice in the Cities*, Philip Winter relates the following experience to his friend Edda: "I'm totally stuck. That was a horrible trip. From the moment you leave New York, nothing changes, everything looks the same so that you cannot imagine any change anymore. I have become a stranger to myself [Ich bin mir selbst fremd geworden]. . . . And yet I went on and listened to the loud-mouth radio, and in the evening I would watch the inhuman television in a motel that looked like the motel from the night before." Echoing statements—at times verbatim—from Wenders's early film reviews, Philip indicts the manipulative powers of television and radio, its reification of art, and the homogenizing effect of mass media. In one scene Philip angrily kicks in the television set because John Ford's *Young Mr. Lincoln*—employed here as an example of authentic art because of its pure images—is mutilated by a commercial. The 1982 film diary *Reverse Angle* continues this critique, now also including contemporary American *film*: "Contemporary American films look more and more like their own trailers. So much here in America has this tendency to become its own publicity, leading to an inflation and invasion of mindless and despotic images. And television, as usual, the poison ivy of the eyes."[26] Wenders's vocabulary is that of Adorno and Horkheimer's *Dialectic of Enlightenment* and their analysis of a world in which the culture industry erases individual experience through homogenization and brainwashing.[27] The long prose poem "The American Dream"—an extensive monologue from 1984 in which Wenders critically assesses his seven-year experience of living in the United States—condemns television as an agent in the subjugation of people and in the destruction of language, and holds it responsible for a hollowing out of the integrity of images. Underlying this notion of critique is the concept of false representation, epitomized for both Wenders and Adorno in television, for it willfully disguises, falsifies, and distorts.[28] "On that screen," Wenders comments during a stay in New York, "there was no longer the slightest connection between reality and its representation in images."[29] This connection *does* exist, Wenders maintains, in films like *Young Mr. Lincoln* and many of the Westerns by Ford, Hawks, and Walsh that follow an ethic of representation where the images are authentic because they "mean themselves"—an ethic that is now lost:

Once there was
the "American Cinema"
and its language
was the legitimate narrative form of America
and, in its finest moments, a fitting expression of the American Dream.
That cinema no longer exists.[30]

The second serious threat to the image is the threat of seduction. According to Jean Baudrillard, the most prominent representative of the theory of simulation, the boundary between representation and reality implodes, and as a result the very experience and ground of the "real" disappear, depriving the critical subject of its foundation. Signs and modes of representation come to constitute reality, signs gain autonomy and, in inter-action with other signs, form a new type of social order—Baudrillard's hy-perreal—in which the distinction between media and reality has been erased: "Simulation . . . is the death sentence of every reference. Whereas representation tries to absorb simulation by interpreting it as false represen-tation, simulation envelops the whole edifice of representation as itself a simulacrum."[31]

What unites Adorno's and Baudrillard's theories of media across their apparent differences is the melancholic undertone mourning the loss of origins and their communal strategy to perceive mass culture as woman. Andreas Huyssen has shown how *Dialectic of Enlightenment* casts mass culture as the female threat. Huyssen cites these telling passages from Adorno and Horkheimer's study: "[Mass culture] cannot renounce the threat of castration . . . mass culture, in her mirror, is always the most beau-tiful in the land."[32] For Baudrillard the attraction—and the threat—of simu-lacra lies in their seductive force—artifice is more seductive than the "real" or "natural." "It is no longer the subject which desires, it is the object which seduces,"[33] writes Baudrillard, and indeed the desire of Wenders's heroes—the search for their identity—is time and again replaced by seduc-tion through landscape—a landscape, to be sure, that itself is a highly cine-matic and cinema-constituted landscape: a second nature much rather than a first or "real" nature.

The threat of the seduction through images within a world of simula-cra is most forcefully presented in *Paris, Texas* and *Until the End of the World*. The first shot of Walt in *Paris, Texas* shows him answering the phone in front of the corner of a skyscraper. When he walks away from the scene we realize that in fact the skyscraper is only a billboard. Later in the film this confusion between reality and its replica occurs again when Travis shows Walt a photograph of his property in Paris, Texas. Walt then asks, "You bought the picture of a vacant lot in the mail?" "No! I bought the land."[34] The entire film is abundant with second nature: highway billboards, neon cowboys, motel signs, a statue of liberty spray-painted on the peep show in Houston, and so on—yet unlike earlier films, these images are pre-sented with little or no irony, not meaning to be parodic or critical, but as "eine Botschaft ins Leere,"[35] that is, a message into the void. As the pro-pelling force for Travis's and Hunter's search for the mother and thus the film's narrative, Jane is reduced to the status of an image: a photo of her and Travis taken in a photomat, a smiling face in a home movie, and ulti-mately a spectacle in a peep show, watched by others but unable to see herself.[36]

The case for the seductive force of images is reiterated in "The American Dream" (written at the time of *Paris, Texas*). Consider the fol-lowing passage:

Pictures and signs everywhere,
on huge boards, photographed, painted, in neon lights.
Nowhere else has this become such an art.
Nowhere else such an inflation of signs and symbols.
Nowhere else the eyes so busy,
so used to working overtime.
Nowhere else is vision harnessed like this,
to the service of seduction.
Nowhere else, therefore, so many longings and needs
because nowhere else are there so many addictions to vision[37]

Finally, *Until the End of the World* represents the strongest moral indictment of the use and abuse of images. The plot revolves around the invention of a contraption that makes the blind see and the serious consequences for all who are involved in this experiment. Edith dies from the images of a damaged world. After Henry Farber refurbishes the machine, enabling it to make visible one's own dreams (only to be taken away himself by the CIA), Sam and Claire become addicted to their dreams—originally conceived to make the blind see, the machine now blinds those who can see. "While originally the camera served to merchandise the dreams which it produced, now it dissolves the dreams by making them visible. Its images have become a drug which devours its victims."[38] Paradoxically, the evil spirit of images is exorcized by images. Chishu Ryu, representing the healing powers of Ozu's cinema, heals Sam Farber of an eye disease inflicted by his machine. Later, when Sam has become addicted to his dream images, his therapy consists of drawing rocks and leaves of grass and painting aquarelles.[39]

Until the End of the World reiterates this paradox on the level of form as well. Equal in length to *Kings of the Road*, it consists of three to four times as many shots. This acceleration of images seems propelled by the director's interest to show more, but it creates the opposite effect—the cities of Paris, Berlin, Lisbon, Tokyo, and San Francisco all look alike, resembling in their gratuity the sets for James Bond thrillers. They are the mere backdrops for the speedy chase across countries and continents, leaving neither time nor space for the camera to discover, that is, to see. It seems that Wenders has taken Cézanne's motto "You've got to hurry up, if you still want to see things"[40] too literally.

The project of discriminating between good and bad images, between false and authentic representation, between autonomy and manipulation or seduction, is omnipresent in the cinema of Wim Wenders. Against the threat of seduction and manipulation, Wenders heroically upholds the notion of the image as something pure, transparent, and autonomous—an image that does not derive its meaning through a network of signification but is meaningful in itself. About *Easy Rider* Wenders remarked that it is a political film not because of its plot but "it is political because it is beautiful."[41] "The American Dream" celebrates the self-sufficiency of a motel sign advertising a Holiday Inn:

> The sign was not there only
> to be seen and to draw attention to
> the hotel that stood behind it.
> It was also there on its own account.
> It was a sheer pleasure to see it.[42]

Elsewhere in the poem he admonishes:

> In German, the two words
> PROJECT and SEDUCE have the same root.
> SEDUCED BY PROJECTION
> the passive form of the active verb TO SEE.

Seeing is what his cinema teaches. His heroes (like those of Peter Handke) preferably assume the position of the spectator; they look on, they witness, they observe; sometimes, like the angels in *Wings of Desire*, they take notes. Their task, and that of Wenders's cinema, is *wahrnehmen*, that is, to perceive and at the same time to authenticate by ascribing truth and beauty. Hence the preserving gesture of many of his films that seek to capture what is about to disappear (sometimes with remarkable foresight): the apartment buildings soon to be torn down in the Hamburg harbor (*The American Friend*); the last functioning cinemas in the provinces (many of which were closed by the time *Kings of the Road* was finished); the borders between the two Germanys and Austria and Hungary; and, most dramatically, the Berlin Wall (in *Wings of Desire*). Time and again his films pay homage to his role models who taught him the art of seeing: the films of Ozu, John Ford, Howard Hawks, and Nicholas Ray; the paintings of Edward Hopper and Caspar David Friedrich; the photography of Walker Evans and August Sander. Time and again these films indict the forces that block vision. Yet as *Paris, Texas* and *Until the End of the World* demonstrate, this enterprise becomes more problematic and ambiguous. His films increasingly become aware of the difficulty and, even, impossibility of combating the power of images through cinema, bringing them closer to a position that Jameson has called the "winner loses" logic. As Richard Kearney comments in an analysis of *Paris, Texas*,

> The more cinema strives to expose the world of pseudo-images, the more it seems to confirm the omnipotence of the very system it wishes to contest. The more striking the portrait of a totalizing system of false imitations, the more impotent the viewer feels. To the extent, therefore, that Wenders *wins* by successfully representing an omnivorous system of mass media representation, to that same extent he *loses*—

"since the critical capacity of his work is thereby paralyzed; and the impulses of negation and revolt, not to speak of those of social transformation, are increasingly perceived as vain and trivial in the face of the model itself."[43]

This is the reason why Wenders's favorite genre is the road movie. Behind the windshield, Wenders's male heroes are safe from the endless flow of images rolling by, and from female seduction and manipulation. They are flaneurs—observing the world, women, and themselves, but not interacting with that which is presented in front of them. The world outside constantly changes, but in their metal containers they enjoy a relative stability outside of time and space, just as the moviegoers do in the dark and air-conditioned theater. This is also the reason why so many of Wenders's male protagonists are involved in framing pictures: the framemaker Jonathan Zimmermann, the photographer Philip Winter, the billboard maker Walt, the painter Derwatt, the projectionist Bruno Winter, the movie director Friedrich Munro, the engineer Sam Farber. Their job is the production of images, but in a more important way, they are involved in stopping the uncontrolled flow of images and in arresting the proliferation of signs and messages. It is their paradox—and Wenders's—that in order to battle images they have to create them.

Notes

1. The poster is reprinted in Frieda Grafe et al., *Wim Wenders* (Hamburg: Hanser, 1992) 69.
2. See Timothy Corrigan, *New German Cinema: The Displaced Image* (Austin: Texas UP, 1983); Dennis Mahoney, "'What's Wrong with a Cowboy in Hamburg?': Narcissism as Cultural Imperialism in Wim Wenders' *The American Friend*," *Journal of Evolutionary Psychology* 7 (1986): 106–16; Kathe Geist, *The Cinema of Wim Wenders: From Paris, France to "Paris, Texas"* (Ann Arbor: U.M.I. Research P, 1988); Thomas Elsaesser, "Germany's Imaginary America: Wim Wenders and Peter Handke," *European Cinema Conference Papers*, ed. Susan Hayward (Birmingham: Aston UP, 1984) 31–52; Eric Rentschler, "How American Is It? The U.S. as Image and Imaginary in German Film," *Persistence of Vision* 2 (1985): 5–18.
3. The only exception is Thomas Elsaesser, "American Graffiti und Neuer Deutscher Film: Filmemacher zwischen Avantgarde und Postmoderne," *Postmoderne: Zeichen eines kulturtellen Wandels*, ed. Andreas Huyssen and Klaus Scherpe (Hamburg: Rowohlt, 1986) 302–28.
4. Wim Wenders, "That's Entertainment: *Hitler*," *Emotion Pictures: Reflections on the Cinema*, trans. Sean Whiteside in association with Michael Hofmann (London: Faber and Faber, 1989) 94ff.
5. Jan Dawson, *Wim Wenders* (New York: Zoetrope, 1976) 12.

6. In the same interview with Dawson Wenders also notes, "My first memories of America were of a mythical country where everything was much better. It was chocolate and chewing gum. One of my cousins had an uncle in the United States and thanks to him I had a toy gun and an Indian headdress that I loved. In Germany at the time there weren't any toys and the only ones I knew were American toys, which were really marvelous. . . . At three or four I didn't know my country was occupied. I had no idea. . . . Certainly I saw troops, soldiers, tanks, but for me it was all spectacle" (12).

7. Wenders's aesthetics are very close to the position of Siegfried Kracauer, who also claims that "the cinema seems to come into its own when it clings to the surface of things"; *Theory of Film: The Redemption of Physical Reality* (New York: Oxford UP, 1965) 285. To my knowledge, there exists yet no analysis of Wenders's relation to Kracauer's film theory.

8. "Emotion Pictures: Slowly Rockin' On," in Wenders, *Emotion Pictures* 49.

9. On Wenders's relation to Nicholas Ray and John Ford see Timothy Corrigan, "Cinematic Snuff: German Friends and Narrative Murders," *Cinema Journal* 24.2 (1985): 9–18.

10. See Wenders's voice-over in *Lightning over Water* (Wim Wenders, Chris Sievernich, *Nick's Film/Lightning over Water* [Frankfurt am Main: Zweitausendeins, 1981]); and Tom Farell, "Nick Ray's German Friend Wim Wenders," *Wide Angle* 5.4 (1983): 62. In the film's version currently circulating in the United States, Wenders tells Ray's wife, Susan, "I'm not his [Ray's] son." Susan then asks back, "Are you sure?" Wenders: "No, I'm not sure. Still, I'm not his son." (The script does not contain this scene.)

11. See Elsaesser, "American Graffiti" 325.

12. "Ich hab' mich immer nur einsam gefühlt in einer Frau. Einsam bis auf die Knochen"; Fritz Müller-Scherz and Wim Wenders, *Im Lauf der Zeit: Drehbuch* (Frankfurt am Main: Zweitausendeins, 1977) 330.

13. Significantly, Wenders deviated from Highsmith's novel *Ripley's Game* by not casting the role of Ripley's wife, Helene.

14. Andreas Huyssen, "Mass Culture as Woman: Modernism's Other," *After the Great Divide: Modernism, Mass Culture, Postmodernism* (Bloomington: Indiana UP, 1987) 47.

15. See Wenders's famous statement to Jan Dawson, "My life was saved by Rock 'n' Roll" (11).

16. Müller-Scherz and Wenders, *Im Lauf der Zeit* 323.

17. See Siegfried Kracauer's famous essay "Die kleinen Ladenmädchen gehen ins Kino," *Das Ornament der Masse*, ed. Karsten Witte (Frankfurt am Main: Suhrkamp, 1977) 279–94. See also Patrice Petro's critique of Kracauer in her study on spectatorship and gender, *Joyless Streets: Women and Melodramatic Representation in Weimar Germany* (Princeton: Princeton UP, 1989).

18. As Wenders commented in an interview: "That was for me the only chance to have him exit from the scene, and together with him all my earlier male characters. All of them have now settled down in a suburb of Paris, Texas"; Taja Gut, "Unterwegs zur Filmkunst von Wim Wenders," *Individualität* 19 (1988): 28.

19. Obviously, this does not apply in equal measure to *Wings of Desire, Until the End of the World*, and *Faraway, So Close!* A discussion of the function of gender in these films would transcend the parameters of my analysis. While Wenders explicitly understands these films as a corrective to his previous centering on the male, I would argue that his revisions do not go beyond the level of narrative. In *Wings of Desire* there remains something deeply disturbing and unsettling about a love story between an artist and an angel whose apparently angelic and benevolent gaze is not only able to see without being seen, but who also invades the private sphere by going through walls and who knows the secret thoughts of the object of his desire. *Until the End of the World* is a love story as well, but without happy end; Claire and Sam's love is destroyed by the catastrophic events around them.

20. "[Helke Sander:] Vielleicht sollten es die Männer überhaupt einmal lassen, sich mit Frauen als Projektionen für ihre eigenen Probleme zu befassen. Sie sollten sich mit sich befassen. Frauen sind in Filmen immer Zeichen für etwas. Wim Wenders hat das in *Im Lauf der Zeit* mal nicht gemacht. Der hat die Frauen ganz herausgelassen. [von Trotta:] Das finde ich auch. Den Vorwurf, daß bei ihm die Frauen zu kurz kommen, verstehe ich nicht. Das ist ganz konsequent, wenn er sagt: 'Mir fällt zu Männern mehr ein, weil da meine Erfahrungen sind' "; Christa Maerker, "Was ich sagen möchte, kann ich so billig sagen: Gespräch mit Margarethe von Trotta und Helke Sander," *Jahrbuch Film 78/79*, ed. Hans Günther Pflaum (München: Hanser, 1978) 81.

21. See Gerd Gemünden, "On the Way to Language: Wenders' *Kings of the Road*," *Film Criticism* 15.2 (1991): 13–28.

22. Wim Wenders, "Impossible Stories" (reprinted in this volume).

23. Geist 93. The following paragraph retraces Geist's analysis.

24. In an obituary on Fritz Lang, Wenders significantly calls him "the lost, no, the missed father"; "Death Is No Solution: The German Film Director Fritz Lang," in Wenders, *Emotion Pictures* 107.

25. Kate is played by the actress Viva Auder, best known for her acting in films by Andy Warhol and Paul Morrissey. It is safe to assume that Viva wrote her own lines for this scene, which would also befit the general improvisational character of the film and its production history.

26. Voice-over by Wenders from *Reverse Angle* (reprinted in this volume). Geist juxtaposes Wenders's text with a passage from Adorno's "Transparencies on Film": "One will have observed that it is difficult, initially, to distinguish the preview of 'coming attractions' from the main film for which one is waiting. This may tell us something about the main attractions. Like the previews and like the pop hits, they are advertisements for themselves, bearing the commodity character like a mark of Cain on their foreheads. Every commercial film is actually only the preview of that which it promises and will never deliver" (106).

27. Max Horkheimer and Theodor W. Adorno, *Dialektik der Aufklärung* (Frankfurt am Main: Fischer, 1969). It should be added that Adorno somewhat revised his views on mass culture in two important essays: "The Culture Industry Reconsidered," trans. Anson G. Rabinbach, *New German Critique* 6 (1975): 12–19;

"Transparencies on Film," trans. Thomas Y. Levin, *New German Critique* 24–25 (1981–82): 199–205. See also the introductions by Andreas Huyssen and Miriam Hansen, respectively, in the same issues.

28. See also *Chambre 666*, a documentary in which fifteen filmmakers address Wenders's concern that a television aesthetics is threatening to permeate and replace a cinema aesthetics. On the relation of television to cinema see also the interview with Reinhold Rau in Reinhold Rau, *Wim Wenders und seine Filme* (Munich: Heyne, 1990) 237–64.

29. Wenders, *Emotion Pictures* 128.

30. Wenders, *Emotion Pictures* 133.

31. Jean Baudrillard, *Simulations*, trans. Pauls Foss, Paul Patton, and Philip Beitchman (New York: Semiotext(e), 1983) 11. The quote continues, "This would be the successive phases of the image: it is the reflection of a basic reality; it masks and perverts a basic reality; it masks the *absence* of a basic reality; it bears no relation to any reality whatever: it is its own pure simulacrum. In the first case, the image is a *good* appearance—the representation is of the order of sacrament. In the second, it is an *evil* appearance—of the order of malefice. In the third, it *plays at being* an appearance—it is of the order of sorcery. In the fourth, it is no longer of the order of appearance at all, but of simulation."

32. Huyssen, "Mass Culture as Woman" 48.

33. Jean Baudrillard, *Selected Writings*, ed. Mark Poster (Stanford: Stanford UP, 1988) 202.

34. Wim Wenders and Sam Shepard, *Paris, Texas*, ed. Chris Sievernich (Greno: Road Movies, 1984) 26.

35. Wim Wenders, *Written in the West: Photographien aus dem amerikanischen Westen* (Munich: Schirmer/Mosel, 1987) 13.

36. Cf. Elsaesser, "American Graffiti" 325.

37. "Bilder und Zeichen überall, / auf riesigen Tafeln, fotografiert, gemalt, in Neonlicht. / Nirgendwo sonst zu solch einer Kunst geworden. / Nirgendwo sonst eine solche Inflation von Zeichen. / Nirgendwo sonst das Auge so beschäftigt, / so überbeschäftigt. / Nirgendwo sonst das Sehenkönnen so in Anspruch genommen, / so im Dienste der Verführung. / Nirgendwo sonst daher so viele Sehnsüchte und Bedürfnisse, / weil nirgendwo sonst solche Seh-Süchte"; Wenders, *Emotion Pictures* 121.

38. Stefan Kolditz, "Kommentierte Filmographie," *Wim Wenders*, Friede Grafe et al., 300.

39. This information is based on my own conversation with Wenders. The presently circulating version of the film with 179 minutes does not contain these scenes. See *Wim Wenders*, Frieda Grafe et al., 89.

40. Used by Wenders in *Reverse Angle* (reprinted in this volume).

41. Wenders, *Emotion Pictures* 29.

42. Wenders, *Emotion Pictures* 126.

43. Richard Kearney, *The Wake of Imagination: Toward a Postmodern Culture* (Minneapolis: U of Minnesota P, 1988) 322. The quote within the quote is from Fredric Jameson, *Postmodernism, or The Cultural Logic of Late Capitalism* (Durham, NC: Duke UP, 1991) 5ff.

Wenders's
Windshields

ALICE KUZNIAR

Objects in mirror are closer than they appear

Jean Baudrillard opens *America* by citing as a caption this familiar warning from a car's passenger-side mirror. As the present study engages Baudrillard in a reading of Wenders's road movies, in particular, of their windshields and car mirrors, it might be profitable to speculate on what prompted Baudrillard to quote this ubiquitous message. Two mutually exclusive possibilities come to mind. First, Baudrillard's initial chapter, entitled "Vanishing Point," concerns what Paul Virilio calls the aesthetics of disappearance, the astral indifference and abstraction of the desert as one speeds through it. The convex side-view mirror confirms this exorcism by speed: by glancing into it we see the vehicle we just passed suddenly far in the distance. The mirror reminds us of our velocity by seeming to accelerate it. Second, Baudrillard could be alluding to his preoccupation with the promiscuous accessibility or availability of American hyperreality. As he writes in *Fatal Strategies*, "Obscenity is the absolute proximity of the thing seen, the gaze stuck in the screen of vision."[1] In other words, when simulated or reproduced in the mirror, reality comes closer; we connect and interface with it. This reading, of course, misinterprets the message, for the curved surface of a convex mirror does not bring the objects it reflects closer but casts them away, making them smaller than when seen in a flat mirror. Baudrillard may not, however, be misreading but playing on the ambiguous wording of the warning. It should say "Objects are closer than they appear in the mirror." As written, the phrase suggests in true Baudrillardian fashion that objects exist not in reality but in the mirror: they do not *appear* in the mirror—they *are* in the mirror. Moreover, they are closer in the mirror than they appear in reality. Regardless of which way we read the warning, the mirror distorts. But then again writing does too, forcing us to mistrust its ambiguity and paradoxically to rely on our eyes instead.

The simulacrum obeys this same paradox: on the one hand, its constant, identical reproduction elicits a sense of familiarity and closeness; on the other hand, its original referent remains indeterminable, lost in an infinitely receding distance. Car mirrors—and, one could add, windshields—function in ways similar to the photographic or cinematic simulacrum. The glass surface, like the lens of a camera, refracts and frames the passing roadside. But the windshield and car mirrors are not only lenses, they are also screens across which images flicker and disappear. More precisely, like the convex side-view mirror (in the alternative reading suggested by Baudrillard), the windshield brings the objects refracted through it closer to the driver. The landscape and cityscape images seem pasted directly before our eyes on the windshield, flattened out on it, not so much as on a movie screen as from inside a television, which, as Jameson writes, "articulates nothing but rather implodes, carrying its flattened image surface within itself."[2] At the same time that it brings objects nearer, however, the windshield shelters the driver and (as in our first reading) distances him or her from the surroundings. The edges of the windshield also make the driver aware of looking through something. This frame self-consciously evokes the camera shot that similarly cuts and selects images.

The mirror and cinema have been linked, of course, in psychoanalytic film criticism since the mid-seventies, when several issues of *Screen* were devoted to Lacanian film analysis. The Lacanian model traces the construction or suturing of the subject in its ambivalent struggle for dominance over the mirror/screen image. The subject alternately identifies with its specular double and distinguishes itself from it. The distance and closeness Baudrillard maps out in the operations of the side-view mirror, however, invert the Lacanian paradigm. For Baudrillard, the object takes precedence over the viewing subject. Existing *in* the mirror, it assumes a status independent from its origin. The flatness of the screen image, moreover, counters the depth model of psychoanalytic identity formation. Following Baudrillard, this essay purports to offer an anti-Lacanian reading of the role windshields, windows, and mirrors assume in Wenders's road movies. In so doing, it focuses on the play of simulacra as a means of diminishing and ultimately subverting interest in the subjectivity and selfhood of Wenders's main characters, who, though they may be loners, prove in postmodern fashion not to be disenchanted or alienated from their surroundings. Instead, they interface with their worlds through the window/mirror/screen.

Windshield reflections of a cowboy in Hamburg—Tom Ripley (Dennis Hopper) in *The American Friend* (1977).

Motion Pictures

Wenders's characters thus do not share his intermittently voiced hostility and aggression against the simulacrum. In essays and interviews Wenders has frequently criticized the cultural ascendancy of commodified images from American advertising and television.[3] His films assume a more ambivalent posture, however. They testify to the prevalence of the endlessly reproducible image—sometimes reluctantly, but sometimes with good-humored abandon. In particular, Wenders indulges his guilty fascination with the simulacrum via the windshield, that is, whenever he takes his characters on the road. With their shots reflecting images in the rear-view mirror or through the windshield, Wenders's road movies are quintessentially about the way we perceive "reality" through photography, film, and video. As Timothy Corrigan summarizes, "If the thriller makes the camera a weapon and the melodrama makes it a family member, in the road movie the camera adopts the framed perspective of the vehicle itself. In this genre, the perspective of the camera comes closest of any genre to the mechanical unrolling of images that defines the movie camera."[4]

Wenders clearly aligns these two kinds of "motion" pictures. In *Alice in the Cities*, for instance, Philip Winter travels by car through America, taking photographs to confirm where he has been. He rides through monotonous landscapes as if watching a film he has seen before. He even shoots through the windshield. Later in the film, he and Alice try to find the same view out of the windshield that is reproduced on a photo Alice props on the dashboard. A similar search takes place in *Paris, Texas* when Travis, who refuses to abandon the car in which he and his brother Walt ride, wants to drive to the identical desert site a photo commemorates.[5] *Tokyo-Ga* saliently compares the windshield with television: Wenders films a night scene out of a cab where a pay television is mounted on the windshield. The black-and-white image flickers like the lights on the freeway ahead. And in *Until the End of the World*, a road movie largely without the road, Claire's car's windshield is shattered at the outset in an accident, only to be replaced by its double, the curved, framed screen of the video terminal, whose aid the heroine enlists as she searches for Trevor/Sam across the globe.

Windshield and film overlap in additional ways. Both entail isolated, solitary viewing. Although Wenders's road movies are simultaneously buddy films (most notably, *Kings of the Road*), his characters chat very little. They travel in a car as if sitting alone in a movie theater, in blank solitude, with the images unfolding before them. They seem stationary, with all else moving instead. Indeed, like spectators in the theater, Wenders's characters do not go anywhere. In an interview, Wenders remarks, "The stability of the characters is something I'm only able to establish by putting them on the road and involving them in a lot of movement. . . . The people in my films don't actually change much, if at all."[6] One could add that they travel aimlessly or astray, relying on sheer contingency. In *Alice in the Cities*, for instance, although Philip and his young companion reach their goal—the house in Alice's photograph—her grandmother does not live there anymore. In *Kings of the Road*, Bruno and Robert hit a dead end as they reach the East German border. As Corrigan aptly points out, "The story of Robert and Bruno itself begins not with the desire to be somewhere or the vision of a new direction, but with the desire not to be somewhere and the choice of no direction."[7] In *The American Friend*, Jonathan dies at the wheel as his car goes out of control up against a dike, another "road sign" marking a dead end. And in *Paris, Texas* Travis first appears not following a road at all as he sets out aimlessly across the desert. Despite their obsessive travel, Wenders's characters do not get very far. Indeed, when they reach the end of the world in his recent film, they only confront a video screen redundantly playing back themselves.

If in these movies direction is unimportant and *Bildung* minimal (as *Wrong Move* suggests in its play on Goethe's classic Bildungsroman, *Wilhelm Meister's Apprenticeship*), then what does count is the sheer flux of images washing over the windshield. These images are hardly spectacular; their engrossing, hypnotizing quality stems more from their familiarity than from their uniqueness. Thus, despite their desolation, Wenders's landscapes eschew the category of the surrealistic, for the mundane objects in them do not suggest unfathomable, esoteric meaning. *Alice in the Cities*, for instance, shows the similarities between American and German towns and streets—the same gas stations, fast-food stands, and roadside telephone booths (all three also playing a prominent role in *Kings of the Road*). Every place looks alike in melancholic re(pro)duction. By filming such a large portion of the movie from the car, Wenders imparts to the viewer a sense of the real time experienced by Alice and Philip as they drive through the Rhineland. Or, more to the point, the monotony of their voyage gives the impression of extended duration that defies precise clock measurement. *Kings of the Road*, too, makes the time Robert and Bruno spend together seem longer because of the uniformity of the road they travel. Jameson, in his essay "Postmodernism, or The Cultural Logic of Late Capitalism," remarks "that we now inhabit the synchronic rather than the diachronic, and . . . that our daily life, our psychic experience, our cultural languages, are today dominated by categories of space rather than by categories of time, as in the preceding period of high modernism."[8] The New York cab driver in *Alice in the Cities* says, "In this city you lose all sense of time." *Until the End of the World* offers numerous such examples of erasure of time by space. When Claire, for instance, asks how long she has slept, Sam Farber replies in kilometers. Her tireless travel through different time zones (signified by the reminder of watch- and clockfaces) further comments ironically on the insignificance of time. And although the two lovers go to the ends of the world together, the end of the world itself, the apocalypse, never occurs (and if it did, a radio broadcaster announces, it would be noticeable only by a flash on the television screen).[9] The end of time appears immaterial, even trivial, in this film.

If Wenders thus measures time by space, it does not follow that space itself is differentiated. The two-dimensional surface of the windshield does not invite articulation. Moreover, because the window frames on the car do not move, they render the landscape uniform. The windshield registers the landscape as if through a camera that does not pan. As Corrigan writes apropos *Kings of the Road*, "The landscape and towns remain the same throughout; shot mostly through the stationary window frames of the truck, the country passes but does not change."[10] The movement registered on the car windows and mirrors thus seems frozen, almost photographic in its stillness. Indeed, if *Kings of the Road* and *Alice in the Cities* lack real, startling events that we have come to expect in the typically action-packed road movie, and if, in postmodern fashion, travel in these films lacks orientation, then it really does not matter what you see in (not through) the windshield: it's all the same anyhow. The flow of signs across it is ceaseless, provisional, and arbitrary. The objects that appear in it seem indifferent; they do not return the gaze.

Surface and Simulacrum

The windshield thus comes to represent a kind of void, a screen on which to record the movement of disappearance. The images on it are as blank and nonreferential as is its reflecting, clear surface. As pure surface or container, this sealed aperture is a paralyzed metonymy. It reflects neither the landscape nor the vehicle's passengers, but only its own surfaces. In *Kings of the Road*, for instance, faint reflections off the windshield of Bruno's truck not only do not reveal the landscape, they also, as Corrigan points out, prevent us from clearly discerning Bruno and Robert.[11] Subjective shots out of the windshield are actually rare in this film, replaced by ones out the side windows. The landscape is thereby seen tangentially through the two prominent side-view mirrors; it is already past, now absent. A night scene in *Tokyo-Ga* shot out of a train window likewise plays with reflections. A barely distinct but noticeable reflection of the train's interior is superimposed on a view of trains passing in other tracks. The reflection calls attention not to what it reflects but to the glass pane itself. At the same time, Wenders's voice-over meditates on the absence in contemporary cinema of moments of truth, when objects are shown, as in Ozu's movies, as they really are. The illusory play of reflections in the train conceivably alludes to the emptiness that Wenders admits he cannot escape—a fate, though, he seems (at least in *Tokyo-Ga*) not terribly to regret. This film documents with less resignation than fascination the prevalence of the simulacrum in the postmodern city—the Coca-Cola billboard dominating downtown Tokyo, the simulated golf on the rooftops of the city's skyscrapers, the Japanese rockers who copy American singers, and the wax food made to look just like its original.

In response to Walter Benjamin, Wenders seems to suggest that we have entered the age of technological reproduction that dulls the experience of shock and surprise.[12] His landscapes not only unfold like a film, they evoke other films, thereby inducing a sense of déjà vu. In a prose poem entitled "The American Dream" he writes about how, when looking for motivic material for a new film (*Paris, Texas*), he encountered decrepit gas stations littering U.S. Route 66.[13] In *Kings of the Road*, the first two gas stations at which Robert and Bruno stop no longer service customers. However small, this detail suggests that in *Kings of the Road* America does not just appear in the rock songs and the abandoned army outpost at the East German border but is inscribed throughout the landscape. The desert(ed) landscapes of *Kings of the Road, Paris, Texas*, and *Until the End of the World* evoke, of course, the precursor of the road movie, the Western. The desert and the movies are inseparably linked for late-twentieth-century travelers. As Baudrillard observes in *America*, "It is useless to seek to strip the desert of its cinematic aspects in order to restore its original essence; those features are thoroughly superimposed upon it and will not go away."[14] To the same effect, Wenders rhetorically asks in "The American Dream," "Is 'America' not an invention of the movies?"[15] He goes on to remark that in American national parks—"as if nature could only exist as a 'park'"—the vistas are already designated where the visitor is to stand, look, and photograph.[16] The landscape is already a simulacrum, or, as *The American Friend* reminds us with Derwatt's paintings, the picture is not authentic, in this case, not even as a true forgery. In other words, as previously noted, the windshield does not open onto the landscape but reproduces it on its screen; this copy then refers not to nature "out there" but to another reproductive medium. Collectively as a genre, road movies seem to capture on camera the transience of the road. This generalization does not apply to Wenders, however, for what one sees through his car windows is not unique but already copied. Even the relatively impromptu-filmed *Kings of the Road* was inspired by other images—by Walker Evans's documentary photographs of the depressed South. To cite Baudrillard again, "Everything is destined to reappear as simulation. Landscapes as photography."[17] Or, as Corrigan observes regarding *Paris, Texas*, "The wild west is a neon landscape where the lack of spatial depth makes everything look a bit like a postcard or a movie quote."[18] This indistinction between what one perceives through the windshield and through the camera perhaps explains why, except for the porno clip, we do not see the big screen in *Kings of the Road*, despite Bruno's profession as a projector repairman: the truck fully substitutes for the cinema. Its windshield is the "Weiße Wand," the name of the last movie theater Bruno visits. Indeed, at the end of the film, the capital neon letters "WW" are reflected in the truck's windshield.

Although the simulacrum does not refer back to reality, it is used in Wenders's films to verify reality. In other words, reality does not gauge the accuracy of the copy; rather, the copy authenticates reality. As Kathe Geist notes with respect to *Alice in the Cities*, for instance, Alice looks at photomat shots of herself and Philip at a moment when she needs to reassure herself that they are still a couple—when Philip has spent the night with another woman.[19] Earlier she photographed him in order, she says, to remind him of what he looks like. Philip's former girlfriend Angela tells him that he takes pictures as proof that he saw something and that he exists. In *The American Friend*, Tom Ripley showers himself with Polaroid photographs while lying on a pool table. He records on tape his anxieties about not knowing who he is, so as to listen to the tapes later in his car. It would be a mistake, though, to see Ripley trying to suture a self-identity via these redundant simulacra; as a con man who consciously dons a cowboy hat abroad and poses like Marilyn Monroe on red satin sheets, he seems to thrive on the pure, self-perpetuating momentum of reproductive play. Travis's dependency on simulacra in *Paris, Texas*, however, is more earnest. He repeatedly verifies his familial origins via the photograph—in the tattered photo of the vacant lot in Paris, Texas (where he believes he was conceived), in the family album, and in the magazine ads that tell him how fathers should look. Hunter seems to see through his father's addiction when he comments, after they have watched home movies together, that it wasn't really his mother on film but "her in a movie . . . a long time ago . . . 'in a galaxy far, far away.'"[20] He confirms that, as simulacrum, the home movie is just as unreal as the science-fiction film.

In *Until the End of the World*, Wenders's fascination with the simulacrum reaches its zenith. In this movie the characters do not even need to verify reality anymore: they do not have to see, because technology does so for them. With either their blank surface or "postcard" familiarity, Wenders's windshields turn vision into a kind of blindness. In *The Aesthetics of Disappearance*, Paul Virilio remarks that with high speeds the landscape vanishes.[21] *Until the End of the World* records precisely this disappearance, especially as Wenders had to edit an originally much longer version. As Claire hops around the globe—from Venice to Paris, Berlin, Lisbon, Tokyo, and San Francisco, to name but a few of the cities she visits—we glimpse only enough of each city to get some local flair. Mostly we stay inside hotels. In fact, Claire does not need to see where she is going, for her computer dashboard drives for her, reminding her of road conditions, speed limits, and so forth.[22] Her car perfectly fits Baudrillard's description of the car as vector in "The Ecstasy of Communication": "The vehicle now becomes a kind of capsule, its dashboard the brain, the surrounding landscape unfolding like a television screen."[23] Like the convex side-view mirror, Claire's dashboard brings what is occurring in the "outside" world closer, at the same time reducing to a minimum what we normally see. The external world is insignificant, for what matters are the directions from the simulated voice on the dashboard. It is no wonder, then, that Claire drives off the road at the outset of the film, for within the first few minutes of the film the road, so to speak, has already vanished.

Claire, moreover, does not so much travel as she traces Sam Farber's travel on computer. In fact, she traces what the bounty hunters are already tracing. As she spies on the simulacrum, her "searching" is best done by an advanced Russian computer program. Precisely speaking, it is not even Sam Farber who is traced, but his credit card number. Again in this movie, travel is simulated, practiced on the video screen. This mediation of vision is underscored by the preponderance of eyeglasses in the film—from corrective eyewear and sunglasses to the videorecorder resembling protectional eyegear that Sam dons to record visual experiences for his blind mother. At one point Henry Farber even wears two pairs of glasses. Repeatedly in *Until the End of the World*, vision is presented as filtered and faulty. But this does not mean that the intervening glass—be it the windshield, side-view mirror, camera, or sunglass lens—sharpens reality. On the contrary, *Until the End of the World* strongly suggests that simulated vision is incomplete. The reconstructed visual memories on the video screen remain fuzzy and fatiguing; their resolution is poor. And although *Until the End of the World* seems to suggest that original, unmediated vision is impossible in postmodernity, it also makes the point that ultimately one cannot see for another.[24] Sam's attempt to be the eyes for his mother not only literally tires his eyes and figuratively blinds him to reality (as he becomes absorbed in his dreams), but it also ends up killing her. When Edith simulates the vision of others through the apparatus her husband designed, the darkness of the world so saddens and weakens her that she dies. Wenders seems thereby to suggest that we should not allow the camera to intervene for us. But he also recognizes the impossibility of a nontechnologized alternative in a postindustrial society.

Dreaming and Driving

It is potentially misleading to speak of these viewing machines—be it the car windshield or Farber's sight simulator—in terms of intervention or filtering. The postmodern interface or symbiosis between self and machine is more fluid than these words suggest. In his reassessment of the logic of driving in "The Ecstasy of Communication," Baudrillard makes the point that the car is no longer "an object of psychological sanctuary": "If one thinks about it, people no longer project themselves into objects, with their affects and representations, their fantasies of possession, loss, mourning, jealousy: the psychological dimension has in a sense vanished, and even if it can be marked out in detail, one feels that it is not really there that things are being played out."[25] Following Baudrillard, we can say that the car no longer is a carapace or shell that the individual enters to drive. It ceases to function as an extension of the self, as its prothesis or "a live-in projectile."[26] The psychoanalytic categories of projection and introjection are thus inadequate. The car in postmodernity does not delineate an interiority; its doors and windows do not mark a boundary between inner and outer.[27] Rather, the windows act as an interface that renders indistinguishable inner and outer. The landscape is no longer "out there" but nearby, flattened onto a screen. That screen, already so close, seems inside us, as if unfolding in a dream.

This is not to say—again in terms of inner and outer—that the landscape on the windshield is a landscape of the mind, revealing the unconscious or projecting it outward. The windshield does not provide a means for self-representation, allowing the subject to view in it his or her own reflection. The metaphor of self-consciousness and inner vision is thus here inappropriate. More fitting is Lacan's observation on the inherent blindness in the dream, where, contrary to expectation, we are not the source or projector of what we see: "In the final resort, our position in the dream is profoundly that of someone who does not see. The subject does not see where it is leading, he follows. He may even on occasion detach himself, tell himself that it is a dream, but in no case will he be able to apprehend himself in the dream in the way in which, in the Cartesian cogito, he apprehends himself as thought. He may say to himself, *It's only a dream.* But he does not apprehend himself as someone who says to himself—*After all, I am the consciousness of the dream.*"[28] As a result, according to Lacan, dreams reduce us to a punctiform, evanescent, defenseless object. In terms of driving, the car takes control and we follow, vulnerable at each moment to sudden accident. At the mercy of the images that flood our ken, "our position . . . is profoundly that of someone who does not see."[29]

Wenders associates driving and sleeping, frequently in ways that highlight the blindness and passivity inherent in both activities. Gerd Gemünden, for instance, notes the link between traveling and dreaming in *Kings of the Road*: "While Robert is racing towards the river, the film cuts to Bruno, who wakes up in his truck saying, 'How can you dream such shit?'—a foreshadowing of the unbelievable scene he is about to witness. Only a few shots later, we see Robert closing his eyes behind the wheel."[30] At the outset of *Alice in the Cities*, shots of Philip sleeping before a turned-on television set in a hotel room are interspliced with a view out of the windshield. Even while sleeping, Philip has no respite from driving. The blink of the windshield wiper marks the rhythm to his blindness, his inability to see while in America, as if he spent his entire time there in a deep sleep, with closed eyes. Indeed, in the next shot of Philip on the road, his eyes are shut. *Tokyo-Ga*, too, links driving, television, and sleeping. The scene already discussed in the television-equipped taxi is followed by a scene of a television running blindly in a hotel room late at night, while Wenders's tired voice-over ruminates on how "images at one with the world are already lost forever." *Until the End of the World* clearly connects the dream with video. As Claire sleeplessly trots around the globe, her video-spying acts as a therapeutic substitute for dreaming. The video image, not the dream image, represents her fantasies. Later in the film, Claire, Sam, and his father become engrossed in viewing their simulated dreams on video. Henry Farber's invention promises to provide what Lacan tells us the dream prohibits, that one can apprehend oneself as seeing instead of passively being given-to-be-seen. The heightened self-consciousness offered by being able to watch one's dreams while awake proves illusory, though, as Claire and the Farbers become progressively estranged from themselves and the world around them while fixated on re-viewing their dreams.

What dreaming and driving have in common, then, is an inability to see and even a forgetting of what one sees. Baudrillard similarly writes in *America*, "Driving is a spectacular form of amnesia. Everything is to be discovered, everything to be obliterated."[31] But driving differs from dreaming in that it does not lead to either a literal or a figurative awakening. In Wenders's films the act of driving fails to reveal psychological depth in the characters. These individuals do not travel to gain experience, and their journeys do not lead to any profound, articulated insight into the self.[32] In fact, these characters seem as monotonous and unobtrusive as the images they watch moving across the windshield. Their depthlessness is represented in the flat image that materializes on the surface of the Polaroids they take (as with Philip Winter in *Alice in the Cities* and Tom Ripley in *The American Friend*). Baudrillard observes that "the polaroid photo is a sort of ecstatic membrane that has come away from the real object."[33] Wenders's characters exist as this membrane. Self-effacing, they seem like afterimages of the movie star.

Symbiosis with the Screen

In "Postmodernism, or The Cultural Logic of Late Capitalism," Jameson compares William Hurt with such older male actors as Steve McQueen and Jack Nicholson: "The immediately preceding generation projected their various roles through and by way of their well-known off-screen personalities, which often connoted rebellion and nonconformism. The latest generation of starring actors continues to assure the conventional functions of stardom (most notably sexuality) but in the utter absence of 'personality' in the older sense, and with something of the anonymity of character acting (which in actors like Hurt reaches virtuoso proportions, yet of a very different kind than the virtuosity of the older Brando or Olivier)."[34] In his performance of Trevor McPhee/Sam Farber in *Until the End of the World*, Hurt confirms Jameson's assessment of him. Like Solveig Dommartin in the role of Claire, he is remarkably indistinctive and nondescript. One could even say the two fail to convince as actors, were it not precisely the point that they are not supposed to engage the spectator. Dullness or tameness indeed characterizes Wenders's protagonists. The actor Rüdiger Vogler, for instance, embodies inertia and passivity in his various roles, as does Harry Dean Stanton as Travis in *Paris, Texas*. "Receptivity" would be too strong a term to designate how these figures interact with their environment; "susceptibility" sounds better. It is crucial, however, that this passivity not be construed as an expression of alienation. These men and women do not represent the alienated heroes and heroines of modernism.

Claire and Alice are certainly at home in the mobile, postmodern, high-tech universe. Claire scores so high on a visual recognition test that she is sent into outer space to decipher the earth's pollution from advanced photographic equipment. Waiting at the airport, Alice amuses herself by flipping through television stations and confesses she likes the nicely packaged food on planes. Peter Falk, from *Wings of Desire*, offers another example of a character who, despite his status as exiled angel, seems at home everywhere, be it America or Berlin. To be sure, other characters, such as Philip at the opening of *Alice in the Cities*, appear estranged and bewildered. Philip relates his nightmarish journey across America: "That was a horrible trip. From the minute you leave New York, nothing changes anymore. I could only imagine that it would continue like this forever." Notwithstanding, Philip affirms his attachment to America when he tells Alice he would just as well stay in New York, and later when he enjoys a Chuck Berry concert in Germany while drinking a Coca-Cola. Wenders exports America around the world: a Hamburg harbor could be New York; the border to East Germany resembles the American South; and Tokyo has its own Disneyland. It is thus not that the experience of America displaces or alienates Wenders's heroes. If anything, the American setting offers the prospect of communication and availability. *Until the End of the World* makes this point by portraying the United States as no longer the signifier of uniqueness and difference; instead, the major cities of the world look alike and are accessible through instantaneous travel and a computerized communications network. In their embrace of technology, these metropolitan centers are already Americanized. Such uniformity counteracts, even contradicts, alienation.

Alienation, of course, characterizes the Lacanian mirror stage, in which the subject oscillates between identification with the specular image and distantiation from it. The subject feels split from his or her selfsame but ultimately fictional double, a division that leads to aggression and fantasies of the fragmented body. The minimalization, if not absence, of alienation and aggression in Wenders's films (especially the later ones) makes the Lacanian model, so ubiquitous in film criticism today, inadequate for the task of defining the identity formation of Wenders's characters. Responding to the current inapplicability of Lacanian dualisms, Baudrillard has provocatively declared that "the mirror phase has given way to the video phase."[35] What this observation means is that we no longer mistrust the mirror image so as to act out a game of attraction and repulsion before it. As Baudrillard writes, we no longer experience "the distance and magic of the mirror."[36] Instead, we are completely immersed in the image, emptied out before it. There is no moment of detachment. Hence, in *Tokyo-Ga* and *Until the End of the World*, the Pachinko players lose themselves in their game; as Wenders says, they play to forget and merge with the machine. Philip voices a similar captivation by the image in *Alice in the Cities* when he compares the Polaroid with reality: "The still picture caught up with reality and overtook it." The video dream also supersedes reality in *Until the End of the World*, where it totally seduces and engulfs its viewer. These various films depict less the identity formation or suturing of the self than its dissolution before the image. The self mirrors not the actual image it sees but the depthlessness and two-dimensionality of the image.

With its peep-show scene between Travis and Jane, *Paris, Texas* invites a Lacanian reading that would highlight its protagonist's voyeurism and specularity. Travis sees what he wants, projecting himself into Jane's life, as his reflection cast on the glass through which he sees her suggests. Corrigan writes, "Like the central shot in the climatic sequence, which superimposes the reflection of his face on her body, he sees her only in the image of his failure to have any history but his own, again blindly in love with his own symptoms."[37] But more convincing than a Lacanian reading, I would argue, is one that would emphasize not Travis's self-imposition on the image but his self-abandonment to it.[38] He does not control the image; it determines him. In addition, it does not so much mold Travis as prevent him from acquiring a sense of individuality. For example, the photo he carries of his imputed place of conception—the vacant lot in Paris, Texas—does not give Travis an image with which to identify. Like the Polaroid taken from the airplane that Alice finds so beautiful, this photo is empty. It signifies only a displacement, a space Travis does not and never will occupy, for the name "Paris, Texas" is merely a disappointing joke. This memento of the family, moreover, cannot make good the family's dysfunctioning. Yet despite its banal emptiness, Travis is captivated by this photograph, just as he is by the billboards his brother designs: "Oh yeah? Oh, you're the one who makes those. I love those. Some of them are just beautiful." Travis also displays no critical distance from the magazines through which he searches for images of the successful father. Although he tries to copy the fashion models, in no way can they be said to define a selfhood for him. As Elsaesser observes, "Space and time, the question 'Who am I? Where do I come from?,' this reality, ever important to the subject and his history, is dissolved in the film into old photographs, into signifiers with multiple meanings (Paris, Texas), transformed into pure signs. The landscape, the buildings, all that Travis and Hunter carry along, eat, speak, see on their journey: all of it is nothing more than stick-on images of other contexts (the neon-cowboy, the painted Statue of Liberty, Travis's pick-up truck)."[39] These images, or "pure signs," as Elsaesser calls them, block access to an interiority. Like the numerous windows in this film, they act as a barrier. Thus, when Travis last catches a glimpse of his son and former wife, the glass wall of a downtown Houston hotel divides him from them. He then leaves, on the road again, still gazing through a window, through the windshield.

The Crack in the Mirror

With the pervasiveness of the simulacrum and the screen in Wenders's movies, the question arises, Does Wenders ever try to counteract the blindness that visual captivation paradoxically induces? Two possible answers come to mind: through the privileging of writing over vision, and through the "buddy system." The first possibility presents itself in various films. As he travels across America, Philip Winter faces the predicament of not being able to write a report of his journey because the sterility of the images he sees overwhelms him. But once he looks at the world through Alice's eyes, he begins to scribble in a notepad. Although the photos he takes represent a certain emptiness, paradoxically it is the script that is invisible: we never hear or see what he writes. Mysteriously, writing helps Philip overcome his addiction to the blank signs he captured on the Polaroids. Writing also surfaces as a metaphor for creativity in *Kings of the Road*. After he abandons his aimless travel with Bruno, Robert exchanges his suitcase for a notebook in which a child has spontaneously written down everything he sees. For children, Robert tells Bruno earlier, writing can be an adventure. In that sense, it substitutes for driving. *Wings of Desire* then foregrounds the written word, thanks in large part to Peter Handke, for whom the act of naming is "a transformation and sheltering of things endangered."[40] In *Wings of Desire*, witnessing—be it on the level of the angels or humans—is intimately tied to the written record: the angels take notes of what they see, as do the humans in the library. Damiel, of course, as the opening and closing shots of the film demonstrate, frames in writing the story he so desperately desired.[41]

The act of writing also frames *Until the End of the World*, but without, as in *Kings of the Road* or *Wings of Desire*, achieving effective closure. Here writing fails to serve as a viable antidote to visual overstimulation. Eugene Fitzpatrick, Claire's former partner, traces her steps around the world and ends up composing the story that we see (as his narrating voice-over intimates). He formulates his thoughts not on the computer, although the instrument abounds in this film, but on an old manual typewriter, as if to underscore the difference between technology and writing. At one point, when Claire has fallen prey to the video simulation of her dreams, Eugene superciliously affirms his belief in stories and words. He then saves her from her addictive habit by caging her and giving her the typescript of their tale to read. This quick resolution is too neat and unmotivated (if not infuriating for women viewers) to possibly consolidate Eugene's position as a mouthpiece for Wenders on the virtues of writing. Eugene appears, furthermore, as a weak, rather pathetic character who is more interested in writing than in gaining back his former girlfriend. Thus, although Wenders once again privileges the written over the visual image, he does so with an undercutting irony not evident in his earlier work.

Does, by contrast, the buddy movie check the dominance of the visual image? *Two for the Road* is a title that could be appended generically to most of Wenders's movies. His protagonists usually set off in pairs: Alice and Philip, Bruno and Robert, Travis and Walt/Hunter, and Claire and Trevor. Even the two angels, Damiel and Cassiel, sit together in a BMW in *Wings of Desire*. In addition, Wenders fantasized about turning *The American Friend*—with its pair Jonathan Zimmermann and Tom Ripley—into a road movie.[42] Although companionship can heighten the sense of adventure, as when Travis and Hunter take off together, usually it alleviates or allays only slightly the blank monotony and solitude of driving. These buddy movies score a delicate counterpoint between the oral and the visual, between minimal conversation and restless glances out the car window. With their gaze distracted by the landscape, these characters rarely look at each other. Their viewing is still isolated. The partnership, moreover, usually ends up being temporary, as in *Kings of the Road, Paris, Texas,* and *Until the End of the World*. Thus, although the buddy films promise to break the spell of the windshield, the predominant silence of the journey accentuates the glass barrier further.

Is there, then, a moment in Wenders's films where the tyranny of this "looking glass" abates? I believe that at least one key, though understated, instance can be found, significantly in an early film—in the closing shot of *Alice in the Cities*. In today's European trains, permanently sealed windows prohibit one from feeling, with the wind on one's face, the joyous exhilaration of speed. But in *Alice in the Cities*, in a simple gesture that displays their freedom, Alice and Philip pull down the train window and lean as far out as they can, directly into the racing landscape. With this interruption of the framed images on the window/screen the movie ends.

Notes

1. Jean Baudrillard, *Fatal Strategies*, trans. Philip Beitchman and W. G. J. Niesluchowski (New York and London: Semiotext(e)/Pluto, 1990) 59.
2. Fredric Jameson, *Postmodernism, or The Cultural Logic of Late Capitalism* (Durham, NC: Duke UP, 1991) 37.
3. See his prose poem "The American Dream" in Wim Wenders, *Emotion Pictures: Reflections on the Cinema,* trans. Sean Whiteside (London and Boston: Faber and Faber, 1989), and in "Reden über Deutschland" in Wim Wenders, *The Act of Seeing: Texte und Gespräche* (Frankfurt am Main: Verlag der Autoren, 1992) 187–98. Appears in English translation in this volume.

4. Timothy Corrigan, *A Cinema without Walls: Movies and Culture after Vietnam* (New Brunswick, NJ: Rutgers UP, 1991) 145–46. Cf. Gerd Gemünden, "On the Way to Language: Wenders' *Kings of the Road*," *Film Criticism* 15 (1991): 24: "This feeling of being behind the screen is also conveyed by the many shots showing the two travellers in the cab, with the windshield being the screen onto which the passing landscape is projected—yet another parallel of travel and film, of voyage and cinema."

5. In both films, the protagonist discovers that he or she cannot go home, for that home exists ironically only in the photo. In other words, once framed by the camera lens or windshield, one's home recedes into the distance.

6. Jan Dawson, *Wim Wenders*, trans. Carla Wartenberg (New York: Zoetrope, 1976) 14.

7. Timothy Corrigan, *New German Film: The Displaced Image* (Austin: U of Texas P, 1983) 27. Corrigan also explores the extensive use *Kings of the Road* makes of circular imagery.

8. Jameson 16.

9. The German title *Bis ans Ende der Welt* carries only the spatial connotation.

10. Corrigan, *New German Film* 33.

11. Corrigan, *New German Film* 32–33.

12. Walter Benjamin, "The Work of Art in the Age of Mechanical Reproduction," *Illuminations*, trans. Harry Zohn (New York: Schocken, 1969) 238: "The painting invites the spectator to contemplation; before it the spectator can abandon himself to his associations. Before the movie frame he cannot do so. No sooner has his eye grasped a scene than it is already changed. It cannot be arrested. . . . This constitutes the shock effect of the film."

13. Wenders, *Emotion Pictures* 145.

14. Jean Baudrillard, *America*, trans. Chris Turner, paperback ed. (London and New York: Verso, 1989) 69.

15. Wenders, *Emotion Pictures* 119.

16. Wenders, *Emotion Pictures* 121.

17. Baudrillard, *America* 32.

18. Corrigan, *A Cinema without Walls* 156.

19. Kathe Geist, *The Cinema of Wim Wenders: From Paris, France to "Paris, Texas"* (Ann Arbor and London: U.M.I. Research P, 1988) 36.

20. Wim Wenders, Sam Shepard, and L. M. Kit Carson, *Paris, Texas* (New York: Ecco, 1984) 42.

21. In fact, Virilio notes that the development of high-speed technology leads to the disappearance of our ability to perceive directly the phenomena that inform us of our existence; *Esthétique de la disparition* (Paris: Balland, 1980) 125.

22. Claire's attachment to the vehicle is concretely demonstrated later in the film when she remains handcuffed to the unhinged airplane door as she tracks across the Australian desert.

23. Jean Baudrillard, "The Ecstasy of Communication," *The Anti-Aesthetic: Essays on Postmodern Culture*, ed. Hal Foster (Port Townsend, WA: Bay Press, 1983) 127.

24. *Wings of Desire* is also ambivalent on this account. On the one hand, the angels' beatific gaze testifies to the camera's gaze by similarly framing the isolated moment and endowing it with significance. On the other hand, Damiel's decision to forfeit this privileged but distanced vision indicates he wants direct, unmediated experience of the world.
25. Baudrillard, "The Ecstasy of Communication" 127.
26. Baudrillard, "The Ecstasy of Communication" 127.
27. An exception might arguably be the mobile home in which Bruno in *Kings of the Road* and Gordon in *The State of Things* live like mollusks. But as this self-equipped unit prevents contact with the outside world; it defines an interiority for its inhabitant only by default. In fact, in *The State of Things* the final long, backward projection of a traveling shot displays the sad, hollow life of Gordon, who has nothing to do but ride around in a mobile home and wait to be blown away.
28. Jacques Lacan, *The Four Fundamental Concepts of Psycho-Analysis*, trans. Alan Sheridan (New York and London: Norton, 1981) 75–76.
29. Virilio writes, "Si tout est mouvement, tout est en même temps accident et notre existence de véhicule métabolique pourrait se résumer à une série de collisions, de traumatismes, les uns prenant l'aspect de caresses lentes et perceptibles, les mêmes suivant l'impulsion qui leur est donnée, devenant des chocs mortels, des apothéoses de feu mais surtout *une autre manière d'être*. La vitesse est une cause de mort dont nous sommes non seulement responsables, mais plus encore créateurs et inventeurs" (123). ("If everything is movement, everything is at the same time accident, and our existence as this metabolical vehicle could be summed up as a series of collisions, of traumatisms, some taking on the aspect of slow and perceptible caresses, the same ones, following the impulse given them, becoming deadly shocks, apotheoses of fire, but above all *another way of being*. Speed is a cause of death for which we are not only responsible but, even more so, the creators and inventors.")
30. Gemünden 20.
31. Baudrillard, *America* 9.
32. Here I disagreee with Kathe Geist, who writes, "Travel, of course, is a metaphor for the search of identity. For Wenders, travel is literally a means of discovering one's identity" (42).
33. Baudrillard, *America* 37.
34. Jameson 20.
35. Baudrillard, *America* 37.
36. Baudrillard, *America* 37.
37. Corrigan, *A Cinema without Walls* 156.
38. *Paris, Texas* is arguably not only post-Lacanian but also post-oedipal. Wenders abandoned his initial plan to portray Travis's encounter with his father in order to focus on Jane instead (see Paul Coates, *The Gorgon's Gaze: German Cinema, Expressionism, and the Image of Horror* [Cambridge and New York: Cambridge UP, 1991] 255). Hence, instead of the son rebelling against the father, the father reunites the son with the mother. There is, moreover, never any oedipal-like struggle for custody of Hunter between the two pseudofathers. Travis

is, after all, less a father than a child himself. Thomas Elsaesser ("American Graffiti und Neuer Deutscher Film—Filmemacher zwischen Avantgarde und Postmoderne," *Postmoderne: Zeichen eines kulturellen Wandels*, ed. Andreas Huyssen and Klaus Scherpe [Hamburg: Rowohlt, 1986] 325) observes: "Da er sich zum Spiegelbild seines Sohnes gemacht hat, kann er nun als Sohn mit seiner Frau vereint sein, und somit ist er gleichzeitig sein eigener Vater und Sohn, während Jane ihm Frau und Mutter ist" ("Because he has made himself into the mirror image of his son, he can only be joined with his wife as a son. Therefore, he is at once his own father and son, while Jane is both wife and mother to him"). It can also be argued that rather than inscribing himself into the family structure, Travis repeatedly removes himself from it. Wenders's other films likewise invite an anti-oedipal reading; for instance, the encounter between Robert and his father in *Kings of the Road* could be read as a parody of oedipal conflict. Further characteristic of Wenders's anti-Symbolic tendency is the absence of the law in films such as *The Goalie's Anxiety at the Penalty Kick, The American Friend*, and *Until the End of the World*, where criminal actions lead one to expect in vain police intervention. I am grateful to Idelber Avelar for suggesting this anti-oedipal view of Wenders.

39. Elsaesser 324. ("Raum und Zeit, die Frage 'Wer bin ich? Woher komme ich?,' diese für das Subjekt und seine Geschichte stets wichtige Realität wird im Film in alte Fotos aufgelöst, in mehrdeutige Signifikanten [Paris, Texas], in pure Zeichen transformiert. Die Landschaft, die Gebäude, alles, was Travis und Hunter auf ihrer Reise tragen, essen, reden, sehen: nichts als Abziehbilder anderer Kontexte [der Neon-Cowboy, die gemalte Freiheitsstatue, Travis' Pick-up-Truck].")

40. Peter Handke, *Slow Homecoming*, trans. Ralph Manheim (New York: Macmillan, 1988) 181.

41. Damiel tells Cassiel that he wants to wrestle a story for himself: "Mir selber eine Geschichte erstreiten"; Wim Wenders and Peter Handke, *Der Himmel über Berlin: Ein Filmbuch* (Frankfurt am Main: Suhrkamp, 1987) 84. See also my "Ephemeral Inscriptions: Wenders's and Handke's Testimony to Writing," *Seminar* 31 (1995): 217–28.

42. See Dawson 14.

Spectators of Life:
Time, Place, and Self in the
Films of Wim Wenders

THOMAS ELSAESSER

All filmmakers are obsessed with the cinema. Their perception of life, of human relationships, of what is possible and what is beautiful, is in some measure determined by the fact that cinema is their life. Since this was true even of many a professional producer in the heyday of the commercial cinema,[1] how much more must it be the case with an independent filmmaker, one who, as in most European countries, has to be scriptwriter, producer, and director all in one, who worries about distribution as much as financing, and who often has to think about and work with his project for several years: vigilant and alert like a wild animal stalking a prey that still has a chance of getting away.[2]

Wim Wenders is such an obsessional filmmaker, in whose life, judging by the meager data he has supplied to inquiring journalists, nothing much seems to have been of significance apart from rock music and movies, first as a spectator-listener, then as a critic, and finally as a director. Completing about twenty films in the last twenty-five years may not seem much for someone who lives, breathes, and dreams cinema day and night, yet it highlights not only the difficulties of both auteur and art cinema in the 1990s, but also the sheer stamina and determination of one who is convinced he has something to say.

Is this determination to shape a "work" the reason why Wenders is, despite a number of critical and commercial setbacks in recent years, still

240

so highly valued, still regarded the most important filmmaker of his generation? After the death of Fellini and Fassbinder and the retreat from cinema of Bergman and Antonioni,[3] it seems that Wenders is inheriting the ambiguous privilege of epitomizing for the American public what a European director is or ought to be. Aware that this international reputation is his cultural capital, and yet hyperconscious of the danger of becoming his own pasticheur and parodist, Wenders's recent films display a kind of gravitas and self-reflexivity perhaps too easily identified as Germanic pomposity and unseemly self-importance.

I want to approach this configuration of a filmmaker at once deeply committed to the cinema and yet determined to make it say something about "life" and "history" via a threefold argument, reflecting a set of interlocking concerns in Wenders's own work: first, there is the outer envelope, as it were, which is Wenders's contribution to the interminable dialogue between European filmmakers and Hollywood; second, the formal-aesthetic issue of "story" and "image," telling and showing, an issue that has often divided the avant-garde from the mainstream in cinema but which is once more of topical relevance as the cinema confronts the technological and aesthetic possibilities of the electronic image; and third, there is a tension, peculiar to Wenders's work, between filmmaking as an active intervention in life and as a more passive recording, a tension that is suggestive of the more general distribution of roles between filmmaker, protagonist, and spectator. These three concerns, which are everywhere in evidence in Wenders's films, I want to probe around two motifs, indeed the two main topics under which Wenders's films tend to be discussed: that of the journey as the central narrative trajectory, and the relation between men and women as the focus for narrative conflict (or lack of it). I will deal with my three headings in reverse order, beginning with the kinds of spectatorship invoked or implied in Wenders's films.

From Addiction to Seduction

Wenders learned his love of the cinema and his craft as a filmmaker by being first possessed by the cinema as a spectator. This is by no means always the case with film directors (it certainly does not apply to Werner Herzog or Hans-Jürgen Syberberg), but in Europe it has its well-documented precedents in the French nouvelle vague of the 1960s (Truffaut, Godard, Rivette, Rohmer). Wenders's work is at the cutting edge of a crucial ambivalence that seems to affect only directors who have experienced going to the cinema as an addiction.

The ambivalence has been called a love-hate relationship—with the cinema in general, and with the American cinema in particular. But one might also call it a fascination, if this term did not suggest too genteel and urbane an interest; what is more typical is not only a moral ambivalence but an absorption to the point of self-oblivion. The moment forever deferred is that of the addict rousing himself from the trance in which he has been living, waking up, and leaving the cinema in disgust, swearing never to return. It is a frequent phenomenon among film critics, who (often in their late thirties) publicly denounce their job as worthless and self-serving and cease writing about films. Some of these renegades become academics. The alternative is to turn the habit inside out and begin to make films, thus mastering the addiction by dedicating one's life to seducing others. The cycle has a name—cinephilia—and among directors Wenders is surely one of its prominent exponents. This is not as frivolous an argument as it might appear, and it is relevant to Wenders. His work (comparable in this only to that of Godard in the 1960s) has created a kind of complicity of identification among his audience, his heroes, and his own persona that rests on the unexamined pleasure the films afford to a certain kind of viewer (who, it has to be said, tends to be male). The films foster the illusion that to be the spectator of a Wenders film is to be its director, since nothing is required except to place oneself in the position of the protagonist. Let me illustrate what I mean by a quotation: It is from the beginning of one of Wenders's short films, *Reverse Angle*, featuring Wenders's voice-over while we see him stepping off a plane at Kennedy Airport, New York:

> "Another night, arriving at another airport, and coming from yet another city: For the first time in his life he was sick and tired of traveling. All cities had become one. Somehow he kept thinking of a book that he must have read as a child. All he remembered of it was this feeling of being lost . . ." That could be the beginning of another story or another film. Just cut to a close-up.[4]

Reverse Angle's protagonist, as one can see, is himself nothing but an observer and a spectator, a weary traveler of life, and the ambivalence that so delicately but decisively multiplies its effects, like a conspiratorial relay passing constantly between film and spectator, is that the illusion of being the creator of the film one is watching is sustained by the equally acute, even if repressed, knowledge of the emptiness of a life whose main aim is going to the cinema. To put it in slightly different terms: the effort it must have taken to break away from being a spectator of films and to become a maker of films is preserved in Wenders's cinema in both obvious and subtle ways, the most obvious being the crisscrossing—aesthetic and geographical—by which he weaves Hollywood, but also television, into the fabric of each of his films.

In the early films, love and loathing seem evenly balanced, or abruptly juxtaposed, as in *Alice in the Cities* where the hero, Philip Winter, uneasily falls asleep in front of the television in his motel room with Henry

Fonda playing a Jew's harp in *Young Mr. Lincoln,* and on waking up kicks in the television set as the film is interrupted by a used-car commercial. The disgust with television voiced throughout *Alice in the Cities* is as eloquent as that of any unreconstructed cinephile, but it is merely the reverse angle of the love that nurtured an earlier infatuation with John Ford, Howard Hawks, Alfred Hitchcock, or Raoul Walsh and which needs a "bad object" in order to keep that love pure. Hence the subtler and darker aspects of the ambivalence. Not, therefore, an ambivalence over whether to make commercial cinema or independent films, whether narrative or experimental, but an attraction and a revulsion more comparable to the probing of a wound that absorbs one's distracted attention. Another, and perhaps more relevant point to make is that the question of cinema—not this or that film, but what it means that the cinema exists—is one Wenders takes utterly seriously:

> I hesitate to talk about myself. Okay, I'm a filmmaker, my films are even very personal; but never private. I was tempted, though, when I was asked if I'd make a sort of New York journal over a couple of weeks for French television. What made me want to do it in the end, was the idea to take a camera myself and shoot something outside the context of a story. Just images.
>
> One should think that after ten feature films I would regard this as my profession: to tell stories through images. But strangely enough, I could never really believe that. Maybe because somehow the images always mattered more to me than the stories, or should I even say that often enough the "story" wasn't more than a pretext to find images. But images, too, aren't very reliable. From time to time . . . they seem to escape me. At least I don't see anything anymore that appears relevant and worth keeping. I totally lose the sense of conceiving images at all, and if I try, during such a time, they seem completely fortuitous, images without any form, because there is no look that could give them one. And the worst look that can happen: the point of view of the tourist.
>
> And now, too, without a story to tell, the images become interchangeable, arbitrary, and their objects in search of their lost form seem to be looking at me directly through the camera saying: "What do you want from us? Leave us alone."[5]

Narrative and Politics

We can put the central problem more sharply still: Wenders's films are always balanced between two orders of being-in-the-world, often quite starkly opposed: image and story, music and language. For instance, his student films were, by his own testimony, a protest against mainstream cinema's need to subordinate its images to a strong plot or story line. But Wenders's shorts did not protest verbally against what the director perceived as the oppressive dominance of Hollywood; they dispensed with words altogether and let music speak in their place, the rock music of the sixties. It was as if for the young filmmaker two languages were inadmissible: Hollywood film dramaturgy and spoken German, so that films like *Same Player Shoots Again* (note the English title, from a pinball machine) appear to be antinarrative films, where long, slow pans and a rock music sound track point an accusing finger at that to which they refer negatively: suspense, action, dialogue. Only English lyrics could be trusted (The Who, Credence Clearwater Revival, Jimmy Hendrix, The Doors, and The Kinks were Wenders's favorite bands), and only a cinema of *temps morts* (dead time), of observation, could reply to the hectic business of a certain Hollywood cinema of car chases and smashups, where action is, according to Wenders, always a form of pornography, a raping of objects, of people, of feelings, landscapes, and spectators. Hollywood of the sixties and the German language: these were the antagonists and mirrors, the implied terms of a stance adopted intuitively in order to get away from a claustrophobia that in time Wenders would read historically as part of the reality of postwar Germany, and even politically as the necessary but nonetheless fateful colonization by American popular culture.

From this rather extreme silence with regard to his own cultural traditions (which Wenders shared with many avant-garde filmmakers of his generation), the gradual appropriation in his films of both spoken language and a Hollywood idiom, however indirectly handled, became indispensable for survival and represents in some respects the recovery from a trauma, a debility, an impotence, a sickness. Wenders's first feature films—*Summer in the City, The Goalie's Anxiety at the Penalty Kick*, and *Wrong Move*—are the testimony to this tension between a moviegoer and a moviemaker slowly finding his way: typically, in all of Wenders's films, right up to *The State of Things*, there are traces of aphasia, insofar as, for instance, in both *Alice in the Cities* and *Kings of the Road* the first ten or fifteen minutes are without dialogue. In *The State of Things*, made after Wenders's disastrous collaboration with Francis Ford Coppola, the tension expresses itself as the opposition between the Hollywood movie industry and European filmmaking. In each case, however, it involves that unresolved relationship with storytelling and narrative already verbalized in *Alice in the Cities* when Philip goes to see his New York editor to show him the pictures he has taken, to be told: "I sent you to get a story, and you come back with a pack of postcards." The conflict turns up again, in almost identical form, in the long scene between the director and his producer in the back of the mobile home cruising around Los Angeles to avoid the hit squad in *The State of Things*.

The fact that such scenes, one from a film made in 1974 and the other made in 1982, are leitmotifs in his work have not only contributed to Wenders's being seen as an auteur who pursues with great consistency a limited but focused set of issues. The emphasis on nationality and the contrast with America have also made Wenders the spokesman for his generation and have helped his protagonists' passing for the quintessential new German, born after the war and radicalized in the late sixties, but in ways that in turn had to be questioned. For instance, radical politics and macho values were challenged in Wenders's films by a sensibility that allowed men to become vulnerable, introspective, and melancholy without being seen as weak. They were radicals, but radically subjective and individual. The connections between this radical subjectivity on the one side, and politics, history, and postwar Germany on the other, was not obvious; it had to be explored and discovered. Above all, it could not be assumed as given in the sociology classes and courses in Marxism taught at the universities: "history," "revolution," and "ideology" became for Wenders so many other languages out of bounds, from which he also had to escape in order to become a filmmaker.

On the Road

The quest and the journey: the hallmarks of Wenders's cinema in the 1970s became ever more globally encompassing in the 1980s. The films were called road movies, but this does not do full justice to the complex set of issues they try to clarify, chief among them that of the relation of the "now" to the "then," the self to others, and, equally fundamental, that between story and image, because it not only played across the Europe-America divide but also defined the modes and qualities of human interaction generally: the active and passive mode, what it means to give and to receive, of establishing contact and refusing conflict. Most nakedly and most explicitly—and therefore exposing almost too raw a nerve—images become the gift that require no acknowledgment in *Until the End of the World*, where the hero neither takes pictures nor tells stories, but entrusts a machine with passing them on.

In a perpetual movement from agoraphobia to claustrophobia, from spaces that are too vast and empty to situations that are too constricting and imprisoning, Wenders is able to suggest that a journey is always a flight away from something and a tentative quest for something else: the central notion would be that of a balance, where a movement forward is also a return, which is to say, these are interior journeys, from self to self. And so the films, in their structure and development, occupy a terrain of borders, boundaries, frontiers, limits, and divisions. In *Summer in the City*, Wenders's first full-length feature film, the escape from Munich to Berlin and the search for once-familiar sites and faces are still motivated by an external threat to the hero, who is being pursued by his former underworld connections. In *The Scarlet Letter*, the immigrants' dilemma is that they are poised between a new land and an old law. In *The Goalie's Anxiety at the Penalty Kick*, the hero skirts the frontier between Austria and Hungary in much the same way as the heroes of *Kings of the Road* trace in their trajectory a parallel course to the divide that then separated East and West Germany. In these last two films the apparently aimless movement conceals a wished-for and impossible return to a place and a situation associated with childhood and adolescence, most explicitly in the symmetrically positioned visits of Kamikaze to his father's printshop and Bruno to his mother's house on the river island in *Kings of the Road*.

Alice in the Cities, too, is the record of a journey of which only the moments of return seem to matter: return to New York at first, from the desert that is (for the protagonist) Middle America, then a return to Europe from the impossible space that is New York, and finally, in Germany itself, a return and search for childhood homes—first for Alice and then for Philip, the journalist-hero himself. In *Alice* the ambivalence of the journey that is both a search and a return is supplied with its implicit and often hidden term, namely, that it is a quest for the many faces and figures of the Mother. This is just as true of Wenders's first film, *Summer in the City*, as of one of his best known, *Paris, Texas*, and becomes in *Until the End of the World* the quest for the mother's sight, so that she can finally see the world through the eyes of the son.

Wenders and Women

On one of the posters that promoted *Kings of the Road* in Germany, one could read in bold capitals "Every Man Is an Adventurer." And underneath, in rather smaller letters: "Women just look on." The words only spell out, in an aggressive-defensive form, what polarizes attitudes toward Wenders's films in Germany and to a lesser extent elsewhere: that Wenders's world is predominantly, even obsessively, a male world, where there is no room for women, except as spectators. But this is a double paradox, insofar as these male protagonists are themselves spectators, and thus adventurers, not of action, but of observation, introspection, of their own passivity, and of their own self-exile from life. And, on the other hand, the goal of their journeys seems to be an obscurely felt, inarticulate, yet persistent desire to be reunited with a woman, *the* woman—often escaping one woman in order to be united with the other, as in *Until the End of the World*, or escaping her "now" in order to find her as she was "then," as in *Paris, Texas*.

Audiences react to Wenders's films largely in direct proportion to their ability to identify with this central paradox or perversity: women spectators who see in the heroes above all the self-absorbed, introspective male whose image of women is nothing but a self-pitying projection of regressive fantasies tend to reject Wenders's films and the closed universe they imply. Male spectators also tend to react quite aggressively against the aimless, drifting element in the characters, when interpreted as a lack of political commitment or an absence of perspective. In this respect, Wenders was ahead of his critics: he anticipated the collapse from within of a certain male subject position in his films even before "masculinity" came onto the gender agenda.

It is true that the Wenders hero began as the existential loner, and occasionally a loner whose only gesture consisted in transforming his status from being the solitary outsider to becoming definitively and irreversibly the outcast, the criminal. This is particularly evident in Bloch, the protagonist of *The Goalie's Anxiety at the Penalty Kick*, but also, in a different sense, of Jonathan, the hero of *The American Friend*: their action fixes for them, however unsatisfactorily, a socially unambiguous identity as a wanted man. More generally, the loner characteristically enters only into temporary relationships with other people—other solitary figures, outsiders, drifters, chance acquaintances, orphans, or men as self-absorbed as the hero. Yet unlike their cinematic uncles—the heroes of Antonioni or Resnais—Wenders's protagonists display their vulnerability and sensitivity as itself a cover, their inability to form relationships with women being bound up with the equally preemptory need to live that relationship as an incestuous bachelor-machine. Thus, Wenders's heroes carry their vulnerability like a shield, or in the words of the ex-girlfriend in *Alice*, they "treat their own emotions like raw eggs"—maybe in the hope that the women will make of them the well-known Lacanian "homelette."

What is the meaning of the neurotic condition that seems to afflict the Wenders hero? It is clearly inadequate to turn this against the filmmaker himself as if he were somehow not aware of what his stories imply. In one sense, Wenders's themes are the stock-in-trade of a certain literary modernism, the portrait of the artist as a sensitive young man, an impression strongly reinforced by his collaboration with the Austrian novelist Peter Handke, whose own work at the time was a commentary and often a kind of updating of Franz Kafka's protagonists or of the existentialist heroes in the novels of Albert Camus and Jean-Paul Sartre.

Yet this interest in unmotivated narrative, in narratives on the margins of narrative, is in Wenders's films less a modernist preoccupation with "exhaustion" than an attempt to rethink narrative from the starting point of images. But these images, as we saw, are taken from or refer to the cinema, which is to say, the images already contain stories—those that the American cinema has told over and over again. To make films is for Wenders in a sense to watch once more and remember the films one had already seen. Action could only be the retelling of action. The point was not to film something that had never been shown before but to show something in such a way that it appeared to be a memory of something one had already seen: once again, an implicit trajectory that *Until the End of the World* takes as its explicit, though not very plausible, plot premise. The student films (*Same Player Shoots Again, Alabama, Silver City, Summer in the City*) were conceived as narratives *after* narrative, when that which made up narrative progress—action, motivation, conflict—is already over, or already elsewhere: "Even the first films I made at film school had the sense of a missing story," Wenders remarked in an interview, meaning that his films are not so much non-narrative as they are post-narrative.[6]

This stance is very noticeable in *The Goalie's Anxiety at the Penalty Kick*, which begins when things are already over for the hero. By murdering Gloria, the cinema usher, Bloch lets his life take the shape of a movie plot, which is to say, the only action he is capable of is to hand over his fate to the mechanism of an already existing narrative. Bloch hardly ever says more than two words, and instead feeds money into a jukebox, a broken phone, or, in one memorable scene, an apartment elevator. His itinerary from player to spectator on the football field is more generally a progress from player to spectator in his life—a progress the film neither moralizes nor associates with any angst-ridden state of modern alienation. The objectification of his own person is experienced as pleasurable by Bloch, and it already indicates the general movement of the hero in virtually all of Wenders's subsequent films. The goal of a Wenders hero is simple: to place himself in a position from which he can become his own spectator, or alternatively, to assume the place of an other, where he had once been, in order to observe himself from that place. Paradigmatically, this is enacted in the final scene of *Paris, Texas*, where Travis manages to send himself—in the person of his son, Hunter—back into Jane's arms, while watching both from the distance of an Edward—not Dennis—Hopper-ish urban darkness, deepened by a shaft of neon coming from a streetlight.

On the other hand, this master narrative of the son's return to the mother is in Wenders (at least prior to *Until the End of the World*) quite timely embedded in some other concerns. For the question of origins as well as of narrative seems at first sight to connect more directly with the lack of motivation in the hero, which (true to the axiom of the classical Hollywood cinema) is equated with the absence of women as direct objects of desire. Where a woman is present, as in *The American Friend*, her presence merely underscores her irrelevance for the resolution of the narrative; where her absence is an issue in the development of the story, as in *Alice in the Cities* (Alice's mother, her grandmother) or *Kings of the Road* (Kamikaze's wife, the woman in the car crash at night), the quest for her becomes a pretext, so that thanks to her absence, something can happen: between two men (*Kings of the Road, The American Friend*), between a man and a little girl (*Alice in the Cities*), between a man and a deaf-mute boy (*The Goalie's Anxiety at the Penalty Kick*), or between a man and his son (*Paris, Texas*).

Emblematically, this is represented in *Kings of the Road*, where desire for the absent woman (for the woman as absent) is displaced onto a desire for adventure ("something is starting to move," as the advertising poster has it), which in turn can be narrated and retold and which has the form and logic of a paratactic sentence, verging on the side of schizophrenia, in order to avoid getting involved in causes and explanations, or mired in conflicts without resolutions, enigmas demanding a search for origins. In this respect, the absence of women directly affects the narrative, making it open-ended, dedramatized, avoiding conventional modes of closure, and instead forcing it into a kind of circularity in which the past is rewritten into the present and vice versa. In *Kings of the Road*, as perhaps nowhere else in Wenders's work, the unavailability of the past is both recognized and opposed by an intense process of rewriting, as Kamikaze prints a "special edition" of his father's newspaper blaming him for his mother's suicide, or cinematic intertextuality, when the return to the childhood home becomes for Philip a return to comics and movies—and Nick Ray's *The Lusty Men*. The paratactic structure of description, with its discrete units, fits very well for one kind of Wenders film, especially the early, black-and-white ones, usually giving themselves as improvisations with a minimum of plot.

The American Friend, on the other hand, is a film where two types of narrative actually come into conflict with each other, and in significant form. The film has sometimes been read metaphorically: as West Germany, in the figure of Jonathan, snubbing the advances of America, represented by Ripley, and responding with high-handed moralism to the glad-handed joviality of the ingenue cowboy. But the relation between these two characters is more ambiguous. Two points seem important: one is that Jonathan's inwardness and self-absorption are challenged and eventually cracked open by Ripley; and the other is that the film is about two kinds of Americas, brought into play and played off against each other. If we take the second aspect first: one kind of America—"violent America," for short—is that of crime, of exploitation, shady deals, power struggles, pornography, labyrinthine international conspiracies, a cold and hostile, cruel and aggressive America. It is associated with plotting, both in the literal and the literary sense, and it is part of the colonizing side of America. It is also that part of the film that can be read metaphorically as the hold—economic as well as in terms of brute force—that the United States has over Europe, and over

249

the European film industries in particular. It is, so to speak, the image of superpower America seen from outside, and to represent it Wenders needs a labyrinthine, paranoid plot and complex narration: precisely, a thriller, more or less expertly retold.

But within this world there is another America, that of Ripley's friendship, where the plot is represented not by the Chinese box puzzle connoting paranoia, but by crisscrossing, by paths converging and overlapping and separating again, without ever joining and merging, already so prevalent in Wenders's films like *Alice in the Cities, Wrong Move,* and *Kings of the Road*: structurally, they are the very epitome of narrative progression when representing all-male relationships, and they invariably suppress direct conflict. In *The American Friend* this is the world of equality, of exchange rather than exploitation: instead of the bribes that the gangster boss Minot makes, we have the gifts that Ripley and Jonathan make each other (inextricably linking sexuality with visual representation, since these are mostly gadgets with lewd pictures), partnership rather than rivalry and competition. The two moments—the exploitative and the egalitarian—are carefully interwoven and contrasted in *The American Friend*; they signify the America of people-oriented behavior, of a casualness that allows individuals to experience each other, learn from each other, tolerate each other in a difference generated from anonymity itself (the glad hand), rather than uniqueness or individuality (the high hand). Exemplary in this respect is the scene of *The American Friend* when Ripley comes into Jonathan's shop, ostensibly to have a picture of Hamburg fitted with a frame, and in the process pays generous tribute to people with skills and a craft.

It is this world that appears as Wenders's utopia, but also as Germany's history with America: the United States as liberator after World War II, and above all as the providers and purveyors of popular culture. There, inwardness can be exchanged for the lightness of touch, where a mutual identification takes place without creating dependency. Contact rather than conflict, identity lived and renewed by interchange rather than by territorial claims, seems to be the goal, but it excludes women. In working this out, *The American Friend* plays through all the possibilities that this relationship could take—most notably also its negative connotations, the Double (Jonathan is always already there before he has arrived, as in the scene at Orly Airport) but also the vampire—the former as the image of one's own death, the latter as the appropriate figuration of the colonizer's role, a colonization in which the victim seeks out the exploiter to find in him the image of his own desire.

Why does Jonathan (who shares his name with the hero of both Bram Stoker's *Dracula* and Murnau's *Nosferatu*) collude so readily, why is he tempted at all? What has this Faust to gain from his Mephisto? In the film, this once more relates to the problematic status of inwardness: Jonathan's cultural superiority, displayed at the auction, is defensive, repressing the knowledge of its own precariousness. Hence it is apt that illness should be the central metaphor of Jonathan's condition: what he represses within him makes him vulnerable. The blood disease, inverting the attraction of the vampire's bite, relates to Jonathan's haughty pride in his workmanship, the illusion of thinking himself above the implications of his trade, the commercialization of culture and of art as a forgery of values. To this disavowal Ripley holds up a mirror, tempts him with the hidden question: what am I really worth, what price can I put on my life, what is the material equivalent of my spiritual pretensions, my rarefied existence: in short, what is my European culture worth in that other world that is the world of the "other"? It is the recognition that such culture and refinement as Jonathan displays in his early dealing with Ripley may be a sham—hollow, already decayed, part of a disease, incurable, terminal: Jonathan's sullen pride is gradually replaced by a kind of other-directedness, until it is finally Ripley who saves him, only for Jonathan to die of his imaginary blood disease after all.

Wenders's America is thus characterized by a double signification: as image for the reality of the self (enacted by popular culture and the cinema), and as the reality of that image (in the form of the film industry and cultural imperialism). Caught up in the dialectic of subject and object, self and other, inside and outside, subjectivity can only be tolerated as image. But this existence as image is itself doubly coded: Wenders, like Handke and others, categorically refuses the polarity involved in the oedipal father-son opposition, on which the old inner-outer divide, as well as the subject-object divisions, were modeled. In this sense, it is the two-dimensionality of the image, its function as mirror, that allows for such a perfect elision of the staging of oedipal conflicts. Yet this also means that the "image" is associated, quite logically, in a world still dominated by oedipal relationships, with either pre-oedipal regression or death. The fascination with the image is, as we have seen, a fascination with one side of America, while the worry over storytelling relates to the other side of America. They find their common denominator in the reinscription and retranslation of the image into the means of its mechanical reproduction, which in turn is associated with a newly regained immediacy: the innocence that joins, in West Germany's history, America and childhood. America, in Wenders, has colonized, even more than the subconscious, the experience of childhood, of Wrigley's chewing gum and Disney cartoons, of Saturday matinees at the movies and rock and roll from the American Forces Network. These experiences in turn are inseparable from jukeboxes and slot machines, movie theaters and record players, gadgets that represent pleasure by metonymic displacement.

In this respect, America's relation to Europe becomes crucial. It is not direct competition, nor is it a father-son rivalry (though as is evident in *Paris, Texas* and taken up more complexly in *Until the End of the World*, there is something of this oedipal nexus in the way the interchange is figured in some of the films). Instead, America is the always re-remembered satisfaction of the image, whose status as memory is safeguarded by access to the means of mechanical reproduction, comparable to the primary and oral satisfaction of the mother's presence, whose capacity to give pleasure is, however, also associated with the anxiety of separation and loss. No wonder, therefore, that sexuality becomes bound up with the technology of moviemaking on the one hand and a totally fantasized image of women on the other: in the world of movie mania, the truth is that women, cinemas, pinball machines, and jukeboxes belong together, and thus, quite logically, women are fascinating in Wenders's films only to the extent that they can also function as substitutes for the pleasure of images and pictures, usually by direct association with cinematic representation, as in the frequent appearance of usherettes in his films, a particularly rich motif in *The Goalie's Anxiety at the Penalty Kick, Wrong Move*, and *Kings of the Road*. Given that an usherette in German is called "Platzanweiserin" (literally, the woman who shows you your place), the motif condenses time, place, and self by tying it to gender.

This motif is both repeated and deconstructed in *Paris, Texas* insofar as the central female character is associated with the Keyhole Club, a peep show that functions as an especially ingenious representation of the cinematic apparatus. To see Nastassja Kinski as a further development of Wenders's usherettes is to say that she is more openly associated with both sides of cinephilia (with maternal satisfaction and childhood but also with death, suicide, and self-oblivion) than any other of Wenders's female characters. In *Paris, Texas* the hero (and the spectator) watches the woman's image through a two-way mirror, without having to encounter her in any other form than as the man's obsessive fantasy. This may well be the point where Sam Shepard's contribution to *Paris, Texas* can be most usefully distinguished from Wenders's use of it: what in Shepard's plays appears as a direct representation of an almost intolerable emotional (and physical) violence in the marital situation, is in Wenders's several times removed, making the film *Paris, Texas* the mise-en-abyme of Shepard's script rather than its transposition onto the screen. Like all of Wenders's men, Travis starts off mute and aimless. And the erotic object even in this film (where for once the woman seems central) is not the woman herself but her specular body, eroticized by an act of pseudocinematic representation and meta-narrative construction.

Paris, Texas is, in Wenders's work, far and away the most complex example of how an entire network of family relations is converted into

The cinematic gaze as peep show—Jane (Nastassja Kinski) and Travis (Harry Dean Stanton) in *Paris, Texas* (1984).

projections and fantasies, each protagonist "de-materializing" the others until they appear as nothing but the products of each other's desires. Travis, the biological father, has to remake himself as father by making himself his son's buddy, playing through the oedipal scenario in reverse, retroactively: first by learning to be the double of Hunter, his son (imitating him: at school, the swap of boots); then by learning to "be" a father in front of the mirror and the approving gaze of the Mexican maid; and finally, by initiating a journey and an adventure where both father and son set out in search for the mother. When she is finally found—represented by that time as the pure product and construct of both men's desiring narratives—the family is not reunited, but the father puts the son in the lover's place, in order to watch himself through the son, returning to the mother. In other words, closure and resolution are attained by elaborate temporal/spatial shifts and displacements, deferrals in time and space through which the father-son scenario is not so much lived as it is reconstructed and reenacted, put on as a kind of dumb show. The film thus dramatizes in its very story development the processes of identification and projection that are typical of classical cinema, by doubling the image of the self. But now it is no longer a matter of the son constructing himself in the image of the "father," as in most Hollywood Westerns, for instance, but instead the father constructing himself in the image of the son.

253

From the narrative that Travis and Jane are telling each other, it is clear that at the core of the film is an unresolved incest fantasy (he did not want to be separate from her, he refused the socialization implied by a steady job, by the role of provider, of adult male and father). This incest fantasy is resolved by being staged, imaged, and narrated in such a way that in the end the family exists purely as an exchange of looks: mother and son are united under the eye of the father, who would like to be in the place where the son is.

Paris, Texas, ostensibly a film about a place, a time, and the self (literally involving the hero's origin, the place where he was conceived), is thus, as are all Wenders's movies, a film about remembering, forgetting, and repressing, but played out across the image, the photo, the fantasy produced by the cinema. Yet while on one level the film shows the nuclear family as a mechanical fiction, there is room for the spectator to become once more a naive viewer and to take the pathos of reconciliation straight, that is to say, as a refiguration of how a father passes on his authority (and his symbolic possession of the mother) to the son. For Travis's goal seems to be to bridge the gap between "Paris" and "Texas," coded as sexual difference in the story of his parents that he tells to Hunter. Except that Travis never attains the full use of language (the reentry into the symbolic). Instead he constructs a kind of speaking and viewing machine made up of a home movie, a tape recorder, a walkie-talkie, and other bits and pieces: all emblems of mechanical reproduction and representation, the cinema. The family functions only in the movies. Equally explicit and equally convoluted, we find the same scenario in *Until the End of the World*. Here, too, it is a machine—image-making, image-recording, image-transmitting—that has to bring the family together, and even more directly, the son's passage (of pictures) to the mother goes via the (reconstruction of the) place of the father: the son has to steal the father's "thing," which has itself been stolen by the superfather, the U.S. government. The oedipal story is twice removed, the phallus in question disguised by an array of gadgets of vision, communication, and presence, only to be reassembled in an apparatus (the image/memory transmitter) every bit as fantastical as Rotwang's laboratory in *Metropolis* or Kafka's self-test apparatus in *The Penal Colony*, the original bachelor machine in Michel Carroughes's *Les machines célibataires*.

Destruction of the past as memory and trauma, and its transformation into scenario and spectacle, are, in Wenders's films, the preconditions for escaping oedipal subjectivity as conceived from the father's perspective, in order to make way for the reconstruction of the pre-oedipal from the perspective of the son, via fantasies of doubling: but because these have become technological fantasies, they are also post-oedipal. The past is resurrected as spectacle through the machines of sound and vision, a definition of nostalgia as retrospective narcissism, in which the other is appropriated not by an act of confrontation or submission but by acts of re-writing, re-production, simulation. Not the imaginary coherence of the film spectator, desired from the fantasy of "full knowledge" at the end of the story, is the point of the fiction, but an endless play of separation and difference, of sub-stitution and deferral, which sustains itself by the simultaneous coexistence of several narrative spaces and time frames: a new geometry of representa-tion.

Wenders's films work out this new geometry not in a vacuum, or as a personal obsession, but under a historical pressure, as it were, namely, the reinscription of the family (and "family values") in contemporary American cinema (*Home Alone, Kindergarten Cop, Honey I Shrunk the Kids*). Such films are at once the disguise of the technological apparatus underpinning the functioning of the family and their expression: just as in *Paris, Texas* the woman as mother, lover, and whore is produced quite literally as an ef-fect of two-way mirrors and a phantasmatic presence, or the mother in *Un-til the End of the World* is wired up to a machine serviced simultaneously by father and son, thus marking one extreme of the all-male obsession with the woman as fetish, so the absent/present family in recent American hits (as well as in the horror film) pushes anxiety about the family to such an extreme that the whole structure is able to make its own mechanisms visi-ble. Yet even this play of family and special effects, of technical gadgetry and electronic wizardry, is itself an inadequate but "hysterically sublime"[7] representation of the processes of the movie business, the blockbuster and the megahit, the global marketing strategies and the tie-ins: "Hollywood, Hollywood. . . ."

We are now, I hope, in a better position to see what unites these vari-ous aspects of Wenders's work. For, it would seem, Wenders is the typical European intellectual, looking to America for the verification or corrobora-tion of his insights into cinema and moviemaking. Across the movie busi-ness, he came to formulate his insights into capitalism and postindustrial society as they are reshaping human relations, especially those centered on the family, at once split apart by modern technology and patched together by its array of user-friendly gadgets. Americans, on the other hand, are tempted by Wenders to mirror their own disquiet about the family, but also about the United States and its role as sole superpower on a global scale, in the image that Europeans project of the United States (or U.S./European re-lations) out of their own cultural and historical situation. To the American experience of American society as both natural and universal corresponds a European sense of Europe's own difference and of America's otherness (Paris/Texas), a conjunction that in turn allows Americans to experience themselves as different across the markers of European cultural specificity. On the other hand, America in turn is for Europeans a mirror, in a displace-ment that is both temporal and spatial, where America is Europe's future as well as its past. This may be what Wenders's films finally have to say to us, and the key to why, despite his many fierce anti-Americanisms (or even, because of them), he is still one of the American cinema's favorite European "sons."

Notes

This essay was first given as a lecture at Middlebury College, Vermont, in May 1991. It is dedicated to Ursula Hardt.

1. An impressive testimony to the movie obsession of a Hollywood mogul is Rudy Behlmer, ed., *Memo from David O. Selznick* (New York: Viking, 1972).
2. See, for instance, Bertrand Tavernier, "I Wake Up, Dreaming: A Journal for 1992," *Projections* 2, ed. John Boorman and Walter Donohue (London: Faber, 1993): 252–378.
3. In an interview I held in July 1994, Wenders spoke about producing a film with and for Antonioni, where he might be acting as "supporting director." Even if it should never come to pass, it is a fantasy fitting in well with the "filial" paradigm that typifies Wenders's relation to film history.
4. See the original English voice-over of *Reverse Angle* in this volume.
5. See the original English voice-over of *Reverse Angle* in this volume.
6. Jan Dawson, *Wim Wenders*, trans. Carla Wartenberg (New York: Zoetrope, 1976), 7.
7. Fredric Jameson, "Pleasure: A Political Issue," *Formations of Pleasure*, ed. Tony Bennet, Victor Burgin, James Donald, et al. (London: Routledge, 1983) 12.

FILMOGRAPHY

Abbreviations:
  d = director
  p = producer
  c = camera
 sc = script
 ed = editor
  m = music
  r = running time
 sd = sound
 lp = leading players

Locations (Schauplätze). (1967)
d/p/c/sc/ed: Wim Wenders. *m:* The Rolling Stones. *r:* 10 min., 16mm, b/w.
No prints exist; the only two surviving shots appear at the beginning of *Same Player Shoots Again.*

Same Player Shoots Again. (1967)
d/p/c/sc/ed: Wim Wenders. *r:* 12 min., 16mm, b/w (differently tinted).
Premiered: October 11, 1967.

Silver City. (1968)
d/p/c/sc/ed: Wim Wenders. *r:* 25 min., 16mm, col.
Premiered: March 7, 1969.

Alabama: 2000 Light Years. (1968)
d/sc/ed: Wim Wenders. *p:* Hochschule für Fernsehen und Film, Munich. *c:* Robby Müller. *m:* The Rolling Stones, Jimi Hendrix, Bob Dylan, John Coltrane. *r:* 21 min., 35mm, b/w. *lp:* Paul Lys, Werner Schroeter, Peter Kaiser, Muriel Schrat, Christian Friedel.
Premiered: May 18, 1969.

Polizeifilm. (1969)

d/c/ed: Wim Wenders. *p:* Bayerischer Rundfunk, Munich. *sc:* Albrecht Göschel, Wim Wenders. *r:* 11 min., 16mm, b/w. *lp:* Jimmy Vogler, Kasimir Esser.
Premiered: May 16, 1969.

3 American LP's (3 amerikanische LP's). (1969)

d/ed/sd: Wim Wenders. *p:* Hessischer Rundfunk, Frankfurt. *sc:* Peter Handke. *m:* Van Morrison, Creedence Clearwater Revival, Harvey Mandel. *r:* 13 min. 16mm, col. *lp:* Wim Wenders, Peter Handke.
Premiered: November 18, 1969.

Summer in the City: Dedicted to the Kinks. (1970)

d/sc: Wim Wenders. *p:* Hochschule für Film und Fernsehen, Munich. *c:* Robby Müller. *ed:* Peter Przygodda. *m:* The Kinks, Lovin' Spoonful, Chuck Berry, Gene Vincent, The Troggs. *r:* 145 min. (first version), 116 min. (second version), 16mm, b/w. *lp:* Hanns Zischler (Hans), Edda Köchl (friend in Munich), Libgart Schwarz (girlfriend in Berlin), Maria Bardischewski (friend in Berlin), Wim Wenders (friend at pool hall).
Premiered: June 2, 1972.

The Goalie's Anxiety at the Penalty Kick (Die Angst des Tormanns beim Elfmeter). (1971)

d: Wim Wenders. *p:* Filmverlag der Autoren, Munich; Telefilm AG, Wien; Westdeutscher Rundfunk Cologne. *sc:* Wim Wenders, after the novel by Peter Handke. *c:* Robby Müller. *ed:* Peter Przygodda. *sd:* Rainer Lorenz, Martin Müller. *m:* Jürgen Knieper. *r:* 100 min., 35mm, col. *lp:* Arthur Brauss (Josef Bloch), Erika Pluhar (Gloria), Kai Fischer (Hertha Gabler), Libgart Schwarz (Anna), Maria Bardischewski (Maria), Rüdiger Vogler (village idiot), Wim Wenders (walks through Vienna bus station).
Premiered: February 29, 1972

The Scarlet Letter (Der scharlachrote Buchstabe). (1972)

d: Wim Wenders. *p:* Filmverlag der Autoren, Munich; Westdeutscher Rundfunk, Cologne; Elias Querejeta, Madrid. *sc:* Wim Wenders, Bernardo Fernandez, after the script by Tankred Dorst and Ursula Ehler, *Der Herr klagt über sein Volk in der Wildnis Amerika*, based on the novel *The Scarlet Letter* by Nathaniel Hawthorne. *c:* Robby Müller. *ed:* Peter Przygodda. *sd:* Christian Schubert. *m:* Jürgen Knieper. *r:* 90 min., 35mm, col. *lp:* Senta Berger (Hester Prynne), Hans Christian Blech (Chillingworth), Lou Castel (Dimmesdale), Yella Rottländer (Pearl), William Layton (Bellingham).
Premiered: March 13, 1973.

Alice in the Cities (Alice in den Städten). (1974)

d: Wim Wenders. *p:* Filmverlag der Autoren, Munich; Westdeutscher Rundfunk, Cologne. *sc:* Wim Wenders, Veith von Fürstenburg. *c:* Robby Müller. *ed:* Peter Przygodda. *sd:* Martin Müller, Paul Schöler. *m:* Can, Chuck Berry, Canned Heat, Deep Purple, Count Five, The Stories. *r:* 110 min., 16mm, b/w. *lp:* Rüdiger Vogler

(Philip Winter), Yella Rottländer (Alice), Lisa Kreuzer (Lisa van Damm), Edda Köckl (Angela, girlfriend in New York), Wim Wenders (man standing at jukebox). *Premiered:* March 3, 1974.

Aus der Familie der Panzerechsen/Die Insel. (1974)

d: Wim Wenders. *p:* Bavaria, Munich, as part of the television series *Ein Haus für alle. sc:* Philippe Pilloid. *c:* Michael Ballhaus. *ed:* Lilian Seng. *sd:* Armin Münch, Walter Hutterer. *m:* arpad bondy. *r:* 50 min., 16mm, col. *lp:* Katja Wulff (Ute), Lisa Kreuzer (social worker), Thomas Braut (director of the school), Marquard Bohm (visitor at the zoo), Nicholas Brieder (father), Hans-Joachim Krietsch (psychologist), Helga Tümper (mother). *Premiered:* July 26, 1977.

Wrong Move (Falsche Bewegung). (1975)

d: Wim Wenders. *p:* Solaris Film, Munich; Westdeutscher Rundfunk, Cologne. *sc:* Peter Handke, freely adapted from Johann Wolfgang von Goethe's *Wilhelm Meister's Apprenticeship. c:* Robby Müller. *ed:* Peter Przygodda. *sd:* Martin Müller, Peter Kaiser, Paul Schöler. *m:* Jürgen Knieper. *r:* 104 min., 35mm, col. *lp:* Rüdiger Vogler (Wilhelm), Hanna Schygulla (Therese), Hans Christian Blech (Laertes), Nastassja Kinski (Mignon), Peter Kern (Landau), Ivan Desny (industrialist), Marianne Hoppe (mother), Lisa Kreuzer (Janine), Wim Wenders (man in dining car). *Premiered:* March 14, 1975.

Kings of the Road (Im Lauf der Zeit). (1976)

d: Wim Wenders. *p:* Wim Wenders Produktion, Munich; Westdeutscher Rundfunk, Cologne. *sc:* Wim Wenders. *c:* Robby Müller. *ed:* Peter Przygodda. *sd:* Martin Müller, Bruno Bollhalder. *m:* Improved Sound Limited, Axel Linstädt. *r:* 176 min., 35mm, b/w. *lp:* Rüdiger Vogler (Bruno), Hanns Zischler (Robert), Lisa Kreuzer (Pauline), Rudolf Schündler (father), Marquard Bohm (husband of the woman who committed suicide), Dieter Traier (Robert's friend from school), Wim Wenders (spectator at Pauline's theater). *Premiered:* March 4, 1976.

The American Friend (Der amerikanische Freund). (1977)

d: Wim Wenders. *p:* Road Movies, Berlin; Les Films du Losange, Paris; Wim Wenders Produktion, Munich; Westdeutscher Rundfunk, Cologne. *sc:* Wim Wenders, after Patricia Highsmith's novel *Ripley's Game. c:* Robby Müller. *ed:* Peter Przygodda. *sd:* Martin Müller, Peter Kaiser. *m:* Jürgen Knieper. *r:* 123 min., 35mm, col. *lp:* Bruno Ganz (Jonathan Zimmermann), Dennis Hopper (Tom Ripley), Lisa Kreuzer (Marianne Zimmermann), Gérard Blain (Raoul Minôt), Nicholas Ray (Derwatt), Samuel Fuller (the American mafioso), Wim Wenders (figure wrapped in plaster bandages in ambulance). *Premiered:* May 26, 1977.

Lightning over Water (Nick's Film). (1980)

d: Nicholas Ray, Wim Wenders. *p:* Road Movies, Berlin; Wim Wenders Produktion, Berlin; Viking-Film, Stockholm. *sc:* Wim Wenders. *c:* Edward Lachmann,

Martin Schäfer (film), Tom Farell (video). *ed:* Peter Przygodda (first version), Wim Wenders (second version). *sd:* Martin Müller, Maryte Kavaliauskas, Gary Steele. *m:* Ronee Blakely. *r:* 116 min. (first version), 90 min. (second version), 35mm, col. *lp:* Nicholas Ray, Wim Wenders, Susan Ray, Timothy Ray, Tom Farrell, Ronee Blakely, Gerry Bauman, Pierre Cottrell, Stephan Czapsky, Becky Johnston, Tom Kaufmann, Craig Nelson, Pat Kirck, Edward Lachmann, Maryte Kavaliauskas, Martin Müller, Martin Schäfer, Chris Sievernich. *Premiered:* November 1, 1980.

Hammett. (1982)

d: Wim Wenders. *p:* Zoetrope Studios, San Francisco; Orion Pictures, New York. *sc:* Ross Thomas, Dennis O'Flaherty, Thomas Pope, Joe Gores, after the novel by Joe Gores. *c:* Philip Lathrop, Joseph Biroc. *ed:* Barry Malkin, Marc Laub, Rober Q. Lovett, Randy Roberts, Andrew London. *sd:* James Webb Jr., Richard Goodman. *m:* John Barry. *r:* 94 min., 35mm, col. *lp:* Frederic Forrest (Hammett), Peter Boyle (Jimmy Ryan), Marilu Henner (Kit Conger, Sue Alabama), Roy Kinnear (Eddie Hagedorn), Elisha Cook Jr. (cab driver), Lydia Lei (Chrystal Ling), R. G. Armstrong (O'Mara), Richard Bradford (Tom Bradford). *Premiered:* May 22, 1982.

The State of Things (Der Stand der Dinge). (1982)

d: Wim Wenders. *p:* Road Movies, Berlin; Wim Wenders Produktion, Berlin; Gray City Inc., New York; Pro-ject Filmproduction, Munich; Zweites Deutsches Fernsehen, Mainz; Pari Films, Paris; Musidora, Madrid; Film International, Rotterdam; Artificial Eye, London. *sc:* Wim Wenders, Robert Kramer. *c:* Henri Alekan, Martin Schäfer, Fred Murphy. *ed:* Barbara von Weitershausen, Peter Przygodda. *sd:* Maryte Kavaliauskas, Martin Müller. *m:* Jürgen Knieper. *r:* 120 min., 35mm, b/w. *lp:* Patrick Bauchau (Friedrich Munro), Isabelle Weingarten (Anna), Rebecca Pauly (Joan), Jeffrey Kime (Mark), Geoffrey Carey (Robert), Camilla Mora (Julia), Alexandra Auder (Jane), Paul Getty III (Dennis), Viva Auder (Kate). *Premiered:* October 29, 1982.

Reverse Angle: New York City, March 1982. (1982)

d/sc: Wim Wenders. *p:* Gray City, New York; Antenne 2, Paris. *c:* Liza Rinsler. *ed:* Jon Neuburger. *sd:* Maryte Kavaliauskas. *m:* Pulic Image, Echo and the Bunnymen, Martha and the Muffins, The Del Byzanteens, Allen Goorwitz. *r:* 17 min., 16mm, col. *lp:* Wim Wenders, Isabelle Weingarten, Tony Richardson, Louis Malle, Francis Ford Coppola. *Premiered:* March 16, 1982.

Chambre 666: Cannes May '82. (1982)

d/sc: Wim Wenders. *p:* Gray City, New York; Antenne 2, Paris. *c:* Agnés Godard. *ed:* Chantal de Vismes. *sd:* Jean-Paul Mugel. *m:* Jürgen Knieper, Berhard Herrmann. *r:* 45 min., 16mm, col. *lp:* Jean-Luc Godard, Paul Morrissey, Mike de Leon, Monte Hellman, Romain Goupil, Susan Seidelman, Noel Simsolo, Rainer Werner Fassbinder, Werner Herzog, Robert Kramer, Ana Carolina, Mahroun Baghbadi,

Steven Spielberg, Michelangelo Antonioni, Wim Wenders, Yilmaz Güney (voice only).
Premiered: June 2, 1982.

Paris, Texas. (1984)

d: Wim Wenders. *p:* Road Movies, Berlin; Argos Films, Paris; Westdeutscher Rundfunk, Cologne; Channel 4, London; Pro-ject Filmproduktion im Filmverlag der Autoren, Munich. *sc:* Sam Shepard. *c:* Robby Müller. *ed:* Peter Przygodda. *sd:* Jean Paul Mugel. *m:* Ry Cooder. *r:* 145 min., 35mm, col. *lp:* Harry Dean Stanton (Travis), Nastassja Kinski (Jane), Dean Stockwell (Walt), Aurore Clément (Anne), Hunter Carson (Hunter), Bernhard Wicki (Dr. Ulmer), John Lurie (Slater), Sam Berry (man at gas station).
Premiered: May 19, 1984.

Tokyo-Ga. (1985)

d/sc: Wim Wenders. *p:* Wim Wenders Produktion, Berlin; Gray City, New York; Chris Sievernich Produktion, Berlin; Westdeutscher Rundfunk, Cologne. *c:* Edward Lachman. *ed:* Wim Wenders, Solveig Dommartin, John Neuburger. *sd:* Hartmut Eichgrün. *m:* Dick Tracy, Loorie Petitgrand, Mechne Mamecier, Chico Rojo Ortega. *r:* 92 min., 16mm, col. *lp:* Chishu Ryu, Yuhara Atsuta, Werner Herzog.
Premiered: April 24, 1985.

Wings of Desire (Der Himmel über Berlin). (1987)

d: Wim Wenders. *p:* Road Movies, Berlin; Argos Films, Paris; Westdeutscher Rundfunk, Cologne. *sc:* Wim Wenders, Peter Handke, Richard Reitinger. *c:* Henri Alekan. *ed:* Peter Przygodda. *s:* Jean-Paul Mugel, Axel Arft. *m:* Jürgen Knieper, Laurent Petitgrand, Laurie Anderson, Crime and the City Solution, Nick Cave and the Bad Seeds, Sprung aus den Wolken, Tuxedomoon, Minimal Compact. *r:* 126 min., 35mm, b/w and col. *lp:* Bruno Ganz (Damiel), Solveig Dommartin (Marion), Otto Sander (Cassiel), Curt Bois (Homer), Peter Falk (Peter Falk), Hans Martin Stier, Elmar Wilms, Sigurd Rachman, Beatriz Mankowski, Lajos Kovacs.
Premiered: May 17, 1987.

Notebooks on Clothes and Cities (Aufzeichungen zu Kleidern und Städten). (1989)

d/sc: Wim Wenders. *p:* Road Movies. *c:* Robby Müller, Muriel Edelstein, Uli Kudicke, Wim Wenders, Musatocki Nakajima, Masasai Chikamori. *ed:* Dominique Auvray, Lenie Saviette, Anne Schnee. *r:* 90 min., 35mm and video, col.
Premiered: December 20, 1989.

Until the End of the World (Bis ans Ende der Welt). (1991)

d: Wim Wenders. *p:* Road Movies, Berlin; Argos Film; Village Roadshow. *sc:* Peter Carvey, Wim Wenders, after an idea by Wim Wenders and Solveig Dommartin. *c:* Robby Müller. *ed:* Peter Przygodda. *m:* Graeme Revell, David Darling, Talking Heads, R.E.M., Lou Reed, Nick Cave, Crime and the City Solution, T-Bone Burnett, Can, Neneh Cherry, Depeche Mode, Robbie Robertson & Blue Nile, The

Kinks, Elvis Costello, Daniel Lanois, Peter Gabriel, U2, Patti & Fred Smith, Jane Siberry, k. d. lang. *r:* 179 min. (Europe), 157 min. (U.S.), 35mm, col. *lp:* Solveig Dommartin (Claire), William Hurt (Sam Farber), Jeanne Moreau (Edith Farber), Max von Sydow (Henry Farber), Chick Ortega (Chico), Sam Neill (Eugene Fitzpatrick), Rüdiger Vogler (Phillip Winter), Eddy Mitchell (Raymond), Ernie Dingo (Burt), Elena Smirnowa (Krasikowa), Ryu Chishu (Mr. Mori), Allen Garfield (Bernie), Lois Chiles (Elsa), David Gulpilil (David), Charlie McMahon (Buzzer), Justine Saunders (Maisie), Jimmy Little (Peter), Kylie Belling (Lydia), Rhoda Roberts (Ronda), Paul Livingston (Karl), Bart Willoughby (Ned).
Premiered: September 10, 1991.

Arisha, the Bear, and the Stone Ring. (1992)

d/sc: Wim Wenders. *p:* Road Movies. *c:* Jürgen Jürges. *ed:* Peter Przygodda. *m:* Nick Cave and the Bad Seeds, The House of Love, Crime and the City Solution, Ed Kuepper. *r:* 45 min. *lp:* Rüdiger Vogler (Bear), Anna Vronskaya (woman), Arina Voznesenskaya (child), Wim Wenders (Santa Claus), Gong Hung Truong, Nam Ha Nguyen, Thi Hoa Nguyen (Vietnamese family).
Premiered: December 21, 1992.

Faraway, So Close! (In weiter Ferne, so nah!). (1993)

d: Wim Wenders. *p:* Road Movies; Tobis Filmkunst. *sc:* Wim Wenders, Ulrich Ziegler, Richard Reitinger. *ed:* Peter Przygodda *m:* U2, Crime and the City Solution, Jane Siberry, Laurie Anderson, Herbert Grönemeyer, Guy Chadwick and the House of Love, Lou Reed. *r:* 146 min. *lp:* Otto Sander (Cassiel), Bruno Ganz (Damiel), Nastassja Kinski (Raphaela), Martin Olbertz (dying man), Lou Reed, Michail Gorbatchov, Heinz Rühmann (Konrad), Horst Buchholz (Tony Baker), Rüdiger Vogler (Phillip Winter), Yella Rottländer (Winter's angel), Hanns Zischler (Dr. Becker), Solveig Dommartin (Marion), Willem Dafoe (Emit Flesti).
Premiered: May 18, 1993.

Lisbon Story. (1994)

d/sc: Wim Wender. *p:* Ulrich Felsberg, Paulo Branco. *c:* Lisa Rinzler. *ed:* Peter Przygodda, Anne Schnee. *m:* Madredeus, Jürgen Knieper. *r:* 105 min. *lp:* Rüdiger Vogler (Phil), Patrick Bauchau (Fritz), Teresa Salgueiro (Teresa), Manuel de Oliveira (guest).
Premiered: December 16, 1994.

Beyond the Clouds (Par-Delà les Nuages) (1995)

d: Michelangelo Antonioni, Wim Wenders. *p:* Philippe Carcasonne, Stephane Tchal Gadjieff. *sc:* Tonino Guerra, Michelangelo Antonioni, Wim Wenders. *c:* Alfio Contini, Robby Mueller. *ed:* Peter Przygodda, Lucian Segura. *m:* Lucio Dalla, Laurent Petitgrand, Van Morrison, U2. *r:* 113 min. *lp:* Fanny Ardant (Patrizia), Chiara Caseli (Olga), Irène Jacob (young woman), John Malkovich (director), Sophie Marceau (young woman), Vincent Perrez (Niccolo), Jean Reno (Carlo), Kim Rossi-Stuart (Silvano), Ines Sastre (Carmen), Peter Weller (Roberto), Marcello Mastroianni (painter), Jeanne Moreau (friend).
Premiered: September 3, 1995.

BIBLIOGRAPHY

Texts by Wenders

"Where's That Joint?" *Filmkritik* July 1969: 408.
"Oh Yeah." *Filmkritik* June 1970: 292.
"The Big TNT Show." *Süddeutsche Zeitung* May 5, 1971: 10.
"Furchtlose Flieger." *Filmkritik* June 1971: 320–22.
"Morning Sun." *Twen* 1–2 (1971): 37–40.
Texte zu Filmen und Musik. Berlin: Freunde der Kinemathek, 1975.
"Photomontages et instantanés." *Positif* 200 (1977): 220.
"Deux textes de Wim Wenders." *Cinema 80* 264 (1980):13–14.
"Pour jeter l'ancre." *Positif* 236 (1980): 14.
"Sur quelques films américains." *Positif* 236 (1980): 20–24.
"Der amerikanische Traum." *Autrement* 79 (1986): 180–201.
Emotion Pictures: Essays und Filmkritiken 1968–1984. Frankfurt am Main: Verlag
    der Autoren, 1986. English translation: *Emotion Pictures: Reflections on the
    Cinema.* Trans. Sean Whiteside in association with Michael Hofmann. Lon-
    don and Boston: Faber and Faber, 1989.
"Briefe an uns Lebendige." *tip* 7 (1987): 50–53
Written in the West: Photographien aus dem amerikanischen Westen. Munich:
    Schirmer/Mosel, 1987.
"Je größer das Budget, umso kleiner wird die Freiheit." *Die Welt* October 24, 1988.
Le souffle de l'ange. Paris: Cahiers du Cinéma, 1988.
Die Logik der Bilder: Essays und Gespräche. Ed. Michael Töteberg. Frankfurt am
    Main: Verlag der Autoren, 1988. English translation: *The Logic of Images:
    Essays and Conversations.* Trans. Michael Hofmann. London and Boston:
    Faber and Faber, 1991.
"Highway durch Moskau." *Die Zeit* (Magazin) April 28, 1989.
"Il cinema secondo Wim." *Grazia* 9 (1989): 133–35.
"Bis ans Ende der Welt: Fotos, Notizen." *Süddeutsche Zeitung* May 11, 1990.

Bibliography

The Act of Seeing: Texte und Gespräche. Frankfurt am Main: Verlag der Autoren, 1992.

"Guilty Pleasures." *Film Comment* 28.1 (1992): 74–77.

Electronic Paintings. Rome: Edizioni Socrates, 1993.

"U2 interviewé par Wenders." *Liberation* June 14, 1993: 57–58, 132–33.

Una Volta. Rome: Edizioni Socrates, 1993. Subsequently published in German as *Einmal: Bilder und Geschichten.* Frankfurt am Main: Verlag der Autoren, 1994.

Die Zeit mit Antonioni: Chronik eines Films. Frankfurt am Main: Verlag der Autoren, 1995.

Scripts and Scenarios

Dorst, Tankred, and Ursula Ehler. *Der Herr klagt über sein Volk in der Wildnis Amerika.* (Unpublished script for *The Scarlet Letter.*)

Handke, Peter. *Falsche Bewegung.* Frankfurt am Main: Suhrkamp, 1975.

Reinhold Rauh. "Falsche Bewegung: Ein Protokoll." *Wim Wenders und seine Filme.* Munich: Heyne, 1990. 129–205.

Wenders, Wim, and Fritz Müller-Scherz. Der Film "Im Lauf der Zeit." Frankfurt am Main: Zweitausendeins, 1976.

————. *The Film by Wim Wenders: "Kings of the Road" (In the Course of Time).* Trans. Christopher Doherty. Munich: Filmverlag der Autoren, 1976.

Wenders, Wim, and Chris Sievernich. *Nick's Film/Lightning over Water.* Frankfurt am Main: Zweitausendeins, 1981.

Alice dans les villes. L'Avant-scène du cinéma 267 (1981): 3–21, 55–74.

Wenders, Wim, and Sam Shepard. *Paris, Texas.* Ed. Chris Sievernich. Nördlingen: Greno, 1984.

Wenders, Wim. *Tokyo-Ga: Ein Reisetagebuch.* Frankfurt am Main: Verlag der Autoren, 1985.

Wenders, Wim, and Sam Shepard. *Der Himmel über Berlin.* Frankfurt am Main: Suhrkamp, 1987.

Wenders, Wim. "Reverse Angle: New York City, March 1982." *Die Logik der Bilder* 32–34

————. "Chambre 666." *Die Logik der Bilder* 35–45.

————. "Aufzeichnungen zu Kleidern und Städten." *The Act of Seeing* 103–15.

Interviews

Adler, Dieter. "Interview mit Wim Wenders." *Filmkritik* December 1978: 673–86.

Audibert, Louis. "Interview with Jean Claude Bonnet and Sylvia Trosa." *Cinematographe* 63 (1980): 50–51.

Bergala, Alain. "A Photographer's Viewpoint: An Interview with Wim Wenders." *UNESCO Courier* April 1988: 4.

Bergala, Alain, Alain Philippon, and Serge Toubiana. "Wenders' À La Recherche D'Un Lieu." *Cahiers du cinéma* 360–61 (1984): 11–17.

Blum, H. R. "Gespräch mit Wim Wenders." *Filmkritik* 16.2 (1972): 69–72.

Brunow, Jochen. "Jukebox Kino: Ein Gespräch über Film und Musik." *Filme* 12 (1981): 38–39.

_____. "Mauern und Zwischenräume: Ein Gespräch über das Schreiben von Dreh-büchern und den Umgang mit ihnen zwischen Jochen Brunow und Wim Wenders." *Schreiben für den Film: Das Drehbuch als eine anders Art des Erzählens*. Ed. Jochen Brunow. Munich: Text und Kritik, 1988. 95–107.

Buchka, Peter. "*Die Angst des Tormanns beim Elfmeter* oder Bilder, wie man sie aus amerikanischen Filmen kennt." *Südeutsche Zeitung* October 9–10, 1971: 17.

Bühler, Wolf-Eckart, and Paul B. Kleiser. Interview with Wim Wenders. *Filmkritik* March 1974: 131–35.

Ciment, Michel. "Entretien avec Wim Wenders." *Positif* 236 (1980): 14–24.

Ciment, Michel, and Hubert Niogret. "Entretien avec Wim Wenders." *Positif* 283 (1984): 8–15.

_____. "Entretien avec Wim Wenders." *Positif* 319 (1987): 9–15.

Clarens, Carlos. "King of the Road: Wim Wenders Interviewed." *Film Comment* 13.5 (1977): 42–46.

Dahan, Lucien. "Interview with Wenders." *Cinematographe* 28 (1977): 12–15.

Daney, Serge, and Oliver Assayas. "Entretien avec Wim Wenders." *Cahiers du cin-éma* 318 (1980): 15–23.

Dawson, Jan. *Wim Wenders*. Trans. Carla Wartenberg. New York: Zoetrope, 1976.

_____. "Filming Highsmith: Wim Wenders August 1976, and Wim Wenders 1977–78." *Sight and Sound* 47.1 (1977–78): 34–36.

Dieckmann, Katherine. "Wim Wenders: An Interview." *Film Quarterly* 38.2 (1984): 2–7.

Donohue, Walter. "An Interview with Wim Wenders." *Sight and Sound* 1.12 (1992): 8–13.

Durançon, Jean. "Entretien avec Wim Wenders." *Camera/Stylo* [Special Issue on Wim Wenders] 1 (1987): 101–6.

Eichenlaub, Hans, and Uwe Künzel. "Ein Gespäch mit Wim Wenders." *Wim Wen-ders: Ein Filmbuch*. Uwe Künzel. Freiburg: Dreisam, 1989. 211–15.

Englebert, A., and H. Auf der Lake. "Forcing the Observer to Begin Asking Ques-tions." Interview with Fritz Cremer. *Tendenzen* (FRG) 134.12 (1981): 52–56.

Fusco, Coco. "Angels, History and Poetic Fantasy: An Interview with Wim Wen-ders." *Cineaste* 16.4 (1988): 14–17.

Gallagher, John. "Wim Wenders." *Films in Review* 34.6 (1983): 355–61.

Gut, Taja. "Das Wahrnehmen einer Bewegung." *Individualität* 19 (1988): 31–50.

Hagen, Charles. "From the End of the World to Smack Dab in the Middle: An Interview with Wim Wenders." *Aperture* 123 (1991): 90, 91.

"Interview about the Making of *Hammett* in the U.S." *KINO* 5 (1980): 18–20.

"Interview with Wenders about *Im Lauf der Zeit*." *German Film Fernsehen* 3 (1974): 155–56.

"Interview with Wim Wenders about Shooting *Hammett* and Nick's Film." *Film-echo/Filmwoche* 9 (1981): 22.

Jost, Jon. "Wrong Move." *Sight and Sound* 50.2 (1981): 94–97.

Kass, Judith M. "At Home on the Road." *Movietone News* 57 (1978): 2–11.

L'Ecuyer, Gerald. "Wim Wenders." *Interview* 15 (1985): 48.

Lehman, Peter. "Making Deals and Matching Actions: An Interview with Edward Lachman." *Wide Angle* 5.4 (1983): 68–74.

Lehman, Peter, Robin Wood, and Edward Lachman. "Wim Wenders: An Interview." *Wide Angle* 2.4 (1978): 73–79.

Maillet, Dominiique. "Entretien avec Wim Wenders." *Lumière de cinéma* 7 (1977): 15–19, 26–31.

Malcolm, Derek. "Interview with Wim Wenders." *Guardian* February 12, 1977.

Masson, Alain, and Hubert Niogret. "Entretien avec Wim Wenders." *Positif* 198 (1977): 21–25.

Müller, André. "Das Kino könnte der Engel sein." *Der Spiegel* 43 (1987): 230–38. Reprinted in a longer version in André Müller, *Im Gespräch*. Reinbek: Rowohlt, 1989. 145–54.

Niogret, Hubert. "Entretien avec Wim Wenders." *Positif* 217 (1976): 25–32.

Nolden, Rainer. "Wim Wenders: Ein Drehbuch zu schreiben, das ist die Hölle." *Die Welt* June 20, 1988.

Petit, Chris. "The Art of Seeing." *Time Out* 361 (1977): 18–24.

Pym, John, and Don Ranvaud. "The Road from Wuppertal: Interview with Wim Wenders and Chris Sievernich." *Sight and Sound* 53.4 (1984): 244–54.

Rabourdin, Dominique. "Entretien avec Wim Wenders." *Cinema 80* 264 (1980): 10–12.

Thompson, Bill. "A Young German Film-Maker and His Road Movie." *Thousand Eyes Magazine* 2.3 (1976): 22–23.

Töteberg, Michael. "Pixel auf der Nase: Ein Gespräch mit Wim Wenders anläßlich der Publikation von *Einmal*." *Tageszeitung* May 19, 1994: 13.

Welsh, James M. "Wim Wenders: An Interview with Peter Lehman, Robin Wood and Edward Lachman." *Wide Angle* 2.4 (1978): 73–79.

Books on Wenders or Containing Chapters on Wenders

Bock, Hans-Michael, ed. *Cinegraph: Lexikon zum deutschsprachigen Film.* Munich: Text and Kritik, 1984.

Boujut, Michel. *Wim Wenders.* Paris: Edilig, 1983.

Buchka, Peter. *Augen kann man nicht kaufen: Wim Wenders und seine Filme.* Frankfurt am Main: Fischer, 1985.

Camera/Stylo. *Wim Wenders.* New enlarged ed. Paris: Ramsay Poche Cinéma, 1987.

Corrente, Giulio, ed. *Wim Wenders.* Rome: CircuitoCinema, 1985.

Corrigan, Timothy. *New German Film: The Displaced Image.* Austin: Texas UP, 1983. Rev. and exp. edition: Bloomington: Indiana UP, 1994.

———. *A Cinema without Walls: Movies and Culture after Vietnam.* New Brunswick, NJ: Rutgers UP, 1991.

D'Angelo, Filippo. *Wim Wenders.* Florence: La nuova Italia, 1982.

Deutsches Filmmuseum Frankfurt am Main. "Schauplätze." Poster with texts for the exhibit "Schauplätze: Kino-Reisen-Bilder von Wim Wenders." September 8– October 30, 1988. Frankfurt am Main: Deutsches Filmmuseum.

Devillers, Jean-Pierre. *Berlin, L.A., Berlin: Wim Wenders.* Paris: Samuel Tastet, 1985.

Elsaesser, Thomas. *New German Cinema: A History.* New Brunswick, NJ: Rutgers UP, 1989.

Estève, Michel, ed. *Wim Wenders.* Paris: Seghers, 1989.

Fischer, Robert, and Joe Hembus. *Der neue deutsche Film 1960–1980.* Munich: Goldman, 1981.

Franklin, James. *New German Cinema: From Oberhausen to Hamburg.* Boston: Twayne, 1983.

Geist, Kathe. *The Cinema of Wim Wenders: From Paris, France to "Paris, Texas."* Ann Arbor: U.M.I. Research P, 1988.

Gemünden, Gerd, and Michael Töteberg, eds. *Wim Wenders: Einstellungen.* Frankfurt am Main: Verlag der Autoren, 1993.

Grob, Norbert. *Die Formen des filmischen Blicks: Wenders—Die frühen Filme.* Munich: Filmland Presse, 1984.

————. *Wenders.* Berlin: Edition Filme, 1991.

Harvey, David. *The Conditions of Postmodernity.* London: Blackwell, 1989.

Hembus, Joe. *Der deutsche Film kann gar nicht besser sein: Ein Pamphlet von gestern. Eine Abrechnung von heute.* Munich: Roger and Bernhard, 1981.

Jansen, Peter W. *The New German Film.* Munich: Goethe Institute, 1982.

Johnston, Sheila, ed. *Wim Wenders: Coming Down from the Mountain.* London: British Film Institute. Dossier No. 10, 1981.

Kearny, Richard. *The Wake of Imagination: Toward a Postmodern Culture.* Minneapolis: U of Minnesota P, 1988.

Kolker, Robert Phillip. *The Altering Eye: Contemporary International Cinema.* New York: Oxford UP, 1983.

Kolker, Robert, and Peter Beicken. *The Films of Wim Wenders: Cinema as Vision and Desire.* Cambridge and New York: Cambridge UP, 1993.

Kuhn, Michael, Johan G. Hahn, and Henk Hoekstra. *Hinter den Augen ein eigenes Bild: Film und Spiritualität.* Zurich: Benziger, 1991.

Künzel, Uwe. *Wim Wenders: Ein Filmbuch.* Freiburg: Dreisam, 1988.

Möbius, Hanno, and Guntram Vogt. *Drehort Stadt: Das Thema "Großstadt" im deutschen Film.* Marburg: Hitzeroth, 1990.

Neumann, Hans-Joachim. *Der deutsche Film heute: Die Macher, das Geld, die Erfolge, das Publikum.* Frankfurt am Main: Ullstein, 1986.

Petit, Catherine, Philippe Dubois, and Claudine Delvaux. *Les voyages de Wim Wenders.* Crisnée: Edition Yellow Now, 1985.

Pflaum, Hans Günther. *Deutschland im Film: Themenschwerpunkte des Spielfilms in der Bundesrepublik Deutschland.* Munich: Hueber, 1985. English translation: *Germany on Film: Theme and Content in the Cinema of the Federal Republic of Germany.* Ed. Robert Picht. Trans. Richard C. Helt and Roland Richter. Detroit: Wayne State UP, 1990.

Pflaum, Hans Günther, and Hans Helmut Prinzler. *Film in der Bundesrepublik Deutschland.* Frankfurt am Main: Fischer, 1982.

————. *Cinema in the Federal Republic of Germany.* Bonn: Inter Nationes, 1983.

Bibliography

Phillips, Klaus, ed. *New German Filmmakers: From Oberhausen through the 1970s.* New York: Ungar, 1983.

Rauh, Reinhold. *Sprache im Film: Die Kombination von Wort und Bild im Spielfilm.* Münster: Maks, 1987.

———. *Wim Wenders und seine Filme.* Munich: Heyne, 1990.

Rentschler, Eric. *West German Film in the Course of Time: Reflections on the Twenty Years since Oberhausen.* Bedford Hills, NY: Redgrave, 1984.

———, ed. *West German Filmmakers on Film.* New York: Holmes and Meier, 1988. In German: *Augenzeugen: 100 Texte deutscher Filmemacher.* Ed. Hans Helmut Prinzler and Eric Rentschler. Frankfurt am Main: Verlag der Autoren, 1988.

Rost, Andreas. *Von einem der auszog das Leben zu lernen: Ästhetische Erfahrung im Kino ausgehend von Wim Wenders' Film "Alice in den Städten."* Munich: Trickster, 1990.

Sandford, John. *The New German Cinema.* New York: Da Capo Press, 1980.

Schleicher, Harald. *Film-Reflexionen: Autothematische Filme von Wim Wenders, Jean-Luc Godard, und Federico Fellini.* Tübingen: Niemeyer, 1991.

Silberman, Marc. *German Cinema: Texts in Context.* Detroit: Wayne State UP, 1995.

Spagnoletti, Giovanni, ed. *Il cinema di Wim Wenders: Incontri Cinematografici di Monicelli Terme.* Parma, 1977.

———. *Wim Wenders.* Rome: Europa Cinema, 1991.

Springer, Bernhard. *Narrative und optische Strukturen im Bedeutungsaufbau des Spielfilms: Methodische Überlegungen entwickelt am Film "Falsche Bewegung" von Peter Handke und Wim Wenders.* Tübingen: Narr, 1987.

Valli, Bernardo. *Lo Sguardo empatico: Wenders e il cinema nella tarda modernità.* Urbino: Quattroventi, 1990.

Weinrichter, Antonio. *Wim Wenders.* Madrid: Ediciones JC, 1986.

Winkler-Bessone, Claude. *Les films de Wim Wenders: La nouvelle naissance des images.* Bern, New York, and Frankfurt am Main: Peter Lang, 1992.

Articles

Adler, Walter. "Wenders en Californie." *Cahiers du cinéma* 301 (1979): 54–64.

Barry, Thomas F. "The Weight of Angels: Peter Handke and *Der Himmel über Berlin.*" *Modern Austrian Literature* 23.3–4 (1990): 53–64.

Bechtold, Gerhard. "Der Fall Wenders oder die Kolonisierung der Gehirne?" *Filmfaust* 37 (1984): 32–39.

Blanchet, Christian. "Au-delà du rêve américain." *Cinéma* 309 (1984): 26–28.

Bloess, Georges. "Entre mensonge et mutisme: Les chemins étroits de l'expression romanesque et filmique chez Peter Handke et Wim Wenders." *Recherches Germaniques* 9 (1979): 234–62.

Bonitzer, Pascal. "Déjà Jadis." *Cahiers du cinéma* 340 (1982): 22–25.

Brunette, Peter. "Filming Words: Wenders' *The Goalie's Anxiety at the Penalty Kick.*" *European Filmmakers and the Art of Adaptation.* Ed. Andrew Horton and Joan Margrette. New York: Ungar, 1981. 188–202.

Caldwell, David, and Paul W. Rea. "Handke's and Wenders' *Wings of Desire:* Transcending Postmodernism." *German Quarterly* 64.1 (1991): 46–60.

Caltvedt, Les. "Berlin Poetry: Archaic Cultural Patterns in Wenders's *Wings of Desire.*" *Literature/Film Quarterly* 20.2 (1992): 121–26.

Carbon, Sabine. "Bis ans Ende der Sehnsucht." *Der Tagesspiegel* 13 (1991): xiv.

Carrere, Emmanuelle. "La distance de la rencontre." *Positif* 283 (1984): 6–7.

"Cinéma ouest-allemand." *Jeune cinéma* 94 (1976): 1–49.

Combs, Richard. "Wim Wenders." *International Film Guide, 1980.* Ed. Peter Cowie. New York: Tantivy Press, 1979. 72–77.

Cook, Roger. "Angels, Fiction, and History in Berlin: Wim Wenders' *Wings of Desire.*" *Germanic Review* 64.1 (1991): 34–47.

Corrigan, Timothy. "The Realist Gesture in the Films of Wim Wenders: Hollywood and the New German Cinema." *Quarterly Review of Film Studies* 5.2 (1980): 205–16.

_____. "Wenders' *Kings of the Road:* The Voyage from Desire to Language." *New German Critique* 24–25 (1981–82): 94–107.

_____. "Cinematic Snuff: German Friends and Narrative Murders." *Cinema Journal* 24.2 (1985): 9–18.

Covino, Michael. "Wim Wenders: A Worldwide Homesickness." *Film Quarterly* 31.2 (1977–78): 9–19.

Curchod, Oliver. "L'ange ou la mouche? Sur *Les ailes de désir.*" *Positif* 319 (1987): 2–4.

Dagneau, Derek. "Voyage au pays de Wenders." *Image et son* 323 (1977): 82–94.

Dawson, Jan. "Filming Highsmith." *Sight and Sound* 47.1 (1977): 30–36.

_____. "German Weasels." *Film Comment* 13.3 (1977): 33–34.

_____. "A Labyrinth of Subsidies: The Origins of the New German Cinema." *Sight and Sound* 50.1 (1980): 14–20.

Delanoe, Nelcya. "La mort à Hollywood: Quelques reflexions sur *L'etat des choses* de Wim Wenders." *Revue francaise d'etudes americaines* 9–10 (1984): 131–38.

Douglas, J. Yellowlees. "American Friends and Strangers on Trains." *Literature/Film Quarterly* 16.3 (1988): 181–90.

Dubroux, Daniéle. "Il n'y aurait plus qu'une seule image." *Cahiers du cinéma* 279–80 (1977): 38–43.

Dupont, Pascal. "Wenders Finds a Star." *World Press* 27 (1980): 64.

Durgnat, Raymond. "From Caligari to Hitler." *Film Comment* 16.4 (1980): 59–70.

Eberwein, Robert T. "Genre and the Writerly Text." *Journal of Popular Film and Television* 13.2 (1985): 63–68.

Ehrlich, Linda C. "Mediations on Wim Wenders's *Wings of Desire.*" *Literature/Film Quarterly* 19.4 (1991): 242–46.

Eidsvik, Charles. "The State as Movie Mogul." *Film Comment* 15.2 (1979): 60–66.

Eisenschitz, Bernard. "Le cinéma allemand, aujourd'hui." *Documents* September 1976: 81–168.

Elsaesser, Thomas. "Germany's Imaginary America: Wim Wenders and Peter Handke." *European Cinema Conference Papers.* Ed. Susan Hayward. Birmingham: Aston UP, 1984. 31–52.

▌ Bibliography

_____. "American Graffiti und neuer deutscher Film: Filmemacher zwischen Avantgarde und Postmoderne." *Postmoderne: Zeichen kulturellen Wandels.* Ed. Andreas Huyssen and Klaus Scherpe. Reinbek: Rowohlt, 1986. 302–28.

Farell, Tom. "Nick Ray's German Friend Wim Wenders." *Wide Angle* 5.4 (1983): 60–67.

Frisch, Shelley. "The Disenchanted Image: From Goethe's *Wilhelm Meister* to Wenders' *Wrong Movement.*" *Literature/Film Quarterly* 7.3 (1979): 208–14.

Garfield, Brian. "Vee Vere Young Then." *Armchair Detective* 17.4 (1984): 420–26.

Geist, Kathe. "West Looks East: The Influence of Yasujiro Ozu on Wim Wenders and Peter Handke." *Art Journal* 43.3 (1983): 234–39.

_____. "Wenders in the Cities." *New German Filmmakers: From Oberhausen through the 1970s.* Ed. Klaus Phillips. New York: Ungar, 1984. 379–404.

_____. "Filmmaking as Research: Wim Wenders' *The State of Things.*" *Post Script* 5.2 (1986): 19–30.

_____. "Women in Wim Wenders's Films: A Structuring Absence." *Schatzkammer* 14.2 (1988): 87–94.

_____. "Mothers and Children in the Films of Wim Wenders." *Gender and German Cinema: Feminist Interventions.* Vol. 1. Ed. Sandra J. Frieden et al. Oxford: Berg, 1993. 11–22.

Gemünden, Gerd. "On the Way to Language: Wenders' *Kings of the Road.*" *Film Criticism* 15.2 (1991): 13–28.

_____. "*Paris, Texas.*" *Metzler Filmlexikon.* Ed. Michael Töteberg. Stuttgart: Metzler, 1995. 447–49.

Ghali, Nourredine. "Les chemins de l'errance et la solitude." *Cinéma 76* 216 (1976): 24–32.

_____. "Wim Wenders: Dossier-auteur." *Cinéma 76* 216 (1976): 33–52.

Goldschmidt, Didier. "Wenders ou la dérive des continents." *Cinématographe* 78 (1982): 25–28.

Grob, Norbert. "Wie die Dauer den Blick verändert: Wanderungen durch die kältere Welt des Wim Wenders." *Filme* 12 (1981): 16–37.

_____. "Sehen, was zu sehen ist." *Filmbulletin* 136 (1984): 24–31.

_____. "Open up the Window: Eine Retrospektive—eine Ausstellung—ein neues Buch: Wim Wenders im Frankfurter Filmmuseum." *Die Zeit* September 30, 1988: 69.

_____. "Wim Wenders." *Cinegraph: Lexikon zum deutschsprachigen Film.* Ed. Hans-Michael Bock. Munich: Text und Kritik, 1988.

Gut, Taja. "Unterwegs zur Filmkunst von Wim Wenders." *Individualität* 19 (1988): 23–30.

Handke, Peter. "Augsburg im August: Trostlos." *Film* January 1969: 30–32.

_____. "Vorläufige Bemerkungen zu Landkinos und Heimatfilmen." *Ich bin ein Bewohner des Elfenbeinturms.* Frankfurt am Main: Suhrkamp, 1972. 146–52.

Harcourt, Peter. "Adaptation through Inversion: Wenders' *Wrong Movement.*" *Modern European Filmmakers and the Art of Adaptation.* Ed. Andrew Horton and Joan Margretta. New York: Ungar, 1982. 263–77.

Helmetag, Charles H. "'. . . Of Men and Angels': Literary Allusions in Wim Wenders' *Wings of Desire.*" *Literature/Film Quarterly* 18.4 (1990): 251–54.

Honickel, Thomas. "Das Comeback des Wim Wenders." *Filmbeobachter* 1 (1983): 11–14.

Horton, Andrew. "Wim Wenders' *Alice in the Cities:* Song of the Open Road." *Ideas of Order in Literature and Film.* Ed. Peter Ruppert. Tallahassee: UP of Florida, 1980. 84–93.

Ishaghpour, Youssef. "Le cinéma de Wim Wenders." *Ecran* 73 (1978): 27–36.

Jacobs, Diane. "Hitler's Ungrateful Grandchildren: Today's German Filmmakers." *American Film* 5.7 (1980): 34–40.

Jaehne, Karen. "Angel Eyes: Wenders Soars." *Film Comment* 24.3 (1988): 18–20.

Johnston, Sheila. "The Author as Public Institution: The 'New' Cinema in the Federal Republic of Germany." *Screen Education* 32–33 (1979–80): 67–78.

———. "Wim Wenders' New Romanticism." *World Press Review* 35.8 (1988): 59.

Jullien, Philippe. "Les variantes d'un seul film jamais réalisé." *Image et son* 384 (1983): 44–48.

Kadish, Doris Y. "Crimes of Domestic Violence in *Paris, Texas.*" *Crime in Motion Pictures.* Ed. Douglas Radcliff-Umstead. Kent, OH: Kent State UP, 1986. 116–24.

Keenan, Richard C., and James M. Welsh. "Wim Wenders and Nathaniel Hawthorne: From *The Scarlet Letter* to *Der scharlachrote Buchstabe.*" *Literature/ Film Quarterly* 6.2 (1978): 175–79.

Kermabon, Jacques. "Pour un cinéma de la stase." *Cinéma* 309 (1984): 25–26.

Kinder, Marsha. "The American Friend." *Film Quarterly* 32.3 (1978–79): 45–50.

Klingmann, Ulrich. "Die Angst des Tormanns beim Elfmeter: Buchtext und Filmtext." *Germanic Review* 70.4 (1995): 164–73.

Koebner, Thomas. "Ein Blick auf Wim Wenders und noch ein Seitenblick auf Volker Schlöndorff." *Augen- Blick* 1.2 (1985): 30–37.

Kolditz, Stefan. "Der Wert des Augenblicks." *Film und Fernsehen* 9 (1990): 36–39.

———. "Sehen und zeigen: Der Regisseur Wim Wenders (1)." *Film und Fernsehen* 7 (1990): 18–21.

Kral, Petr. "Détour par l'Amerique (sur les traces de Wim Wenders)." *Positif* 236 (1980): 14–24.

Kuzniar, Alice. "Ephemeral Inscriptions: Wenders' and Handke's Testimony to Writing." *Seminar* 31.3 (1995): 217–28.

Kuzniar, Alice, and Xavier Vila. "Witnessing Narration in *Wings of Desire.*" *Film Criticism* 16.3 (1992): 53–65.

La Pavec, Jean-Pierre. "*Nick's Movie:* Un cinéma au Carré." *Cinema 80* 264 (1980): 6–8.

Levine, June Perry. "Wim Wenders: The State of Stories." *National Traditions in Motion Pictures.* Ed. Douglas Radcliff-Umstead. Kent, OH: Kent State UP, 1985. 101–6.

Levy, Shawn. "*Until the End of the World:* Wim Wenders' Dance around the Planet." *American Film* 17.1 (1992): 51–52.

Linville, Susan, and Kent Casper. "Imitations, Dreams, and Origins in Wim Wenders' *The American Friend.*" *Literature/Film Quarterly* 13.4 (1985): 234–39.

Luft, Edmund. "*Der amerikanische Freund.*" *International Film Guide.* Ed. Peter Cowie. New York: A.S. Barnes/Tantivy, 1976. 153–58.

▌Bibliography

Luprecht, Mark. "Freud at Paris, Texas: Penetrating the Oedipal Sub-Text." *Literature/Film Quarterly* 20.2 (1992): 115–20.

Mahoney, Dennis F. "'What's Wrong with a Cowboy in Hamburg?': Narcissism as Cultural Imperialism in Wim Wenders' *American Friend.*" *Journal of Evolutionary Psychology* 7.1 (1986): 106–16.

Mairesse, Emmanuel. "Le cinémasse de Wim Wenders." *Cahiers du cinéma* 281 (1977): 61, 62.

Markgraf, Nikolaus. "Wenders dreht in Portugal und verfilmt Frischs *Stiller.*" *Frankfurter Rundschau* 24 (1981): 11.

Martin, John W. "Humor and Malevolence in Wenders' *The American Friend.*" *Michigan Academician* 12.2 (1980): 145–53.

Mason, Deborah. "Will the Real Wim Wenders Please Stand Up?" *Vogue* 173.5 (1983): 52.

Mitchell, Tony. "Wim Wenders and *The State of Things.*" *Film Criticism* 7.3 (1983): 47–50.

Möbius, Hanno, and Guntram Vogt. "Wim Wenders' filmische Stadtlandschaften oder *Der Himmel über Berlin.*" *Drehort Stadt.* Marburg: Hitzeroth, 1990. 149–64.

Narboni, Jena. "Traquenards." *Cahiers du cinéma* 279–80 (1977): 28–32.

Oksiloff, Assenka. "Eden Is Burning: Wim Wenders's Techniques of Synaesthesia." *German Quarterly* 69.1 (1996): 32–47.

Paneth, Ira. "Wim and His Wings." *Film Quarterly* 42.1 (1988): 2–8.

Payne, Robert. "New German Cinema/Old Hollywood Genres." *Critical Studies* (School of Cinema- Television, USC) 5.1 (1985): 8–11.

Peling, Mireille. "Les chemins de Wim Wenders." *Jeune cinéma* 187 (1988): 3–14.

Petat, Jacques. "Le cinéma ou la raison d'être." *Cinéma* (Paris) 234 (1978): 51.

Pflaum, Hans Günther. "Der Traum vom Kino: Wim Wenders." *Europäische Filmkunst.* Ed. Jörg-Dieter Kogel. Frankfurt am Main: Fischer, 1990. 197–207.

Philippon, Alain. "The Day of the Hunter." *Cahiers du cinéma* 360–61 (1984): 7–9.

Plater, Edward M. V. "The Temptation of Jonathan Zimmermann: Wim Wenders' *The American Friend.*" *Literature/Film Quarterly* 16.3 (1988): 191–200.

Prill, Meinhard. "Wim Wenders und seine Erfahrung in Hollywood." *Medien und Erziehung* 4 (1983): 222–31.

Radcliff-Umstead, Douglas. "Wenders: The Filmic Language of Loss." *National Traditions in Motion Pictures.* Ed. Douglas Radcliff-Umstead. Kent, OH: Kent State UP, 1985. 92–100.

Rayns, T. "Forms of Address." *Sight and Sound* 44.1 (1974): 2–7.

Rentschler, Eric. "American Friends and the New German Cinema: Patterns of Reception." *New German Critique* 24–25 (1981–82): 7–35.

_____. "How American Is It: The U.S. as Image and Imaginary in German Film." *Persistence of Vision* 2 (1985): 5–18.

Rogowski, Christian. "'To Be Continued': History in Wim Wenders' *Der Himmel über Berlin* and Thomas Brasch's *Domino.*" *German Studies Review* 15.3 (1992): 547–63.

_____. "'Der liebevolle Blick': Gender and Love in Wim Wenders' *Wings of Desire.*" *Seminar* 29.4 (1993): 398–409.

Ruppert, Peter. "Audience Engagement in Wenders's *The American Friend* and Fassbinder's *Ali: Fear Eats the Soul.*" *Narrative Strategies: Original Essays in Film and Prose Fiction.* Ed. Sydney M. Conger and Janice R. Welsch. Macomb: Western Illinois UP, 1980. 61–77.

Scheel, Kurt. "Oberammergau, Bayern: Wim Wenders und die Filmkritik." *Merkur* 39.3 (1985): 263–66.

Scheib, Ronnie. "Angst for the Memories." *Film Comment* 26.4 (1990): 9–17.

Schlunk, Jürgen. "The Image of America in German Literature and in the New German Cinema: Wim Wenders' *The American Friend.*" *Literature/Film Quarterly* 7.3 (1979): 215–22.

Schneider, Roland. "Wim Wenders: L'homme atlantique." *CinémAction* (1984): 60–65.

Seidenberg, Robert. "The Man Who Fell to Earth: No More Angst and Alienation for Wim Wenders." *American Film* 13.8 (1988): 28–32.

Sharrett, Christopher. "'No More Going Back and Forth as in the Past': Notes on the Fate of History in Recent European Film." *Persistence of Vision* 8 (1990): 29–44.

Simsolo, Noël, Danièle Parra, and Pascal Mérigeau. "Wim Wenders." *Image et son* 397 (1984): 63–74.

Sineux, Michael. "L'évidence des choses." *Positif* 283 (1984): 2–5.

Snyder, Stephen. "Wim Wenders: The Hunger Artist in America." *Post Script* 6.2 (1987): 54–62.

Steinborn, Bion. "Der deutsche Filmnachwuchs." *Filmfaust* 17–18 (1980): 49–62.

Thoms, A. "German Underground." *Afterimage* 1.1 (1972): 45–55.

Toubiana, Serge. "Cannes en Proie à l'Ogre." *Cahiers du cinéma* 360–61 (1984): 4–5.

_____. "Wenders in California." *Cahiers du cinéma* 301 (1979): 53–64.

Vogt, Guntram. "Der entäuschte Entdecker: Wim Wenders in den USA." *Augen-Blick* 12 (1992): 79–95.

Watt, Stephen. "Simulation, Gender, and Postmodernism: Sam Shepard and *Paris, Texas.*" *Perspectives on Contemporary Literature* 13 (1987): 73–82.

Welsh, Henry. "Wim Wenders cinéaste de la subjectivité." *Jeune cinéma* 94 (1976): 27–28.

Whalen, Tom. "'When You Think You've Got There, You Haven't': Wim Wenders' *Alice in the Cities.*" *New Orleans Review* 15.2 (1988): 80–83.

Winkler, Willi. "Der Intellektuelle auf der Suche nach der verlorenen Naivität: Wim Wenders und seine Filme." *Merkur* 38.4 (1984): 473–77.

Zavarzadeh, Mas'ud. "Biology and Ideology: The 'Natural' Family in *Paris, Texas.*" *CineAction* 8 (1987): 25–30.

Reviews

Adler, Walter. "Das grosse Geld, die Angst und der Traum vom Geschichten Erzählen." *Filmkritik* December 1978: 673–86.

▌ Bibliography

"Der amerikanische Freund (The American Friend)." *Variety* June 8, 1977: 26, 30.

Andrews, Nigel. "Wim Wenders: *The Goalkeeper's Fear of the Penalty.*" *Sight and Sound* 42.1 (1972–73): 6–7.

Ansen, David. "Poor Murderer." *Newsweek* October 3, 1977: 71–72.

_____. "*Wings of Desire.*" *Newsweek* May 23, 1988: 70–71.

Arnold, Gary. "A Major Talent Takes Shape in Wenders' *American Friend.*" *Washington Post* January 5, 1978: F9.

Baker, R. "*Alice in the Cities.*" *Soho Weekly News* April 28, 1977: 40.

_____. "*American Friend*—German Masterpiece." *Soho Weekly News* September 29, 1977.

Baroncelli, Jean de. "Wim Wenders." *Le monde* July 14, 1979.

Bassan, Raphaël. "*L'angoisse du gardien de but au moment de penalty.*" *Ecran* 73 (1978): 37.

Baumbach, Jonathan. "Festival Report: New York." *American Film* 3.4 (1978): 66–67.

_____. "*Wings of Desire.*" *The Nation* 246.19 (1988): 691–92.

Baxter, Brian. "*Kings of the Road.*" *BFI National Film Theatre* November 15–December 5, 1976: 15.

Bégramian, Alain. "*Faux mouvement.*" *Lumière du cinéma* 11 (1978): 26–29.

Benson, Sheila. "*Hammett.*" *Los Angeles Times* May 20, 1983, sec. 6: 1.

Bergala, Alain. "*L'angoisse du gardien de but au moment du penalty.*" *Cahiers du cinéma* 294 (1978): 55–56.

Biette, Jean-Claude. "*Faux mouvement.*" *Cahiers du cinéma* 286 (1978): 54–55.

Blum, H. R. "*Die Angst des Tormanns beim Elfmeter* oder Bilder, wie man sie aus amerikanischen Filmen kennt." *Süddeutsche Zeitung* October 9, 1971: 124.

Blumenberg, Hans C. "Bildschirm contra Leinwand." *Die Zeit* June 23, 1978: 28.

_____. "Von Caligari bis Coppola: Junge deutsche Filmemacher in Hollywood auf den Spuren von Lubitsch, Murnau und Lang." *Die Zeit* February 22, 1980: 9–11.

_____. "Ripley in den Städten." *Kino Zeit: Aufsätze und Kritiken zum modernen Film, 1976–1980.* Frankfurt am Main: Fischer, 1980. 84–88.

_____. "Der Aufstand der Trittbrettfahrer." *tip* August 12, 1983: 6.

_____. "Odysseus auf Umwegen." *Gegenschuß: Texte über Filmemacher und Filme, 1980–1983.* Frankfurt am Main: Fischer, 1984. 41–45.

_____. "Hammett kam nur bis Hollywood." *Gegenschuß: Texte über Filmemacher und Filme 1980–1983.* Frankfurt am Main: Fischer, 1984. 227–31.

Buchka, Peter. ". . . in die leere Welt hinein." *Süddeutsche Zeitung* September 13, 1973: 71.

_____. "Suche nach Heimat." *Expression* 2 (1989): 86.

Buhler, W. E., and P. B. Kleiser. "*Alice in den Städten.*" *Filmkritik* 18.3 (1974): 131–35.

Canby, Vincent. "*The Goalie's Anxiety:* Lonely Madness." *New York Times* January 14, 1977: C4.

_____. "Film Festival: *American Friend* Tops Day's Fare." *New York Times* September 24, 1977: 15.

————. "This Festival Could Turn Out to Be a Real Smash." *New York Times* September 25, 1977: D15.

————. "This Was the Year Comedy Was the King." *New York Times* December 25, 1977: D15.

————. "Series at Modern Is Presenting *Radio On*." *New York Times* April 30, 1980, sec. 1: 49.

————. "Midterm Festival Report." *New York Times* October 11, 1981: D19.

————. "The Last Months of Nicholas Ray's Life." *New York Times* September 26, 1981: L13.

————. "Wim Wenders's *Hammett*." *New York Times* July 1, 1983: C8.

————. *"Reverse Angle."* *New York Times* January 23, 1985: C14.

————. *"Toky-Ga."* *New York Times* April 26, 1985: C13.

Carroll, Kathleen. "This Gun for Short-Term Hire." *New York Daily News* September 27, 1977.

Castro, Antonio. "Sobre dos films de Wim Wenders." *Insula* April 1983: 14–15.

Clarke, Gerald. "Seeking Planets That Do Not Exist." *Time* March 20, 1978: 51–53.

Cocks, Jay. "More a Famine Than a Festival." *Time* October 25, 1976: 81.

Codelli, Lorenzo. *"Die Angst des Tormanns beim Elfmeter."* *Positif* 144–45 (1972): 85–86.

Cohn, Lawrence. "Gray City Films as Wim Wenders' N.Y. Distribution and Production Base." *Variety* September 30, 1981: 6.

Combs, Richard. *"Im Lauf der Zeit (Kings of the Road)."* *Monthly Film Bulletin* July 1977: 148–49.

"Coppola, Wenders Set Film for Orion." *Hollywood Reporter* March 30, 1978: 1.

Corliss, Richard. *"Wings of Desire."* *Time* May 9, 1988: 79.

Curchod, Olivier. "L'ange ou la mouche? Sur *Les ailes du désir*." *Positif* 319 (1987): 2–4.

Daney, Serge, and Oliver Assayas. "Wim's Movie." *Cahiers du cinéma* 318 (1980): 15–17.

Denby, David. "New York Festival: Wenders." *Boston Phoenix* October 4, 1977.

————. *"Wings of Desire."* *New York* May 9, 1988: 68–69.

Dionne, E. J., Jr. "Wenders's Film, *Paris, Texas*, Wins at Cannes." *New York Times* May 24, 1984: 22.

Domecq, Jean-Philippe. "L'Europe vue d'ici. Sur *Les ailes du désir*." *Positif* 319 (1987): 7–8.

Donner, Wolf. "Film around the World: The Germans Are Coming." *Atlas* 23.3 (1976): 29–30.

————. "Kein Engel über Wenders: *In weiter Nähe, so fern!*" *Frankfurter Allgemeine Zeitung* September 9, 1993.

Dowling, Tom. *"American Friend* Is a Thriller á la Hitchcock." *Washington Star* January 5, 1978: C1–2.

Dupont, Pascal. "Wenders Finds a Star." *World Press Review* 27 (1980): 64.

Ebert, Jürgen. *"Im Lauf der Zeit I."* *Filmkritik* 235 (1976): 306–7.

Ebert, Roger. "Impressive Festival Features *Kings of the Road*." *Chicago Sun-Times* November 14, 1976: Show 2.

▌ Bibliography

"Ein Kampf um *Paris, Texas*: Warum der neue Wenders Film erst jetzt in die deutschen Kinos kommt." *Der Spiegel* 2 (1985): 137–38.

Elley, Derek. *"Alice in the Cities."* Films and Filming 22.3 (1975): 35–36.

———. *"The Goalkeeper's Fear of the Penalty."* Films and Filming 22.5 (1976): 36–37.

"Flattern für Deutschland." *Der Spiegel* 21 (1993): 214–15.

Feldmann, Sebastian. *"Im Lauf der Zeit II."* Filmkritik 235 (1976): 308–9.

Feldvoß, Marlie. "Damit der Zufall eingreifen kann: Ein Gespräch mit dem Fotografen und Filmregisseur Wim Wenders." *Frankfurter Rundschau* July 23, 1994: ZB2.

Fell, John L. *"The Wrong Movement."* Film Quarterly 32.2 (1978): 49–50.

Fox, Terry Curtis. "Wim Wenders Crosses the Border." *Village Voice* October 3, 1977: 42, 43, 46.

Geist, Kathe. *"Lightning over Water."* Film Quarterly 35.2 (1981–82): 46–51.

Gies, Martin. *"Alice in den Städten."* Jugend Film Fernsehen 3 (1974): 155–56.

Gonzalez, Carlos Benito. *"La Letra Escarlata."* Cinema 2002 46 (1978): 14–15.

Grant, Jacques. *"Au fil du temps* (au temps du film)." *Cinéma 76* 210 (1976): 117–22.

Green, Peter. "Germans Abroad." *Sight and Sound* 57.2 (1988): 126–30.

Greenspun, Roger. "Cannes: Seeing and Selling." *American Film* September 2, 1977: 60–63.

Greiner, Ulrich. "Erscheinung des Engels." *Die Zeit* 39 (1993): 65.

Grob, Norbert. "Konflikte im Schnitt verschwunden: *In weiter Nähe, so fern!" Tageszeitung* September 9, 1993: 12–13.

Harris, Art. "Hopper's Riding Easy in New Film." *Washington Post* January 6, 1978: 15.

Haskell, Molly. *"Wings of Desire."* Vogue June 1988: 52.

Heinrich, Nathalie. *"La lettre écarlate."* Cahiers du cinéma 305 (1979): 54–55.

Hofmann, Michael. *"Wings of Desire."* Times Literary Supplement June 24–30, 1988: 706.

———. *"Until the End of the World."* Times Literary Supplement May 8, 1992: 17.

hooks, bell. "Representing Whiteness: Seeing *Wings of Desire.*" Zeta Magazine 2.3 (1989): 36–39. Reprinted in Bell Hooks, *Yearning: Race, Gender, and Cultural Politics.* Boston: West End, 1990. 165–71.

Jacobs, Karen. "Angel Eyes: Wenders Soars." *Film Comment* 24.3 (1988): 18–20.

Jaehne, Karen. "The American Fiend." *Sight and Sound* 47.2 (1978): 101–3.

Jeremias, Brigitte. "Wenders/Handke Re-vamp *Wilhelm Meister.*" German Tribune 680 (1975): 10–11.

Johnston, Sheila. "Wim Wenders' New Romanticism." *World Press Review* 35 (1988): 59.

Kael, Pauline. "Heart/Soul." *New Yorker* October 1977: 173–79.

———. *"Wings of Desire."* New Yorker May 1988: 77–78.

Kauffmann, Stanley. "Wenders." *New Republic* January 29, 1977: 26–27.

———. "A Cost of Freedom." *New Republic* October 1, 1977: 26–27.

Kilb, Andreas. "Die Erde vom Himmel aus betrachtet." *Die Zeit* August 24, 1990: 13–14.

_____. "So weit, so fern, so nah—vorbei." *Die Zeit* [Overseas Edition] 22 (1993): 13.

Knight, Julia. *"Bis ans Ende der Welt." Sight and Sound* 2.1 (1992): 45–46.

Körte, Peter. *"Falsche Bewegung.* Ein gesperrter Film, ein neues Buch: Wim Wenders, wohin?" *Frankfurter Rundschau* May 7, 1994: 7.

Legrand, Gérard. "Les deux testaments." *Positif* 232–33 (1980): 94–98.

Le Pavec, Jean-Pierre. "Economie chronique." *Cinéma* 264 (1980): 4.

_____. *"Nick's Movie:* Un cinéma au carré." *Cinéma* 264 (1980): 6–8.

Light, Alan. "Star-Studded Soundtrack." *Rolling Stone* January 9, 1992: 34.

Linett, Richard. *"The State of Things." Cineaste* 13.1 (1983): 26.

Magny, Joël. "Profile of Wenders and Review of *Falsche Bewegung." Cinéma 80* 256 (1980): 11–12.

_____. "Wim Wenders entre classicisme et modernité." *Cinéma* 309 (1984): 21–24.

Mason, Deborah. "Will the Real Wim Wenders Please Stand Up?" *Vogue* May 1983: 52.

Masson, Alain. "Hermés au verso." *Positif* 183–84 (1976): 104–6.

_____. "Le romanesque et le spectaculaire." *Positif* 198 (1977): 18–20.

_____. "Conversion à la vie: Sur *Les ailes du désir." Positif* 319 (1987): 5–6.

McCarthy, Todd. "Wenders' 'Texas' Leads to Cannes." *Variety* May 9, 1984: 347.

_____. "Governments Trying to Start 'End of World': Big Wenders Film Has Problems in Oz." *Variety* October 12, 1988: 5.

McCourt, James. "Festivlog: *Im Lauf der Zeit." Film Comment* 12.6 (1977): 37.

_____. "New York Film Festival Review I." *Film Comment* 13.6 (1977): 38–41.

McCreadie, Marsha. *"American Friend." Films in Review* 28.10 (1977): 632–33.

Milne, Tom. *"Der amerikanische Freund." Monthly Film Bulletin* January 1978: 3.

Monaco, James. *"Alice in the Cities:* Alice Is Alive and Well." *Take One* 4.11 (1975): 30–31.

Nadotti, Maria. *"Wings of Desire." Artforum International Magazine* 26.10 (1988): 10–11.

Paneth, Ira. "Wim and His Wings." *Film Quarterly* 42.1 (1988): 2–8.

Pollock, Dale. " 'Paris,' 'America' Lead Cannes Pack." *Los Angeles Times* May 22, 1984, sec. 6: 2–3.

_____. *"Paris, Texas* Wins Palme d'Or." *Los Angeles Times* May 24, 1984, sec. 6: 1, 6.

Porter, Milinda Camber. "Wenders in the U.S.: A European Explores America's Changing Landscape." *World Press Review* 31 (1984): 59.

Powers, John. *"Until the End of the World." New York* 25.3 (1992): 58.

Pym, John. *"Falsche Bewegung." Monthly Film Bulletin* July 1977: 145.

Rechtshaffen, Michael. *"Wings of Desire." Maclean's* May 16, 1988: 62.

Reilly, Charles Phillips. "1977's Ten Best." *Films in Review* 29.2 (1978): 65–72.

Rich, Frank. "The Goalie Saved by a Long Shot." *New York Post* January 14, 1977.

_____. "Wenders' *Alice in the Cities* Is a Wonderland of Images." *New York Post* April 29, 1977: 35.

▌Bibliography

Röhl, Bettina, and Klaudius Seidl. "Die Wim-Bibel. Worte des großen Vorsitzenden Wim Wenders. Aus Anlaß seines neuen Films *Der Himmel über Berlin.*" *Tempo* November 1987: 86–90.

"Ronee Blakley Goes Up to the Mountain—And Returns with a Husband, Director Wim Wenders." *People* September 17, 1979: 34.

Roud, Richard. "Cannes 77." *Sight and Sound* 46.3 (1977): 149.

———. "Journals: Berlin Festival." *Film Comment* 10.5 (1974): 4.

Rousuck, J. Wynn. "9th International Film Festival Here Attracts 150 Entries." *Baltimore Sunday Sun* April 9, 1978: D1, D3.

"Ruf in die Wüste. Wim Wenders' Erfahrungen mit Hollywood." *Der Spiegel* 2 (1985): 139.

Sabouraud, Frédéric. "Lorsque l'ange atterrit." *Cahiers du cinéma* 397 (1987): 8.

Sante, Luc. *"Wings of Desire."* *Interview* 18 (1988): 122.

Scheib, Ronnie. "Angst for the memories." *Film Comment* 26.4 (1990): 9–16.

Schober, Siegfried. "Die Leiden des Wilhelm M." *Der Spiegel* 11 (1975): 134–37.

Schütte, Wolfram. "Absturz in Begleitung von Engeln: *In weiter Ferne, so nah!*" *Frankfurter Rundschau* September 9, 1993: 7

Seidenberg, Robert. "The Man Who Fell to Earth: No More Angst and Alienation for Wim Wenders." *American Film* 13.8 (1988): 28.

Simon, John. *"Wings of Desire."* *National Review* 40.11 (1988): 54–55.

Solman, Gregory. *"The State of Things."* *Films in Review* 34.3 (1983): 175–76.

Springer, Gregory, Ron Epple. "Festivals: 12th Chicago International Film Festival." *Filmmakers Newsletter* 10.5 (1977): 57.

Stamelman, Peter. "Wenders at Warners." *Sight and Sound* 47.4 (1978): 225.

Stein, Elliott. "New York Film Festival Review II: Salomagundi." *Film Comment* 13.6 (1977): 42–46.

Sterritt, David. "German Director in U.S. Tradition." *Christian Science Monitor* January 15, 1979: 19.

———. "Vivid Visuals in an Otherwise Sparkleless *Hammett.*" *Christian Science Monitor* July 26, 1983: 8.

Stone, Judy. "Moving Tale of Journalist, Child." *San Francisco Chronicle* September 16, 1976: 5.

———. "An Exploration of Loneliness." *San Francisco Examiner.* June 22, 1977: 49.

———. *"The State of Things* in Film Making." *Los Angeles Times* July 20, 1983, sec. 6: 5.

Storch, U. "Die Filmographie—Wim Wenders." *Die Information* February 23, 1974: 28–29.

Stratton, David. "Wenders Plans His *End of World* as Oz-Francecoprod." *Variety* June 8, 1988: 17.

Theuring, Gerhard. "Filme von Wim Wenders." *Filmkritik* May 1969: 315–17.

Travers, Peter. *"Until the End of the World."* *Rolling Stone* 25.3 (1992): 50.

Van Gelder, Lawrence. "Alice in Jet Land." *New York Times* April 29, 1977: C6.

Webb, Michael. "Festival Report: Cannes." *American Film* 1.9 (1976): 69.

Welsh, James M. "Baltimore Film Festival II: Watkins, Wenders, and Resnais." *Salisbury Advertiser* May 3, 1978: 7.

"Wenders' Film Wins at Venice Festival." *New York Times* September 9, 1982: 23.

"Wenders Sets *Hammett*, His First American Film." *Variety* April 19, 1978: 40.

Westerbeck, Colin L., Jr. "The Screen." *Commonweal* October 28, 1977: 687–88.

Wiegand, Wilfried. "Kunstfigur aus Fleisch und Blut: Handkes *Angst des Tormanns von Wim Wenders verfilmt.*" *Frankfurter Allgemeine Zeitung* 52 (1972): 22.

———. "Wenders." *Frankfurter Allgemeine Zeitung* (Magazin). January 28, 1983: 10–14.

Youngblood, Gene. "A New Nostalgia." *Take One* 5.4 (1976): 33–34.

INDEX

Books in the Contemporary Film and Television Series